HIDEYUKI FURUHASHI

In this volume, Master's story comes to a head. Part of me wanted him to be this man of mystery forever, but at some point I had to portray him as vulnerable and human...

BETTEN COURT

As others have pointed out, every *Vigilantes* volume cover is an homage to a corresponding *My Hero Academia* cover.

Which was this one inspired by? Might be fun to go back and compare.

MY HERO ACADEMIA VIGILANTES

VOLUME 4
SHONEN JUMP Manga Edition

STORY: HIDEYUKI FURUHASHI
ART: BETTEN COURT
ORIGINAL CONCEPT: KOHEI HORIKOSHI

Translation & English Adaptation/Caleb Cook
Touch-Up Art & Lettering/John Hunt
Designer/Julian [JR] Robinson
Editor/Mike Montesa

VIGILANTE -BOKU NO HERO ACADEMIA ILLEGALS-
© 2016 by Hideyuki Furuhashi, Betten Court, Kohei Horikoshi
All rights reserved.
First published in Japan in 2016 by SHUEISHA Inc., Tokyo.
English translation rights arranged by SHUEISHA Inc.

The stories, characters and incidents mentioned in this publication
are entirely fictional.

Printed in the U.S.A.

Published by VIZ Media, LLC
P.O. Box 77010
San Francisco, CA 94107

10 9 8 7 6 5 4 3 2 1
First printing, April 2019

 **VIZ** MEDIA
viz.com

 SHONEN JUMP
shonenjump.com

PARENTAL ADVISORY
MY HERO ACADEMIA: VIGILANTES is rated
T for Teen and is recommended for ages
13 and up. This volume contains fantasy
violence.

RATED T TEEN
ratedgs.viz.com

MY HERO ACADEMIA
VIGILANTES

Writer / Letterer
Hideyuki Furuhashi

Penciller / Colorist
Betten Court

Original Concept
Kohei Horikoshi

noun | idol

: an image or representation of an object of worship; a performer who capitalizes on his or her charm and personality

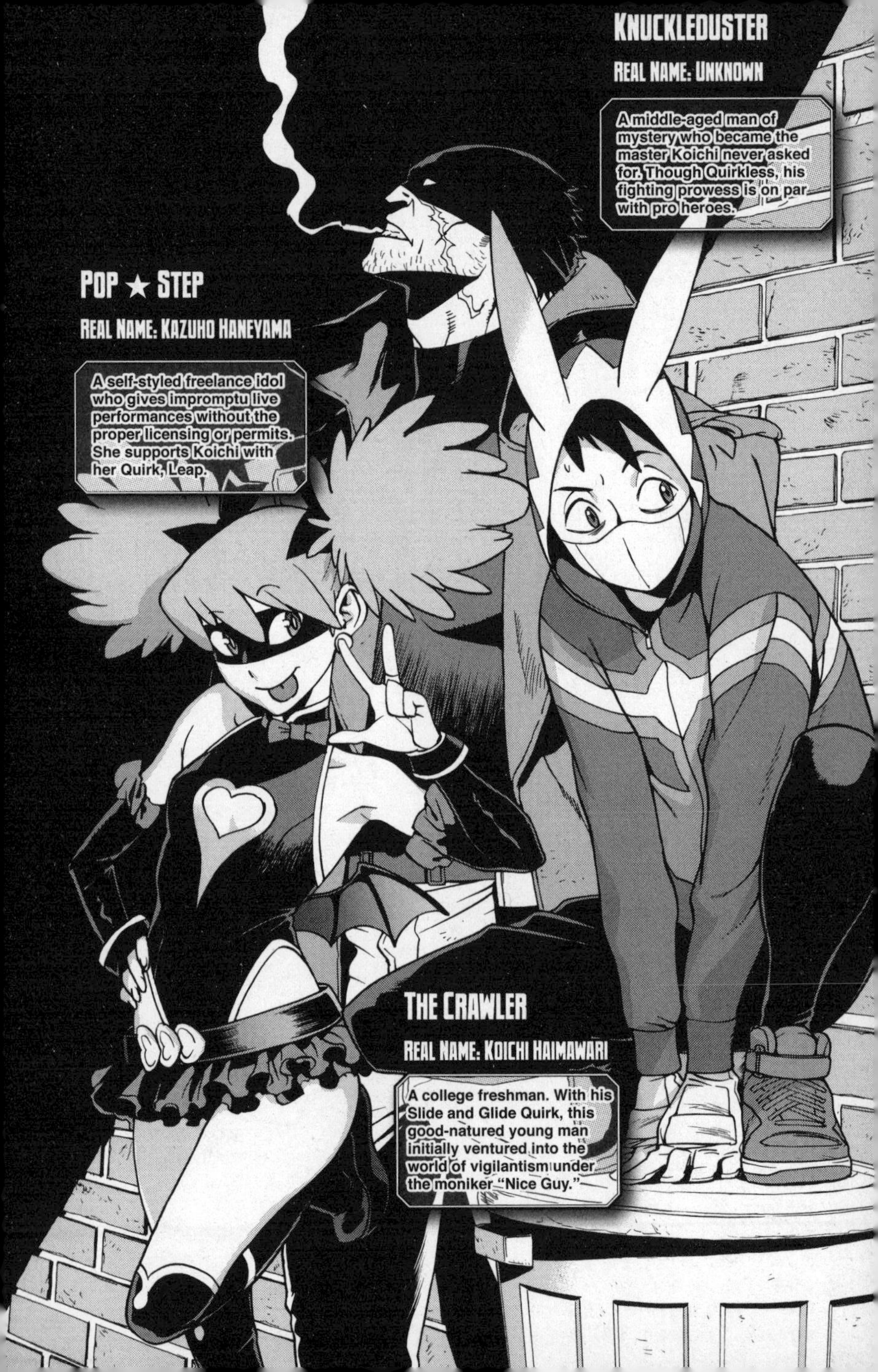
KNUCKLEDUSTER
REAL NAME: UNKNOWN
A middle-aged man of mystery who became the master Koichi never asked for. Though Quirkless, his fighting prowess is on par with pro heroes.
POP ★ STEP
REAL NAME: KAZUHO HANEYAMA
A self-styled freelance idol who gives impromptu live performances without the proper licensing or permits. She supports Koichi with her Quirk, Leap.
THE CRAWLER
REAL NAME: KOICHI HAIMAWARI
A college freshman. With his Slide and Glide Quirk, this good-natured young man initially ventured into the world of vigilantism under the moniker "Nice Guy."

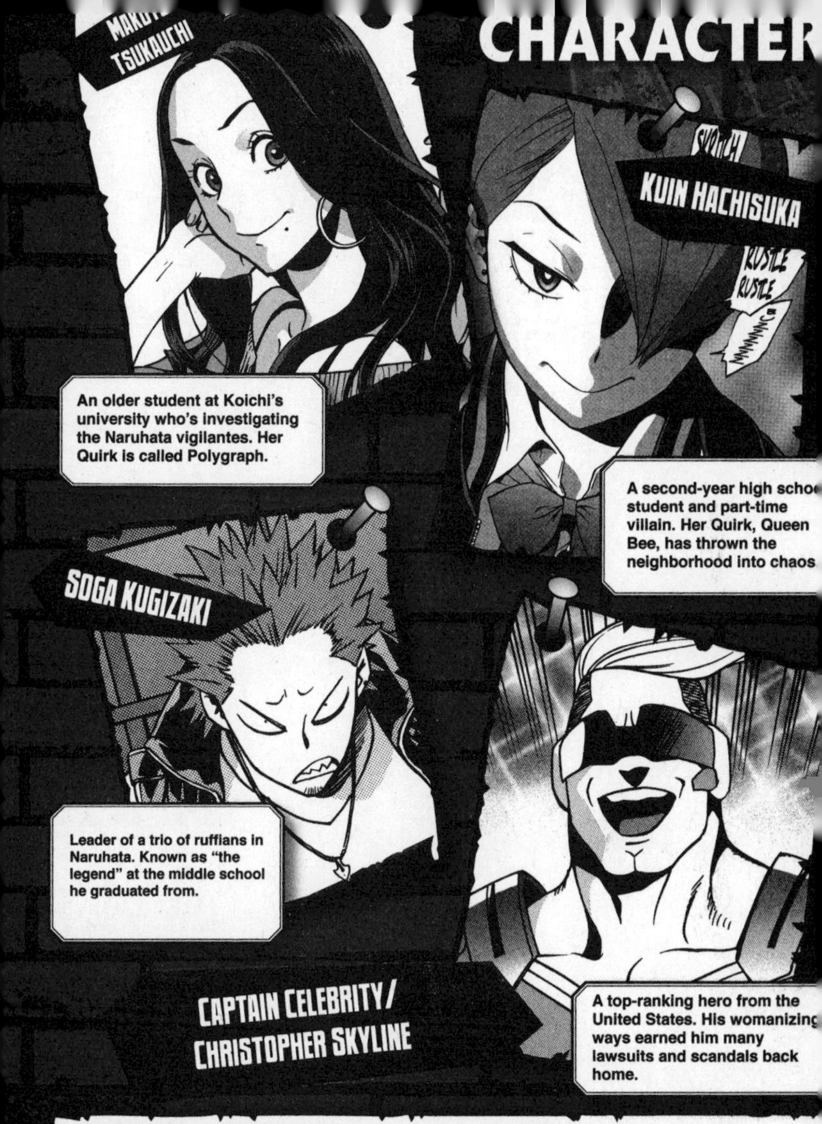
CHARACTER
TSUKAUCHI
An older student at Koichi's university who's investigating the Naruhata vigilantes. Her Quirk is called Polygraph.
KUIN HACHISUKA
RUSTLE
RUSTLE
A second-year high scho
student and part-time
villain. Her Quirk, Queen
Bee, has thrown the
neighborhood into chaos
SOGA KUGIZAKI
Leader of a trio of ruffians in Naruhata. Known as "the legend" at the middle school he graduated from.
CAPTAIN CELEBRITY/
CHRISTOPHER SKYLINE
A top-ranking hero from the United States. His womanizing ways earned him many lawsuits and scandals back home.

STORY

What is "justice" anyway? Get ready for a PLUS ULTRA spin-off set in the world of *My Hero Academia*!!

Heroes. The chosen ones who, with explicit government permission, use their natural talents, or Quirks, to aid society. However, not everyone can be chosen, and some take action of their own accord, becoming illegal heroes. What does justice mean to them? And can we really call them heroes? This story takes to the streets in order to follow the exploits of those known as *vigilantes.*

MY HERO ACADEMIA VIGILANTES

4

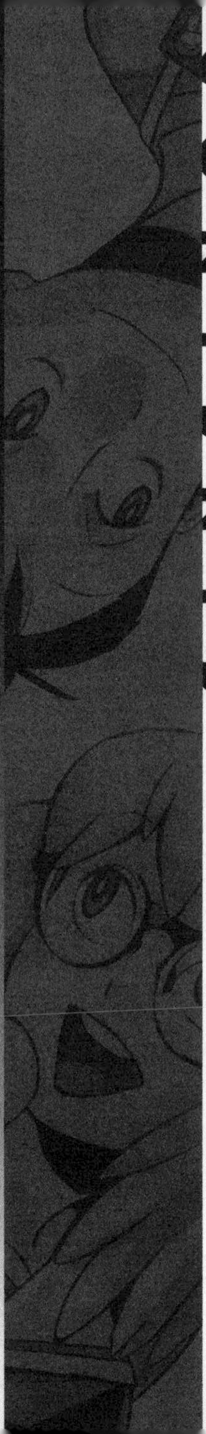

CONTENTS

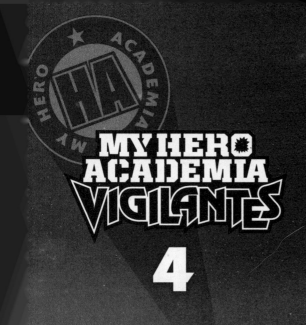

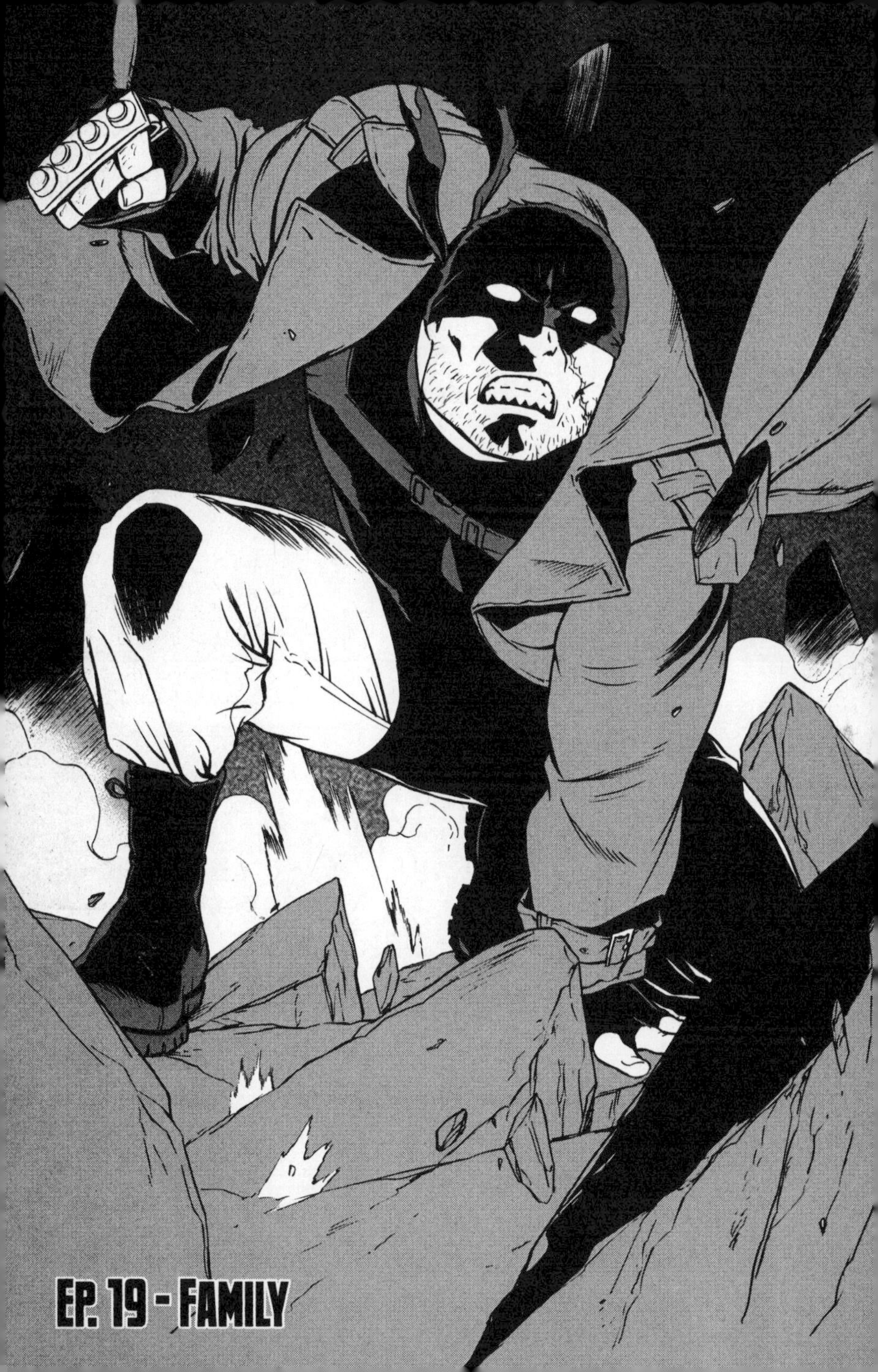
EP. 19 - FAMILY

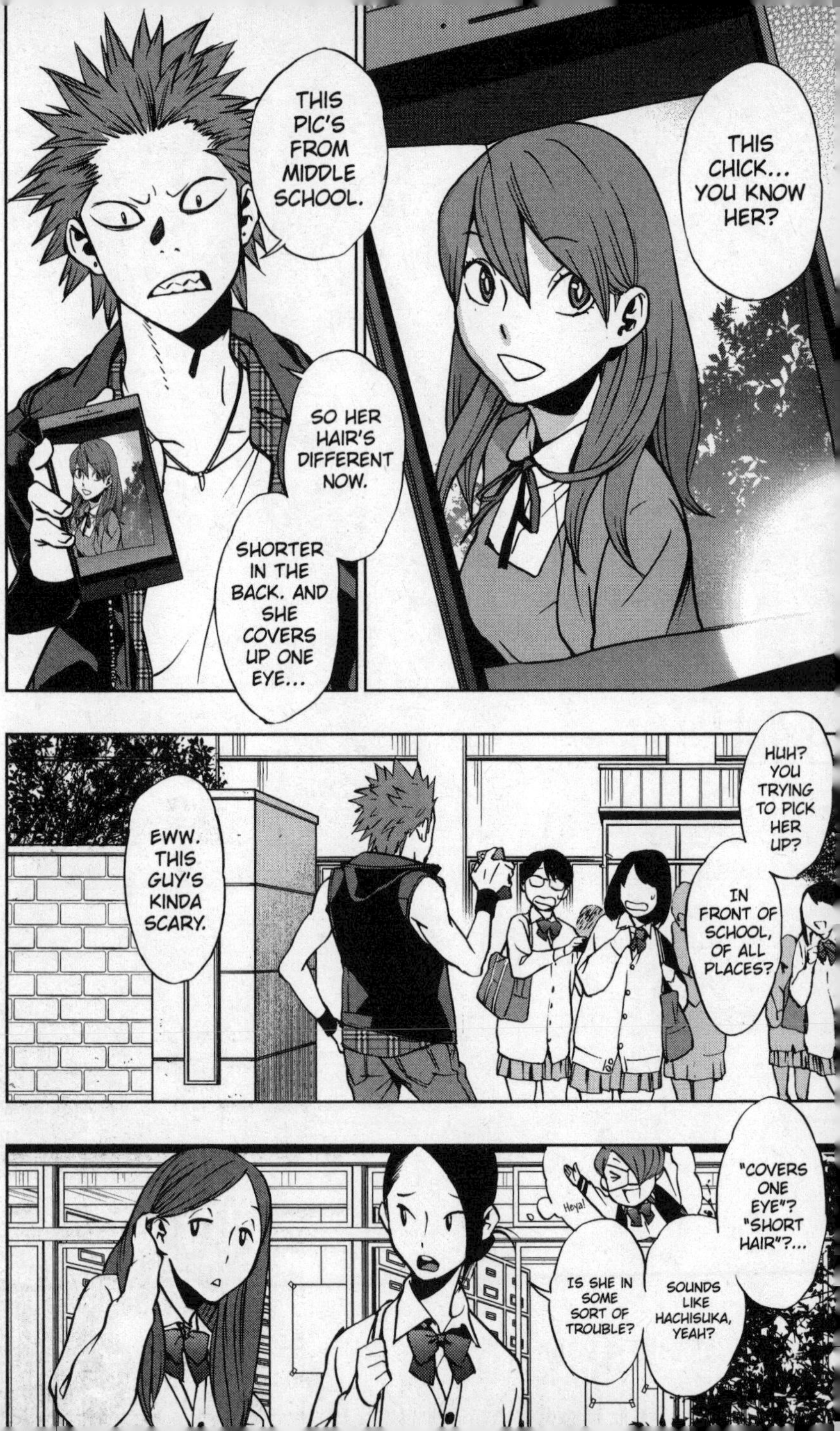
THIS CHICK... YOU KNOW HER?
THIS PIC'S FROM MIDDLE SCHOOL.
SO HER HAIR'S DIFFERENT NOW.
SHORTER IN THE BACK. AND SHE COVERS UP ONE EYE...
HUH? YOU TRYING TO PICK HER UP?
IN FRONT OF SCHOOL, OF ALL PLACES?
EWW. THIS GUY'S KINDA SCARY.
"COVERS ONE EYE"? "SHORT HAIR"?...
Heya!
SOUNDS LIKE HACHISUKA, YEAH?
IS SHE IN SOME SORT OF TROUBLE?

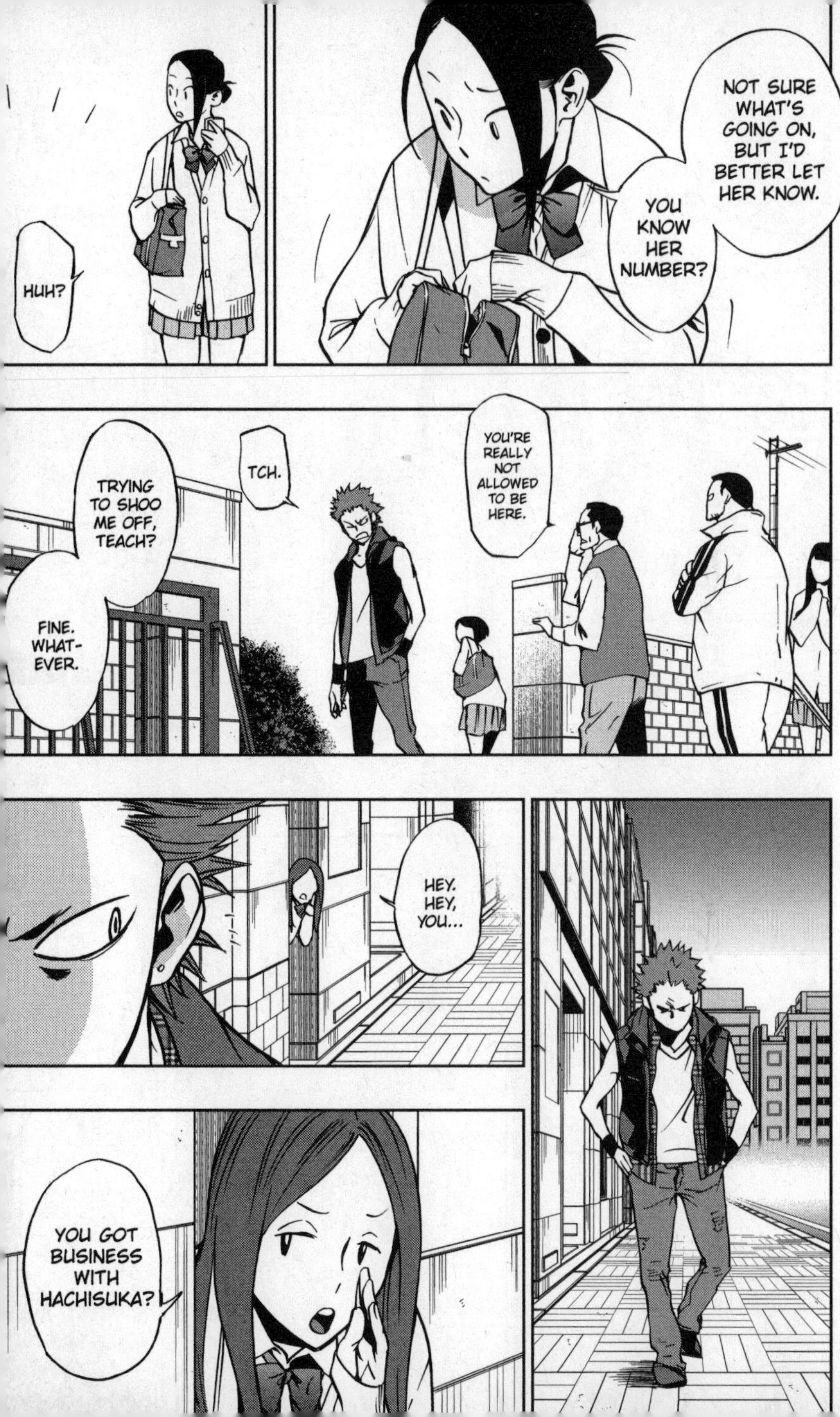
NOT SURE WHAT'S GOING ON, BUT I'D BETTER LET HER KNOW.
YOU KNOW HER NUMBER?
HUH?
YOU'RE REALLY NOT ALLOWED TO BE HERE.
TCH.
TRYING TO SHOO ME OFF, TEACH?
FINE. WHAT-EVER.
HEY. HEY, YOU...
YOU GOT BUSINESS WITH HACHISUKA?

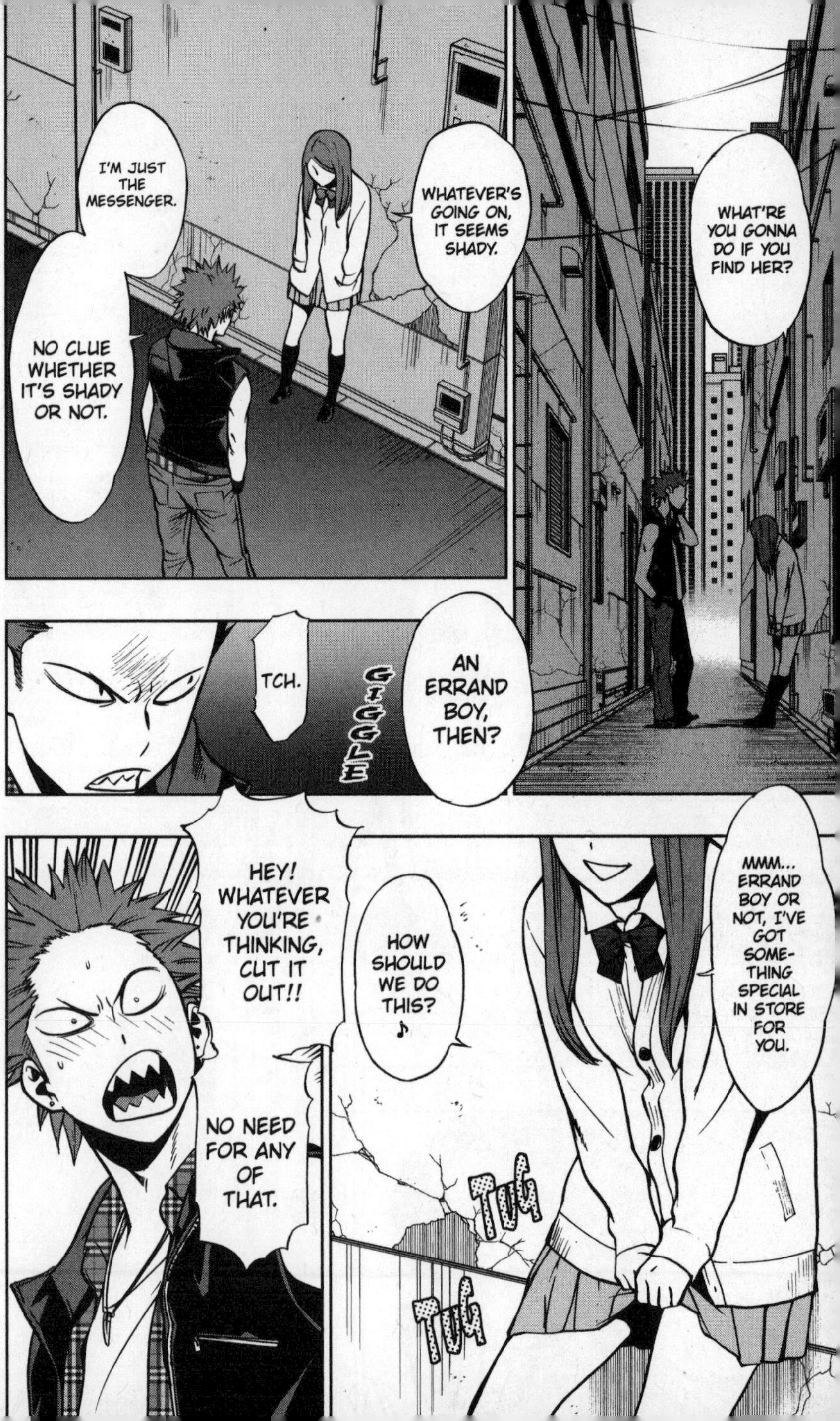
WHAT'RE YOU GONNA DO IF YOU FIND HER?
I'M JUST THE MESSENGER.
WHATEVER'S GOING ON, IT SEEMS SHADY.
NO CLUE WHETHER IT'S SHADY OR NOT.
AN ERRAND BOY, THEN?
GIGGLE
TCH.
MMM... ERRAND BOY OR NOT, I'VE GOT SOME-THING SPECIAL IN STORE FOR YOU.
HOW SHOULD WE DO THIS? ♪
TUG
TUG
HEY! WHATEVER YOU'RE THINKING, CUT IT OUT!!
NO NEED FOR ANY OF THAT.

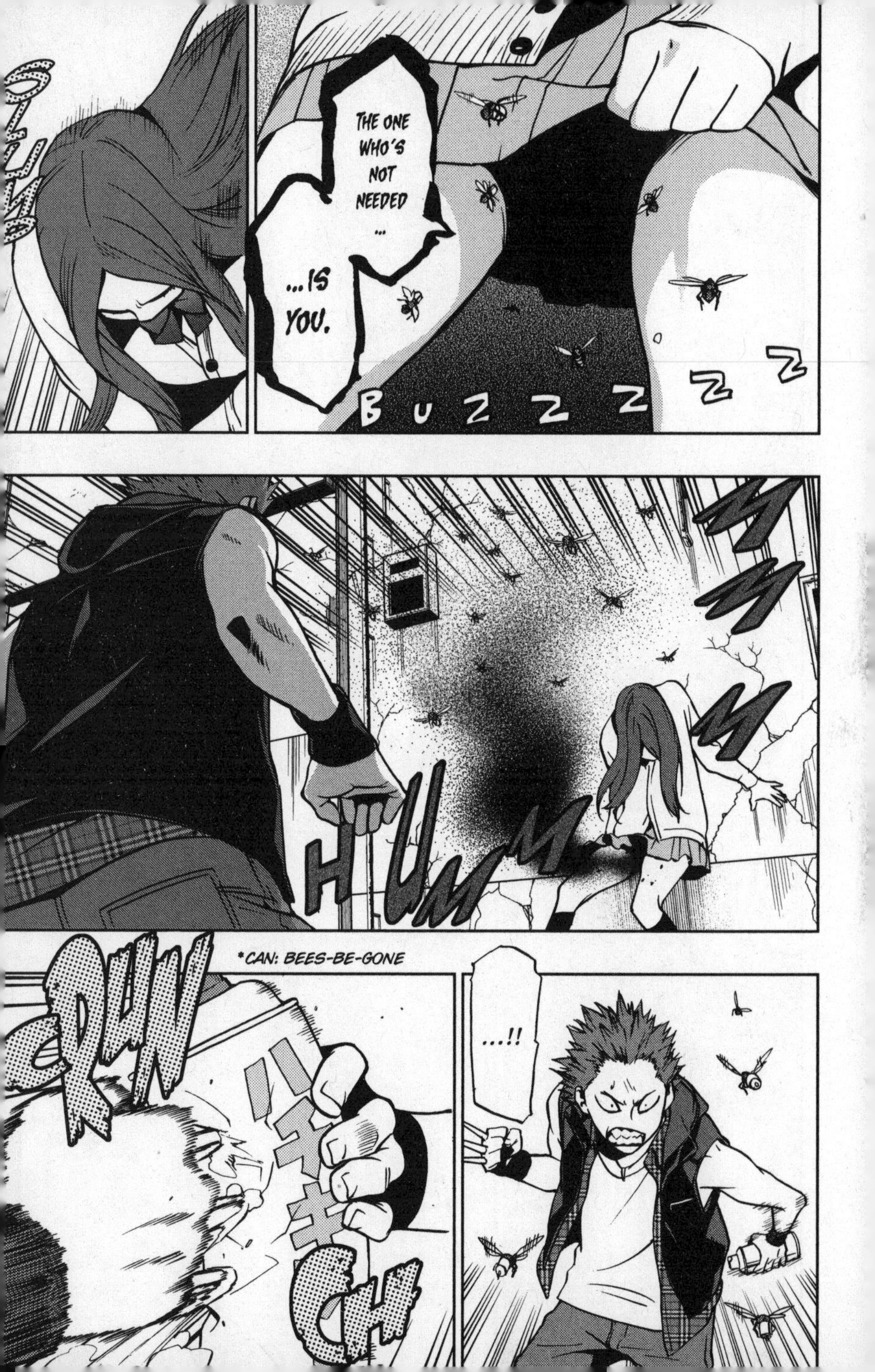
THE ONE WHO'S NOT NEEDED ...
...IS YOU.
BUZZZZZZ
HUMM
MMMM
...!!
CRUNCH
*CAN: BEES-BE-GONE

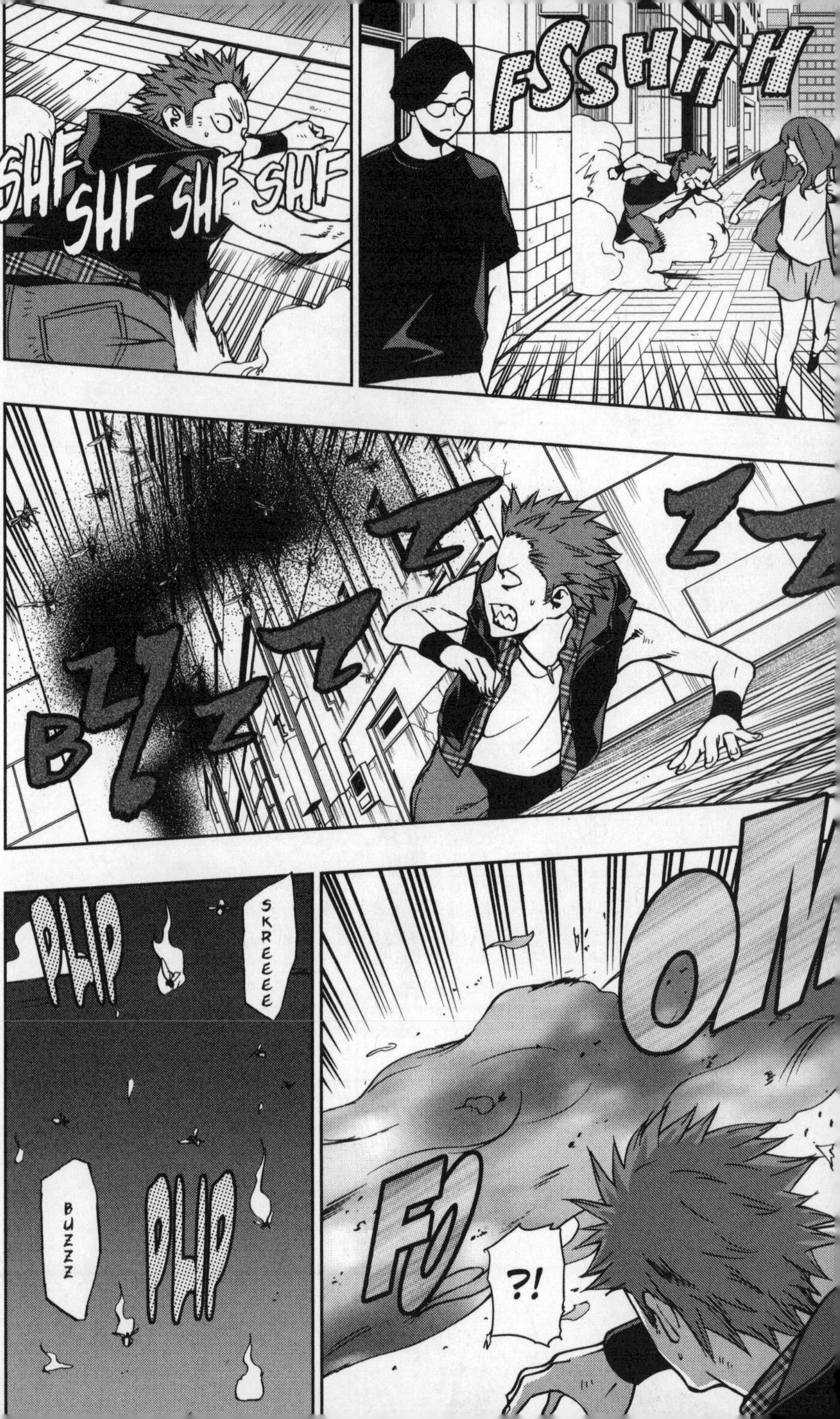
FSSHHHH
SHF SHF SHF SHF
BZZZZ
ZZ
?!
SKREEEE
DLIP
BUZZZ
DLIP

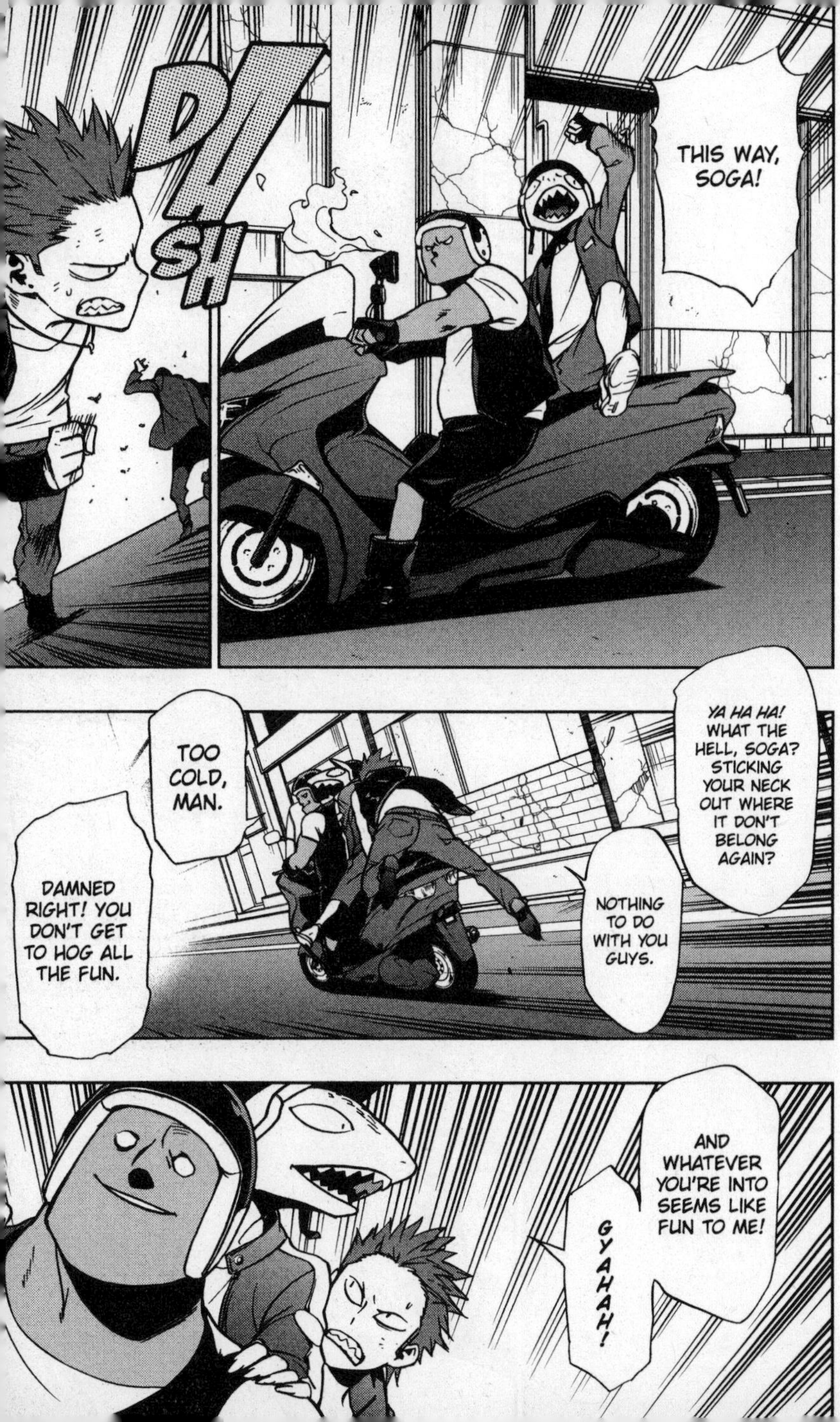
THIS WAY, SOGA!
DASH
YA HA HA! WHAT THE HELL, SOGA? STICKING YOUR NECK OUT WHERE IT DON'T BELONG AGAIN?
NOTHING TO DO WITH YOU GUYS.
TOO COLD, MAN.
DAMNED RIGHT! YOU DON'T GET TO HOG ALL THE FUN.
AND WHATEVER YOU'RE INTO SEEMS LIKE FUN TO ME!
GYAHAH!

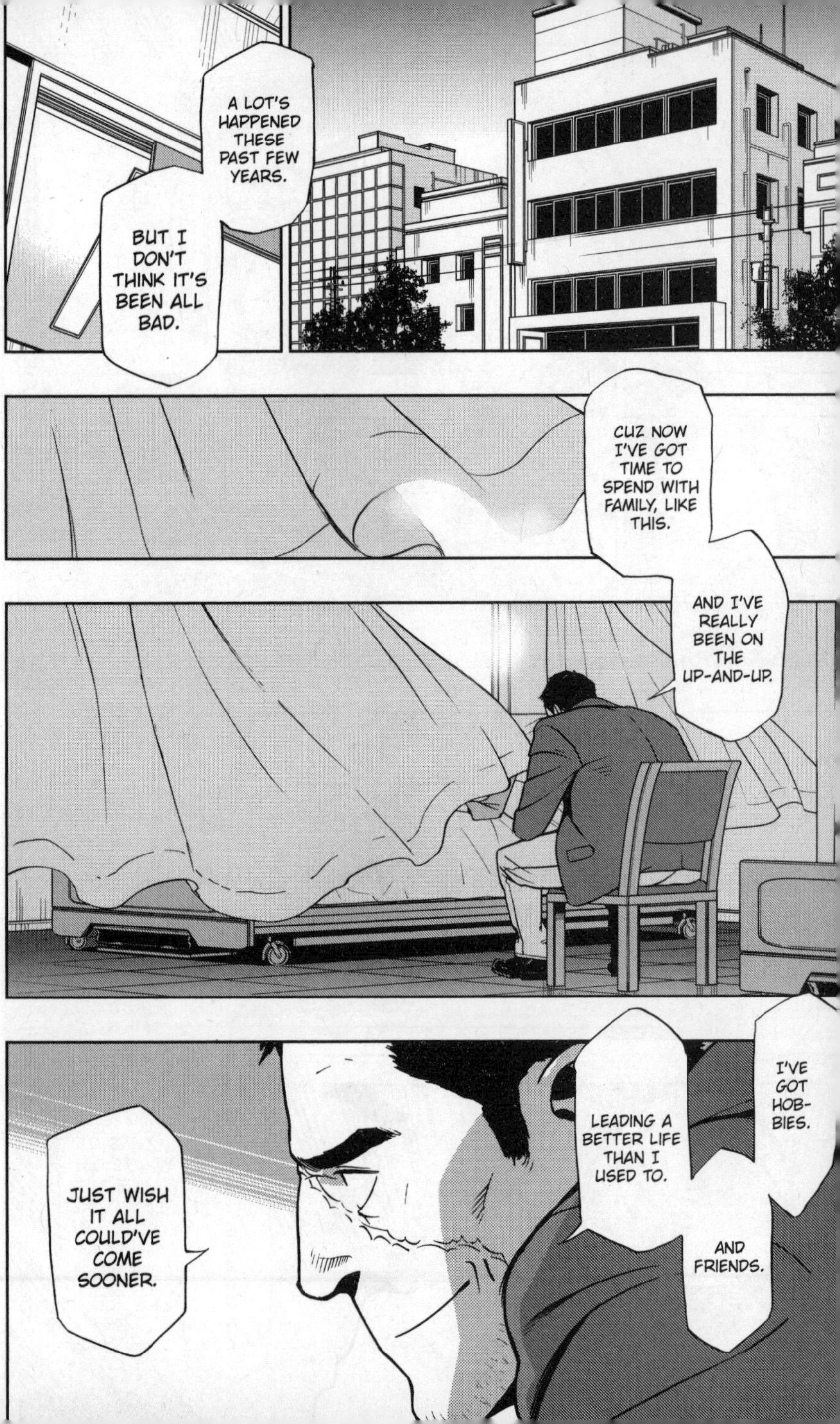
A LOT'S HAPPENED THESE PAST FEW YEARS.
BUT I DON'T THINK IT'S BEEN ALL BAD.
CUZ NOW I'VE GOT TIME TO SPEND WITH FAMILY, LIKE THIS.
AND I'VE REALLY BEEN ON THE UP-AND-UP.
I'VE GOT HOB-BIES.
AND FRIENDS.
LEADING A BETTER LIFE THAN I USED TO.
JUST WISH IT ALL COULD'VE COME SOONER.

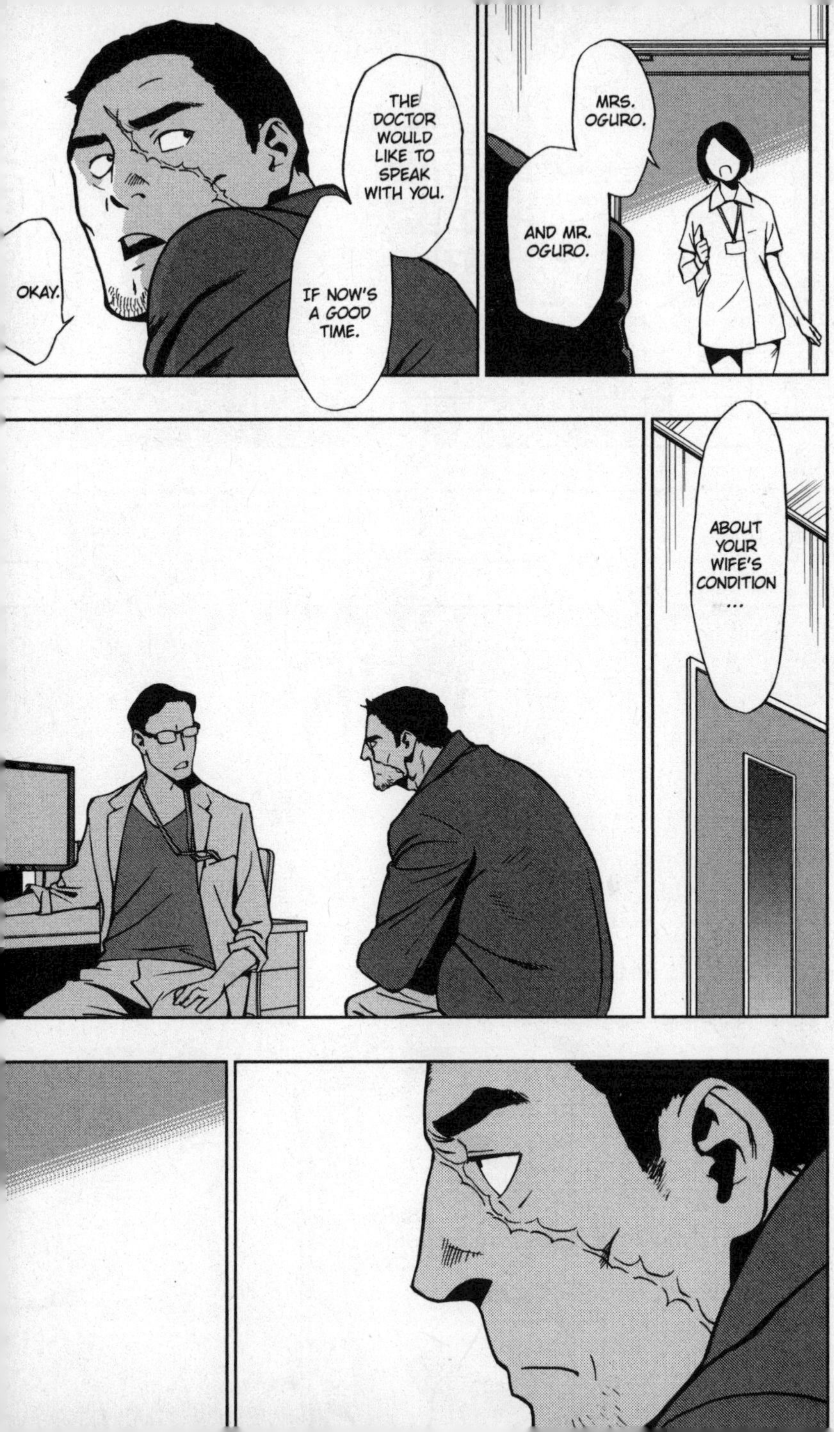
MRS. OGURO.
AND MR. OGURO.
THE DOCTOR WOULD LIKE TO SPEAK WITH YOU.
IF NOW'S A GOOD TIME.
OKAY.
ABOUT YOUR WIFE'S CONDITION ...

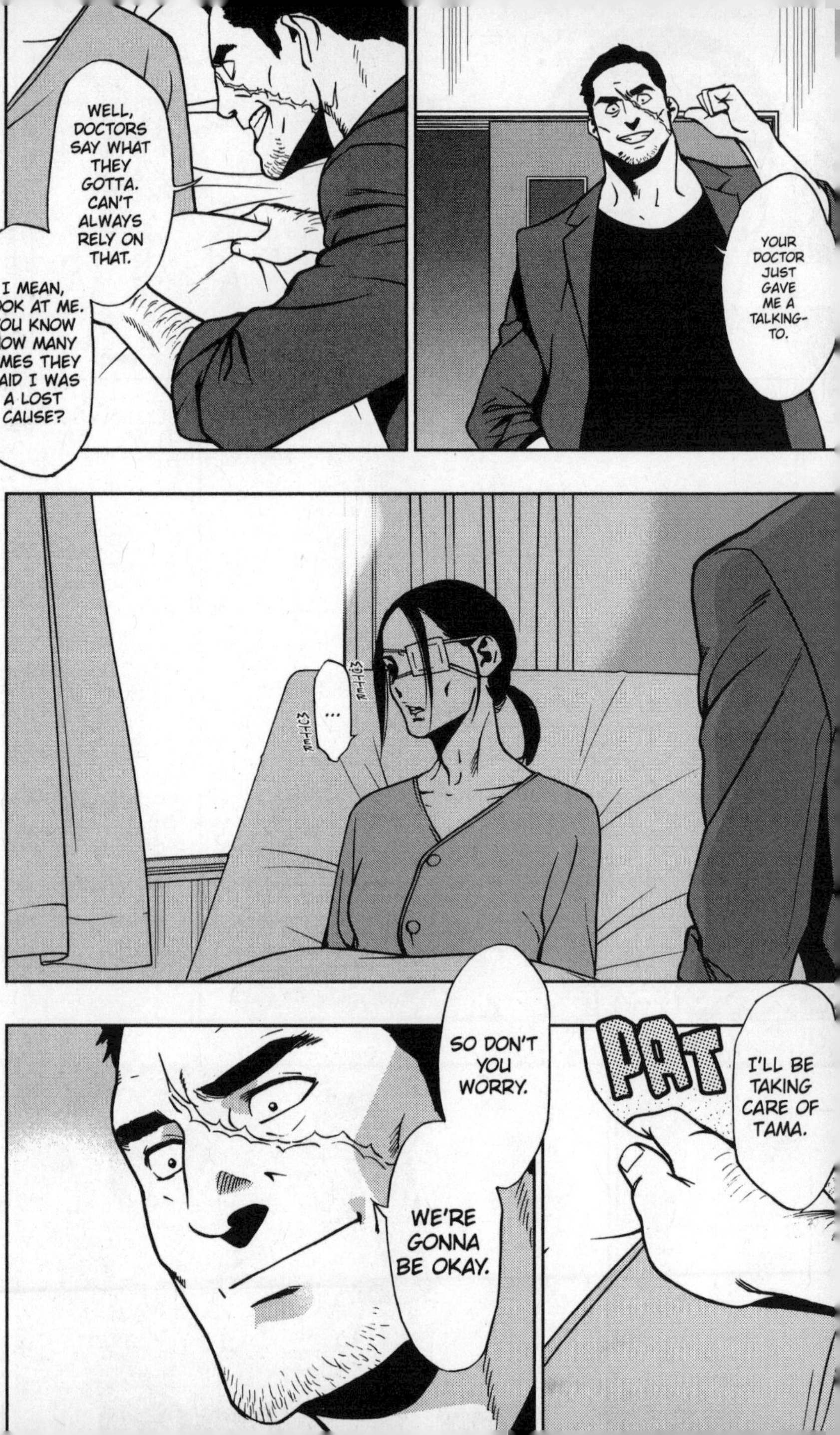
YOUR DOCTOR JUST GAVE ME A TALKING-TO.
WELL, DOCTORS SAY WHAT THEY GOTTA. CAN'T ALWAYS RELY ON THAT.
I MEAN, LOOK AT ME. YOU KNOW HOW MANY TIMES THEY SAID I WAS A LOST CAUSE?
...
PAT
I'LL BE TAKING CARE OF TAMA.
SO DON'T YOU WORRY.
WE'RE GONNA BE OKAY.

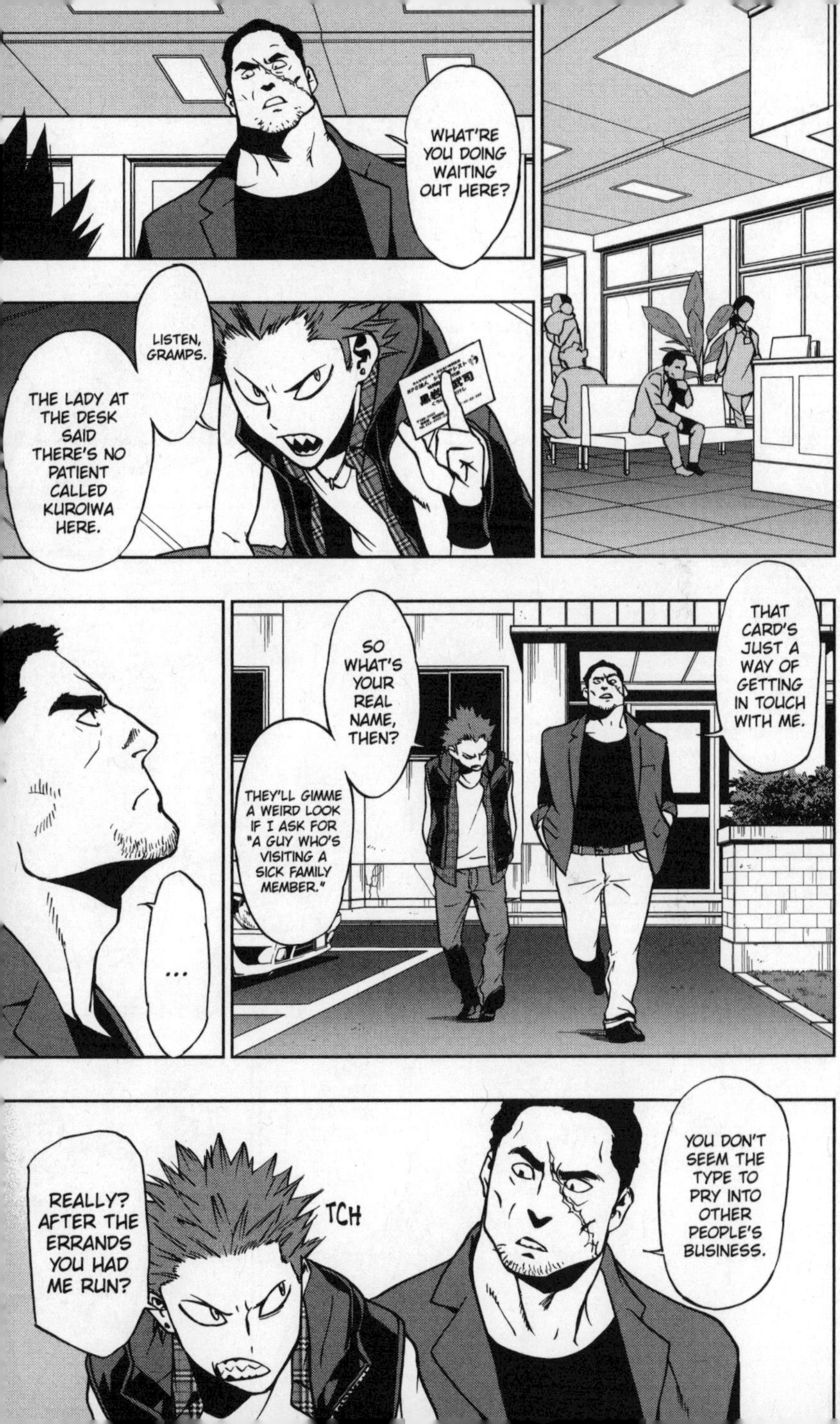
WHAT'RE YOU DOING WAITING OUT HERE?
LISTEN, GRAMPS.
THE LADY AT THE DESK SAID THERE'S NO PATIENT CALLED KUROIWA HERE.
THAT CARD'S JUST A WAY OF GETTING IN TOUCH WITH ME.
SO WHAT'S YOUR REAL NAME, THEN?
THEY'LL GIMME A WEIRD LOOK IF I ASK FOR "A GUY WHO'S VISITING A SICK FAMILY MEMBER."
...
YOU DON'T SEEM THE TYPE TO PRY INTO OTHER PEOPLE'S BUSINESS.
TCH
REALLY? AFTER THE ERRANDS YOU HAD ME RUN?

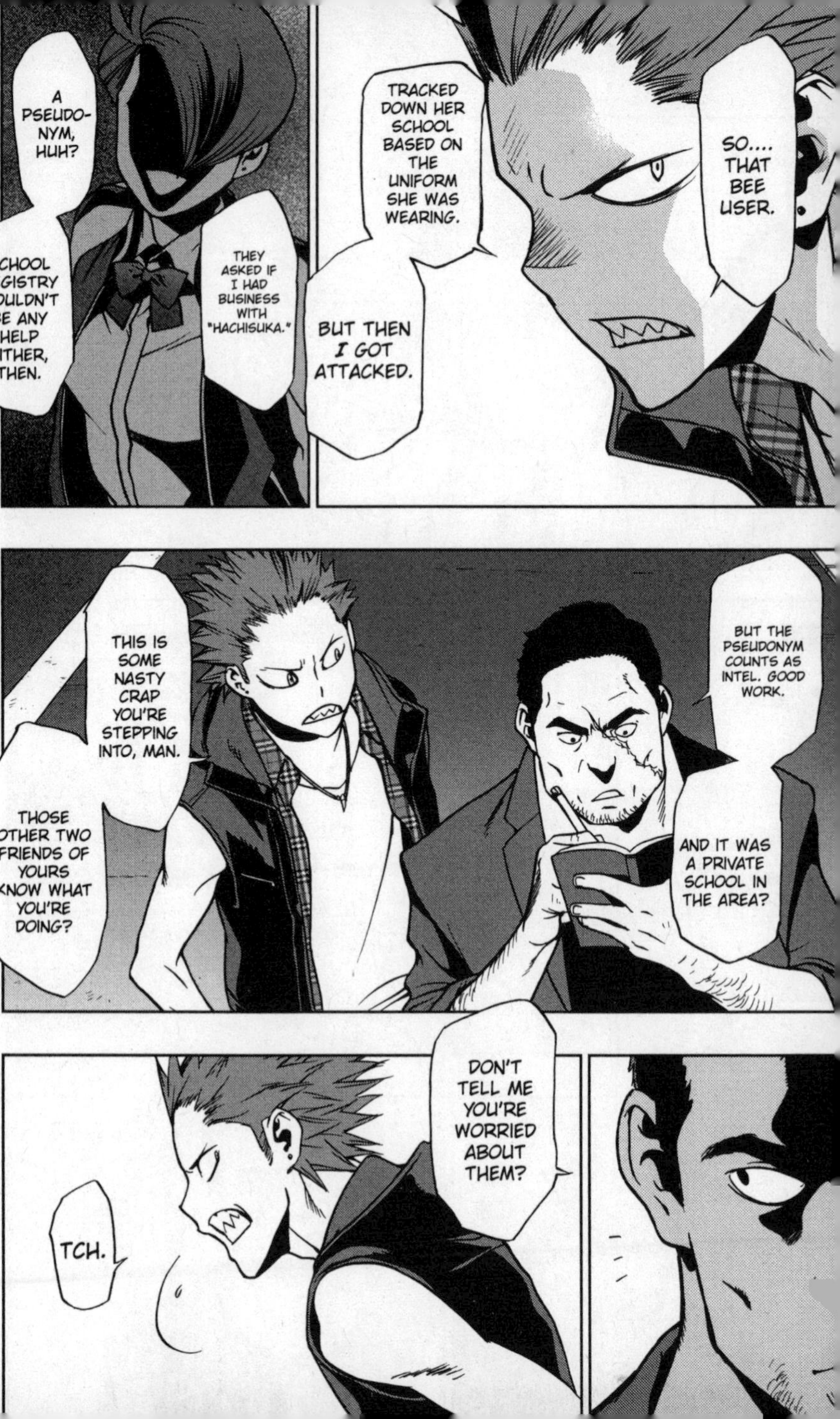
SO.... THAT BEE USER.
TRACKED DOWN HER SCHOOL BASED ON THE UNIFORM SHE WAS WEARING.
BUT THEN *I* GOT ATTACKED.
A PSEUDO-NYM, HUH?
THEY ASKED IF I HAD BUSINESS WITH "HACHISUKA."
SCHOOL REGISTRY WOULDN'T BE ANY HELP EITHER, THEN.
BUT THE PSEUDONYM COUNTS AS INTEL. GOOD WORK.
AND IT WAS A PRIVATE SCHOOL IN THE AREA?
THIS IS SOME NASTY CRAP YOU'RE STEPPING INTO, MAN.
THOSE OTHER TWO FRIENDS OF YOURS KNOW WHAT YOU'RE DOING?
DON'T TELL ME YOU'RE WORRIED ABOUT THEM?
TCH.

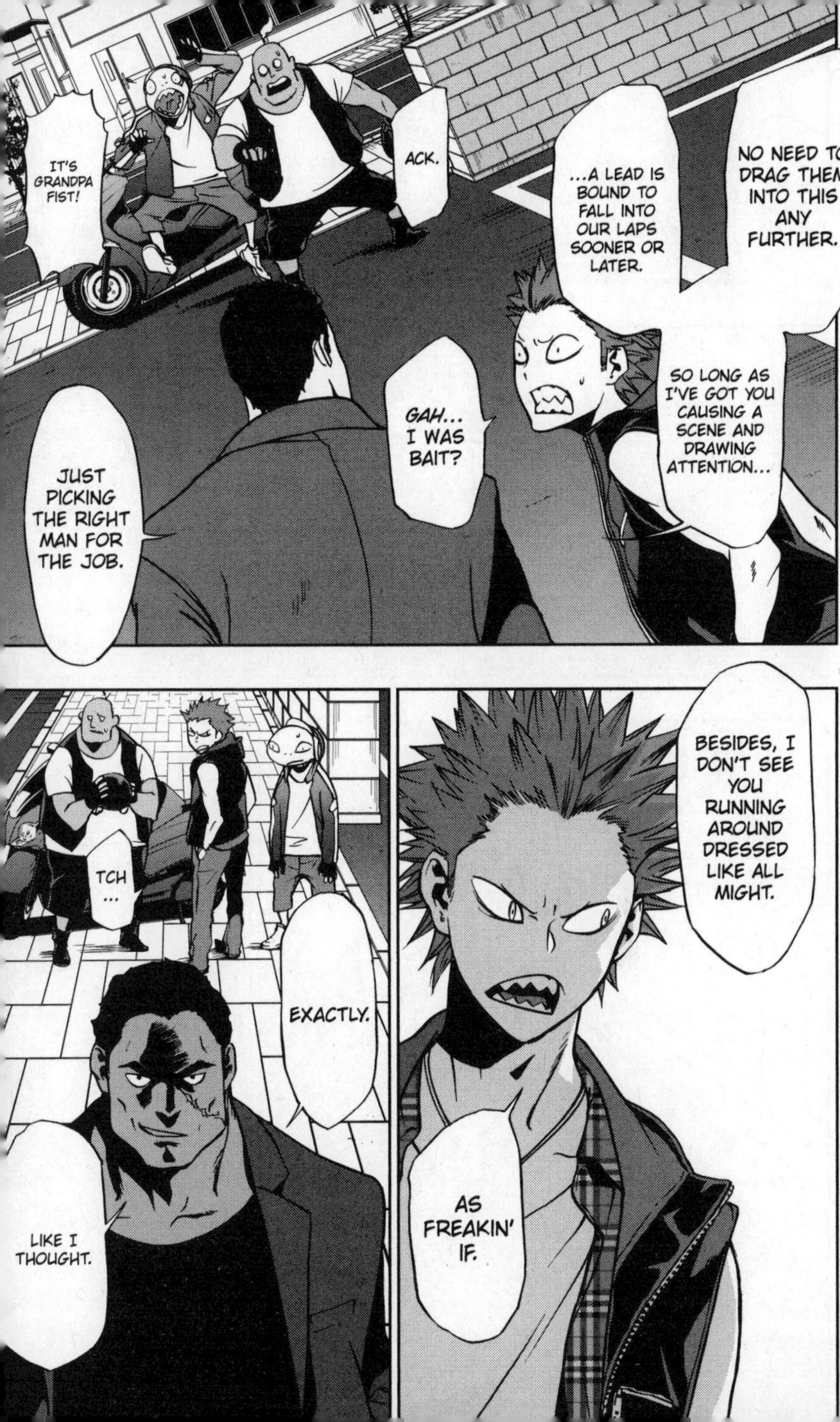
NO NEED TO DRAG THEM INTO THIS ANY FURTHER.
SO LONG AS I'VE GOT YOU CAUSING A SCENE AND DRAWING ATTENTION...
...A LEAD IS BOUND TO FALL INTO OUR LAPS SOONER OR LATER.
ACK.
IT'S GRANDPA FIST!
GAH... I WAS BAIT?
JUST PICKING THE RIGHT MAN FOR THE JOB.
BESIDES, I DON'T SEE YOU RUNNING AROUND DRESSED LIKE ALL MIGHT.
AS FREAKIN' IF.
TCH ...
EXACTLY.
LIKE I THOUGHT.

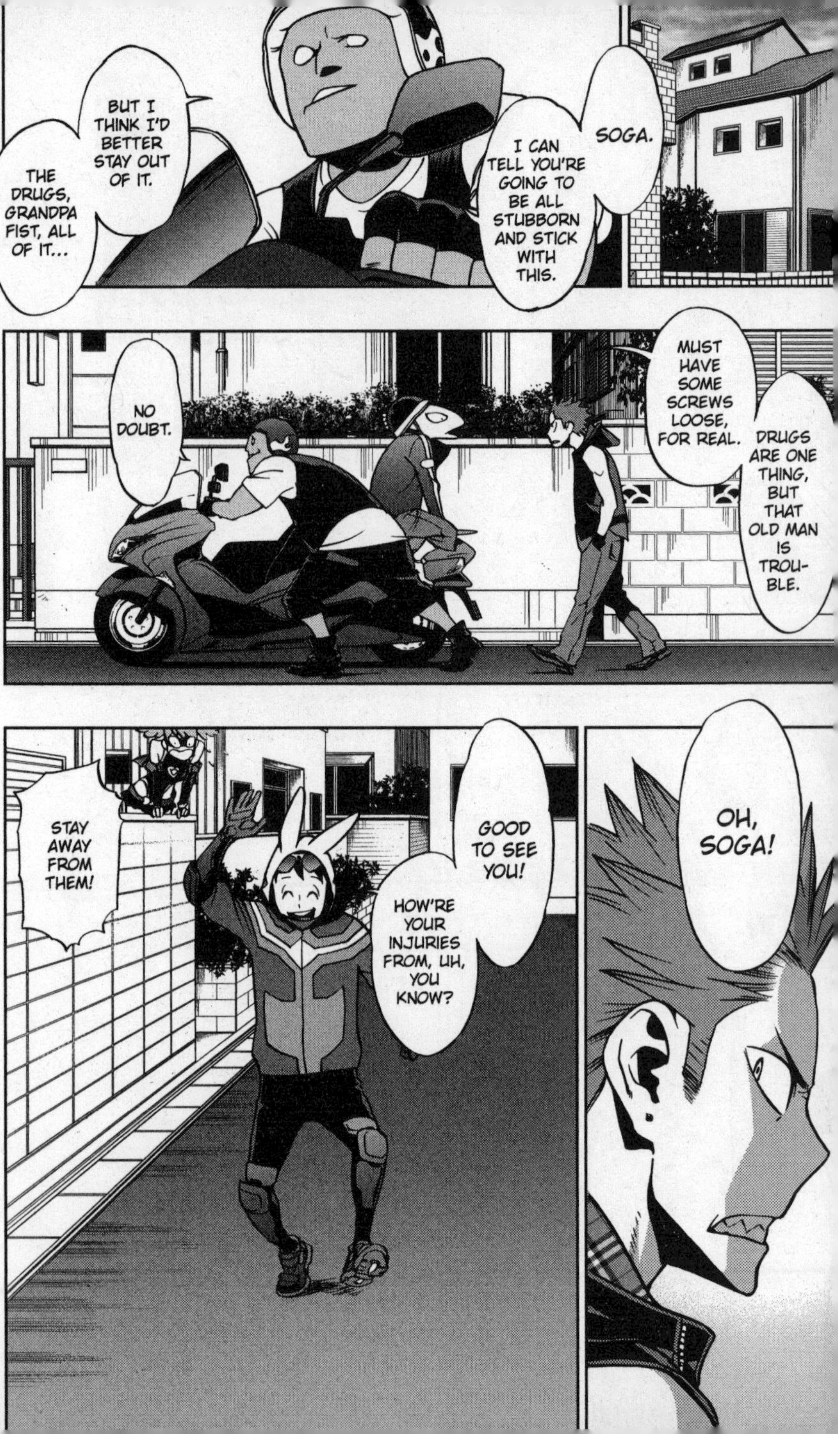
SOGA.
I CAN TELL YOU'RE GOING TO BE ALL STUBBORN AND STICK WITH THIS.
BUT I THINK I'D BETTER STAY OUT OF IT.
THE DRUGS, GRANDPA FIST, ALL OF IT...
MUST HAVE SOME SCREWS LOOSE, FOR REAL.
DRUGS ARE ONE THING, BUT THAT OLD MAN IS TROU-BLE.
NO DOUBT.
OH, SOGA!
GOOD TO SEE YOU!
HOW'RE YOUR INJURIES FROM, UH, YOU KNOW?
STAY AWAY FROM THEM!

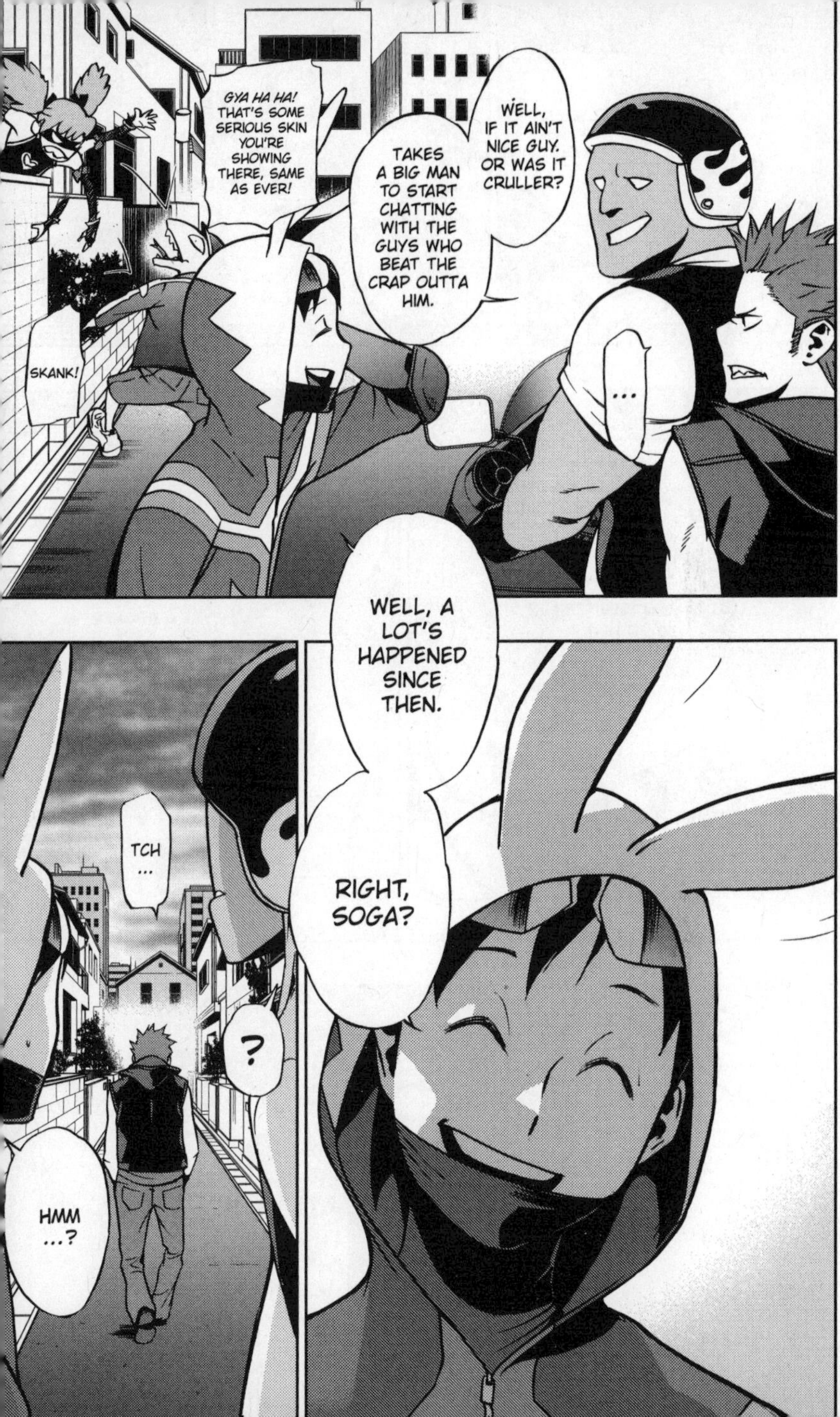
WELL, IF IT AIN'T NICE GUY. OR WAS IT CRULLER?
TAKES A BIG MAN TO START CHATTING WITH THE GUYS WHO BEAT THE CRAP OUTTA HIM.
GYA HA HA! THAT'S SOME SERIOUS SKIN YOU'RE SHOWING THERE, SAME AS EVER!
...
SKANK!
WELL, A LOT'S HAPPENED SINCE THEN.
RIGHT, SOGA?
TCH ...
?
HMM ...?

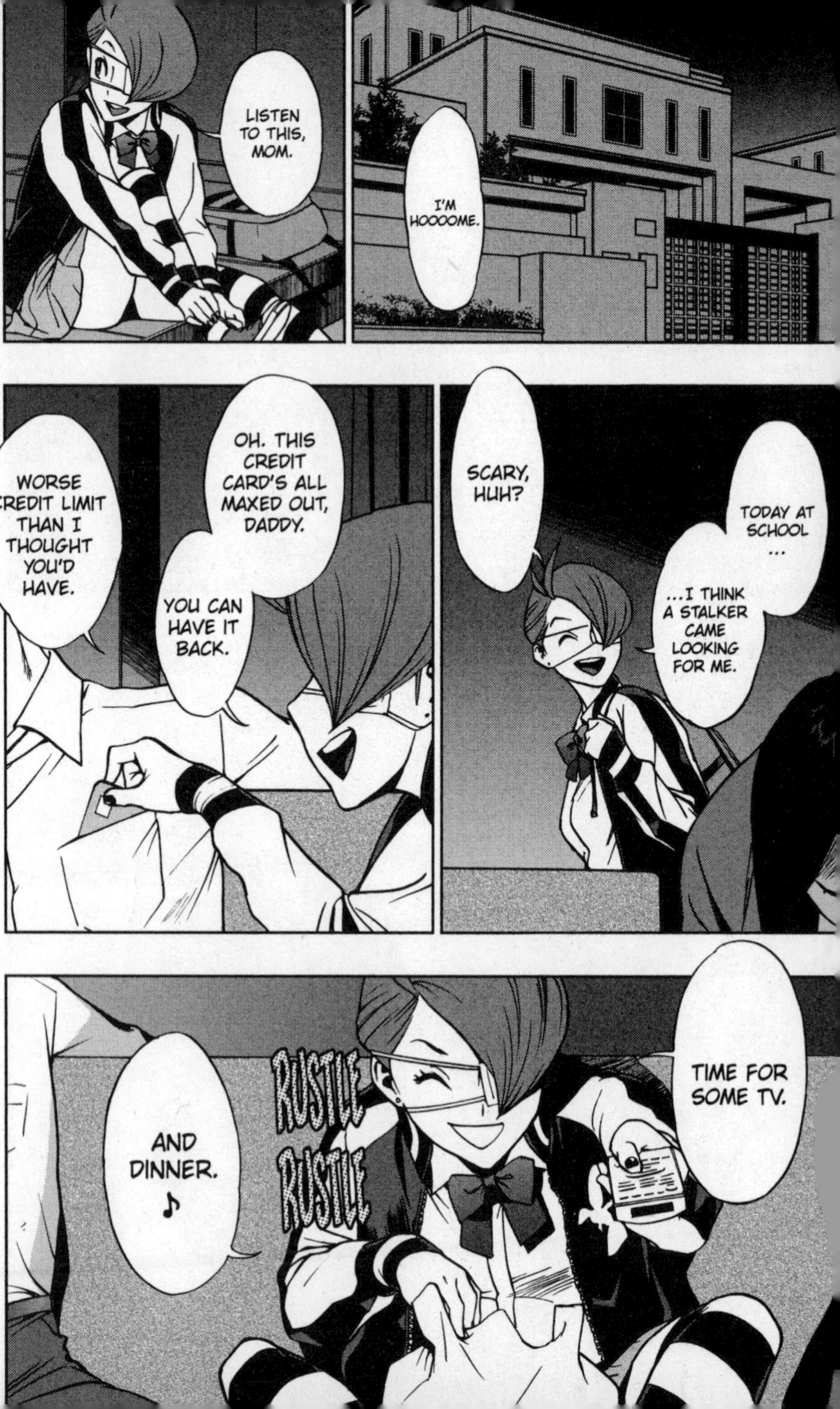
I'M HOOOOME.
LISTEN TO THIS, MOM.
TODAY AT SCHOOL ...
...I THINK A STALKER CAME LOOKING FOR ME.
SCARY, HUH?
OH. THIS CREDIT CARD'S ALL MAXED OUT, DADDY.
WORSE CREDIT LIMIT THAN I THOUGHT YOU'D HAVE.
YOU CAN HAVE IT BACK.
TIME FOR SOME TV.
RUSTLE
RUSTLE
AND DINNER. ♪

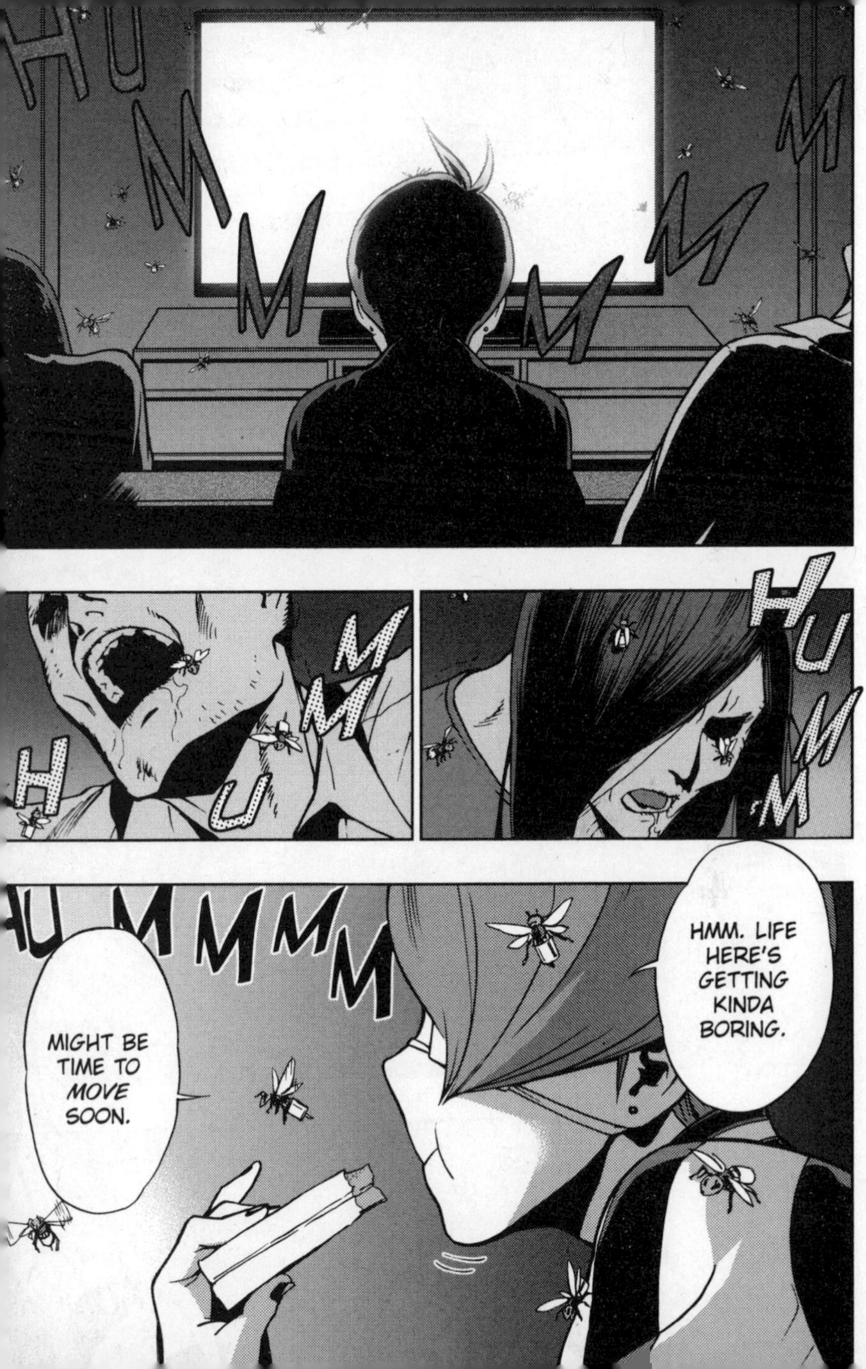
HUMMMM
MMM
HUMMM
HUMMM
HUMMMMM
HMM. LIFE HERE'S GETTING KINDA BORING.
MIGHT BE TIME TO *MOVE* SOON.

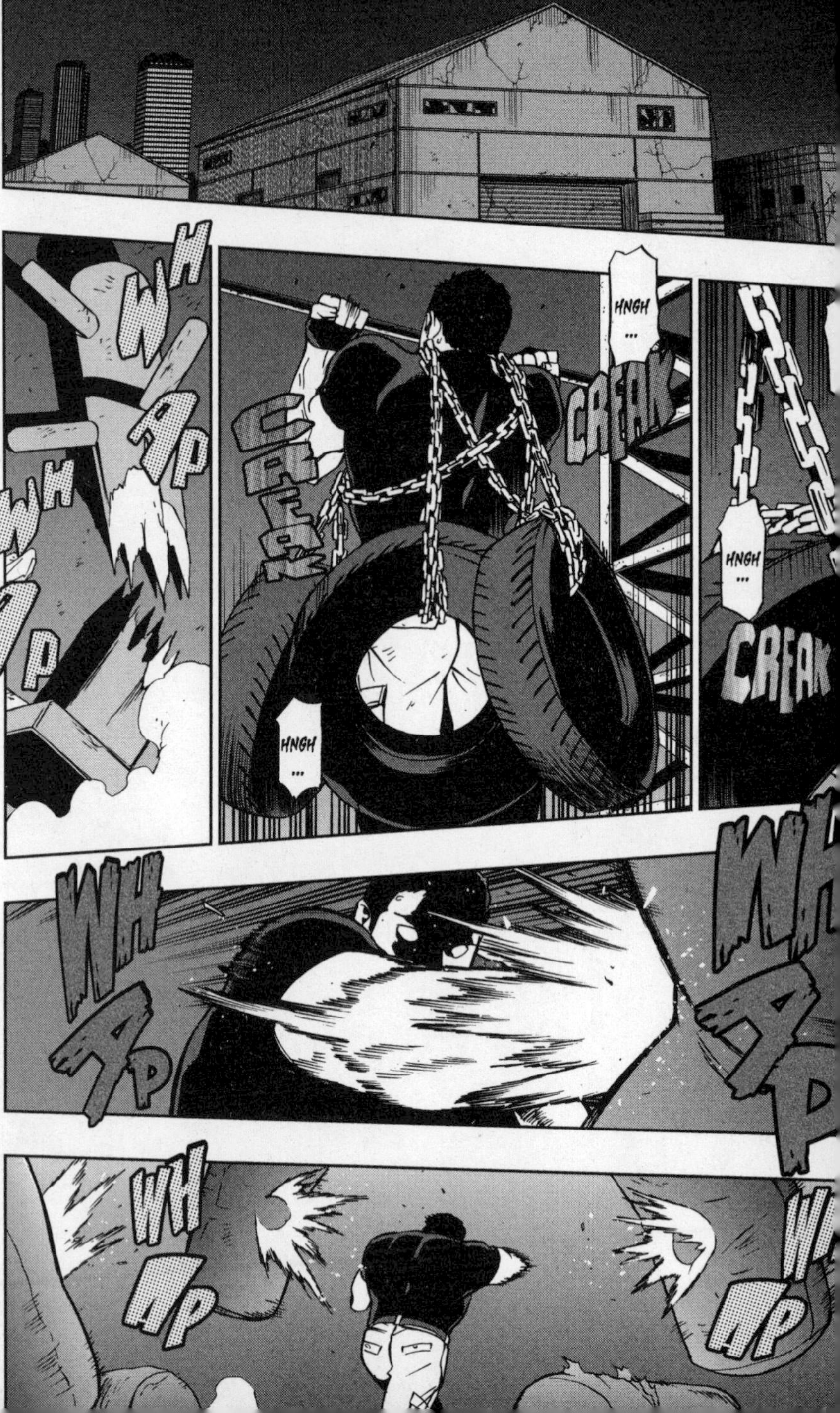
HNGH ...
CREAK
HNGH ...
CREAK
CREAK
HNGH ...
WHAP
WHAP
WHAP
WHAP
WHAP
WHAP

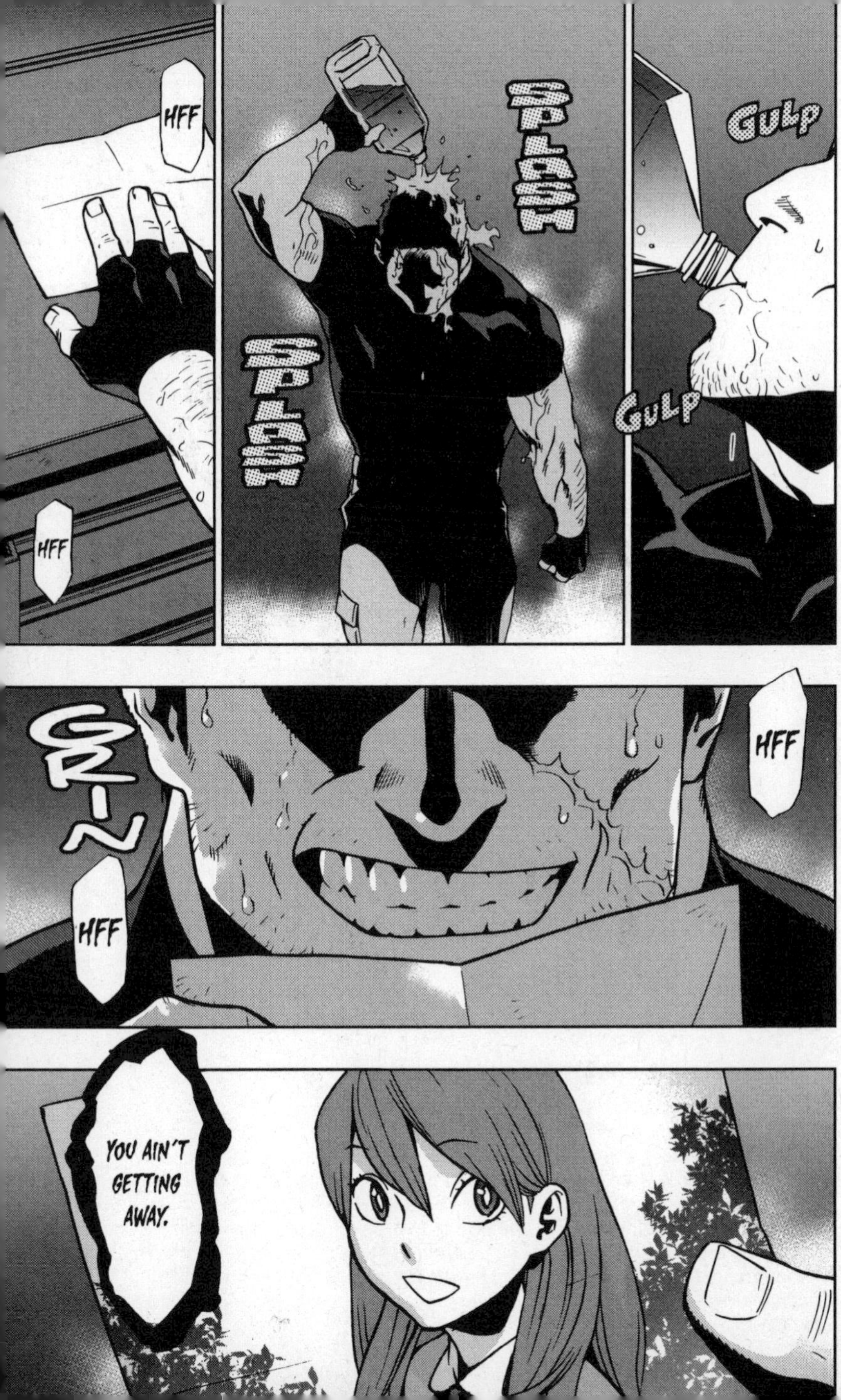
GULP
GULP
SPLASH
SPLASH
HFF
HFF
HFF
GRIN
HFF
YOU AIN'T GETTING AWAY.

THE COLUMN

ABOUT HACHISUKA

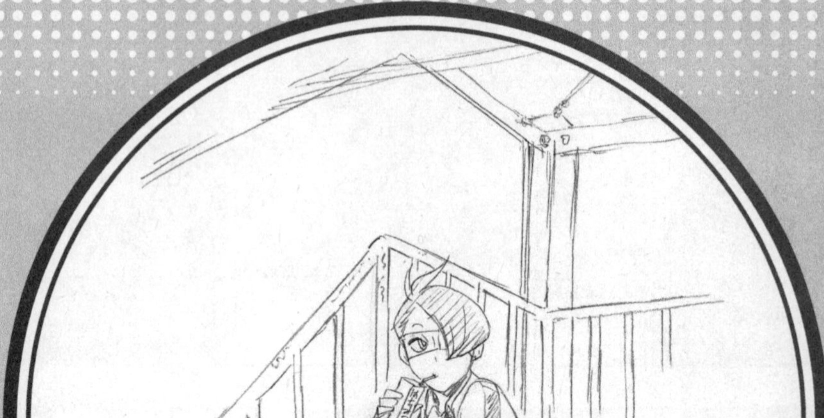

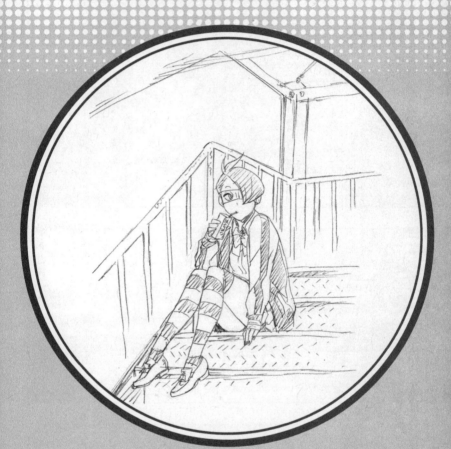

My early concept notes for Hachisuka were things like "high school girl who's a villain on the side" and "always shrewd and competent—as a villain she's a smooth operator who clearly shows how hollow she is inside." Afterwards, I added elements like "eeriness about her that's hard to pin down" and "familial connection to Master." The point that really defines her as a prototypical *Vigilantes* villain is how she acts on whims and doesn't have much of a pro mind-set. I often had her eating and drinking when she first showed up, as a way of emphasizing that she's committing evil in the midst of her everyday life.

—Furuhashi

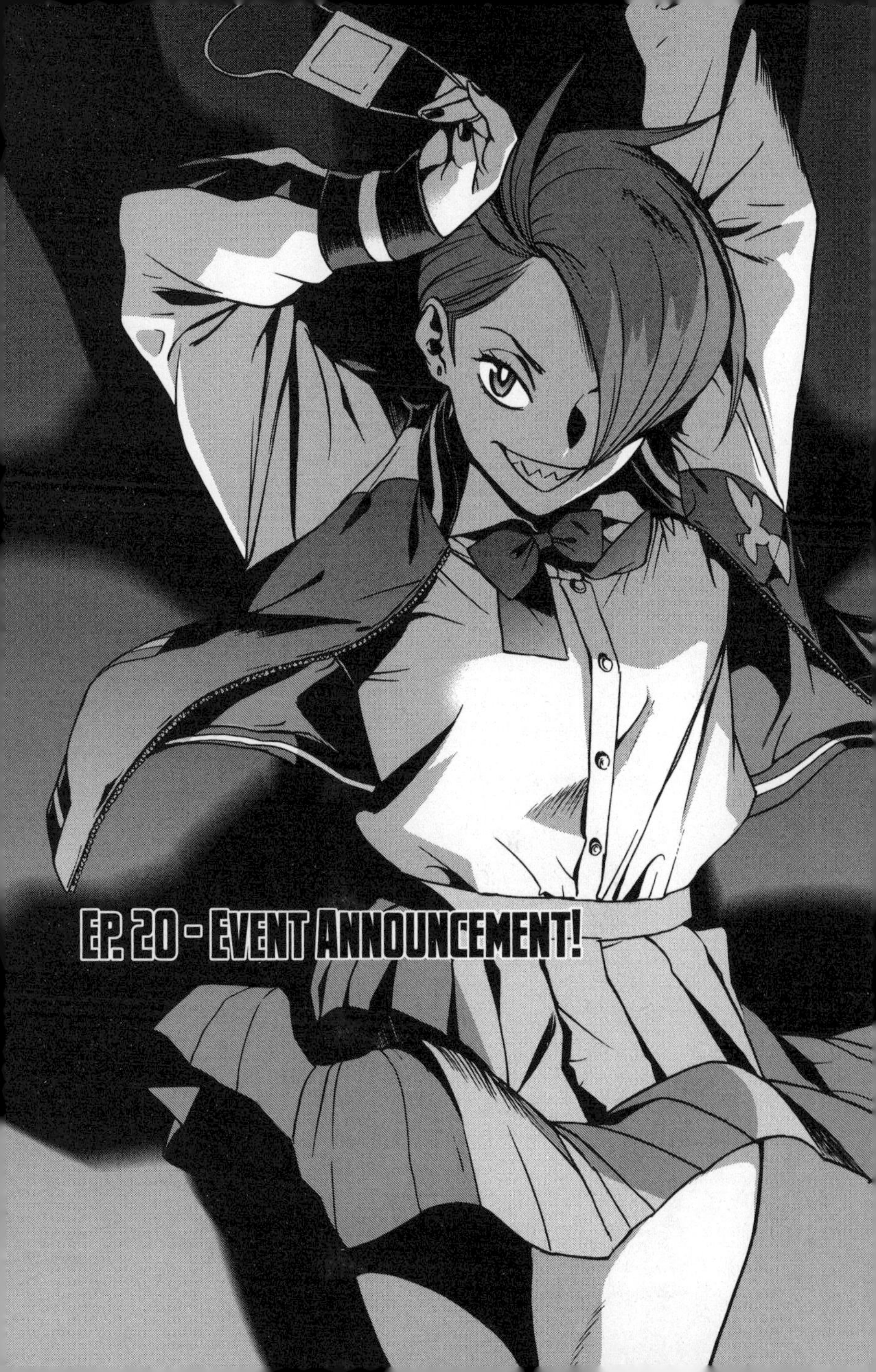
EP. 20 - EVENT ANNOUNCEMENT!

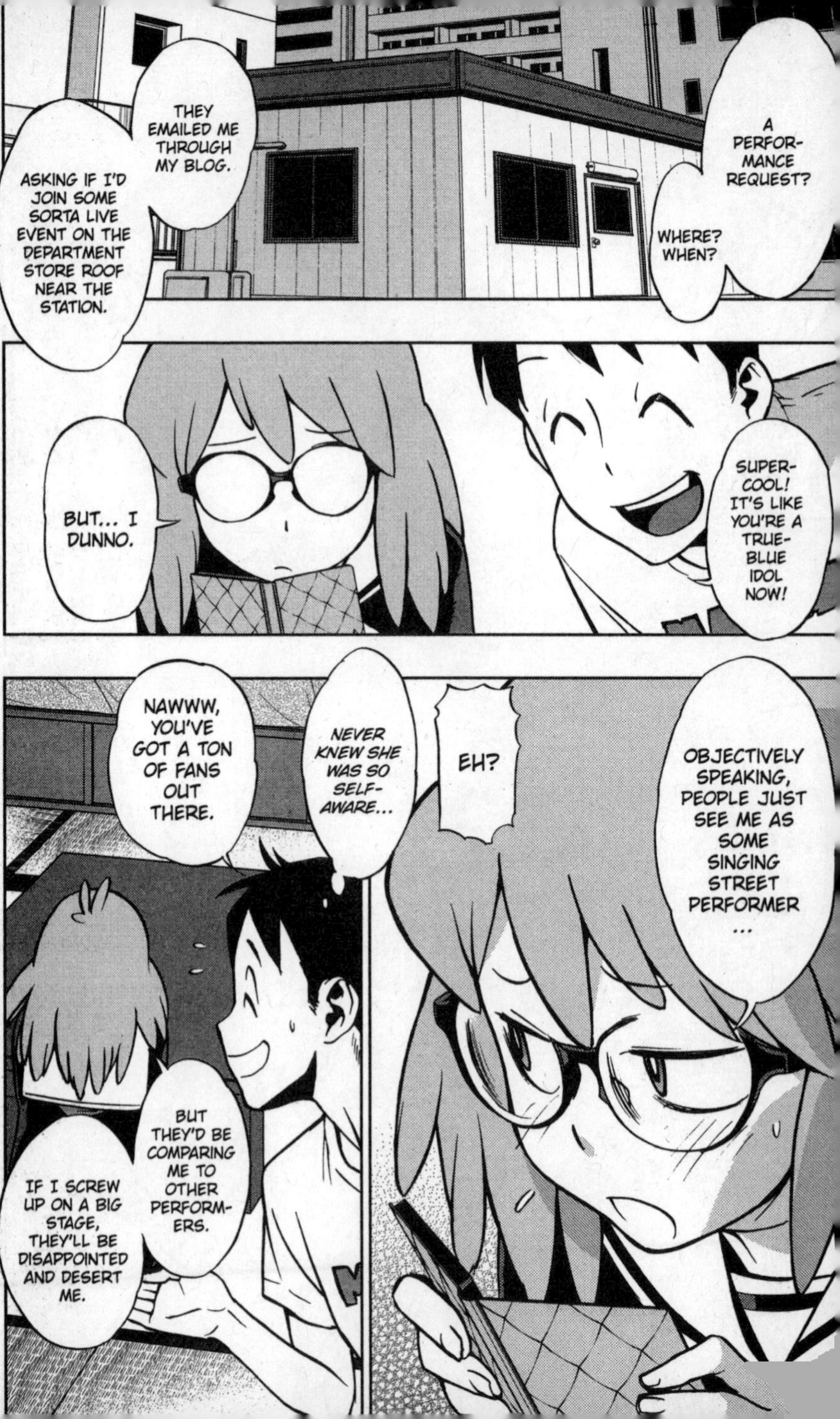
A PERFORMANCE REQUEST?
WHERE? WHEN?
THEY EMAILED ME THROUGH MY BLOG.
ASKING IF I'D JOIN SOME SORTA LIVE EVENT ON THE DEPARTMENT STORE ROOF NEAR THE STATION.
SUPER-COOL! IT'S LIKE YOU'RE A TRUE-BLUE IDOL NOW!
BUT... I DUNNO.
OBJECTIVELY SPEAKING, PEOPLE JUST SEE ME AS SOME SINGING STREET PERFORMER...
EH?
NEVER KNEW SHE WAS SO SELF-AWARE...
NAWWW, YOU'VE GOT A TON OF FANS OUT THERE.
BUT THEY'D BE COMPARING ME TO OTHER PERFORMERS.
IF I SCREW UP ON A BIG STAGE, THEY'LL BE DISAPPOINTED AND DESERT ME.

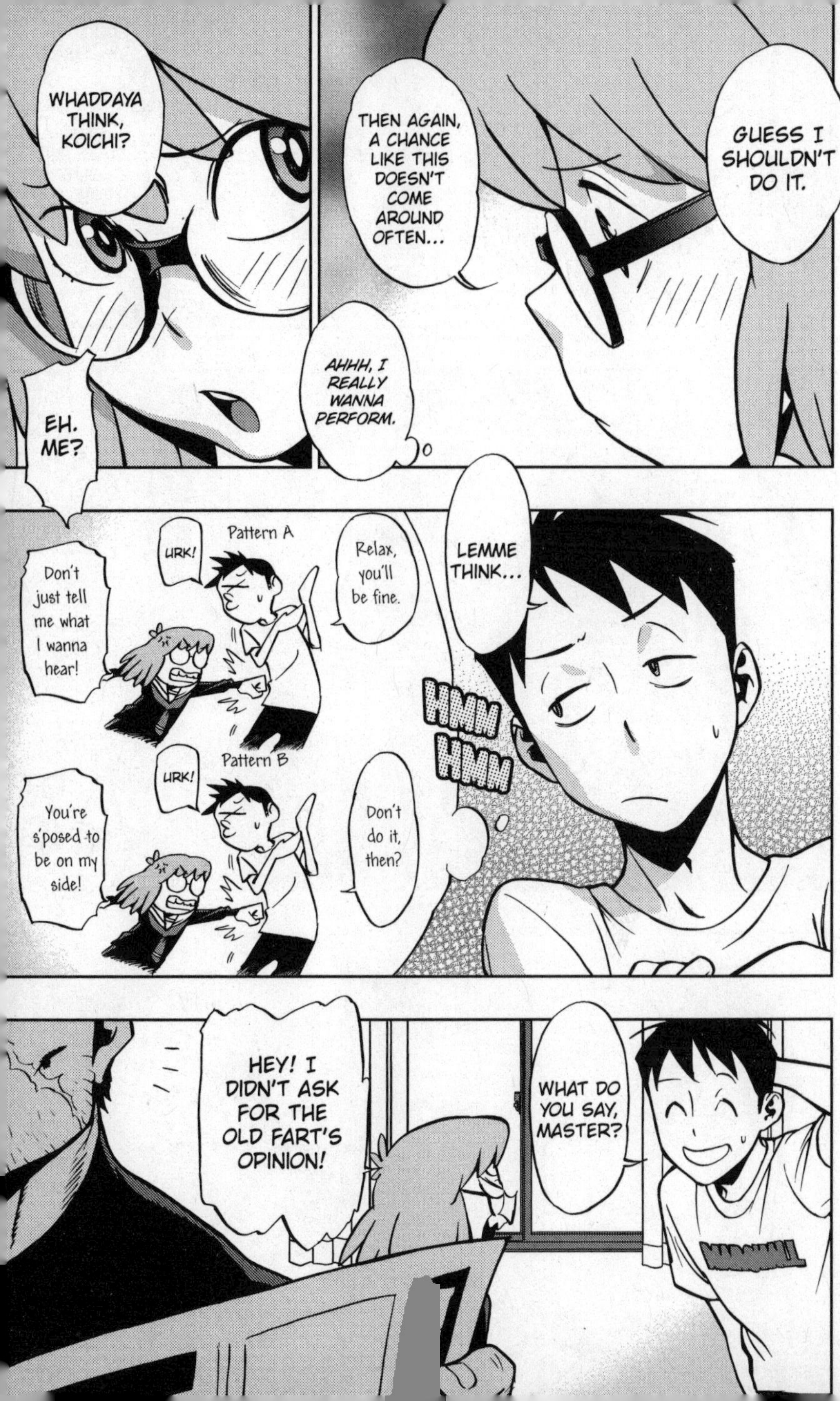
GUESS I SHOULDN'T DO IT.
THEN AGAIN, A CHANCE LIKE THIS DOESN'T COME AROUND OFTEN...
AHHH, I REALLY WANNA PERFORM.
WHADDAYA THINK, KOICHI?
EH. ME?
LEMME THINK...
HMM HMM
Relax, you'll be fine.
Pattern A
URK!
Don't just tell me what I wanna hear!
Don't do it, then?
Pattern B
URK!
You're s'posed to be on my side!
WHAT DO YOU SAY, MASTER?
HEY! I DIDN'T ASK FOR THE OLD FART'S OPINION!

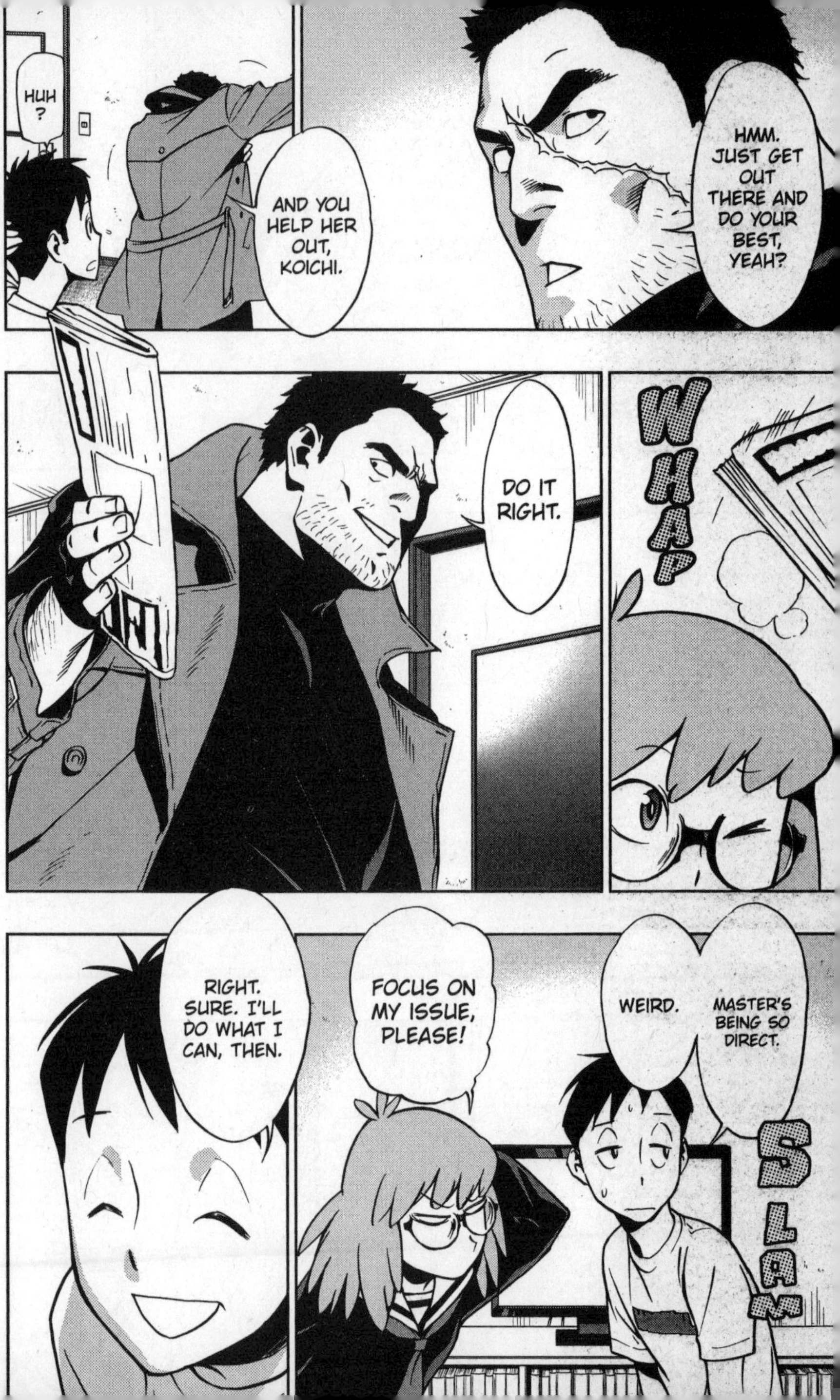
HMM. JUST GET OUT THERE AND DO YOUR BEST, YEAH?
AND YOU HELP HER OUT, KOICHI.
HUH?
WHAP
DO IT RIGHT.
MASTER'S BEING SO DIRECT.
WEIRD.
SLAM
FOCUS ON MY ISSUE, PLEASE!
RIGHT. SURE. I'LL DO WHAT I CAN, THEN.

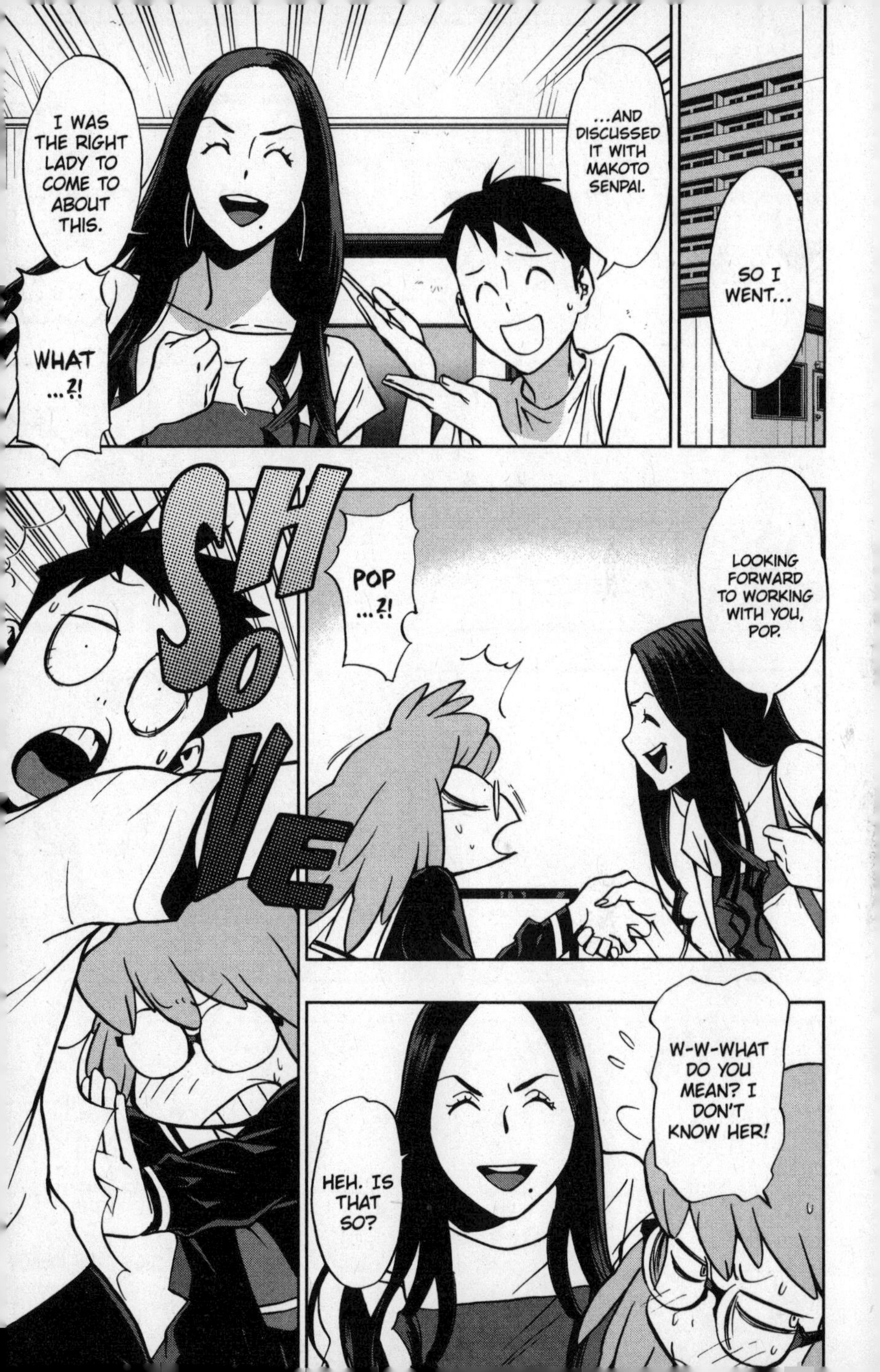
SO I WENT...
...AND DISCUSSED IT WITH MAKOTO SENPAI.
I WAS THE RIGHT LADY TO COME TO ABOUT THIS.
WHAT ...?!
LOOKING FORWARD TO WORKING WITH YOU, POP.
POP ...?!
W-W-WHAT DO YOU MEAN? I DON'T KNOW HER!
HEH. IS THAT SO?
SHOVE

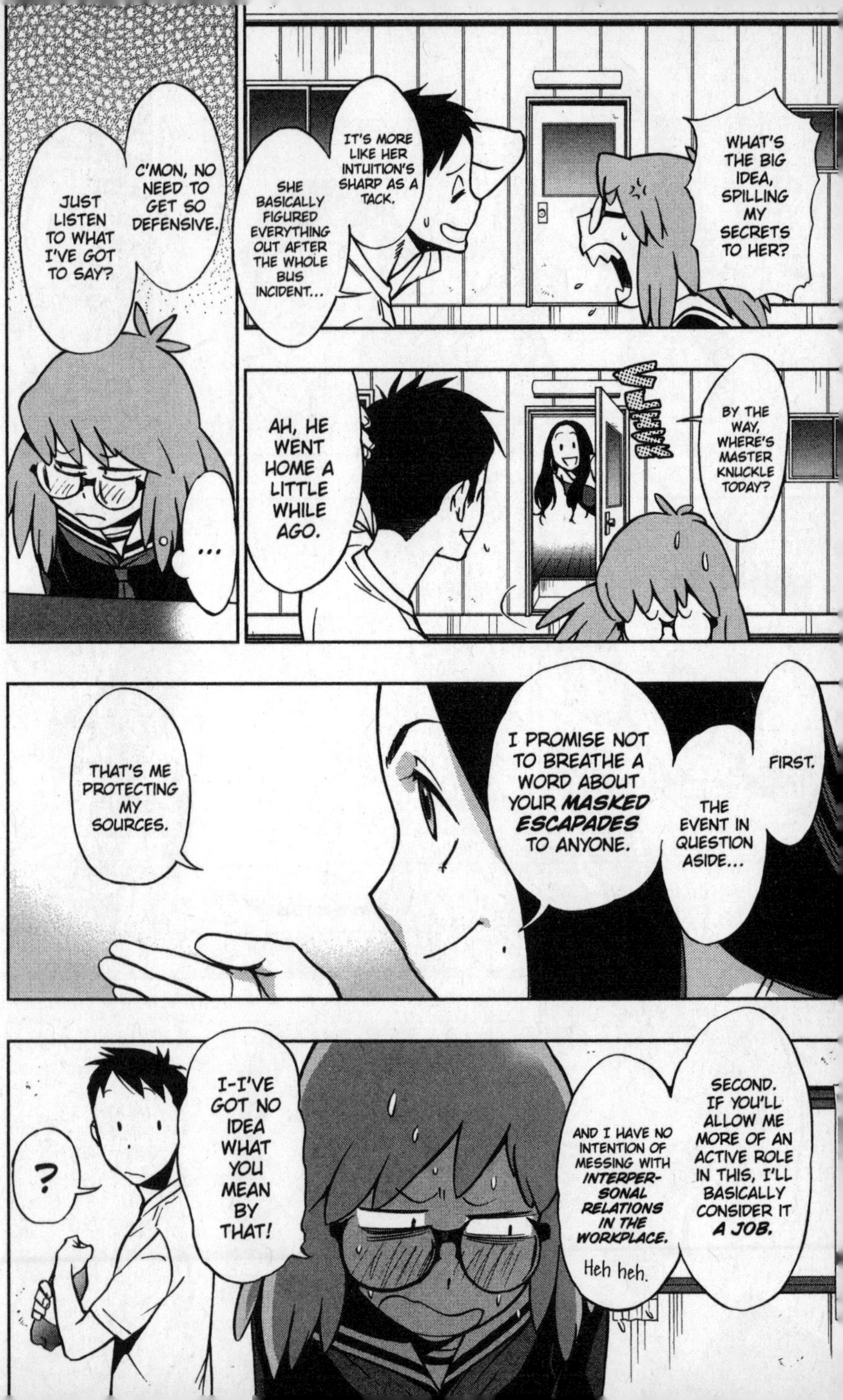
WHAT'S THE BIG IDEA, SPILLING MY SECRETS TO HER?
IT'S MORE LIKE HER INTUITION'S SHARP AS A TACK.
SHE BASICALLY FIGURED EVERYTHING OUT AFTER THE WHOLE BUS INCIDENT...
BY THE WAY, WHERE'S MASTER KNUCKLE TODAY?
AH, HE WENT HOME A LITTLE WHILE AGO.
C'MON, NO NEED TO GET SO DEFENSIVE.
JUST LISTEN TO WHAT I'VE GOT TO SAY?
...
FIRST.
THE EVENT IN QUESTION ASIDE...
I PROMISE NOT TO BREATHE A WORD ABOUT YOUR *MASKED ESCAPADES* TO ANYONE.
THAT'S ME PROTECTING MY SOURCES.
SECOND. IF YOU'LL ALLOW ME MORE OF AN ACTIVE ROLE IN THIS, I'LL BASICALLY CONSIDER IT *A JOB.*
AND I HAVE NO INTENTION OF MESSING WITH *INTERPERSONAL RELATIONS IN THE WORKPLACE.*
Heh heh.
I-I'VE GOT NO IDEA WHAT YOU MEAN BY THAT!
?

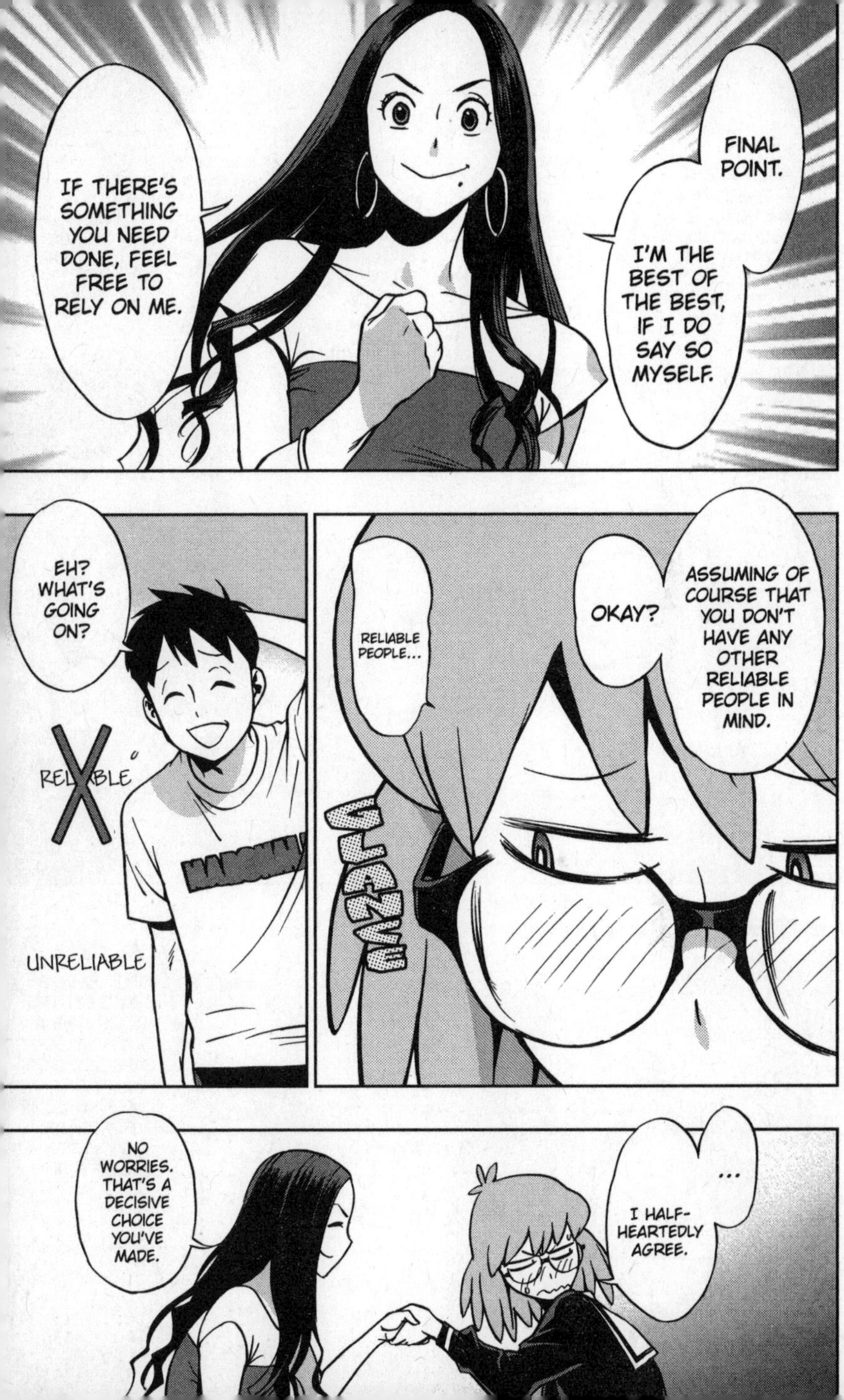
FINAL POINT.
I'M THE BEST OF THE BEST, IF I DO SAY SO MYSELF.
IF THERE'S SOMETHING YOU NEED DONE, FEEL FREE TO RELY ON ME.
ASSUMING OF COURSE THAT YOU DON'T HAVE ANY OTHER RELIABLE PEOPLE IN MIND.
OKAY?
RELIABLE PEOPLE...
EH? WHAT'S GOING ON?
RELIABLE
UNRELIABLE
...
I HALF-HEARTEDLY AGREE.
NO WORRIES. THAT'S A DECISIVE CHOICE YOU'VE MADE.

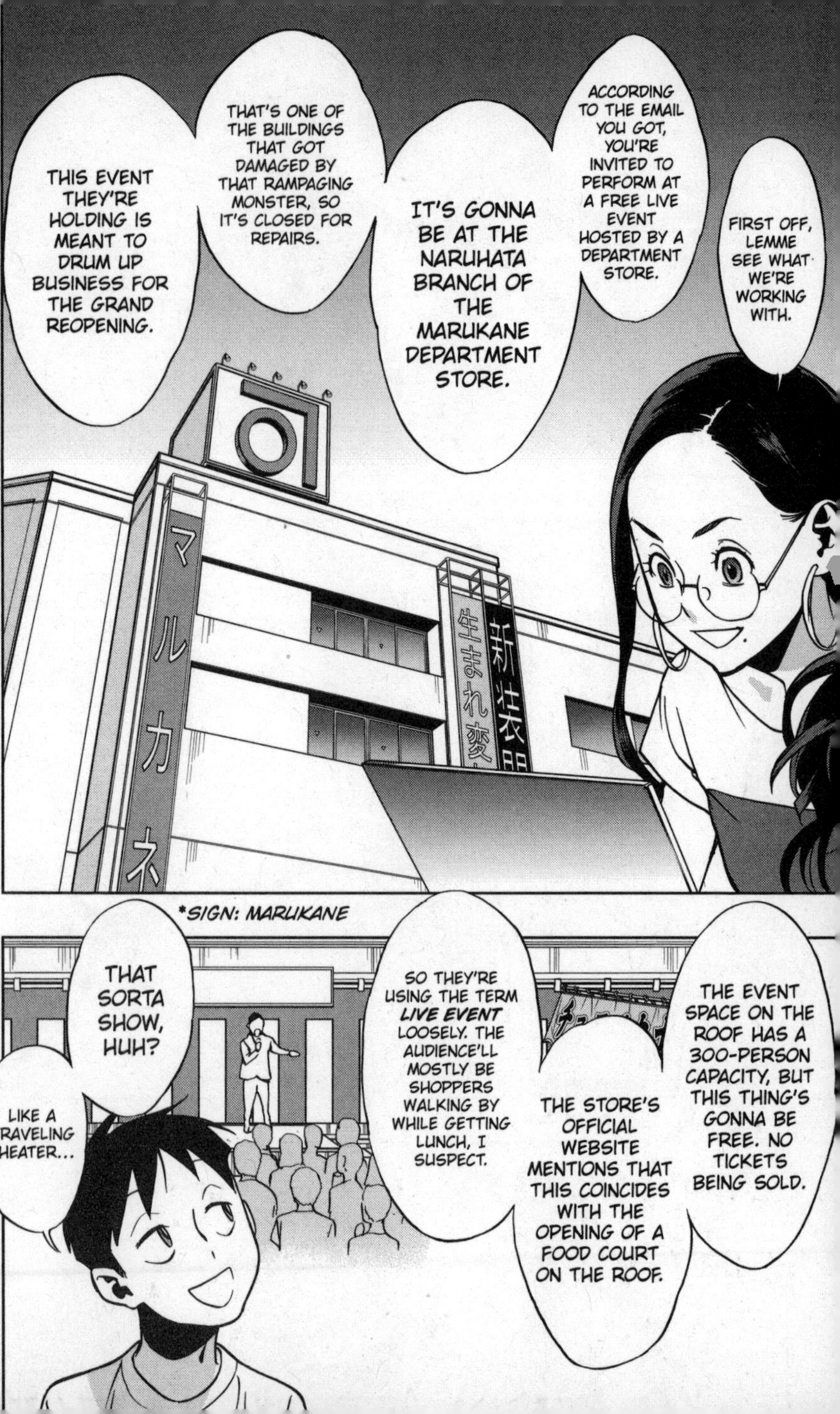
FIRST OFF, LEMME SEE WHAT WE'RE WORKING WITH.
ACCORDING TO THE EMAIL YOU GOT, YOU'RE INVITED TO PERFORM AT A FREE LIVE EVENT HOSTED BY A DEPARTMENT STORE.
IT'S GONNA BE AT THE NARUHATA BRANCH OF THE MARUKANE DEPARTMENT STORE.
THAT'S ONE OF THE BUILDINGS THAT GOT DAMAGED BY THAT RAMPAGING MONSTER, SO IT'S CLOSED FOR REPAIRS.
THIS EVENT THEY'RE HOLDING IS MEANT TO DRUM UP BUSINESS FOR THE GRAND REOPENING.
マルカネ
*SIGN: MARUKANE
THE EVENT SPACE ON THE ROOF HAS A 300-PERSON CAPACITY, BUT THIS THING'S GONNA BE FREE. NO TICKETS BEING SOLD.
THE STORE'S OFFICIAL WEBSITE MENTIONS THAT THIS COINCIDES WITH THE OPENING OF A FOOD COURT ON THE ROOF.
SO THEY'RE USING THE TERM *LIVE EVENT* LOOSELY. THE AUDIENCE'LL MOSTLY BE SHOPPERS WALKING BY WHILE GETTING LUNCH, I SUSPECT.
THAT SORTA SHOW, HUH?
LIKE A TRAVELING THEATER...

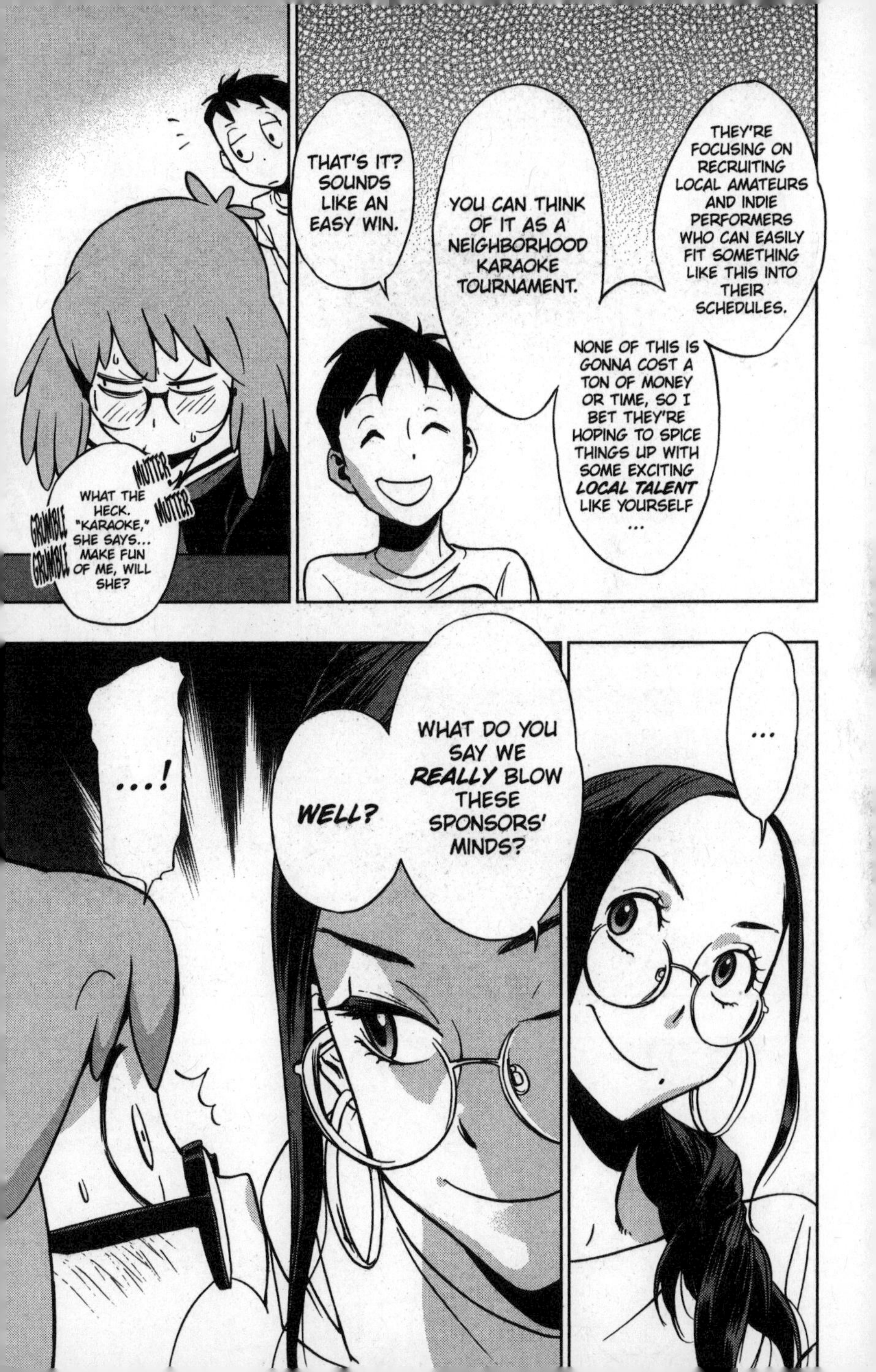
THEY'RE FOCUSING ON RECRUITING LOCAL AMATEURS AND INDIE PERFORMERS WHO CAN EASILY FIT SOMETHING LIKE THIS INTO THEIR SCHEDULES.
YOU CAN THINK OF IT AS A NEIGHBORHOOD KARAOKE TOURNAMENT.
THAT'S IT? SOUNDS LIKE AN EASY WIN.
NONE OF THIS IS GONNA COST A TON OF MONEY OR TIME, SO I BET THEY'RE HOPING TO SPICE THINGS UP WITH SOME EXCITING ***LOCAL TALENT*** LIKE YOURSELF ...
MUTTER MUTTER
WHAT THE HECK. "KARAOKE," SHE SAYS... MAKE FUN OF ME, WILL SHE?
GRUMBLE GRUMBLE
...
WHAT DO YOU SAY WE ***REALLY*** BLOW THESE SPONSORS' MINDS?
WELL?
...!

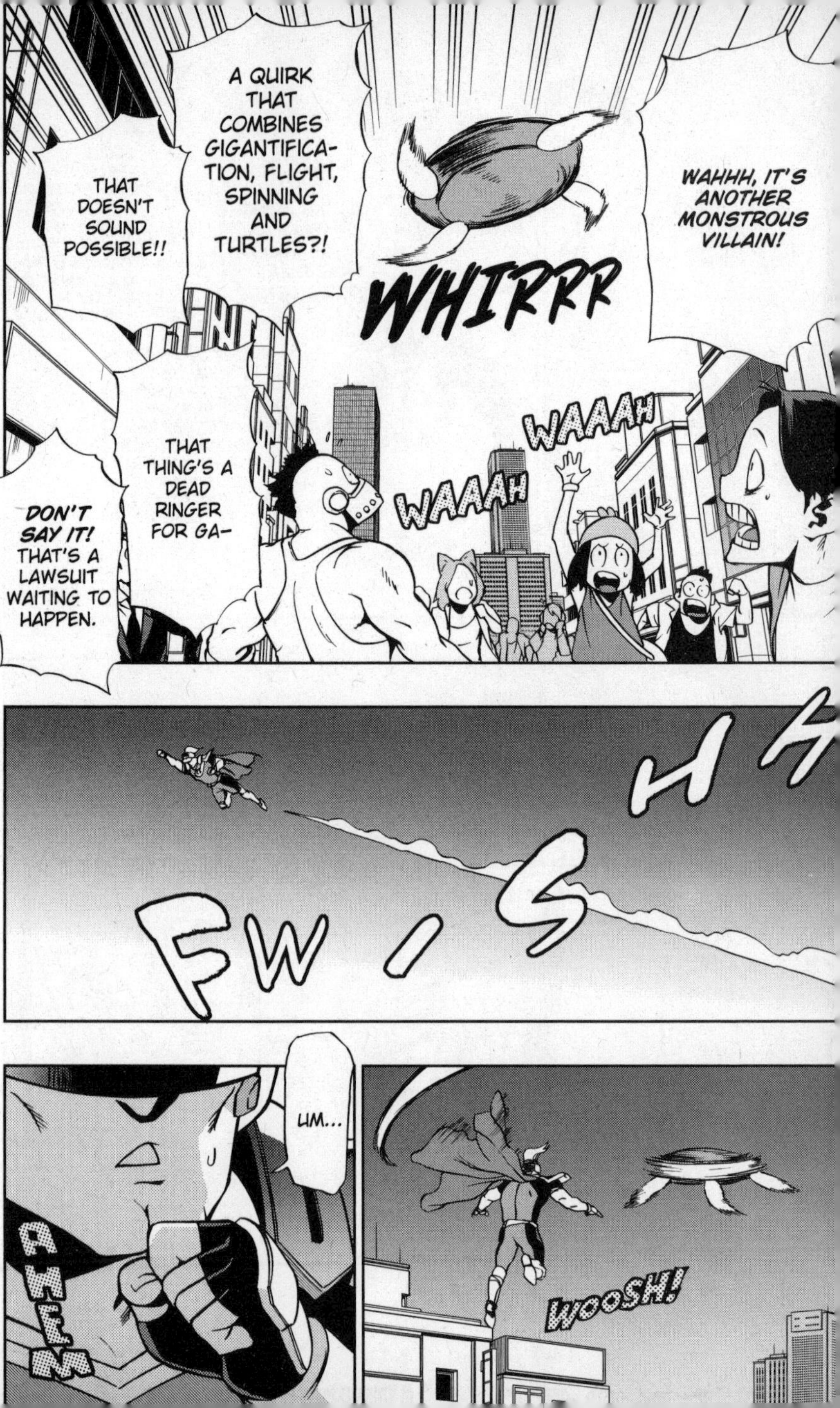
WAHHH, IT'S ANOTHER MONSTROUS VILLAIN!
A QUIRK THAT COMBINES GIGANTIFICATION, FLIGHT, SPINNING AND TURTLES?!
THAT DOESN'T SOUND POSSIBLE!!
WHIRRR
WAAAH
WAAAH
THAT THING'S A DEAD RINGER FOR GA-
DON'T SAY IT! THAT'S A LAWSUIT WAITING TO HAPPEN.
FWISH
WOOSH!
UM...
AHEM

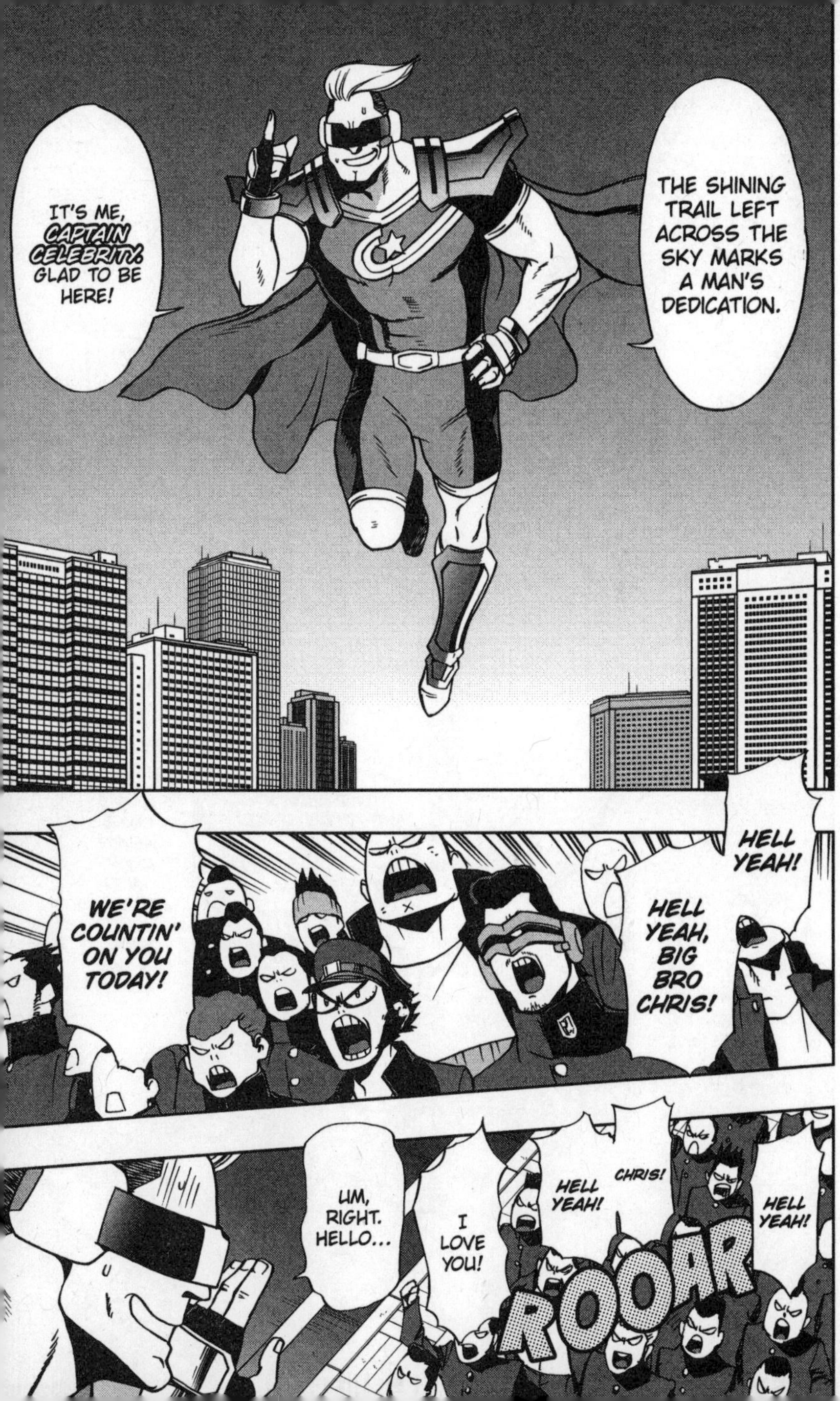
THE SHINING TRAIL LEFT ACROSS THE SKY MARKS A MAN'S DEDICATION.
IT'S ME, CAPTAIN CELEBRITY. GLAD TO BE HERE!
HELL YEAH!
HELL YEAH, BIG BRO CHRIS!
WE'RE COUNTIN' ON YOU TODAY!
HELL YEAH!
CHRIS!
HELL YEAH!
ROOAR
I LOVE YOU!
UM, RIGHT. HELLO...

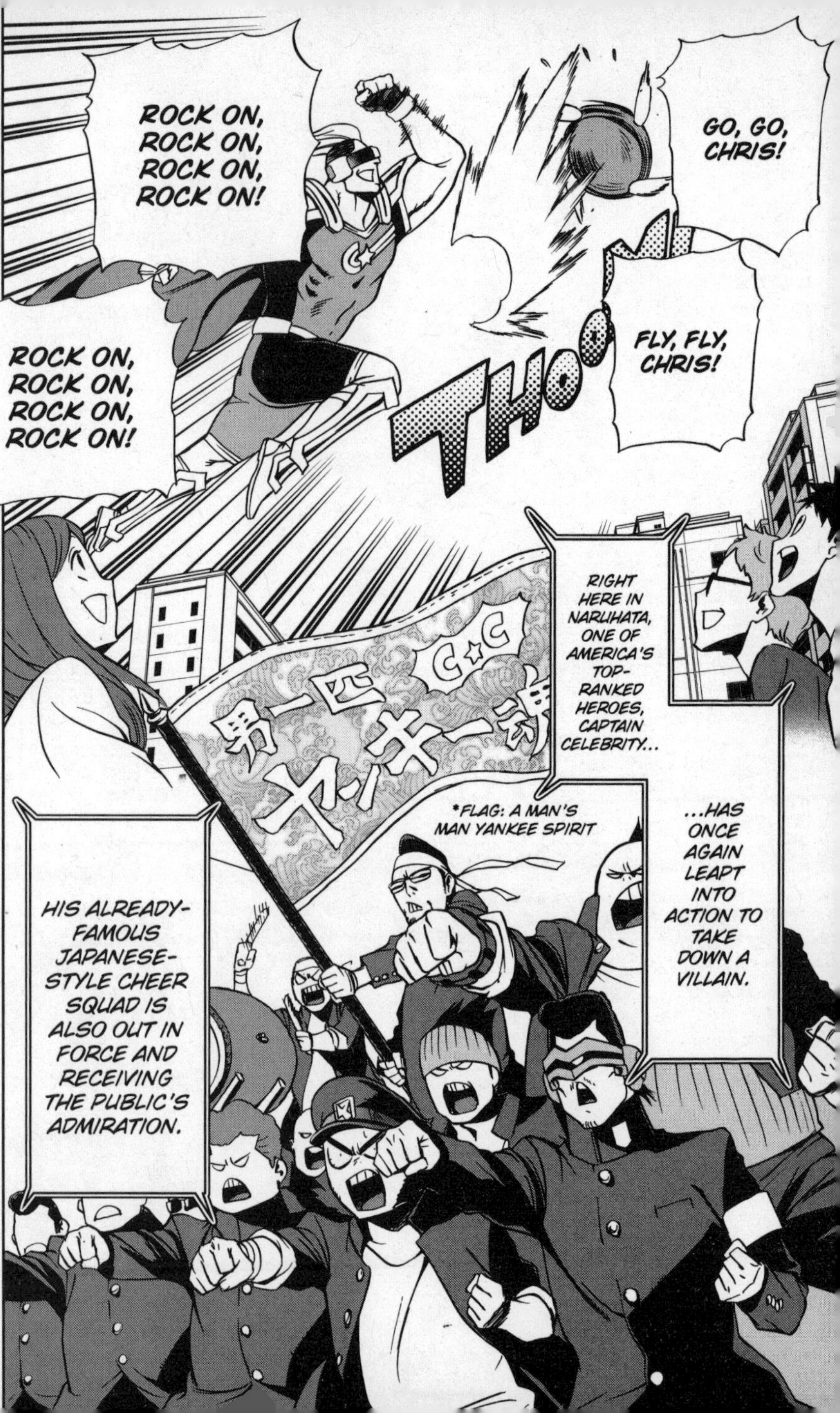
GO, GO, CHRIS!
ROCK ON, ROCK ON, ROCK ON, ROCK ON!
FLY, FLY, CHRIS!
THOOM
ROCK ON, ROCK ON, ROCK ON, ROCK ON!
RIGHT HERE IN NARUHATA, ONE OF AMERICA'S TOP-RANKED HEROES, CAPTAIN CELEBRITY...
...HAS ONCE AGAIN LEAPT INTO ACTION TO TAKE DOWN A VILLAIN.
*FLAG: A MAN'S MAN YANKEE SPIRIT
HIS ALREADY-FAMOUS JAPANESE-STYLE CHEER SQUAD IS ALSO OUT IN FORCE AND RECEIVING THE PUBLIC'S ADMIRATION.

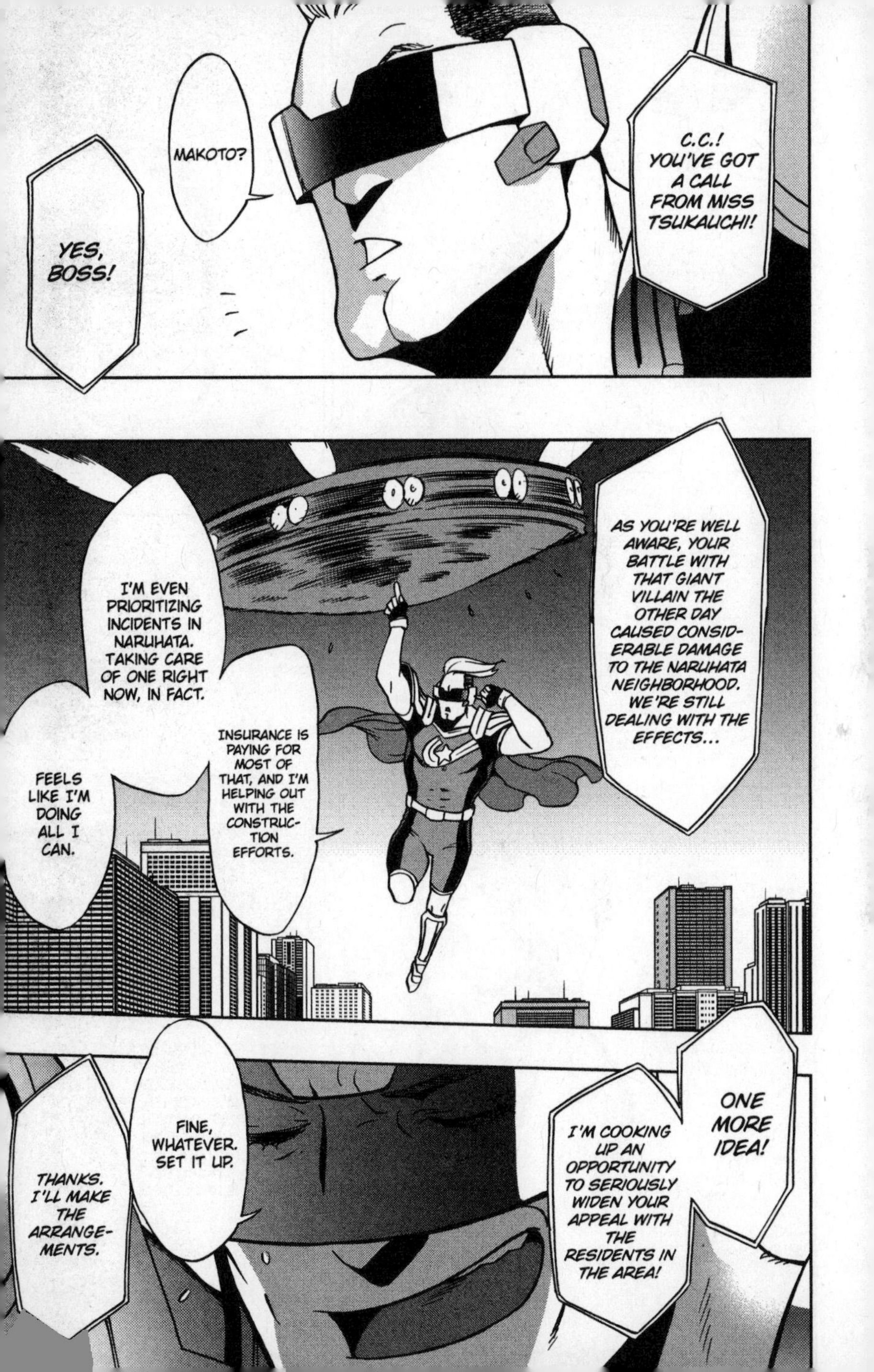
C.C.! YOU'VE GOT A CALL FROM MISS TSUKAUCHI!
MAKOTO?
YES, BOSS!
AS YOU'RE WELL AWARE, YOUR BATTLE WITH THAT GIANT VILLAIN THE OTHER DAY CAUSED CONSIDERABLE DAMAGE TO THE NARUHATA NEIGHBORHOOD. WE'RE STILL DEALING WITH THE EFFECTS...
I'M EVEN PRIORITIZING INCIDENTS IN NARUHATA. TAKING CARE OF ONE RIGHT NOW, IN FACT.
INSURANCE IS PAYING FOR MOST OF THAT, AND I'M HELPING OUT WITH THE CONSTRUCTION EFFORTS.
FEELS LIKE I'M DOING ALL I CAN.
ONE MORE IDEA!
I'M COOKING UP AN OPPORTUNITY TO SERIOUSLY WIDEN YOUR APPEAL WITH THE RESIDENTS IN THE AREA!
FINE, WHATEVER. SET IT UP.
THANKS. I'LL MAKE THE ARRANGEMENTS.

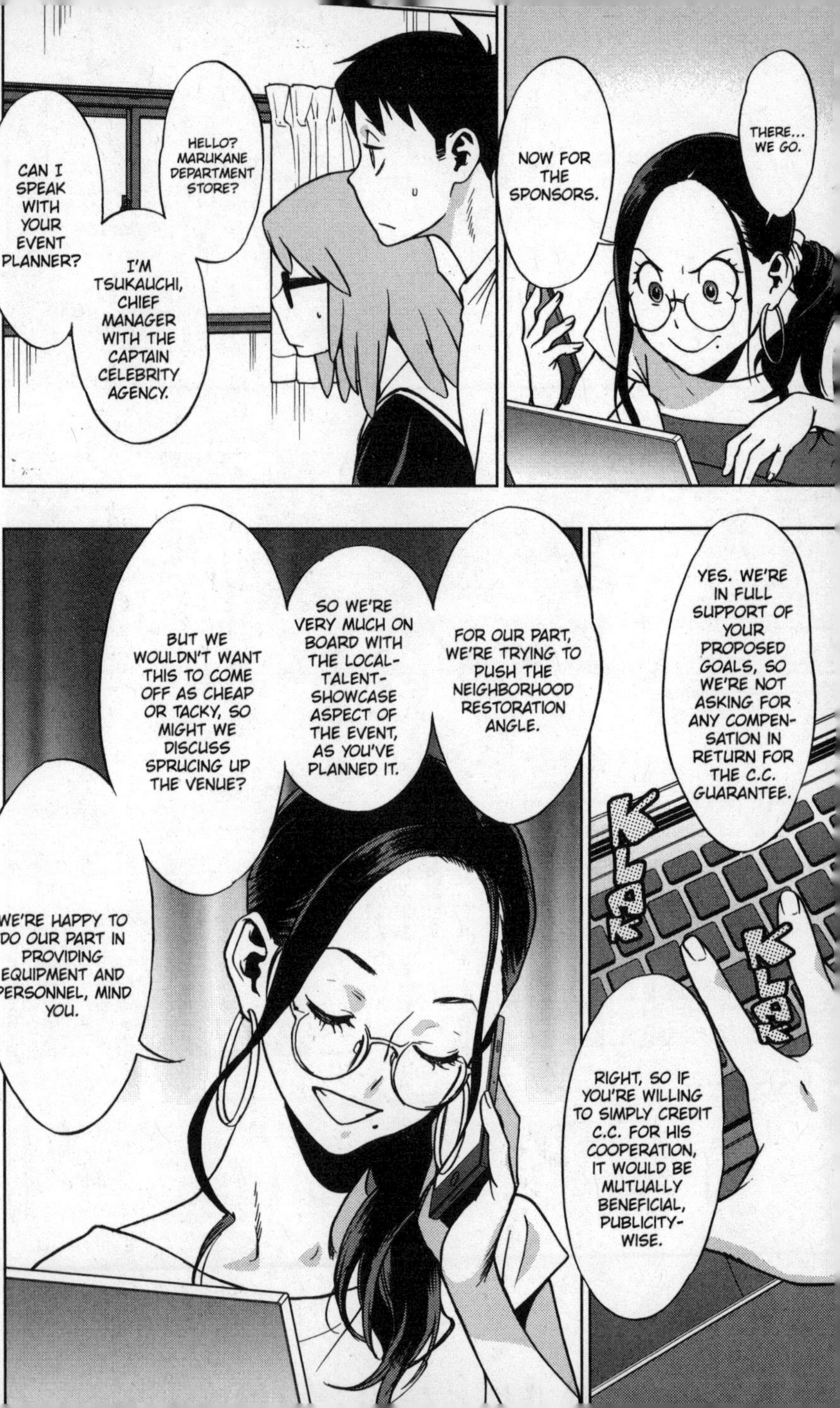
THERE... WE GO.
NOW FOR THE SPONSORS.
HELLO? MARUKANE DEPARTMENT STORE?
I'M TSUKAUCHI, CHIEF MANAGER WITH THE CAPTAIN CELEBRITY AGENCY.
CAN I SPEAK WITH YOUR EVENT PLANNER?
YES. WE'RE IN FULL SUPPORT OF YOUR PROPOSED GOALS, SO WE'RE NOT ASKING FOR ANY COMPENSATION IN RETURN FOR THE C.C. GUARANTEE.
KLAK
KLAK
RIGHT, SO IF YOU'RE WILLING TO SIMPLY CREDIT C.C. FOR HIS COOPERATION, IT WOULD BE MUTUALLY BENEFICIAL, PUBLICITY-WISE.
FOR OUR PART, WE'RE TRYING TO PUSH THE NEIGHBORHOOD RESTORATION ANGLE.
SO WE'RE VERY MUCH ON BOARD WITH THE LOCAL-TALENT-SHOWCASE ASPECT OF THE EVENT, AS YOU'VE PLANNED IT.
BUT WE WOULDN'T WANT THIS TO COME OFF AS CHEAP OR TACKY, SO MIGHT WE DISCUSS SPRUCING UP THE VENUE?
WE'RE HAPPY TO DO OUR PART IN PROVIDING EQUIPMENT AND PERSONNEL, MIND YOU.

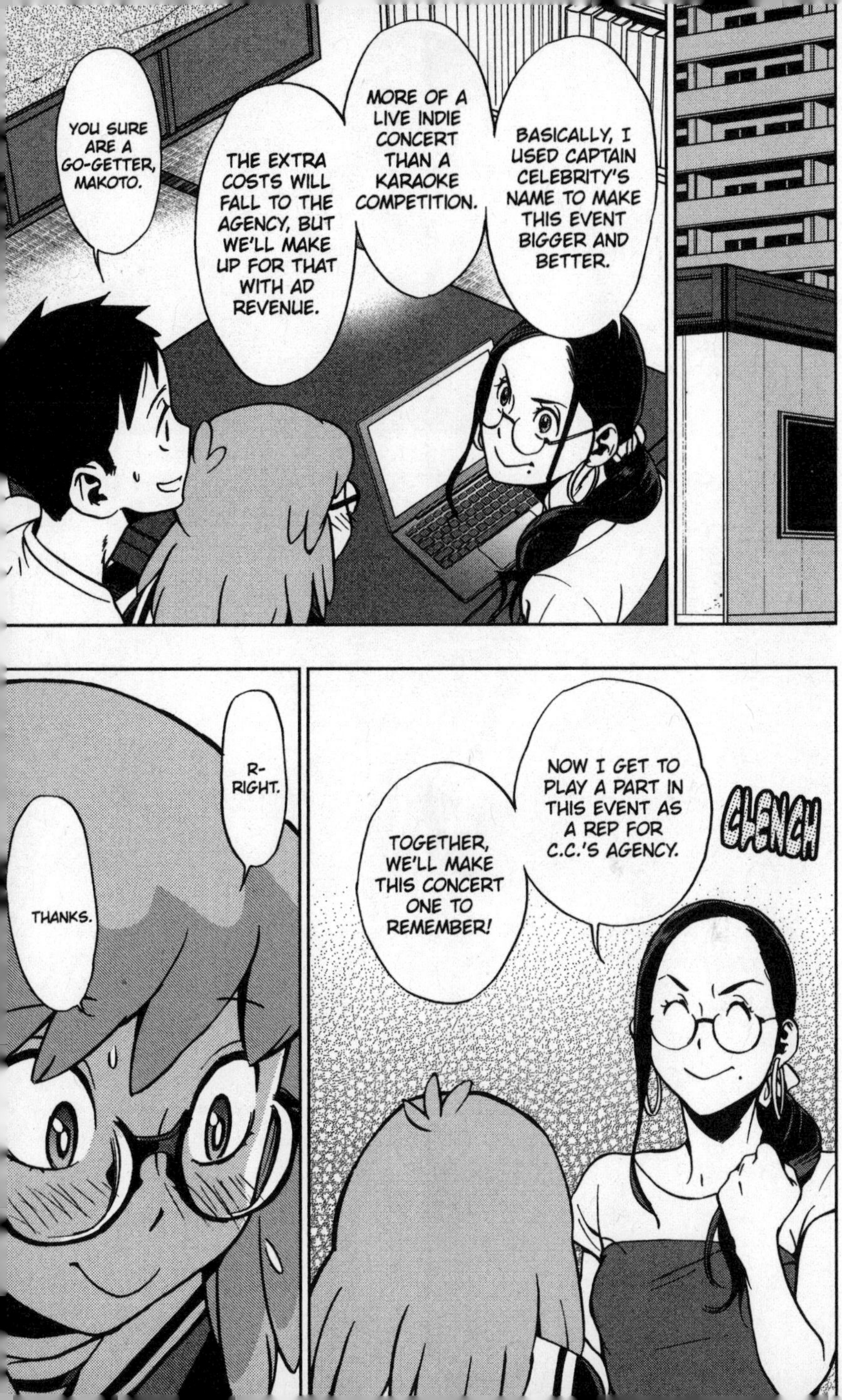
BASICALLY, I USED CAPTAIN CELEBRITY'S NAME TO MAKE THIS EVENT BIGGER AND BETTER.
MORE OF A LIVE INDIE CONCERT THAN A KARAOKE COMPETITION.
THE EXTRA COSTS WILL FALL TO THE AGENCY, BUT WE'LL MAKE UP FOR THAT WITH AD REVENUE.
YOU SURE ARE A GO-GETTER, MAKOTO.
CLENCH
NOW I GET TO PLAY A PART IN THIS EVENT AS A REP FOR C.C.'S AGENCY.
TOGETHER, WE'LL MAKE THIS CONCERT ONE TO REMEMBER!
R-RIGHT.
THANKS.

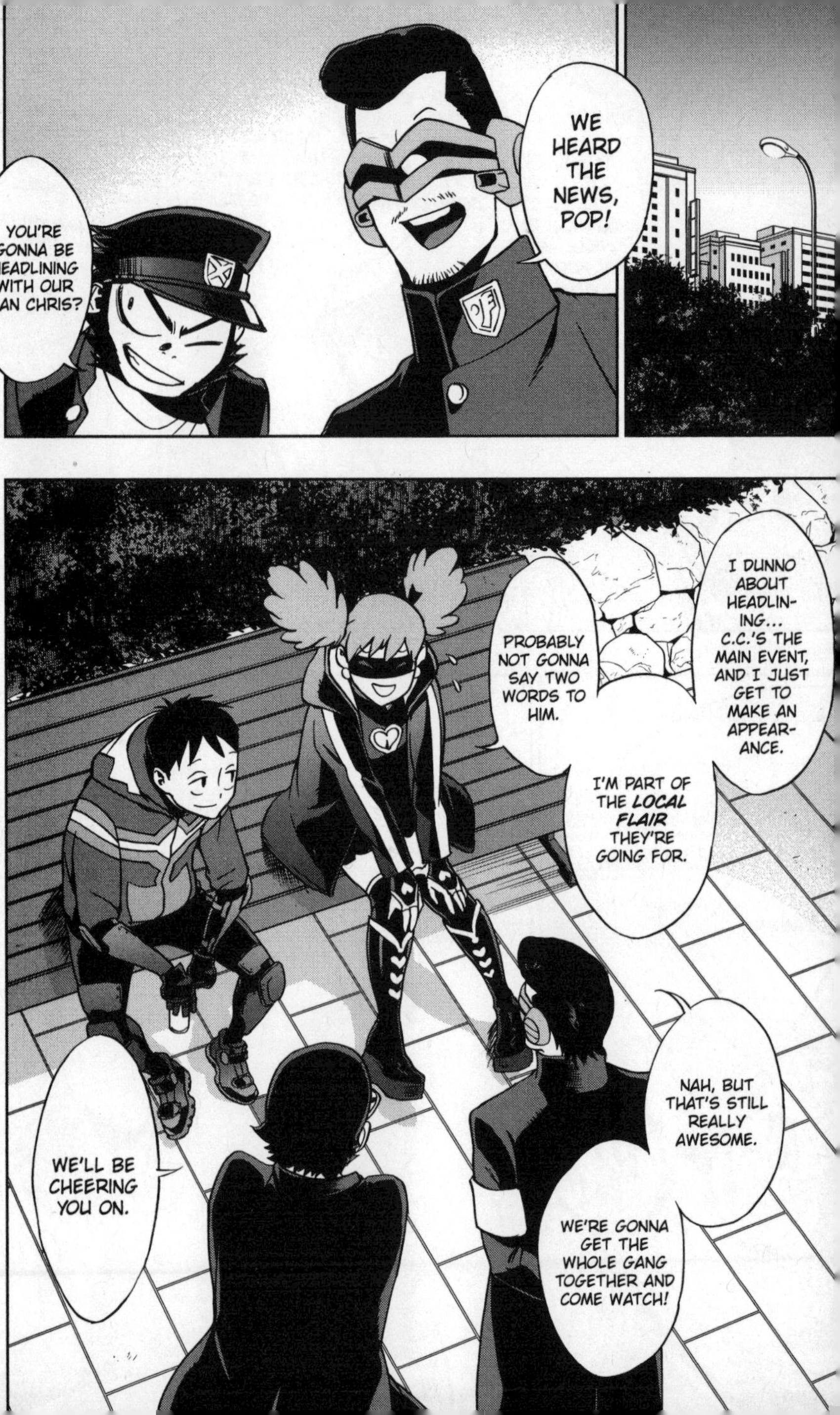
WE HEARD THE NEWS, POP!
YOU'RE GONNA BE HEADLINING WITH OUR MAN CHRIS?
I DUNNO ABOUT HEADLINING... C.C.'S THE MAIN EVENT, AND I JUST GET TO MAKE AN APPEARANCE.
I'M PART OF THE *LOCAL FLAIR* THEY'RE GOING FOR.
PROBABLY NOT GONNA SAY TWO WORDS TO HIM.
NAH, BUT THAT'S STILL REALLY AWESOME.
WE'RE GONNA GET THE WHOLE GANG TOGETHER AND COME WATCH!
WE'LL BE CHEERING YOU ON.

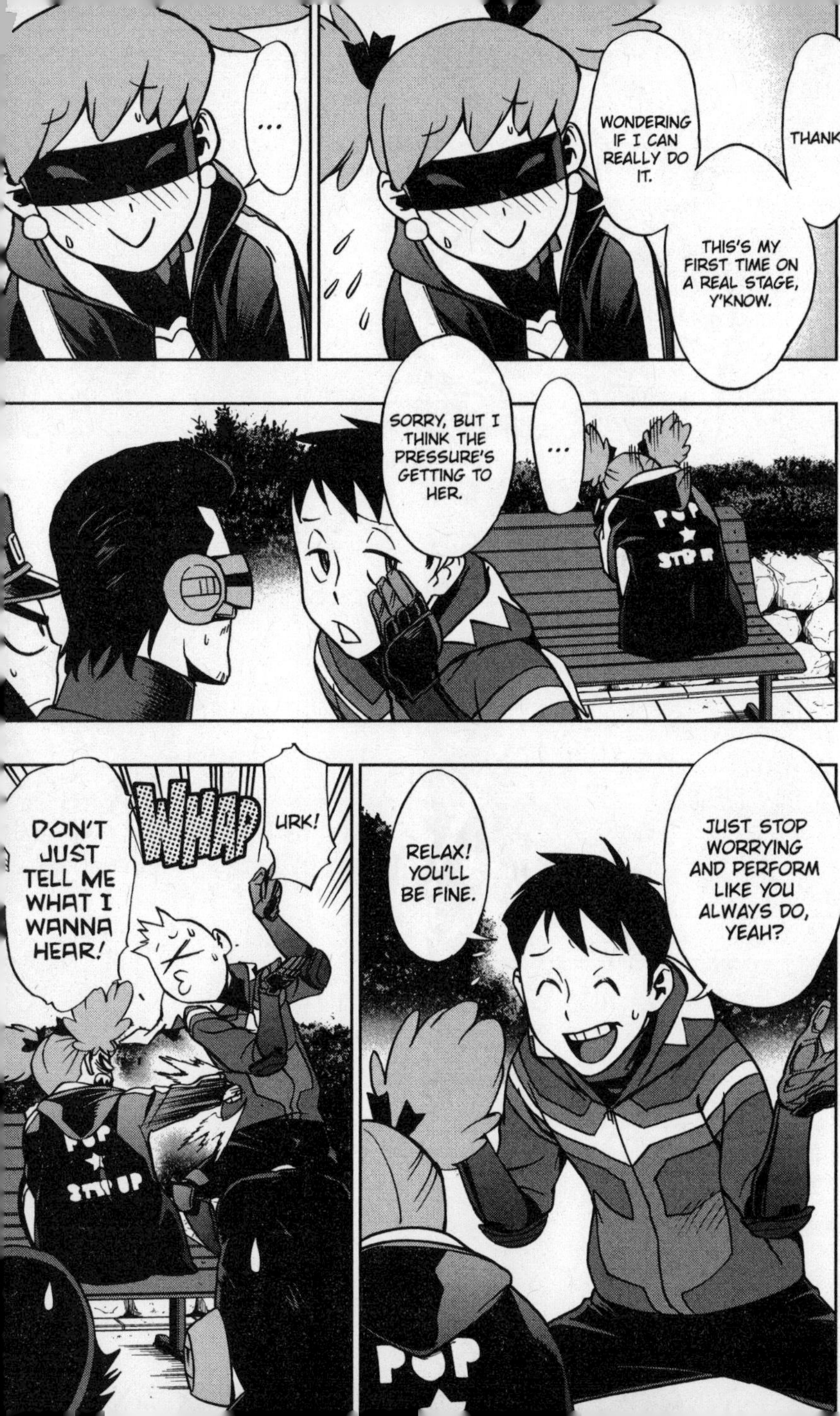
THANKS.
WONDERING IF I CAN REALLY DO IT.
THIS'S MY FIRST TIME ON A REAL STAGE, Y'KNOW.
...
...
SORRY, BUT I THINK THE PRESSURE'S GETTING TO HER.
JUST STOP WORRYING AND PERFORM LIKE YOU ALWAYS DO, YEAH?
RELAX! YOU'LL BE FINE.
URK!
WHAP
DON'T JUST TELL ME WHAT I WANNA HEAR!

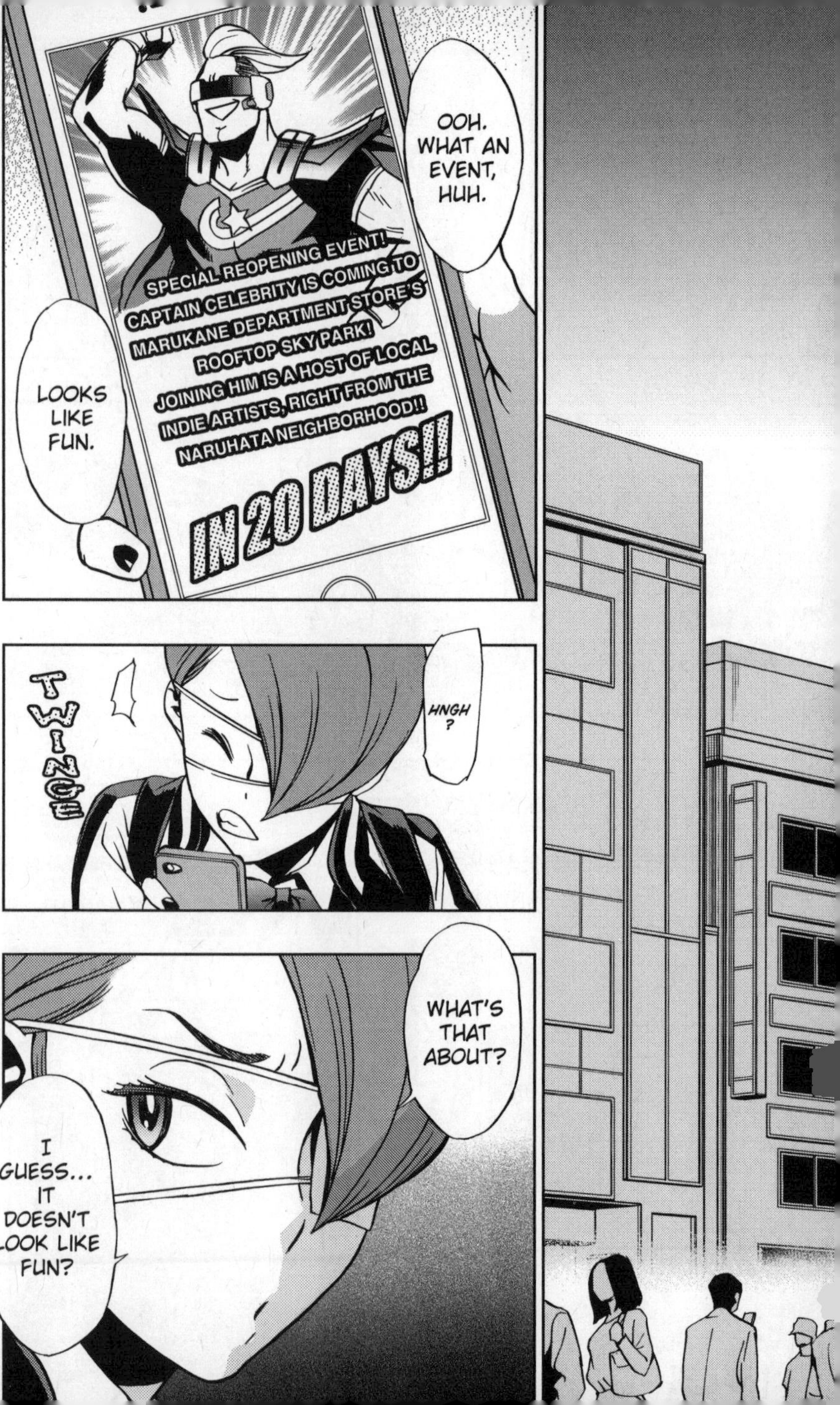
OOH. WHAT AN EVENT, HUH.
SPECIAL REOPENING EVENT! CAPTAIN CELEBRITY IS COMING TO MARUKANE DEPARTMENT STORE'S ROOFTOP SKY PARK! JOINING HIM IS A HOST OF LOCAL INDIE ARTISTS, RIGHT FROM THE NARUHATA NEIGHBORHOOD!!
IN 20 DAYS!!
LOOKS LIKE FUN.
HNGH?
TWINGE
WHAT'S THAT ABOUT?
I GUESS... IT DOESN'T LOOK LIKE FUN?

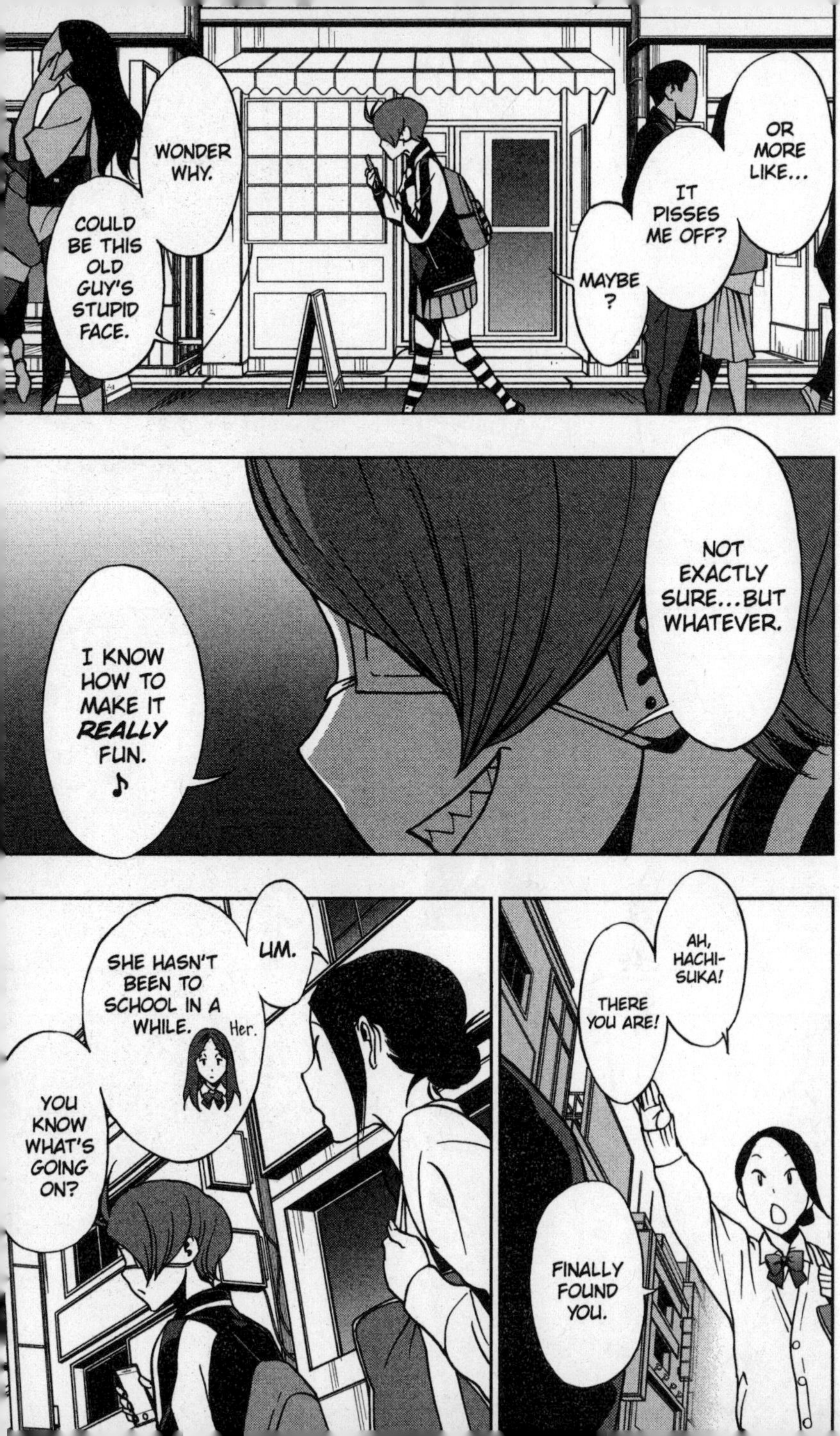
OR MORE LIKE...
IT PISSES ME OFF?
MAYBE ?
WONDER WHY.
COULD BE THIS OLD GUY'S STUPID FACE.
NOT EXACTLY SURE...BUT WHATEVER.
I KNOW HOW TO MAKE IT *REALLY* FUN. ♪
AH, HACHI-SUKA!
THERE YOU ARE!
FINALLY FOUND YOU.
UM.
SHE HASN'T BEEN TO SCHOOL IN A WHILE.
Her.
YOU KNOW WHAT'S GOING ON?

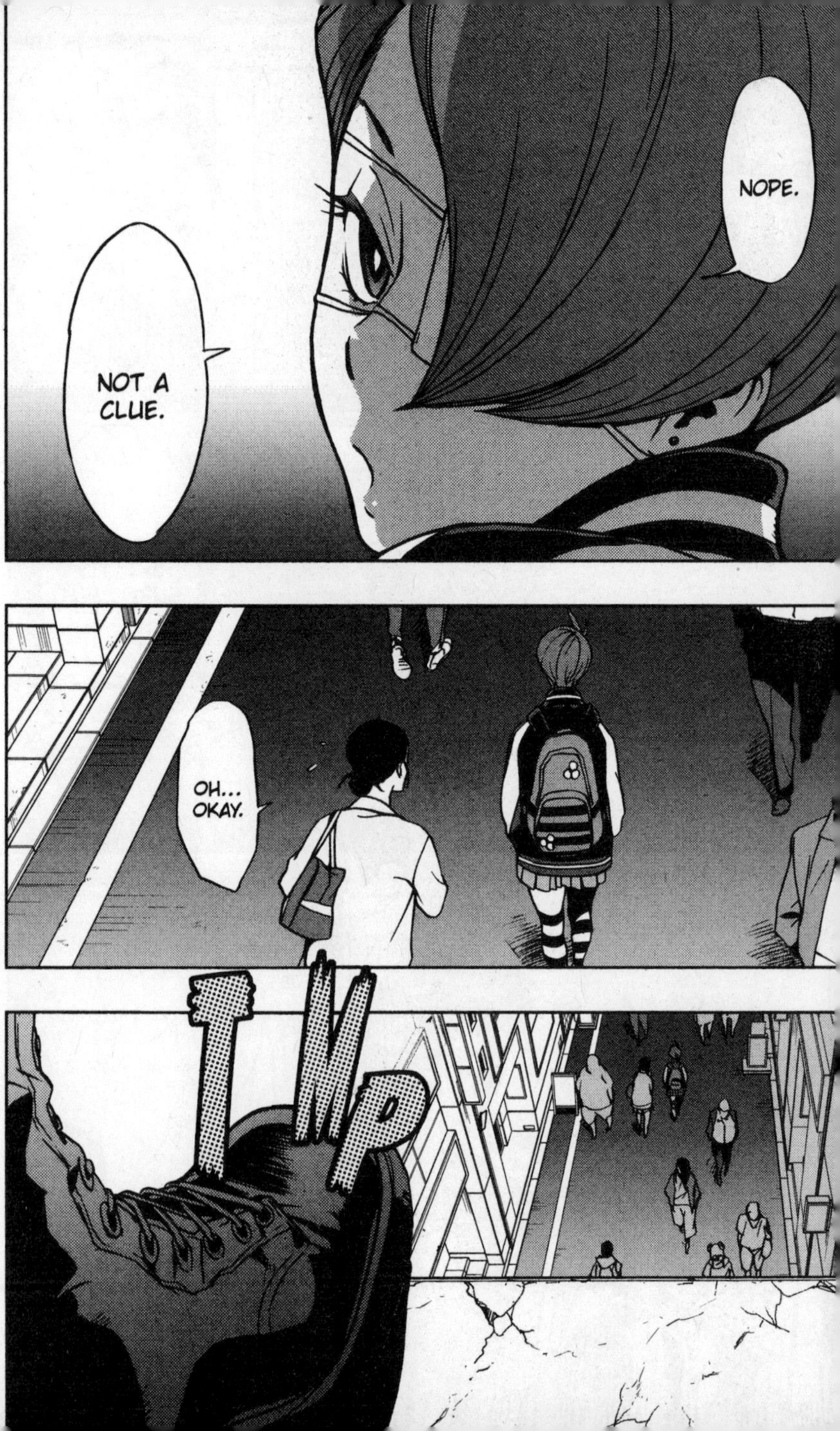
NOPE.
NOT A CLUE.
OH... OKAY.
TMP

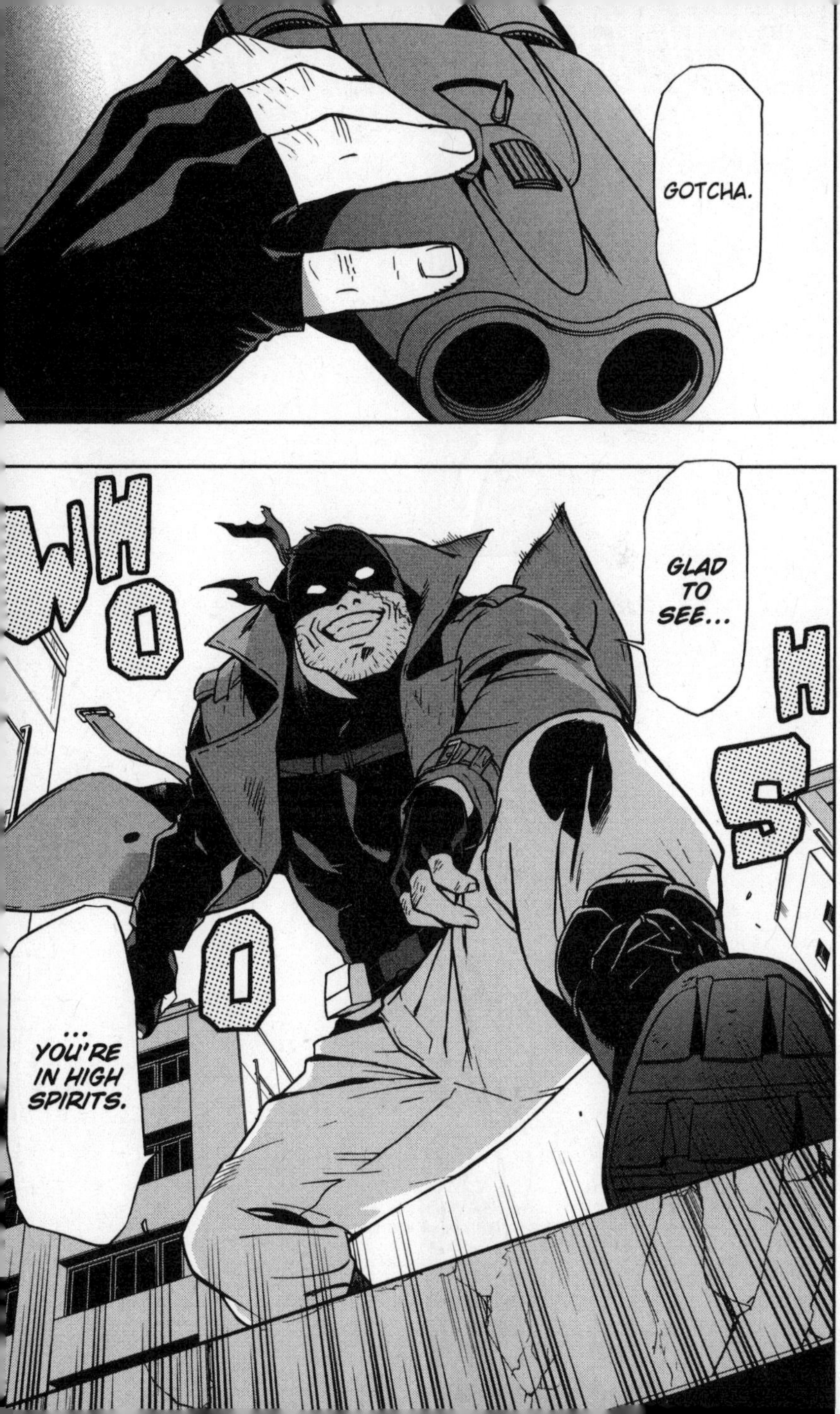
GOTCHA.
GLAD TO SEE...
WHOOSH
... YOU'RE IN HIGH SPIRITS.

KOICHI AND POP IN STREET CLOTHES

THE ROUGH DESIGN

Sand ro 1/2

40/

40/

10%

Gradation

40%

30%

BEHIND THE SCENES

The outfits they wore when tailing C.C. in the previous volume. When Pop is in street clothes she's usually walking around with Koichi. It's charming how much they look like close siblings.

—Furuhashi

Koichi's casual style is the ultimate in safe, inoffensive choices. (LOL) Pop's style isn't *lame*, per se, but it's hardly sophisticated. I struggle with her.

—Betten

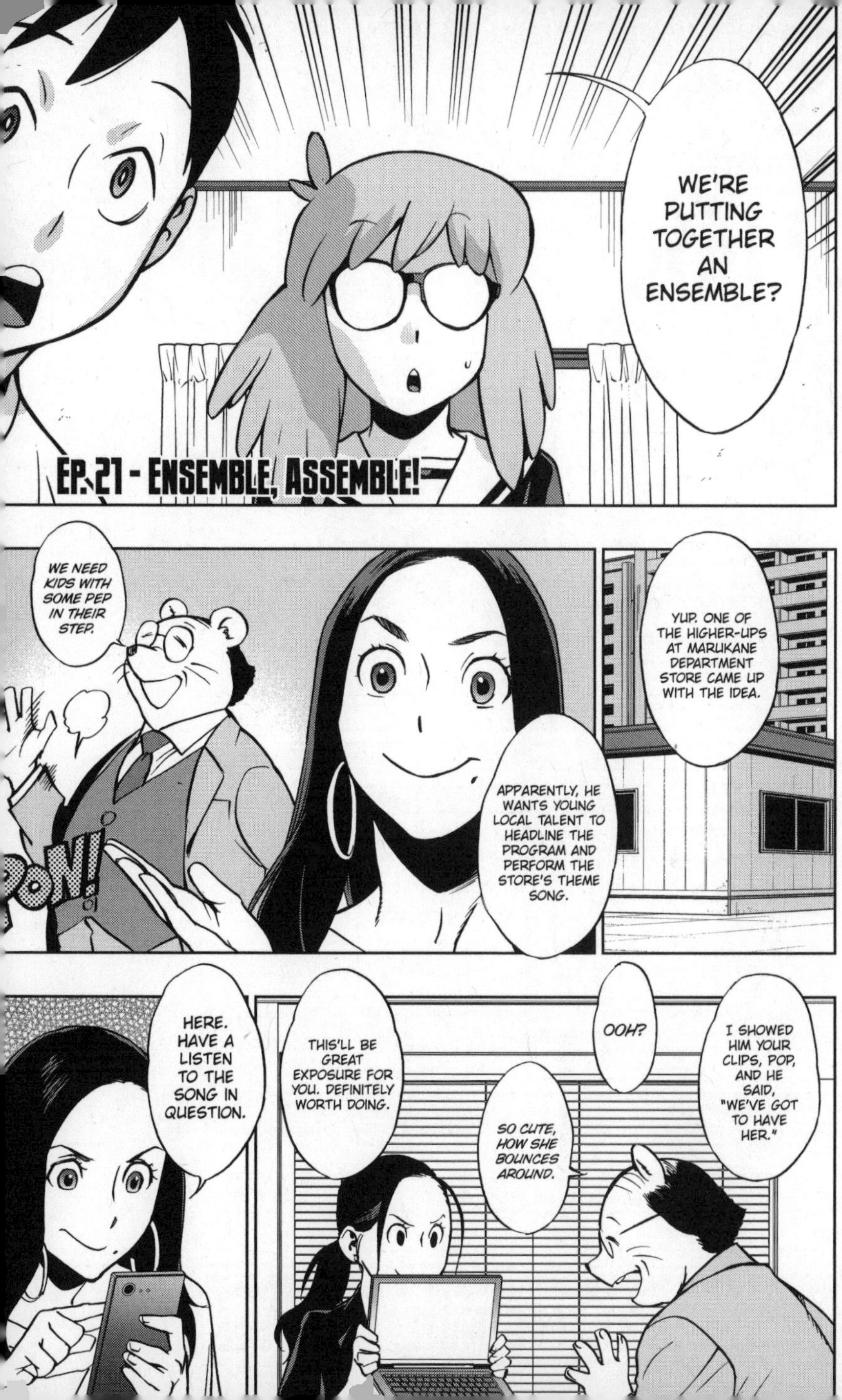
WE'RE PUTTING TOGETHER AN ENSEMBLE?
EP. 21 - ENSEMBLE, ASSEMBLE!
YUP. ONE OF THE HIGHER-UPS AT MARUKANE DEPARTMENT STORE CAME UP WITH THE IDEA.
APPARENTLY, HE WANTS YOUNG LOCAL TALENT TO HEADLINE THE PROGRAM AND PERFORM THE STORE'S THEME SONG.
WE NEED KIDS WITH SOME PEP IN THEIR STEP.
PON!
I SHOWED HIM YOUR CLIPS, POP, AND HE SAID, "WE'VE GOT TO HAVE HER."
OOH?
SO CUTE, HOW SHE BOUNCES AROUND.
THIS'LL BE GREAT EXPOSURE FOR YOU. DEFINITELY WORTH DOING.
HERE. HAVE A LISTEN TO THE SONG IN QUESTION.

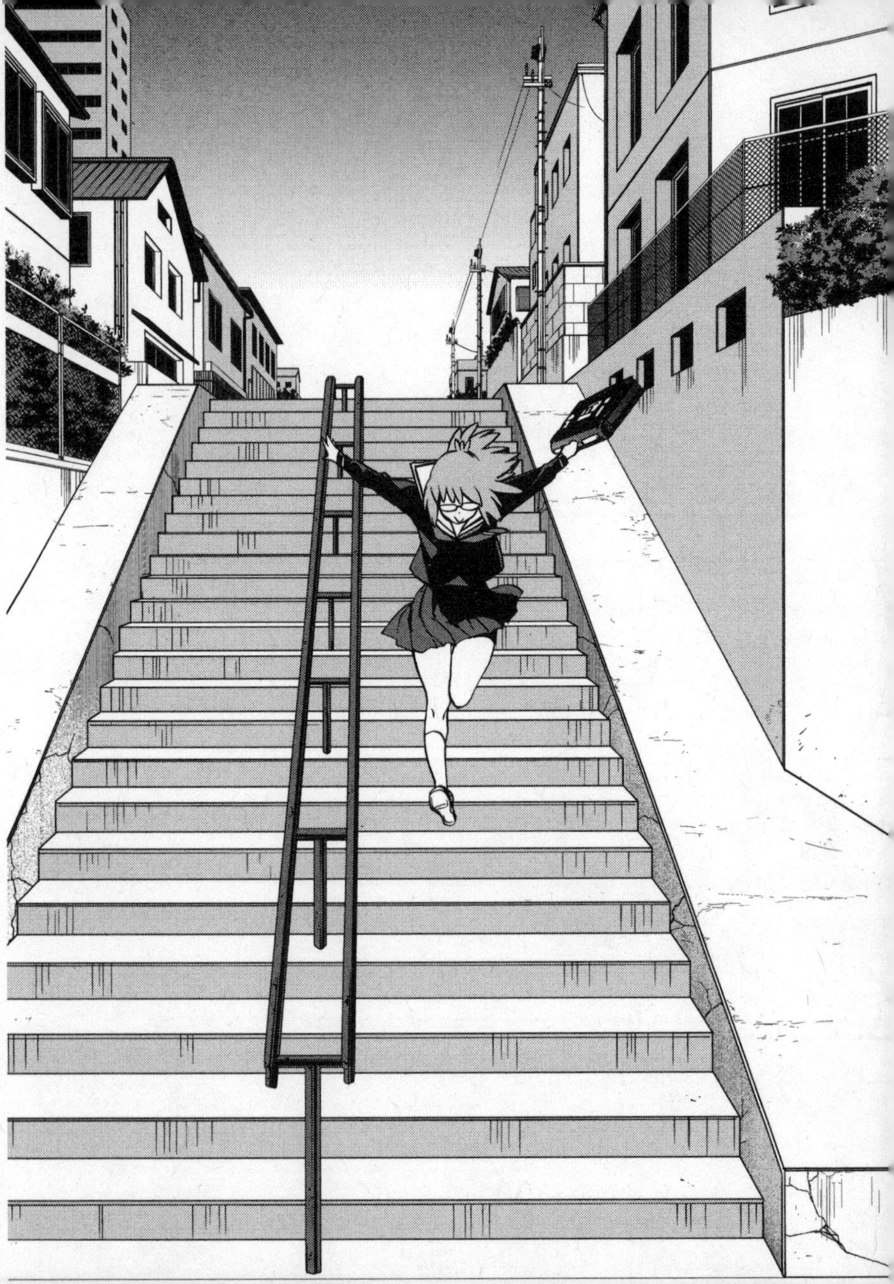

Ep. 21 - Ensemble, Assemble!

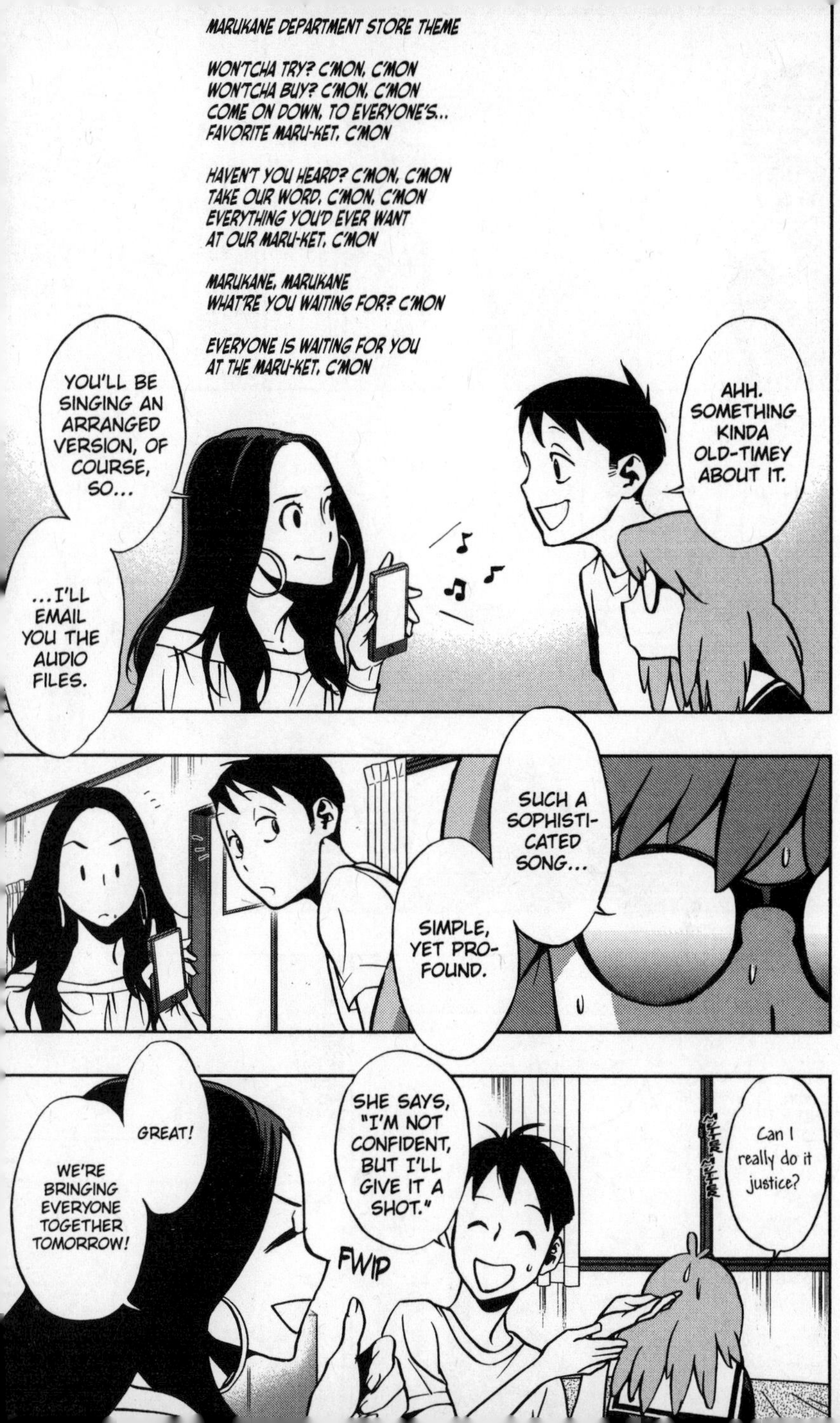
MARUKANE DEPARTMENT STORE THEME
WON'TCHA TRY? C'MON, C'MON
WON'TCHA BUY? C'MON, C'MON
COME ON DOWN, TO EVERYONE'S...
FAVORITE MARU-KET, C'MON
HAVEN'T YOU HEARD? C'MON, C'MON
TAKE OUR WORD, C'MON, C'MON
EVERYTHING YOU'D EVER WANT
AT OUR MARU-KET, C'MON
MARUKANE, MARUKANE
WHAT'RE YOU WAITING FOR? C'MON
EVERYONE IS WAITING FOR YOU
AT THE MARU-KET, C'MON
AHH. SOMETHING KINDA OLD-TIMEY ABOUT IT.
YOU'LL BE SINGING AN ARRANGED VERSION, OF COURSE, SO...
...I'LL EMAIL YOU THE AUDIO FILES.
SUCH A SOPHISTICATED SONG...
SIMPLE, YET PROFOUND.
Can I really do it justice?
SHE SAYS, "I'M NOT CONFIDENT, BUT I'LL GIVE IT A SHOT."
FWIP
GREAT!
WE'RE BRINGING EVERYONE TOGETHER TOMORROW!

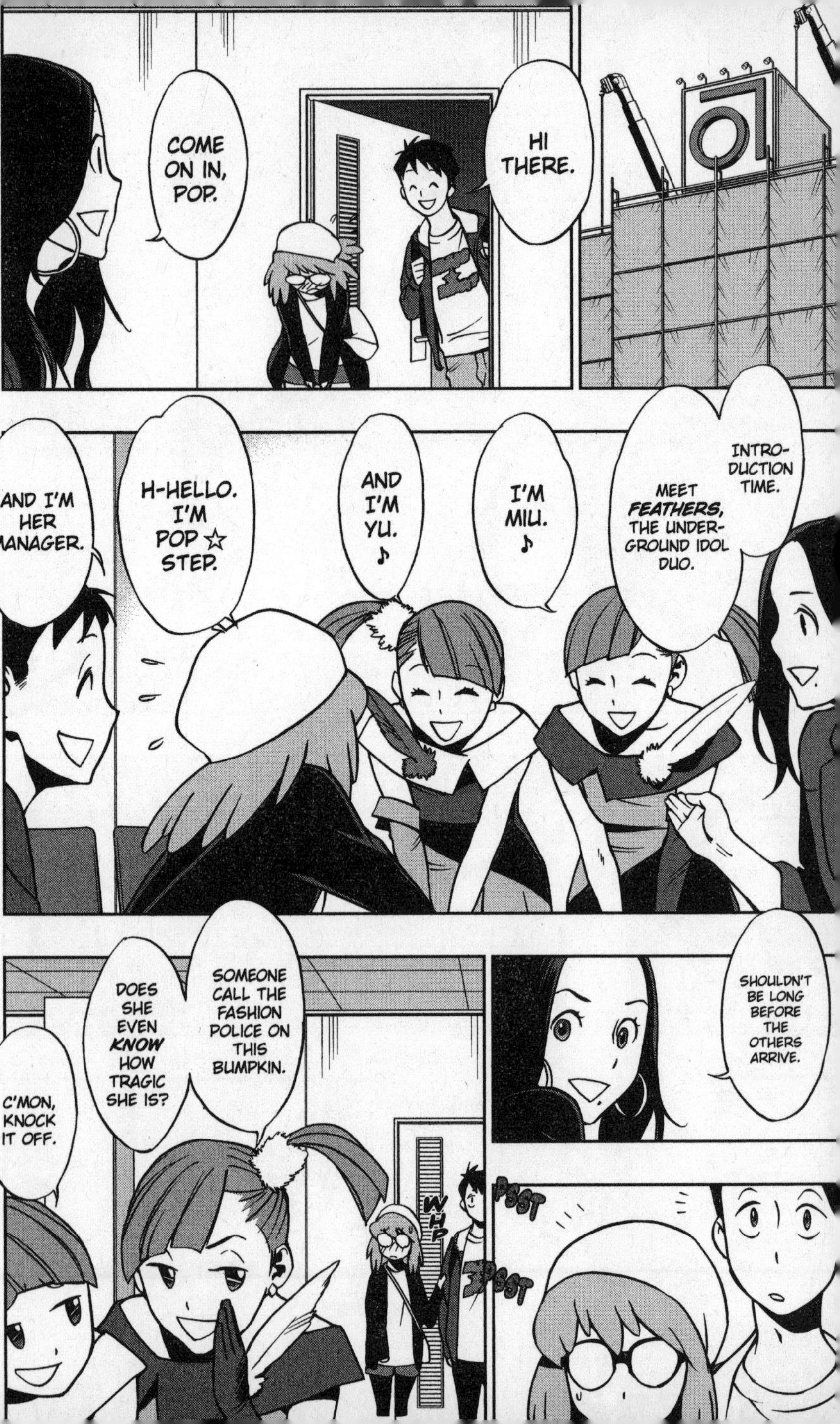
HI THERE.
COME ON IN, POP.
INTRO-DUCTION TIME.
MEET **FEATHERS,** THE UNDER-GROUND IDOL DUO.
I'M MIU. ♪
AND I'M YU. ♪
H-HELLO. I'M POP☆STEP.
AND I'M HER MANAGER.
SHOULDN'T BE LONG BEFORE THE OTHERS ARRIVE.
PSST
PSST
SOMEONE CALL THE FASHION POLICE ON THIS BUMPKIN.
DOES SHE EVEN ***KNOW*** HOW TRAGIC SHE IS?
C'MON, KNOCK IT OFF.
WHP

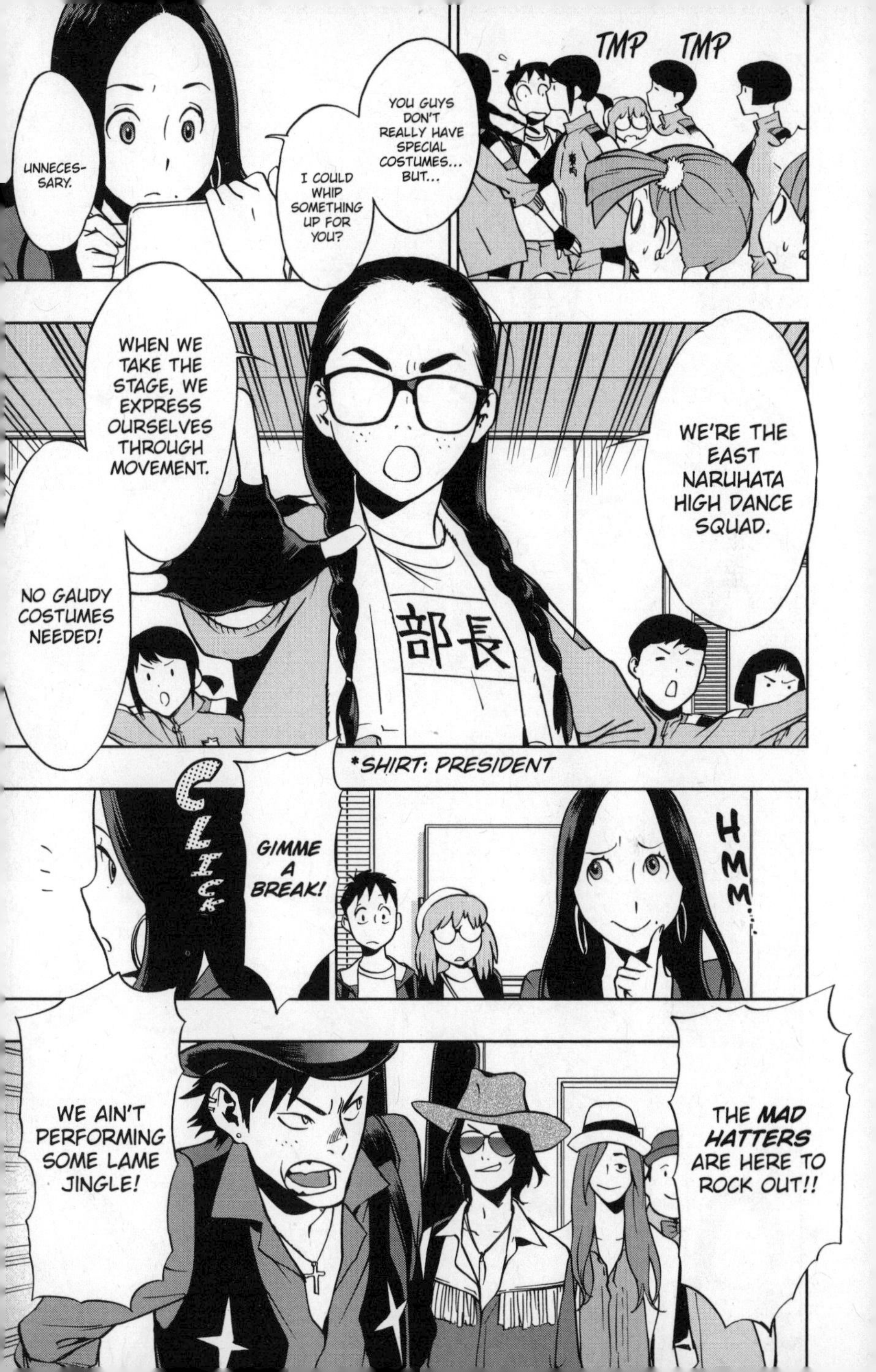
TMP TMP
YOU GUYS DON'T REALLY HAVE SPECIAL COSTUMES... BUT...
I COULD WHIP SOMETHING UP FOR YOU?
UNNECES-SARY.
WE'RE THE EAST NARUHATA HIGH DANCE SQUAD.
WHEN WE TAKE THE STAGE, WE EXPRESS OURSELVES THROUGH MOVEMENT.
NO GAUDY COSTUMES NEEDED!
部長
*SHIRT: PRESIDENT
HMM...
GIMME A BREAK!
CLICK
THE MAD HATTERS ARE HERE TO ROCK OUT!!
WE AIN'T PERFORMING SOME LAME JINGLE!

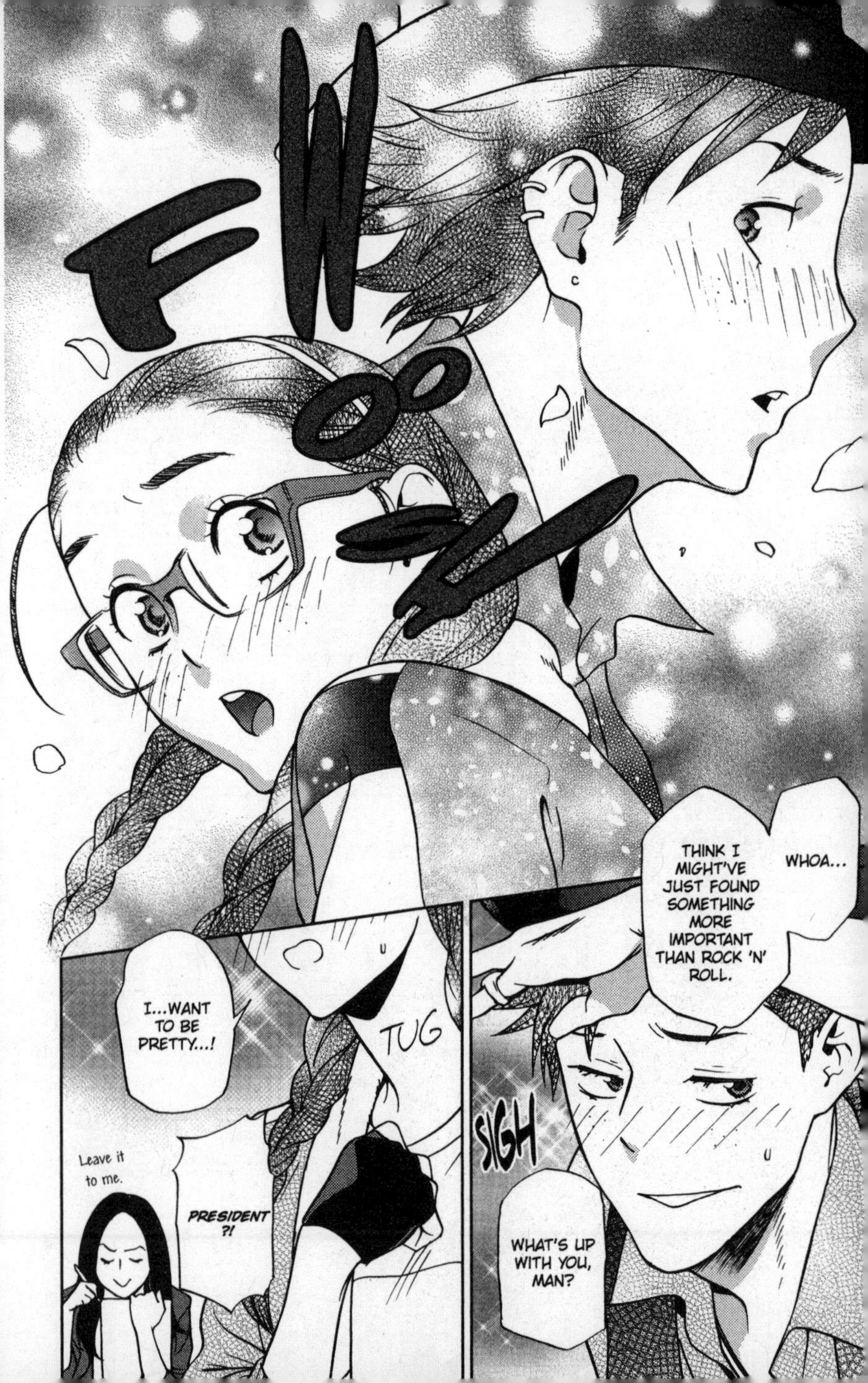
FWOOSH!
WHOA...
THINK I MIGHT'VE JUST FOUND SOMETHING MORE IMPORTANT THAN ROCK 'N' ROLL.
SIGH
WHAT'S UP WITH YOU, MAN?
I...WANT TO BE PRETTY...!
TUG
Leave it to me.
PRESIDENT ?!

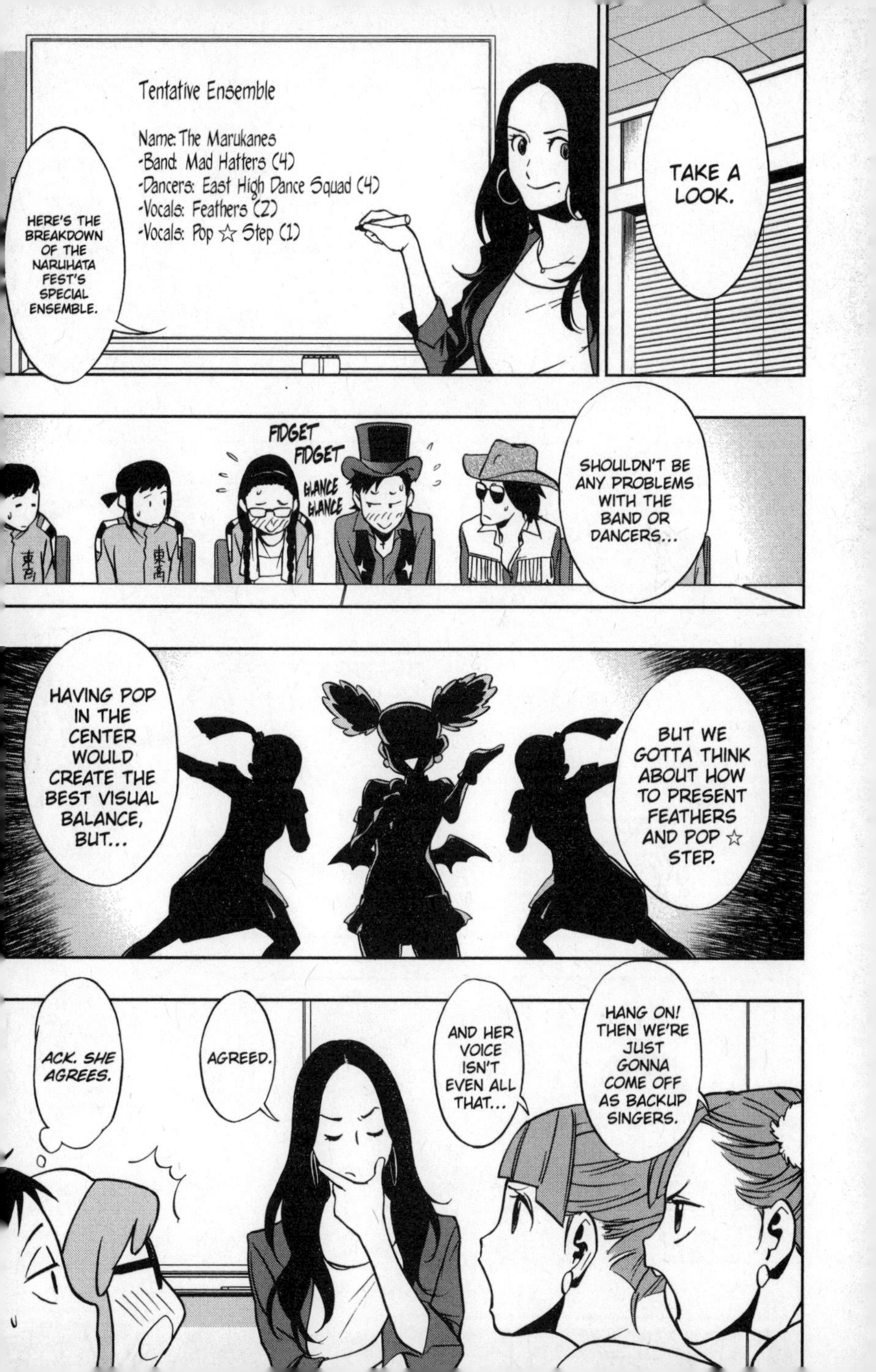
TAKE A LOOK.
Tentative Ensemble
Name: The Marukanes
-Band: Mad Hatters (4)
-Dancers: East High Dance Squad (4)
-Vocals: Feathers (2)
-Vocals: Pop ☆ Step (1)
HERE'S THE BREAKDOWN OF THE NARUHATA FEST'S SPECIAL ENSEMBLE.
SHOULDN'T BE ANY PROBLEMS WITH THE BAND OR DANCERS...
FIDGET FIDGET
GLANCE GLANCE
BUT WE GOTTA THINK ABOUT HOW TO PRESENT FEATHERS AND POP ☆ STEP.
HAVING POP IN THE CENTER WOULD CREATE THE BEST VISUAL BALANCE, BUT...
HANG ON! THEN WE'RE JUST GONNA COME OFF AS BACKUP SINGERS.
AND HER VOICE ISN'T EVEN ALL THAT...
AGREED.
ACK. SHE AGREES.

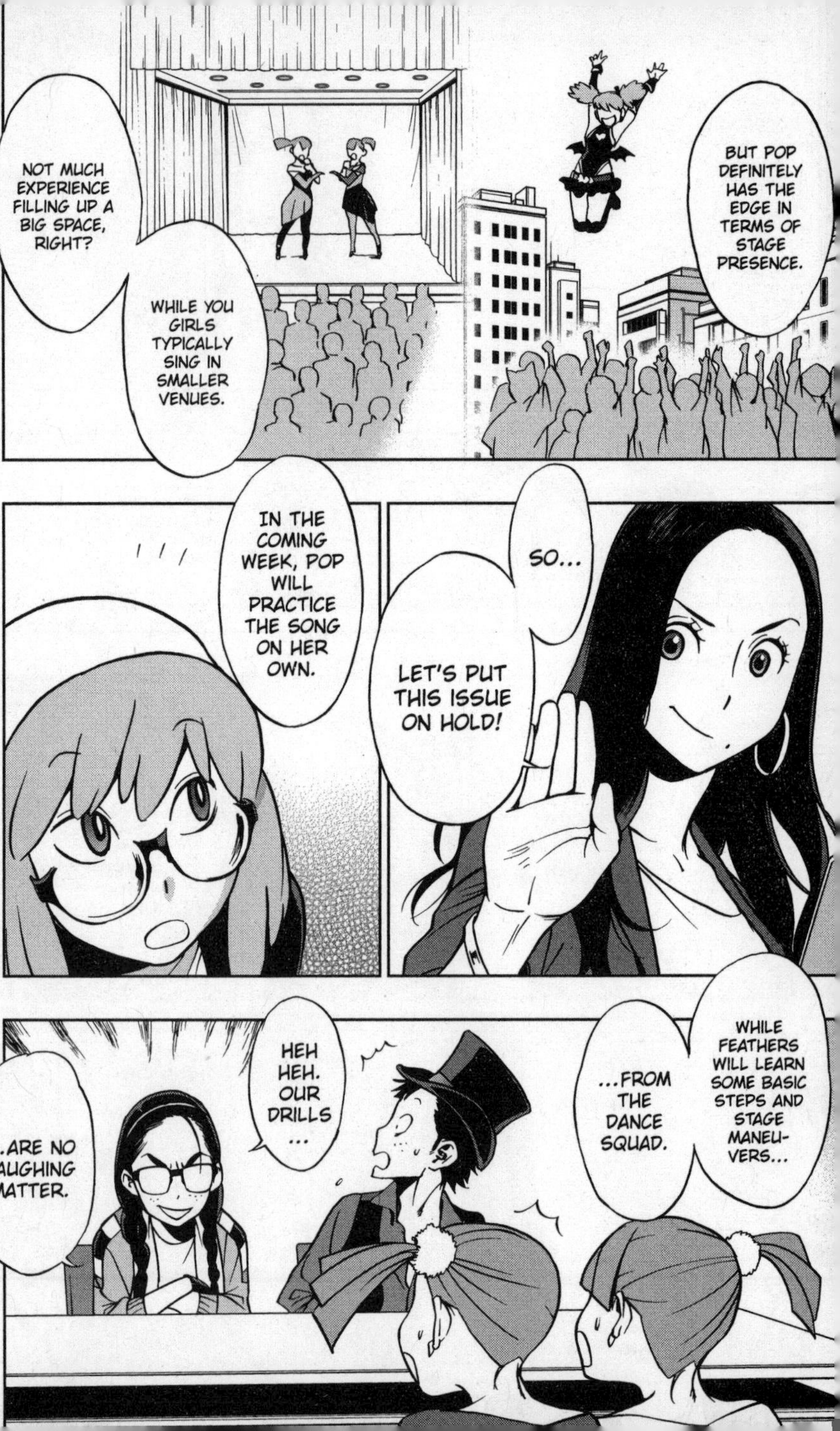
BUT POP DEFINITELY HAS THE EDGE IN TERMS OF STAGE PRESENCE.
NOT MUCH EXPERIENCE FILLING UP A BIG SPACE, RIGHT?
WHILE YOU GIRLS TYPICALLY SING IN SMALLER VENUES.
SO...
LET'S PUT THIS ISSUE ON HOLD!
IN THE COMING WEEK, POP WILL PRACTICE THE SONG ON HER OWN.
WHILE FEATHERS WILL LEARN SOME BASIC STEPS AND STAGE MANEU-VERS...
...FROM THE DANCE SQUAD.
HEH HEH. OUR DRILLS...
...ARE NO LAUGHING MATTER.

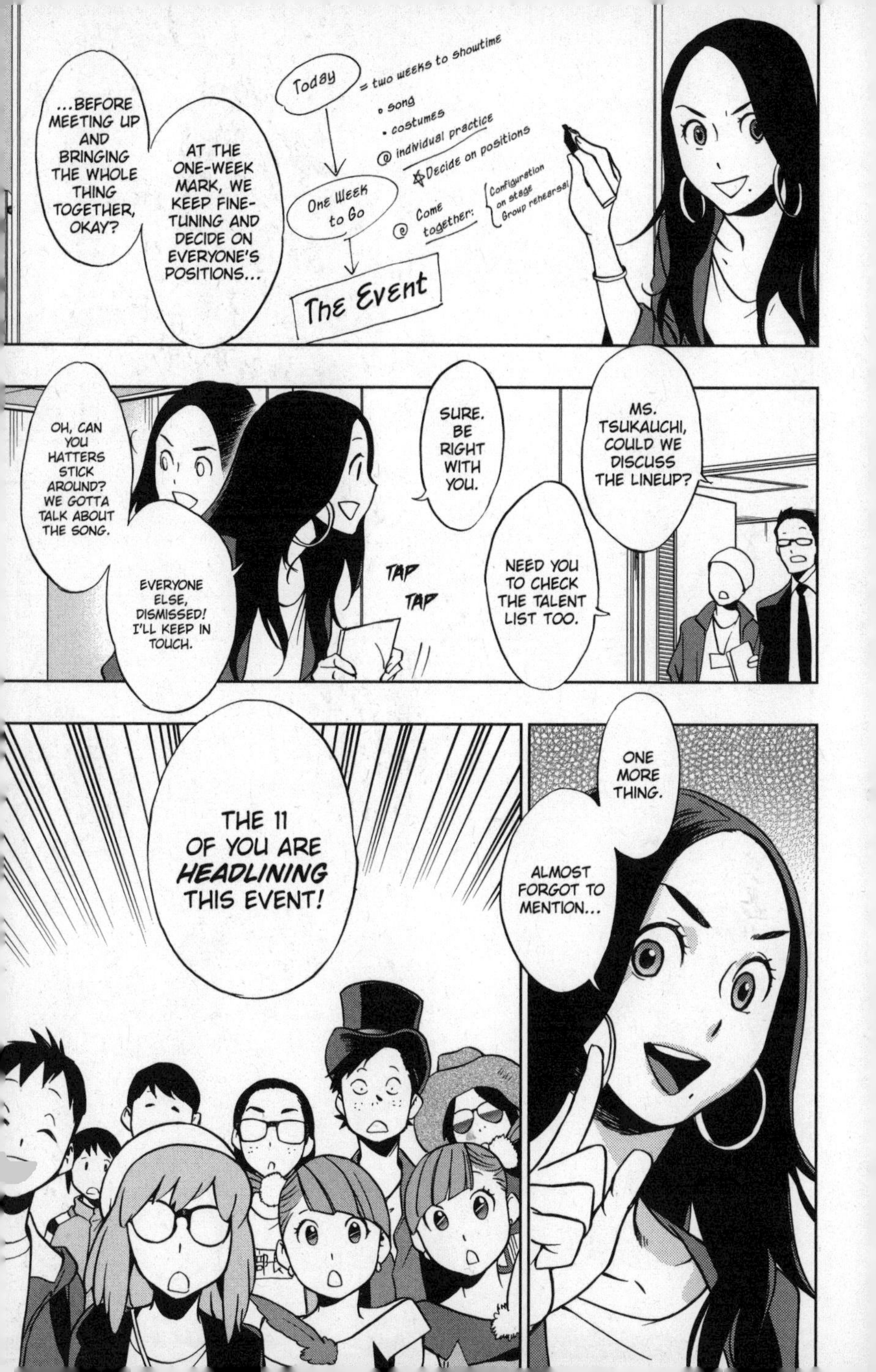
Today = two weeks to showtime
• song
• costumes
@ individual practice
☆ Decide on positions
One Week to Go
@ Come together: Configuration on stage Group rehearsal
The Event
AT THE ONE-WEEK MARK, WE KEEP FINE-TUNING AND DECIDE ON EVERYONE'S POSITIONS...
...BEFORE MEETING UP AND BRINGING THE WHOLE THING TOGETHER, OKAY?
MS. TSUKAUCHI, COULD WE DISCUSS THE LINEUP?
NEED YOU TO CHECK THE TALENT LIST TOO.
SURE. BE RIGHT WITH YOU.
OH, CAN YOU HATTERS STICK AROUND? WE GOTTA TALK ABOUT THE SONG.
TAP TAP
EVERYONE ELSE, DISMISSED! I'LL KEEP IN TOUCH.
ONE MORE THING.
ALMOST FORGOT TO MENTION...
THE 11 OF YOU ARE *HEADLINING* THIS EVENT!

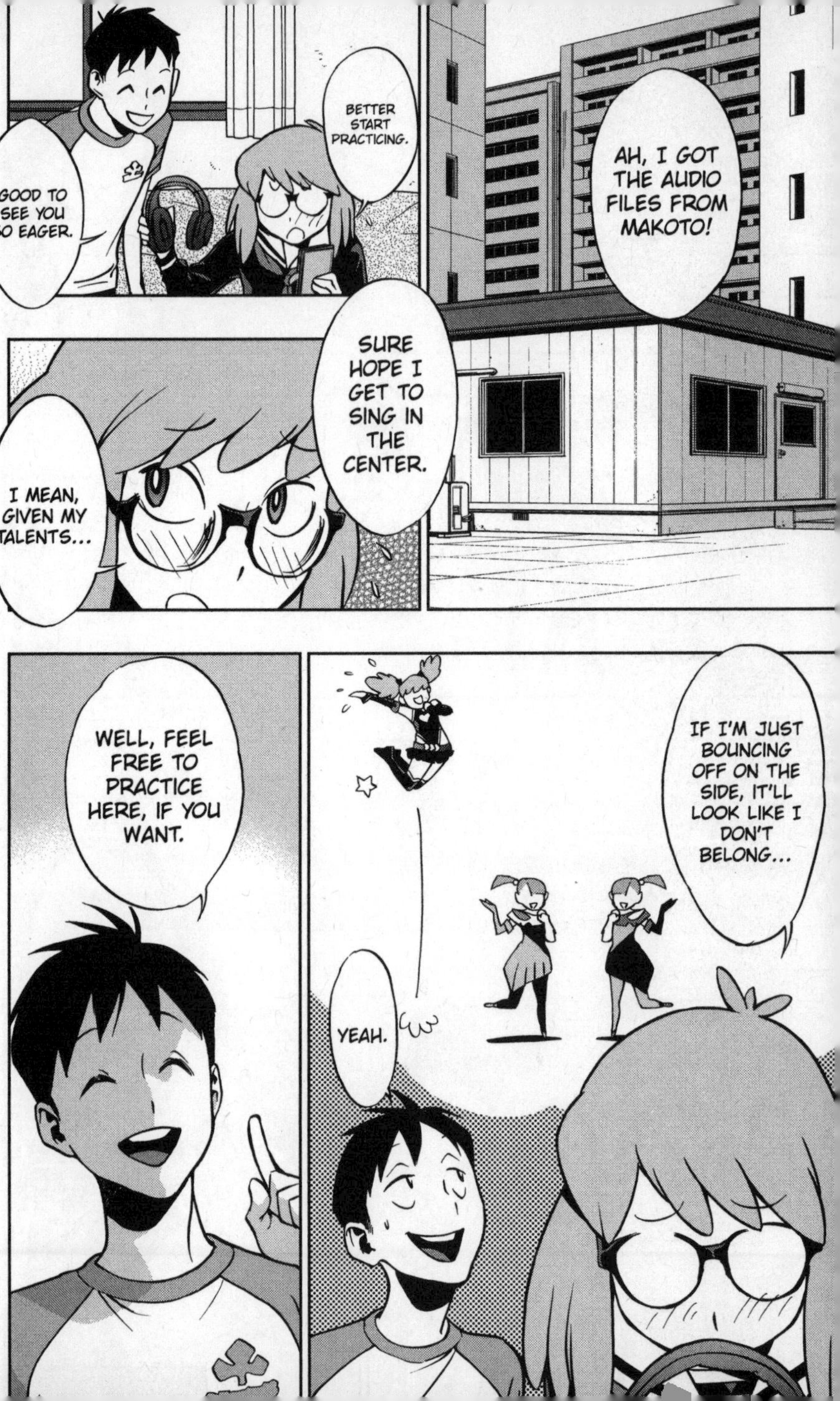
AH, I GOT THE AUDIO FILES FROM MAKOTO!
BETTER START PRACTICING.
GOOD TO SEE YOU SO EAGER.
SURE HOPE I GET TO SING IN THE CENTER.
I MEAN, GIVEN MY TALENTS...
IF I'M JUST BOUNCING OFF ON THE SIDE, IT'LL LOOK LIKE I DON'T BELONG...
YEAH.
WELL, FEEL FREE TO PRACTICE HERE, IF YOU WANT.

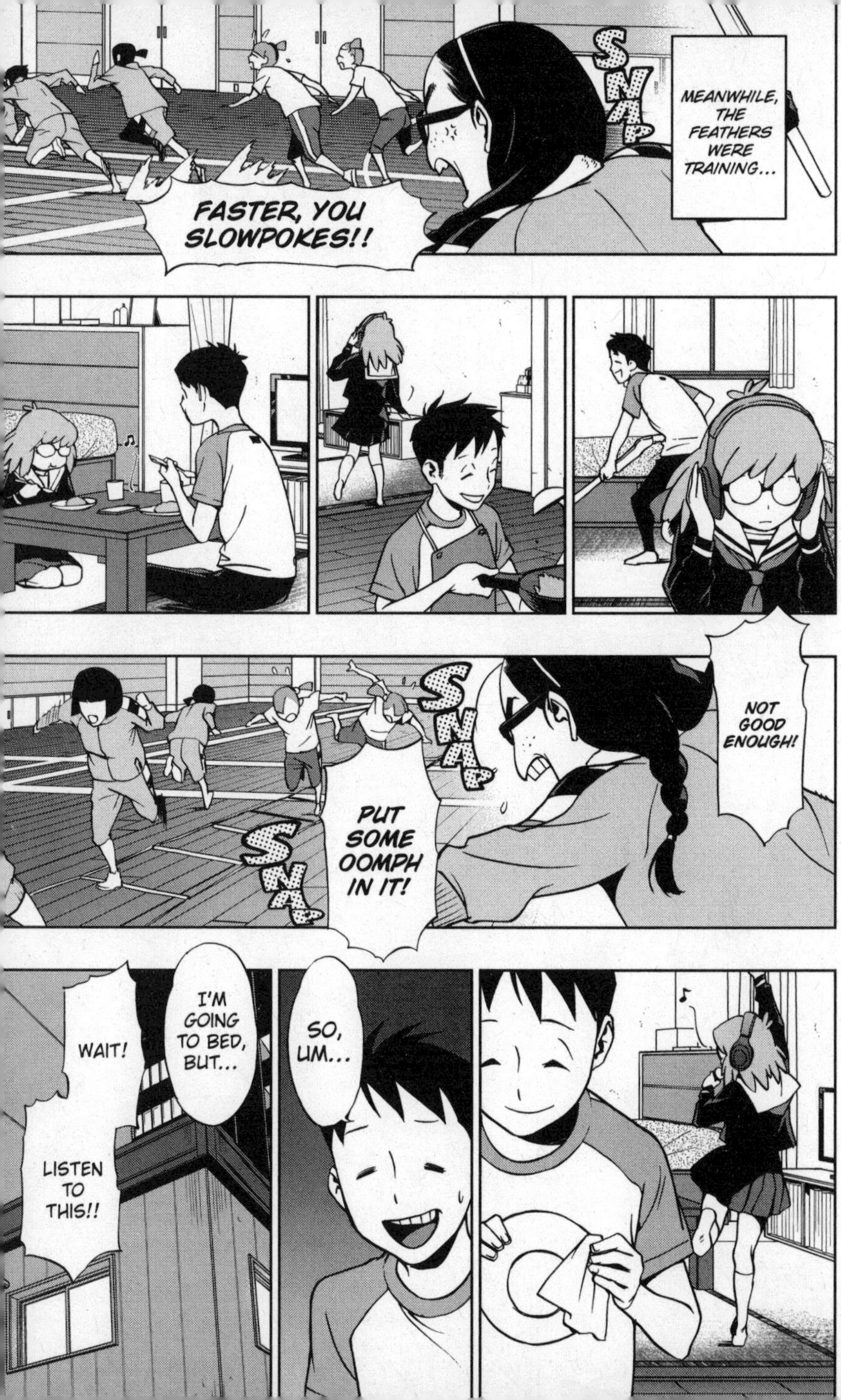
MEANWHILE, THE FEATHERS WERE TRAINING…
SNAP
FASTER, YOU SLOWPOKES!!
NOT GOOD ENOUGH!
SNAP
PUT SOME OOMPH IN IT!
SNAP
SO, UM…
I'M GOING TO BED, BUT…
WAIT!
LISTEN TO THIS!!

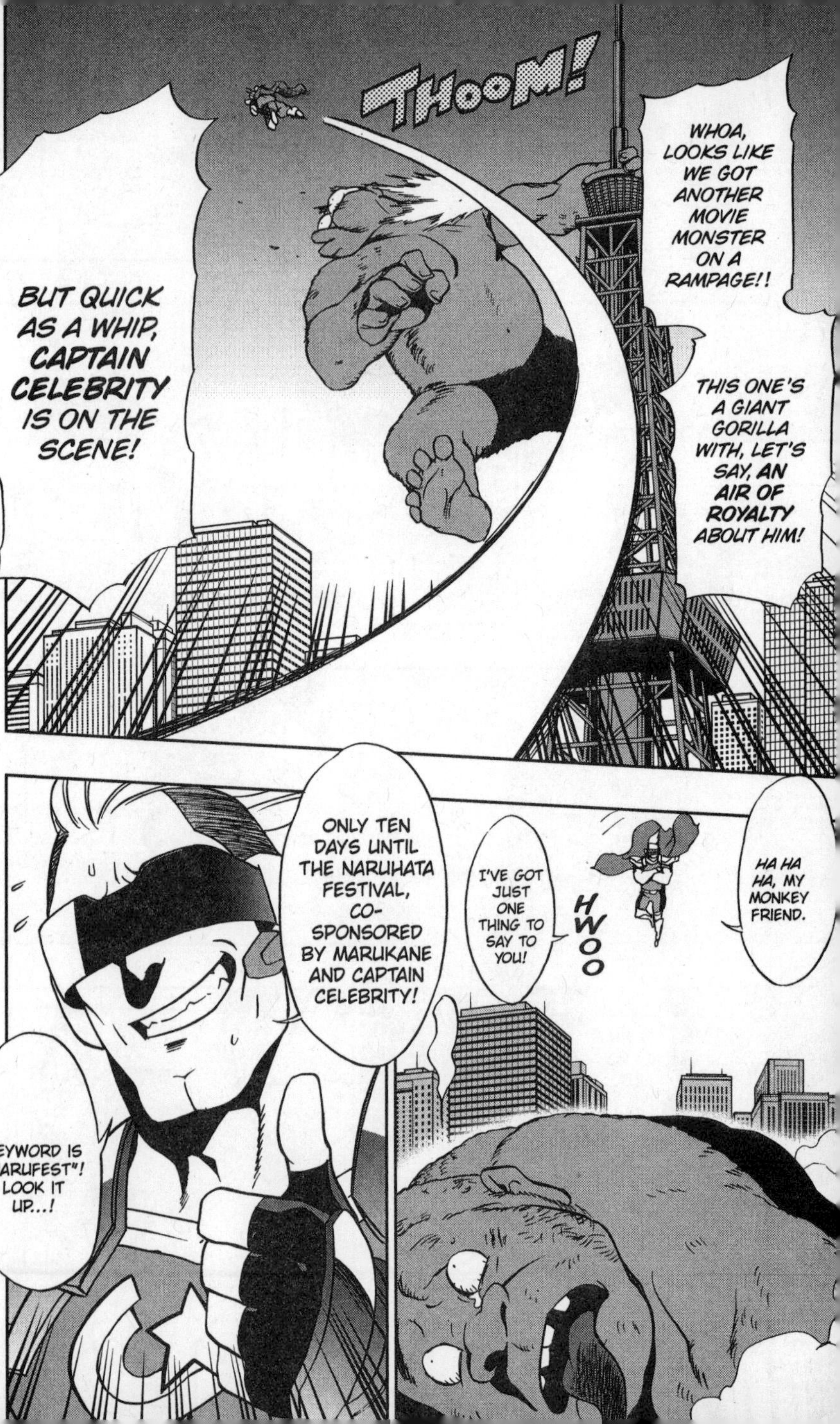
THOOM!
WHOA, LOOKS LIKE WE GOT ANOTHER MOVIE MONSTER ON A RAMPAGE!!
THIS ONE'S A GIANT GORILLA WITH, LET'S SAY, AN AIR OF ROYALTY ABOUT HIM!
BUT QUICK AS A WHIP, CAPTAIN CELEBRITY IS ON THE SCENE!
HA HA HA, MY MONKEY FRIEND.
HWOO
I'VE GOT JUST ONE THING TO SAY TO YOU!
ONLY TEN DAYS UNTIL THE NARUHATA FESTIVAL, CO-SPONSORED BY MARUKANE AND CAPTAIN CELEBRITY!
KEYWORD IS "NARUFEST"! LOOK IT UP...!

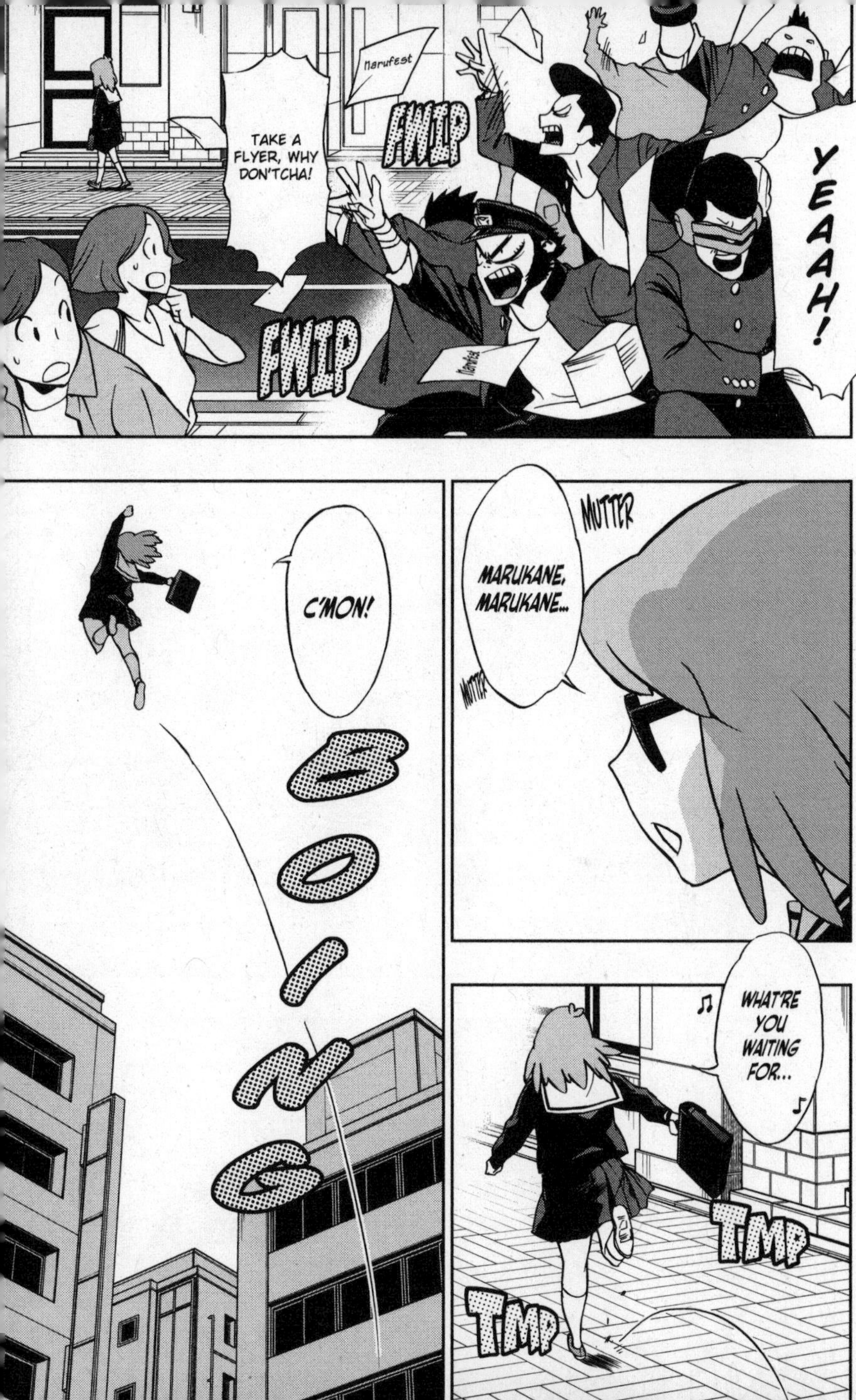
Marufest
YEAAAH!
FWIP
TAKE A FLYER, WHY DON'TCHA!
FWIP
MUTTER
MARUKANE, MARUKANE...
MUTTER
WHAT'RE YOU WAITING FOR...
TMP
TMP
C'MON!
BOING

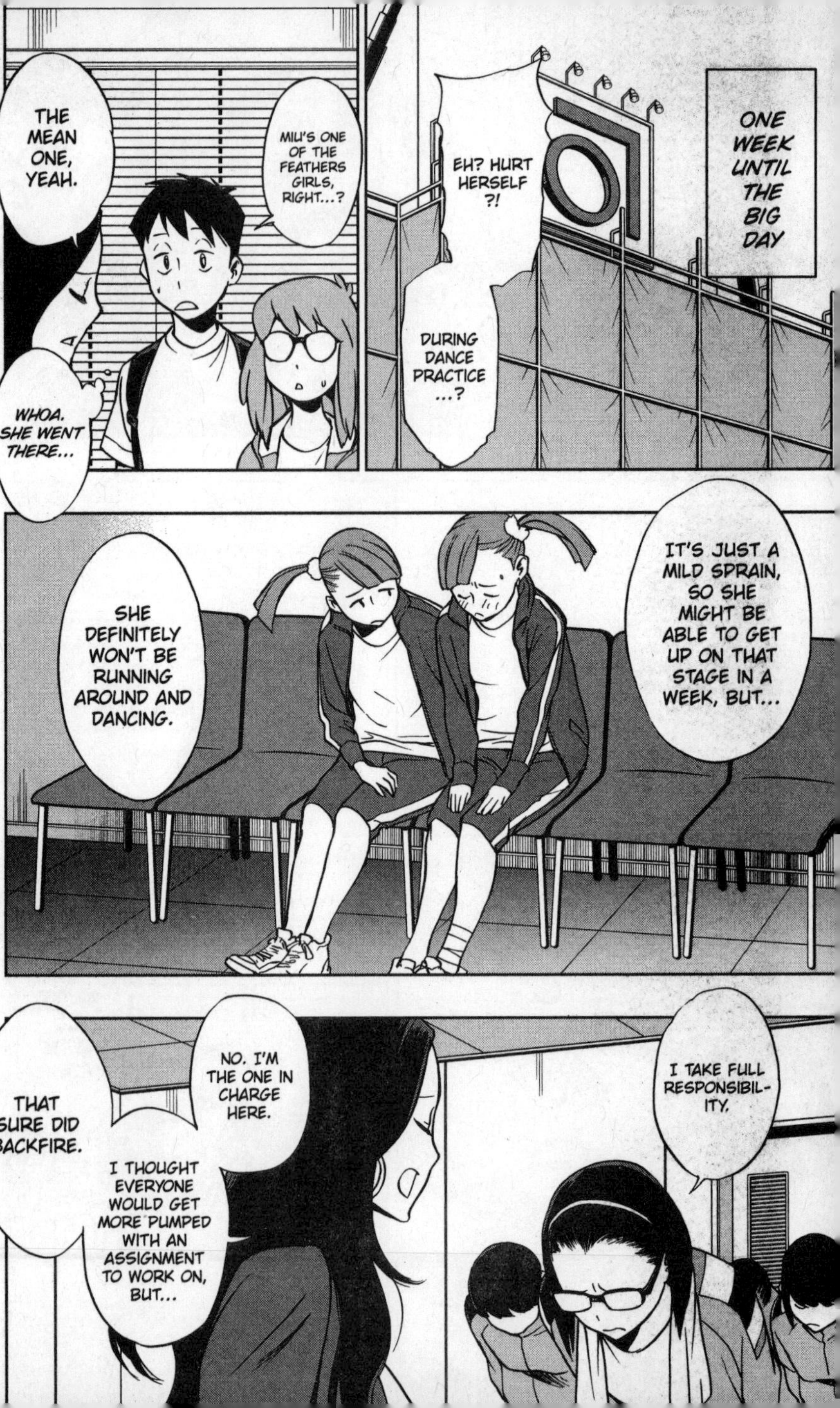
ONE WEEK UNTIL THE BIG DAY
EH? HURT HERSELF ?!
DURING DANCE PRACTICE ...?
MIU'S ONE OF THE FEATHERS GIRLS, RIGHT...?
THE MEAN ONE, YEAH.
WHOA. SHE WENT THERE...
IT'S JUST A MILD SPRAIN, SO SHE MIGHT BE ABLE TO GET UP ON THAT STAGE IN A WEEK, BUT...
SHE DEFINITELY WON'T BE RUNNING AROUND AND DANCING.
I TAKE FULL RESPONSIBIL-ITY.
NO. I'M THE ONE IN CHARGE HERE.
THAT SURE DID BACKFIRE.
I THOUGHT EVERYONE WOULD GET MORE PUMPED WITH AN ASSIGNMENT TO WORK ON, BUT...

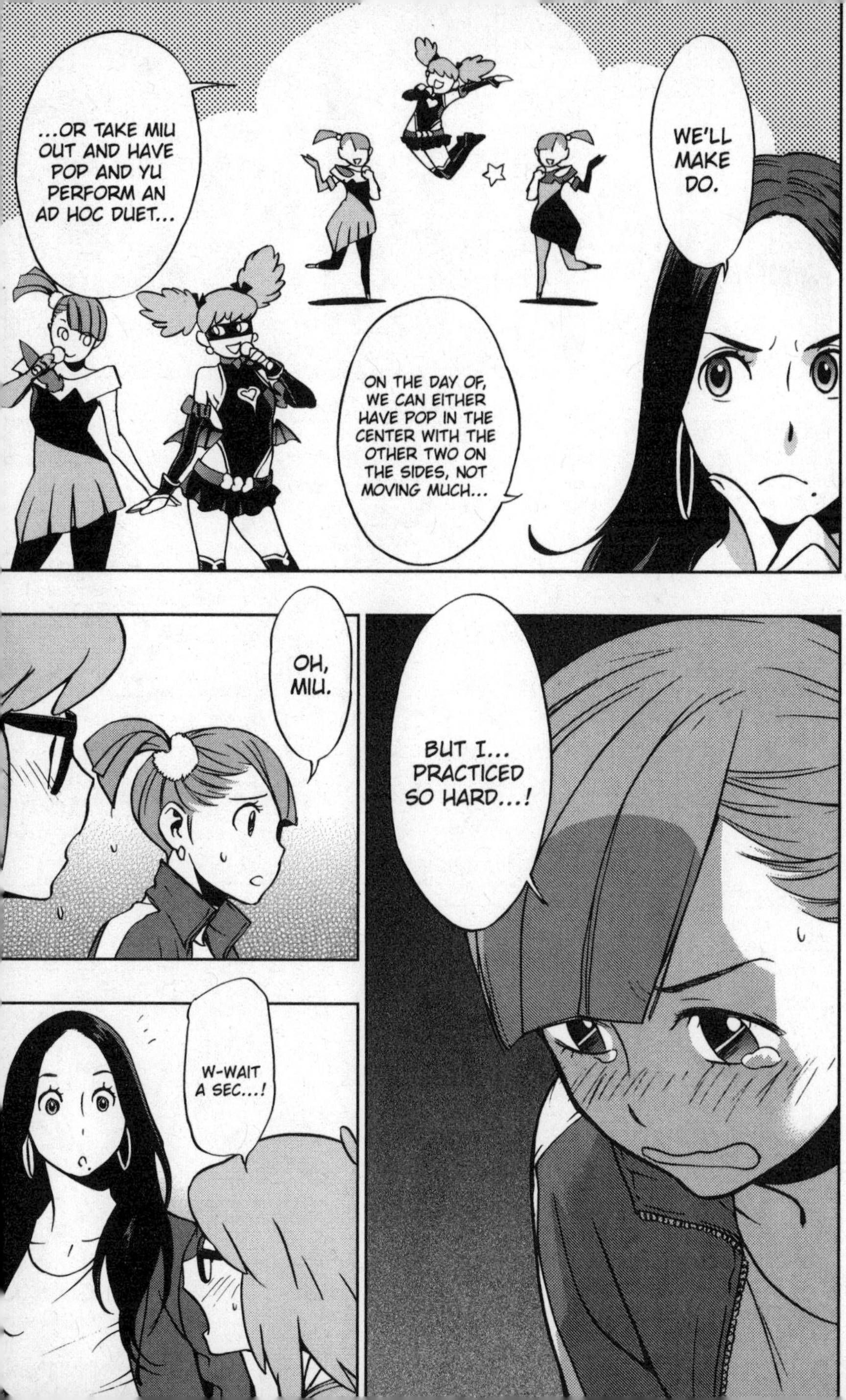
WE'LL MAKE DO.
ON THE DAY OF, WE CAN EITHER HAVE POP IN THE CENTER WITH THE OTHER TWO ON THE SIDES, NOT MOVING MUCH...
...OR TAKE MIU OUT AND HAVE POP AND YU PERFORM AN AD HOC DUET...
BUT I... PRACTICED SO HARD...!
OH, MIU.
W-WAIT A SEC...!

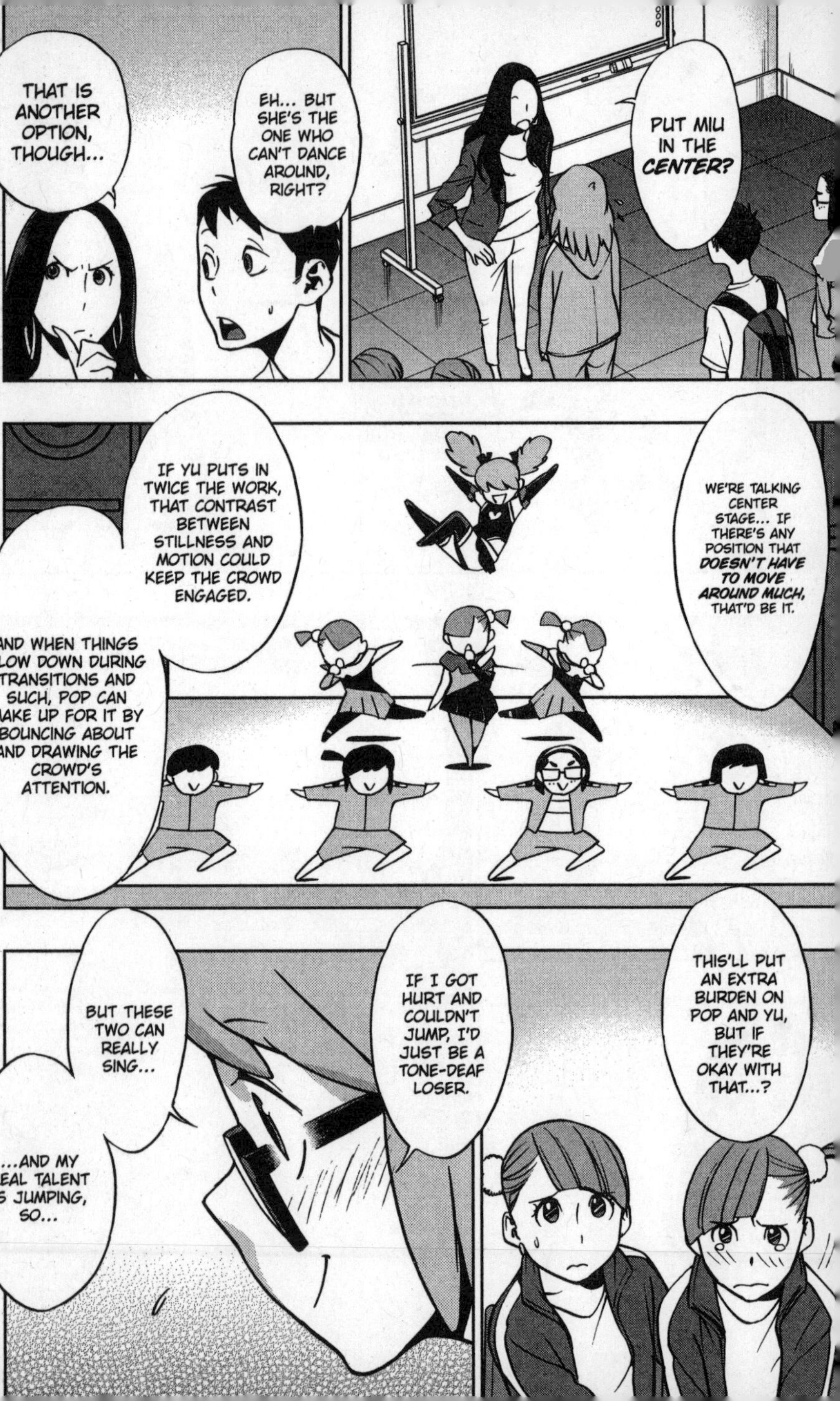
PUT MIU IN THE *CENTER?*
EH... BUT SHE'S THE ONE WHO CAN'T DANCE AROUND, RIGHT?
THAT IS ANOTHER OPTION, THOUGH...
WE'RE TALKING CENTER STAGE... IF THERE'S ANY POSITION THAT *DOESN'T HAVE TO MOVE AROUND MUCH,* THAT'D BE IT.
IF YU PUTS IN TWICE THE WORK, THAT CONTRAST BETWEEN STILLNESS AND MOTION COULD KEEP THE CROWD ENGAGED.
AND WHEN THINGS SLOW DOWN DURING TRANSITIONS AND SUCH, POP CAN MAKE UP FOR IT BY BOUNCING ABOUT AND DRAWING THE CROWD'S ATTENTION.
THIS'LL PUT AN EXTRA BURDEN ON POP AND YU, BUT IF THEY'RE OKAY WITH THAT...?
IF I GOT HURT AND COULDN'T JUMP, I'D JUST BE A TONE-DEAF LOSER.
BUT THESE TWO CAN REALLY SING...
...AND MY REAL TALENT IS JUMPING, SO...

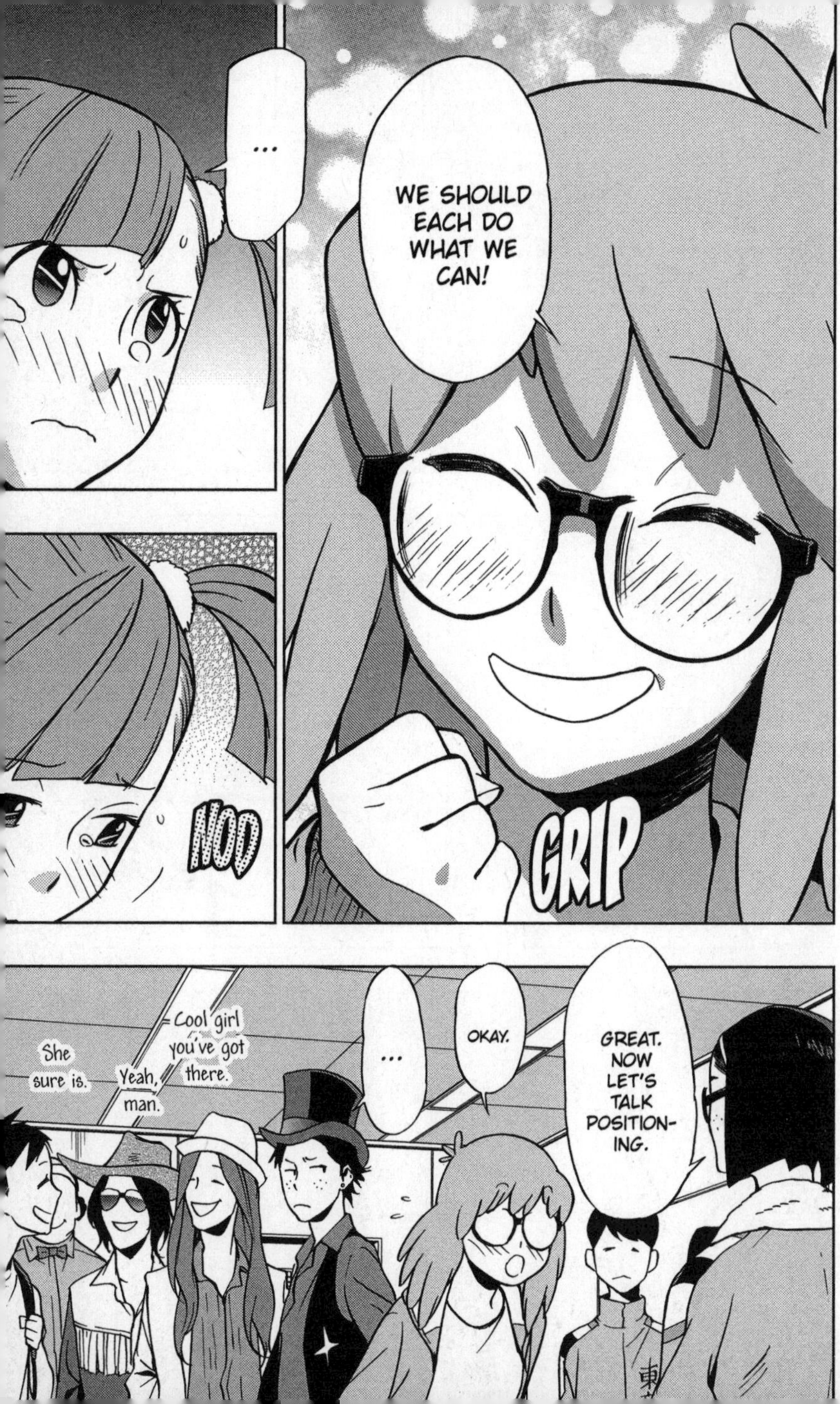
WE SHOULD EACH DO WHAT WE CAN!
GRIP
...
NOD
GREAT. NOW LET'S TALK POSITIONING.
OKAY.
...
Cool girl you've got there.
Yeah, man.
She sure is.

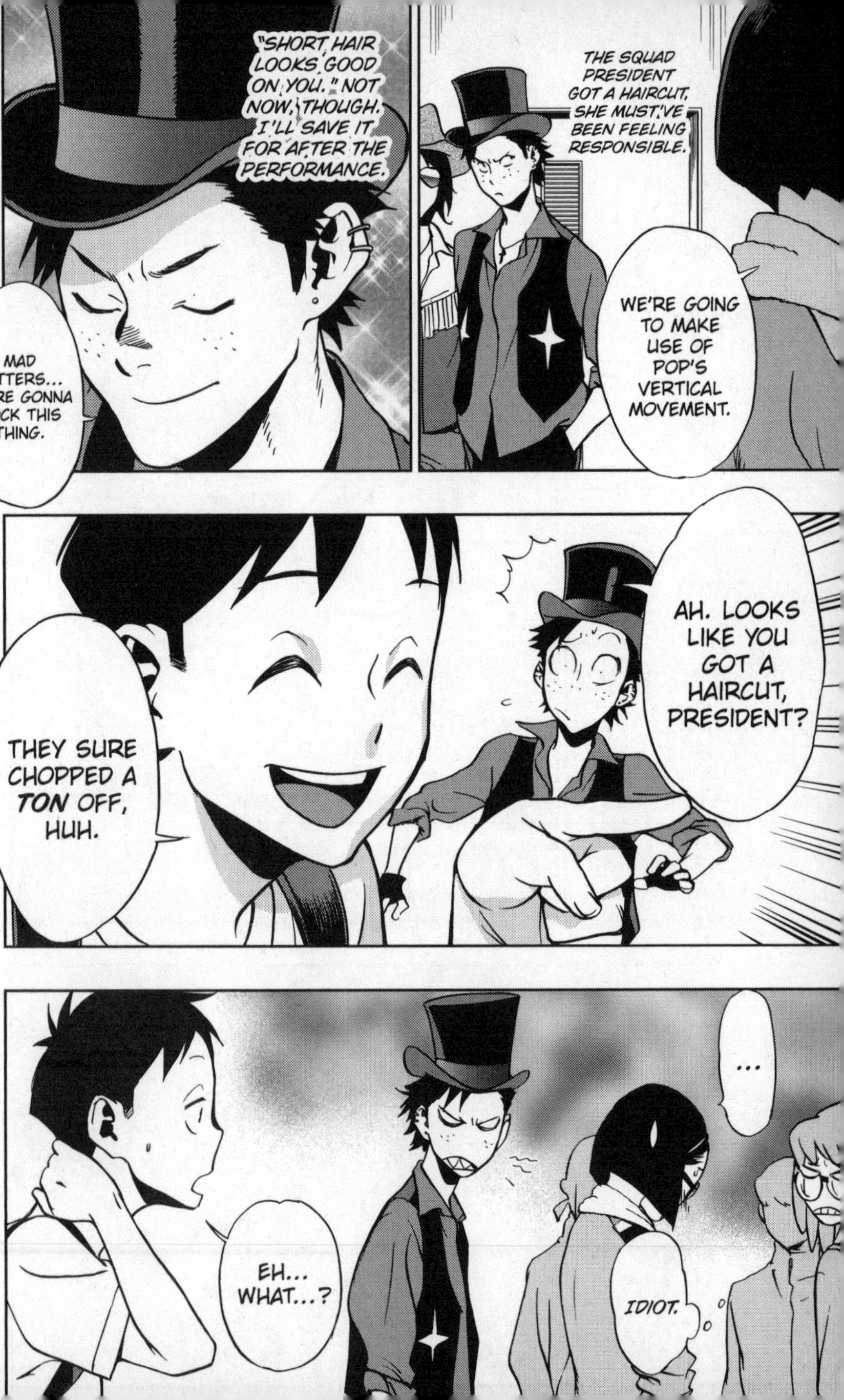
THE SQUAD PRESIDENT GOT A HAIRCUT. SHE MUST'VE BEEN FEELING RESPONSIBLE.
WE'RE GOING TO MAKE USE OF POP'S VERTICAL MOVEMENT.
"SHORT HAIR LOOKS GOOD ON YOU." NOT NOW, THOUGH. I'LL SAVE IT FOR AFTER THE PERFORMANCE.
MAD HATTERS... WE'RE GONNA ROCK THIS THING.
AH. LOOKS LIKE YOU GOT A HAIRCUT, PRESIDENT?
THEY SURE CHOPPED A *TON* OFF, HUH.
...
IDIOT.
EH... WHAT...?

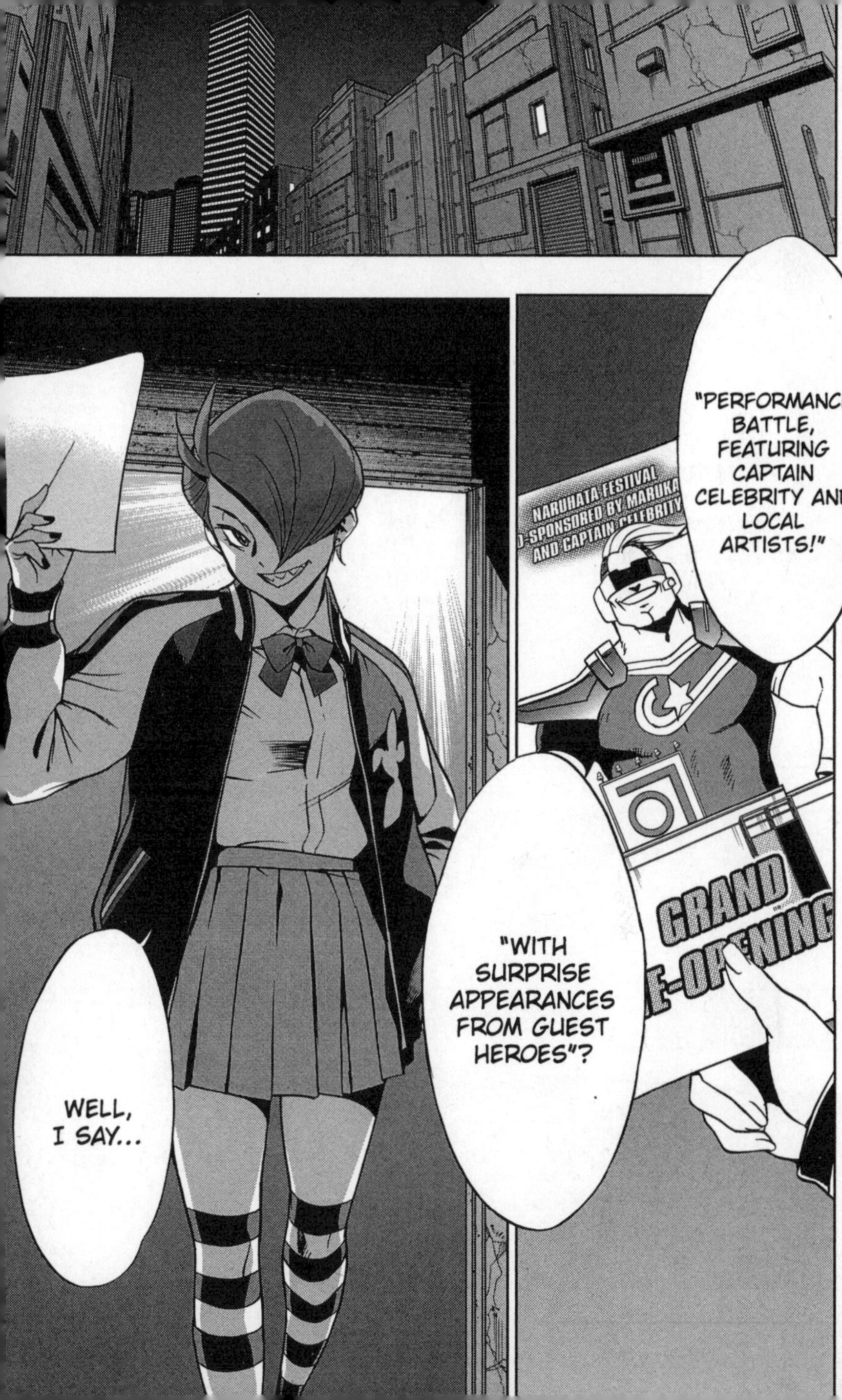
"PERFORMANCE BATTLE, FEATURING CAPTAIN CELEBRITY AND LOCAL ARTISTS!"
NARUHATA FESTIVAL
AND CAPTAIN CELEBRITY
GRAND
"WITH SURPRISE APPEARANCES FROM GUEST HEROES"?
WELL, I SAY...

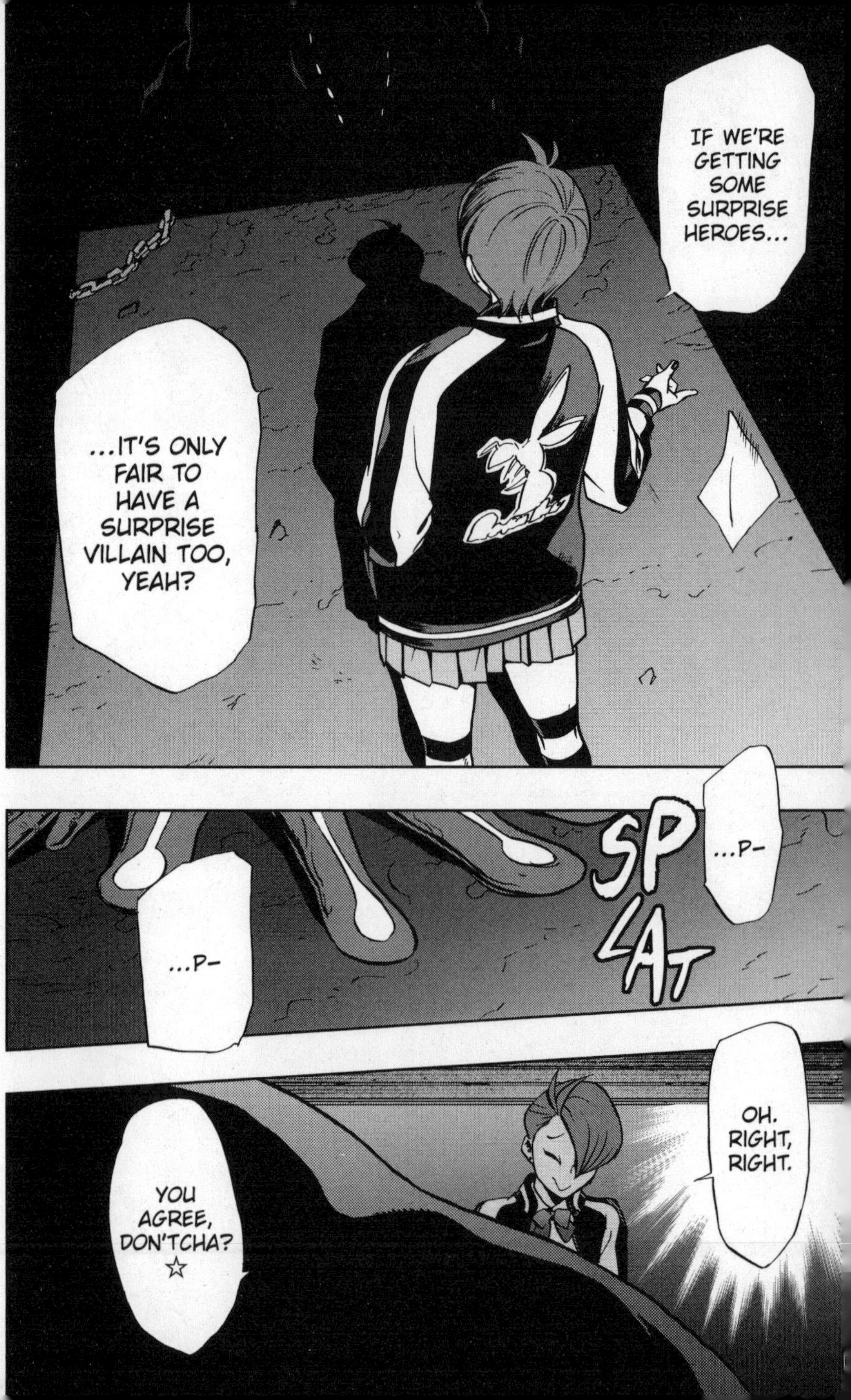
IF WE'RE GETTING SOME SURPRISE HEROES...
...IT'S ONLY FAIR TO HAVE A SURPRISE VILLAIN TOO, YEAH?
...P-
SPLAT
...P-
OH. RIGHT, RIGHT.
YOU AGREE, DON'TCHA? ☆

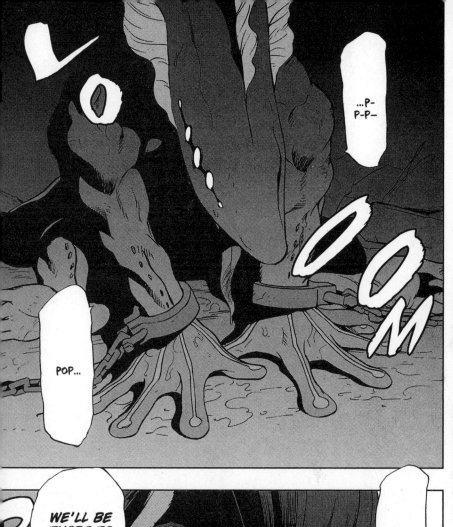

...P-
P-P-

OOM

POP...

WE'LL BE THERE TO CHEER ON LITTLE MISS POP! ♪

YESSS.

U
Z
Z
Z
Z

FEATHERS

THE ROUGH DESIGN

Feathers

Yu

Miu

Fundamentally the same face, since they're twins, but Miu has sharper expressions.

Electropop motif

BEHIND THE SCENES

The twins, Miu and Yu. Personality-wise, Miu is the…less pleasant of the two, but since they're dividing the twin labor, Yu also asserts herself to an extent.

As far as their background, I pictured them less as indie idols and more like girls who got thrown up onstage when some family member was putting on a live event. They're not too different from Pop, honestly…

—Furuhashi

The concept here was that you need both of them for that left-right symmetry.

Thinking back, I had wings in mind when designing them, rather than feathers. I wish I'd given them slightly softer-looking edges.

—Betten

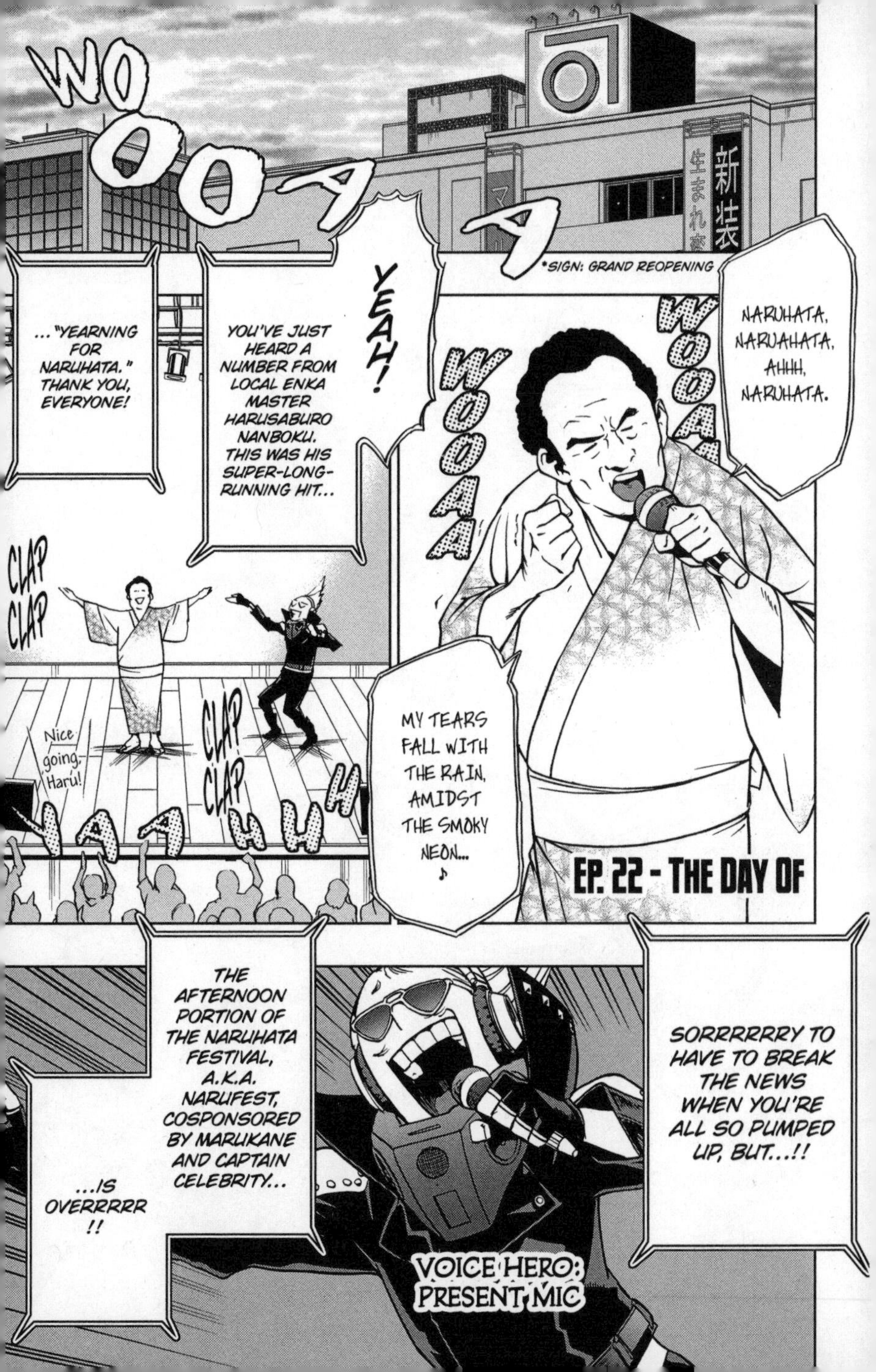
WOOOAAA
新装
YEAH!
*SIGN: GRAND REOPENING
NARUHATA, NARUAHATA, AHHH, NARUHATA.
WOOOAA
WOOOAA
MY TEARS FALL WITH THE RAIN, AMIDST THE SMOKY NEON... ♪
EP. 22 - THE DAY OF
YOU'VE JUST HEARD A NUMBER FROM LOCAL ENKA MASTER HARUSABURO NANBOKU. THIS WAS HIS SUPER-LONG-RUNNING HIT...
..."YEARNING FOR NARUHATA." THANK YOU, EVERYONE!
CLAP CLAP
CLAP CLAP
Nice going, Haru!
YAAAHHHH
SORRRRRRY TO HAVE TO BREAK THE NEWS WHEN YOU'RE ALL SO PUMPED UP, BUT...!!
THE AFTERNOON PORTION OF THE NARUHATA FESTIVAL, A.K.A. NARUFEST, COSPONSORED BY MARUKANE AND CAPTAIN CELEBRITY...
...IS OVERRRRR!!
VOICE HERO: PRESENT MIC

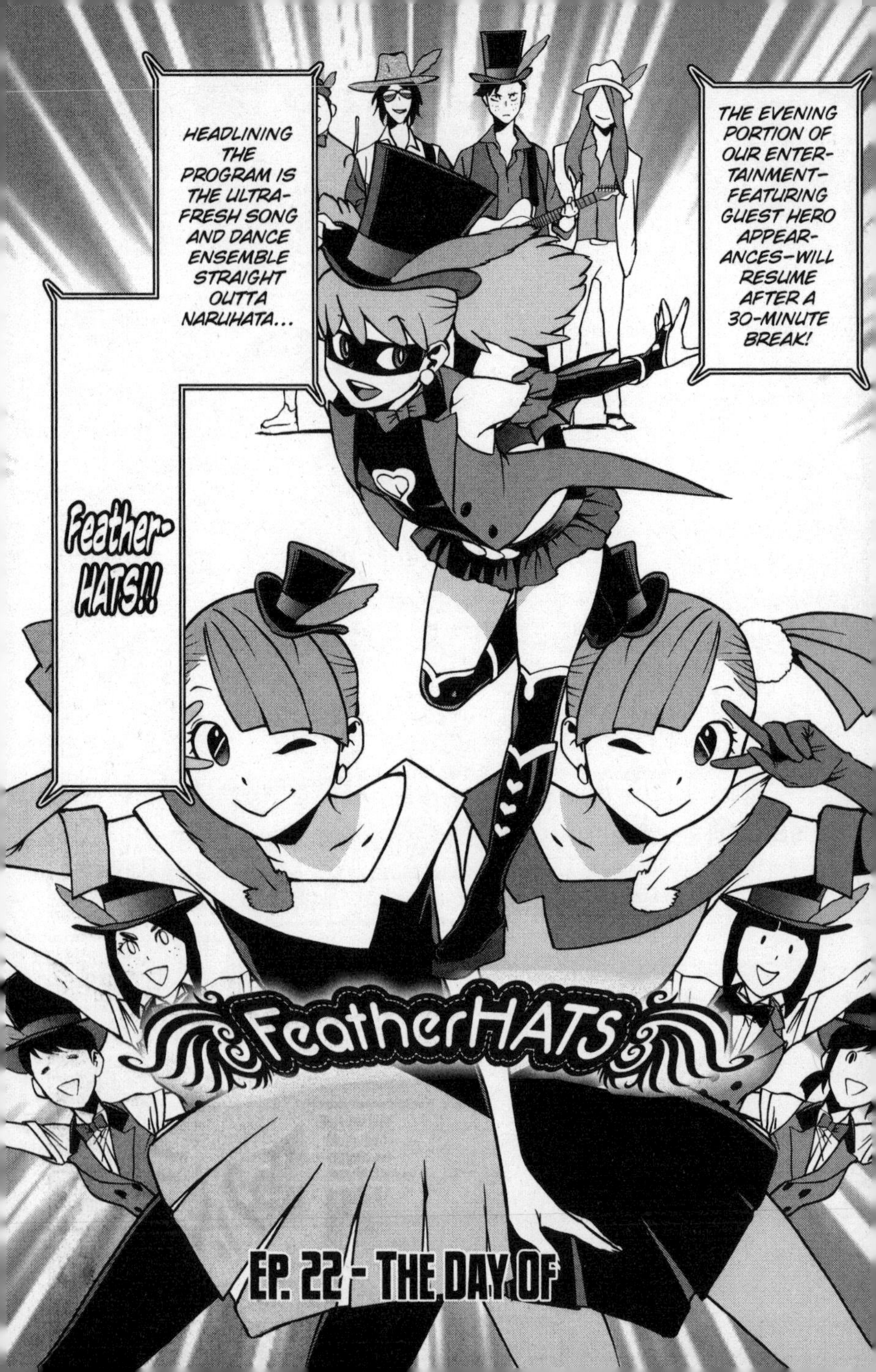
THE EVENING PORTION OF OUR ENTER-TAINMENT—FEATURING GUEST HERO APPEAR-ANCES—WILL RESUME AFTER A 30-MINUTE BREAK!
HEADLINING THE PROGRAM IS THE ULTRA-FRESH SONG AND DANCE ENSEMBLE STRAIGHT OUTTA NARUHATA...
Feather-HATS!!
FeatherHATS
EP. 22 - THE DAY OF

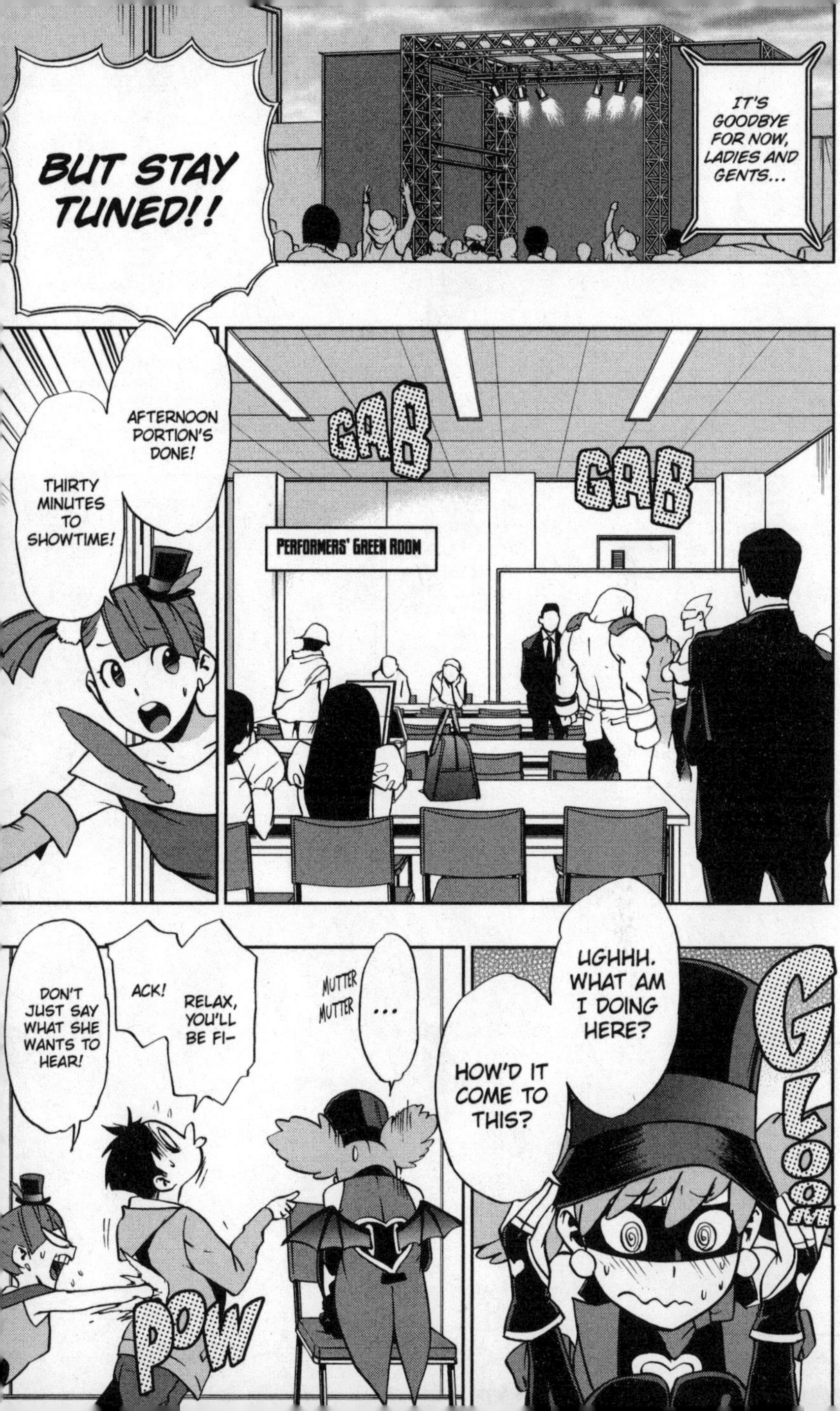
IT'S GOODBYE FOR NOW, LADIES AND GENTS...
BUT STAY TUNED!!
GAB
GAB
PERFORMERS' GREEN ROOM
AFTERNOON PORTION'S DONE!
THIRTY MINUTES TO SHOWTIME!
GLOOM
UGHHH. WHAT AM I DOING HERE?
HOW'D IT COME TO THIS?
...
MUTTER MUTTER
RELAX, YOU'LL BE FI-
ACK!
DON'T JUST SAY WHAT SHE WANTS TO HEAR!
POW

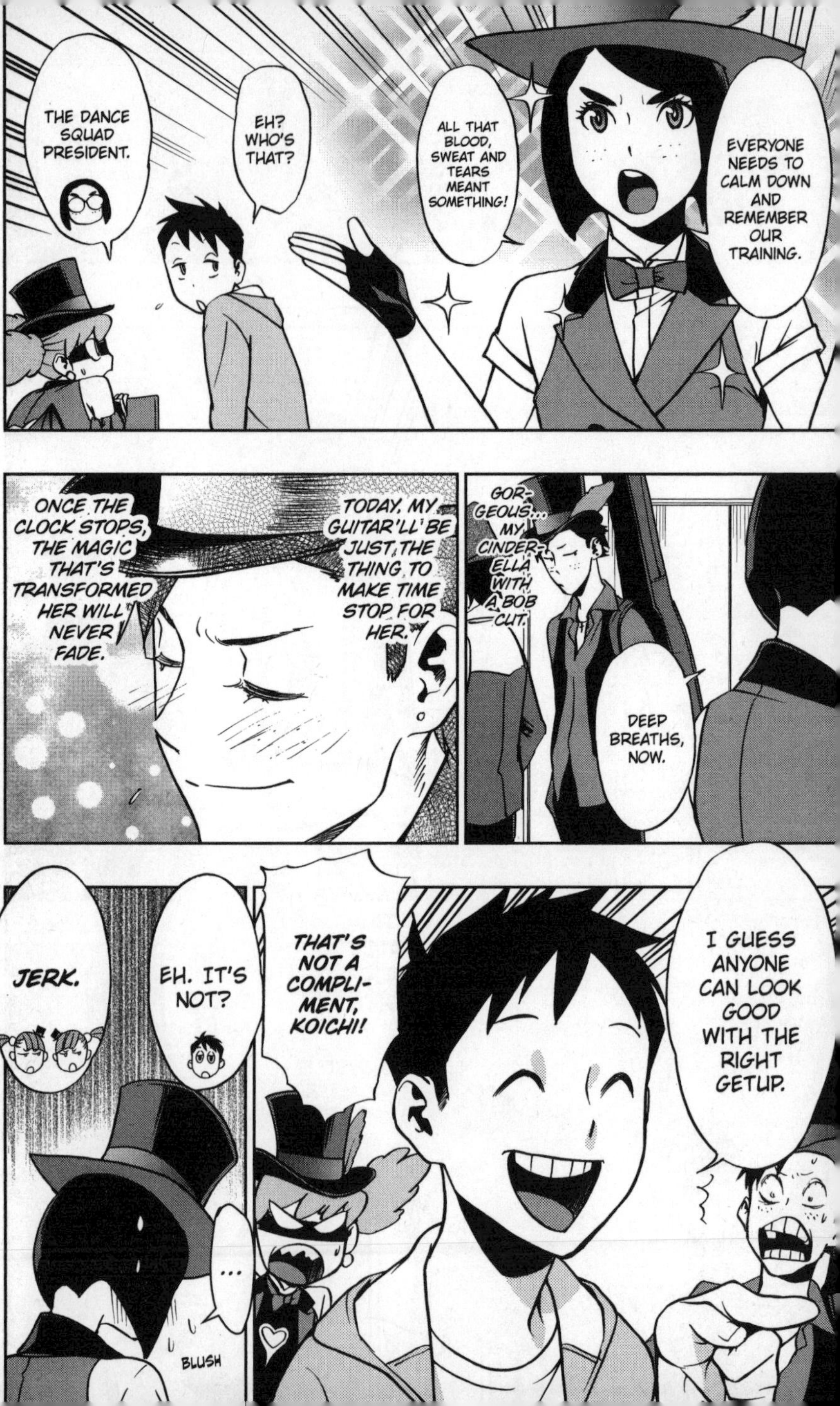
EVERYONE NEEDS TO CALM DOWN AND REMEMBER OUR TRAINING.
ALL THAT BLOOD, SWEAT AND TEARS MEANT SOMETHING!
EH? WHO'S THAT?
THE DANCE SQUAD PRESIDENT.
GOR-GEOUS... MY CINDER-ELLA WITH A BOB CUT.
DEEP BREATHS, NOW.
TODAY, MY GUITAR'LL BE JUST THE THING TO MAKE TIME STOP FOR HER.
ONCE THE CLOCK STOPS, THE MAGIC THAT'S TRANSFORMED HER WILL NEVER FADE.
I GUESS ANYONE CAN LOOK GOOD WITH THE RIGHT GETUP.
THAT'S NOT A COMPLI-MENT, KOICHI!
EH. IT'S NOT?
JERK.
...
BLUSH

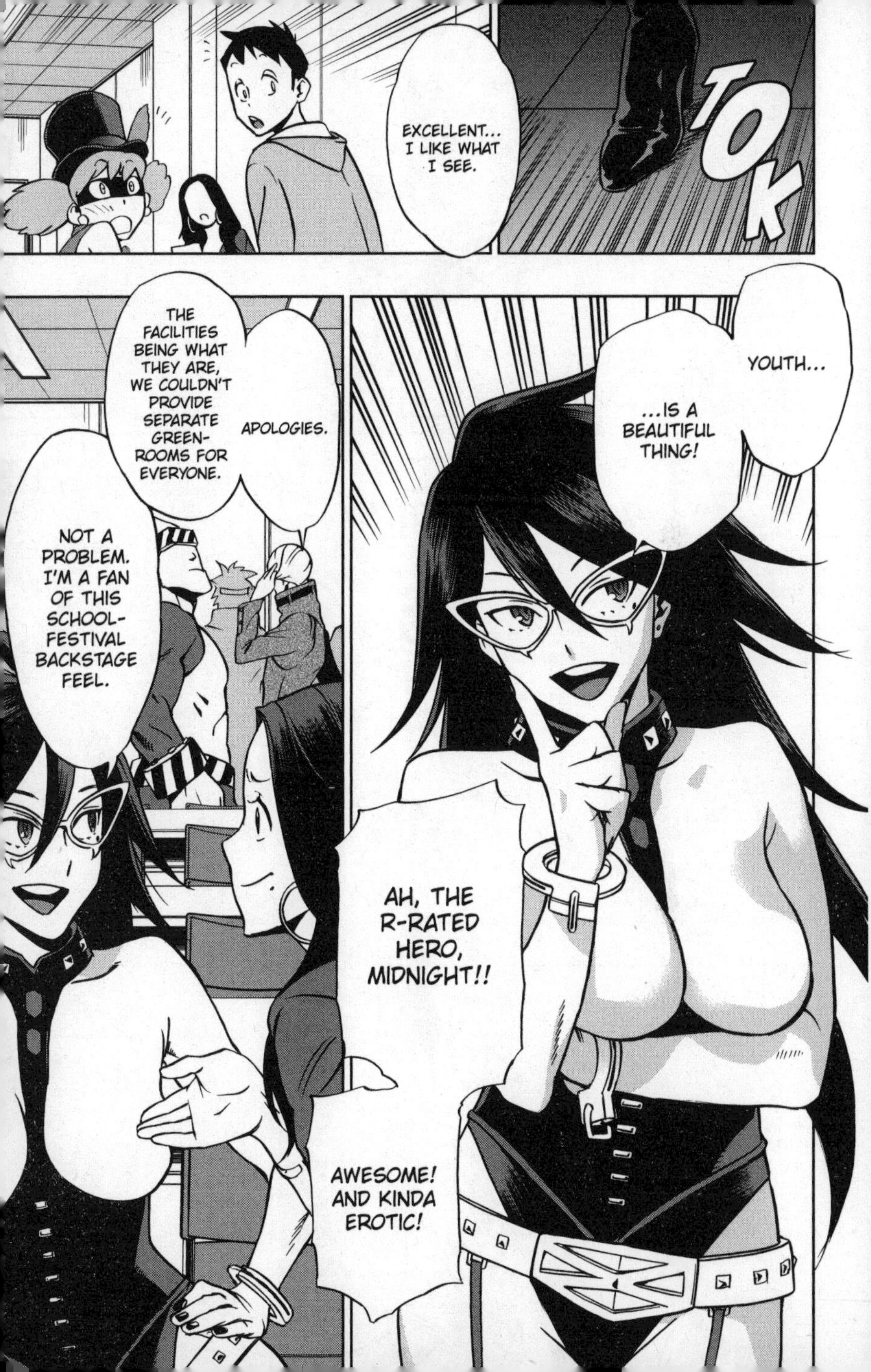
TOK
EXCELLENT... I LIKE WHAT I SEE.
YOUTH...
...IS A BEAUTIFUL THING!
AH, THE R-RATED HERO, MIDNIGHT!!
AWESOME! AND KINDA EROTIC!
THE FACILITIES BEING WHAT THEY ARE, WE COULDN'T PROVIDE SEPARATE GREEN-ROOMS FOR EVERYONE.
APOLOGIES.
NOT A PROBLEM. I'M A FAN OF THIS SCHOOL-FESTIVAL BACKSTAGE FEEL.

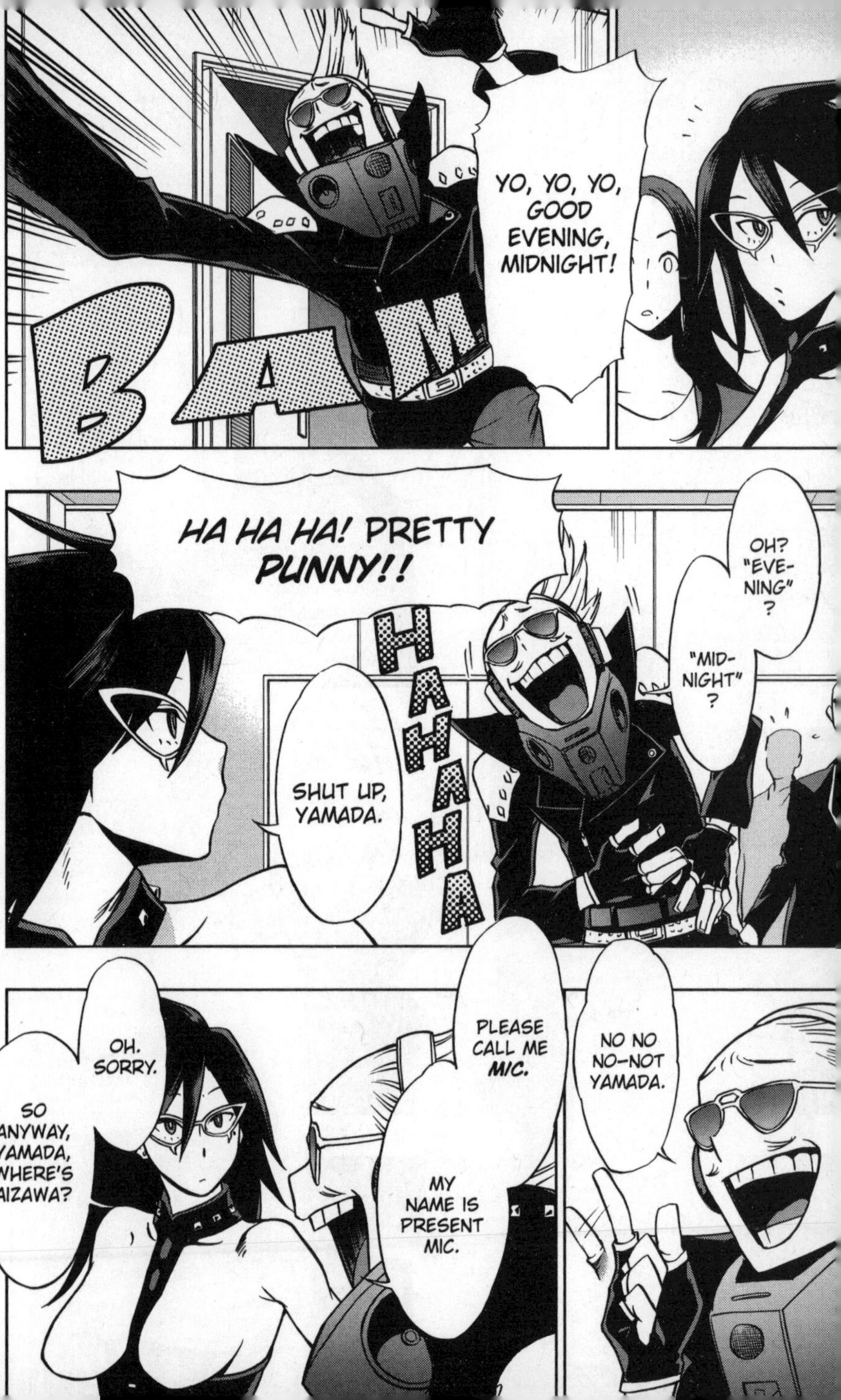
YO, YO, YO, GOOD EVENING, MIDNIGHT!
BAM
OH? "EVE-NING"?
"MID-NIGHT"?
HA HA HA! PRETTY PUNNY!!
HAHAHAHAHA
SHUT UP, YAMADA.
NO NO NO-NOT YAMADA.
PLEASE CALL ME MIC.
MY NAME IS PRESENT MIC.
OH. SORRY.
SO ANYWAY, YAMADA, WHERE'S AIZAWA?

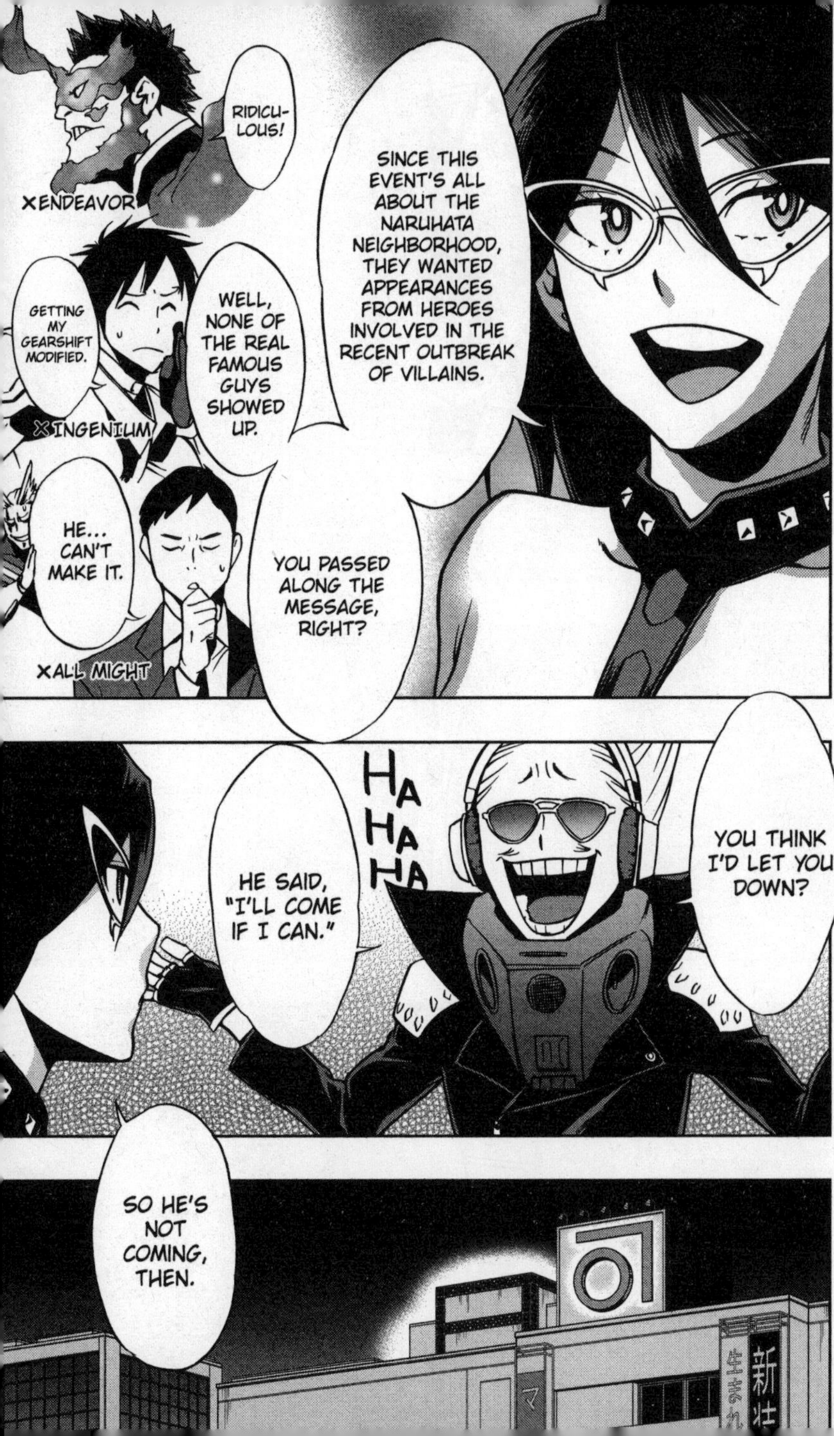
SINCE THIS EVENT'S ALL ABOUT THE NARUHATA NEIGHBORHOOD, THEY WANTED APPEARANCES FROM HEROES INVOLVED IN THE RECENT OUTBREAK OF VILLAINS.
WELL, NONE OF THE REAL FAMOUS GUYS SHOWED UP.
RIDICU-LOUS!
×ENDEAVOR
GETTING MY GEARSHIFT MODIFIED.
×INGENIUM
HE... CAN'T MAKE IT.
×ALL MIGHT
YOU PASSED ALONG THE MESSAGE, RIGHT?
YOU THINK I'D LET YOU DOWN?
HA HA HA
HE SAID, "I'LL COME IF I CAN."
SO HE'S NOT COMING, THEN.

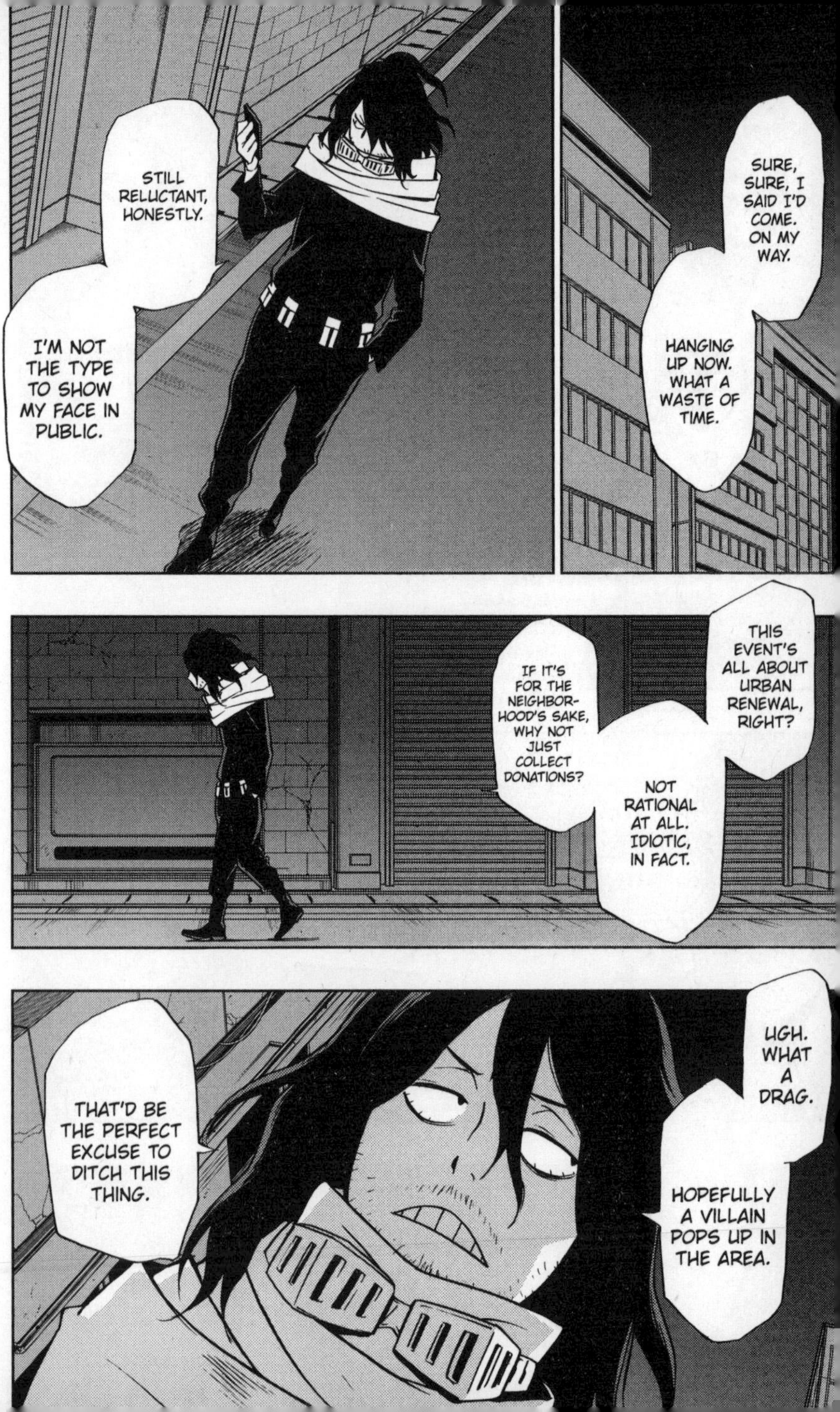
SURE, SURE, I SAID I'D COME. ON MY WAY.
HANGING UP NOW. WHAT A WASTE OF TIME.
STILL RELUCTANT, HONESTLY.
I'M NOT THE TYPE TO SHOW MY FACE IN PUBLIC.
THIS EVENT'S ALL ABOUT URBAN RENEWAL, RIGHT?
IF IT'S FOR THE NEIGHBOR-HOOD'S SAKE, WHY NOT JUST COLLECT DONATIONS?
NOT RATIONAL AT ALL. IDIOTIC, IN FACT.
UGH. WHAT A DRAG.
HOPEFULLY A VILLAIN POPS UP IN THE AREA.
THAT'D BE THE PERFECT EXCUSE TO DITCH THIS THING.

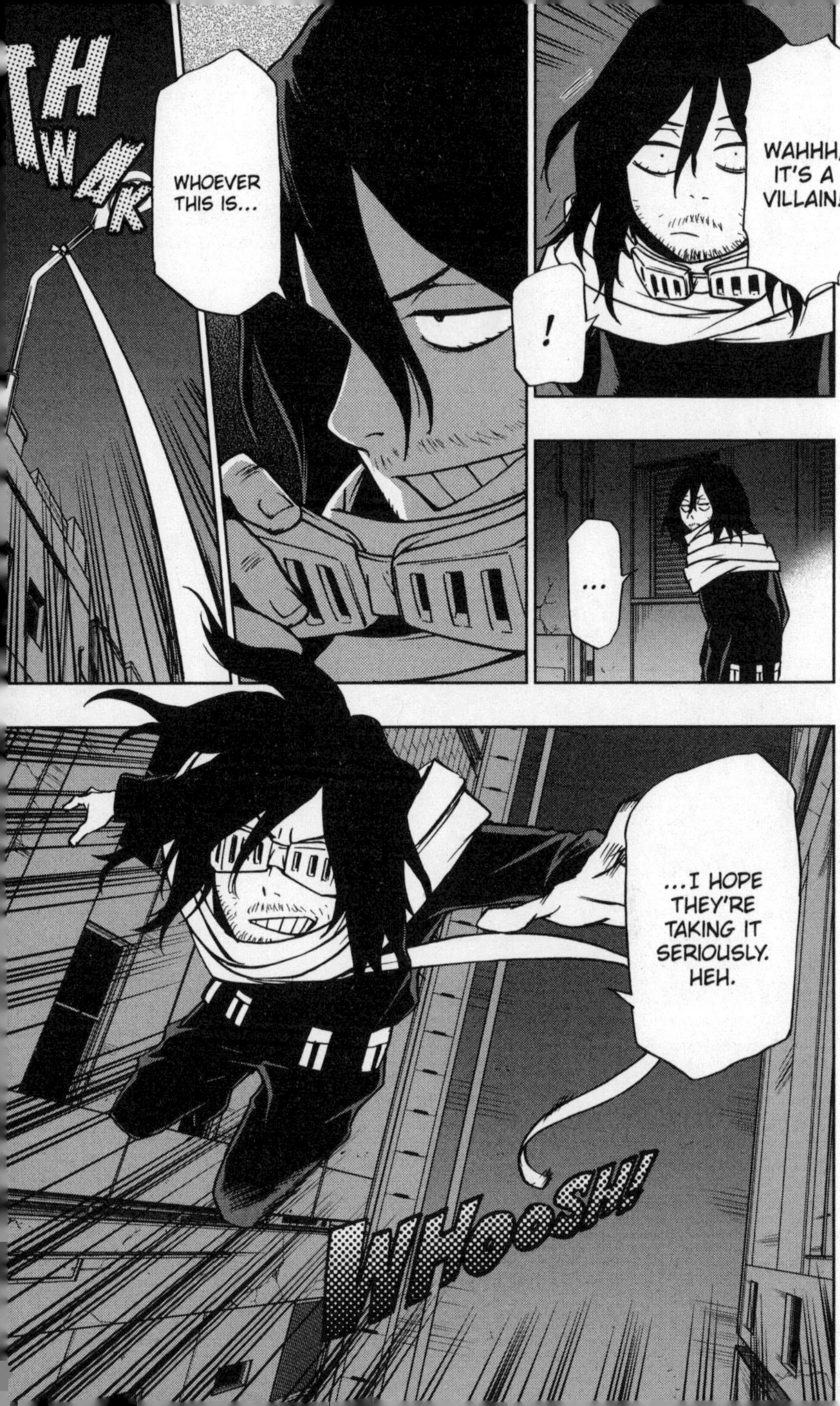
WAHHH, IT'S A VILLAIN!
!
...
THWAK
WHOEVER THIS IS...
...I HOPE THEY'RE TAKING IT SERIOUSLY. HEH.
WHOOSH!

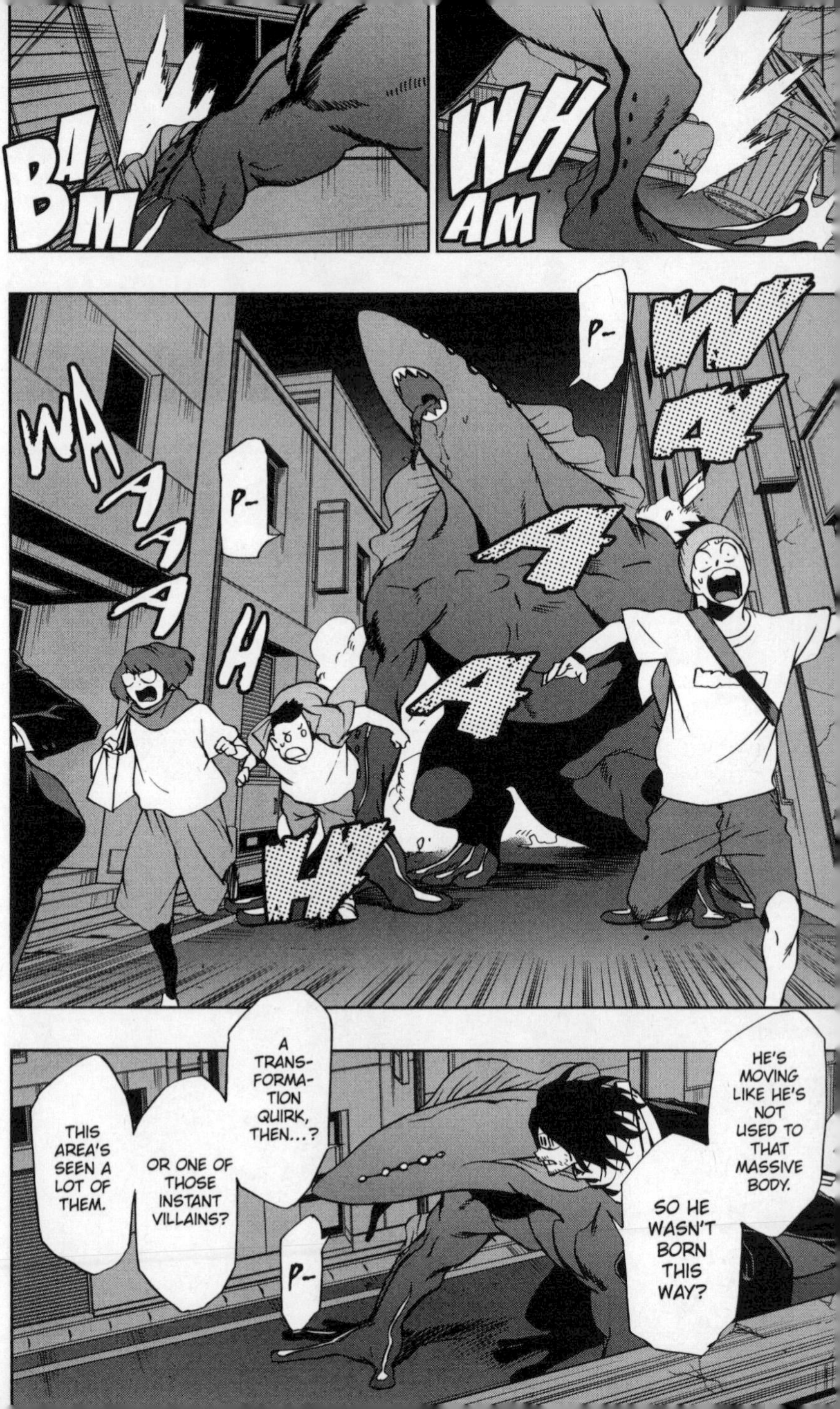
WHAM
BAM
P-
WAAAAH
WAAAAAH
P-
HE'S MOVING LIKE HE'S NOT USED TO THAT MASSIVE BODY.
SO HE WASN'T BORN THIS WAY?
A TRANSFORMATION QUIRK, THEN...?
OR ONE OF THOSE INSTANT VILLAINS?
THIS AREA'S SEEN A LOT OF THEM.
P-

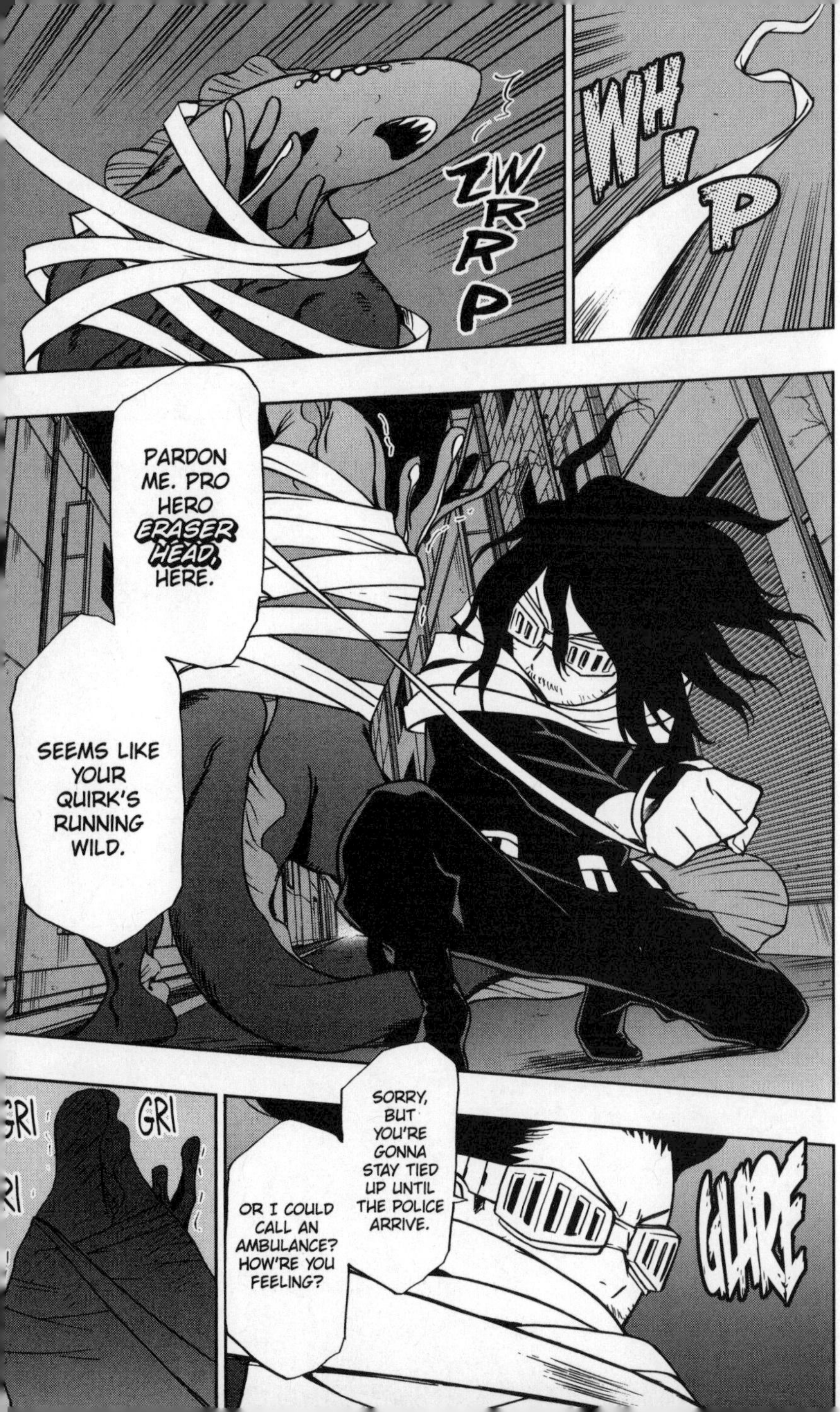
WHIP
ZWRRP
PARDON ME. PRO HERO ERASER HEAD, HERE.
SEEMS LIKE YOUR QUIRK'S RUNNING WILD.
SORRY, BUT YOU'RE GONNA STAY TIED UP UNTIL THE POLICE ARRIVE.
OR I COULD CALL AN AMBULANCE? HOW'RE YOU FEELING?
GLARE
GRI
GRI
GRI

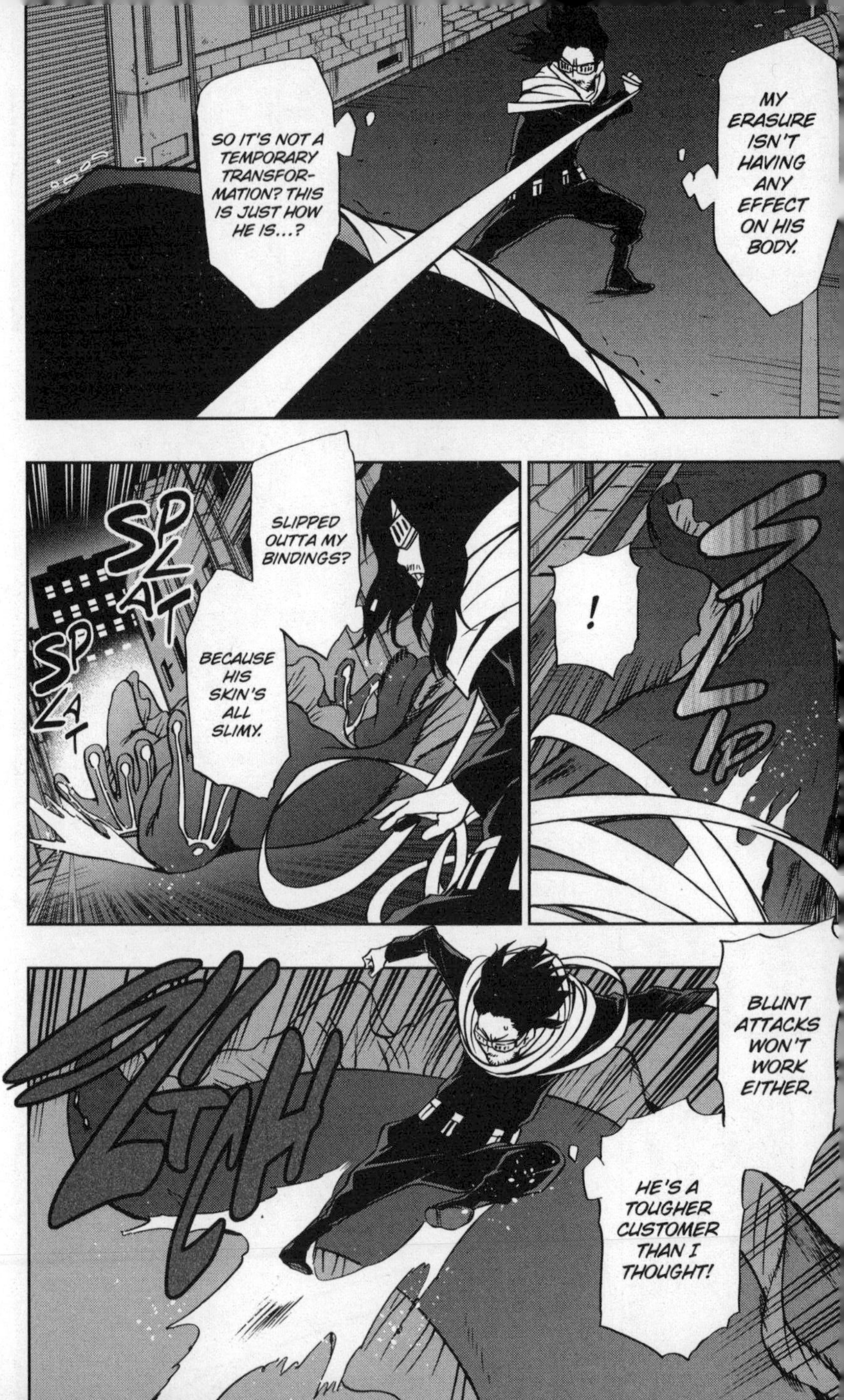
MY ERASURE ISN'T HAVING ANY EFFECT ON HIS BODY.
SO IT'S NOT A TEMPORARY TRANSFORMATION? THIS IS JUST HOW HE IS...?
!
SLIP
SLIPPED OUTTA MY BINDINGS?
BECAUSE HIS SKIN'S ALL SLIMY.
SPLAT
SPLAT
BLUNT ATTACKS WON'T WORK EITHER.
HE'S A TOUGHER CUSTOMER THAN I THOUGHT!

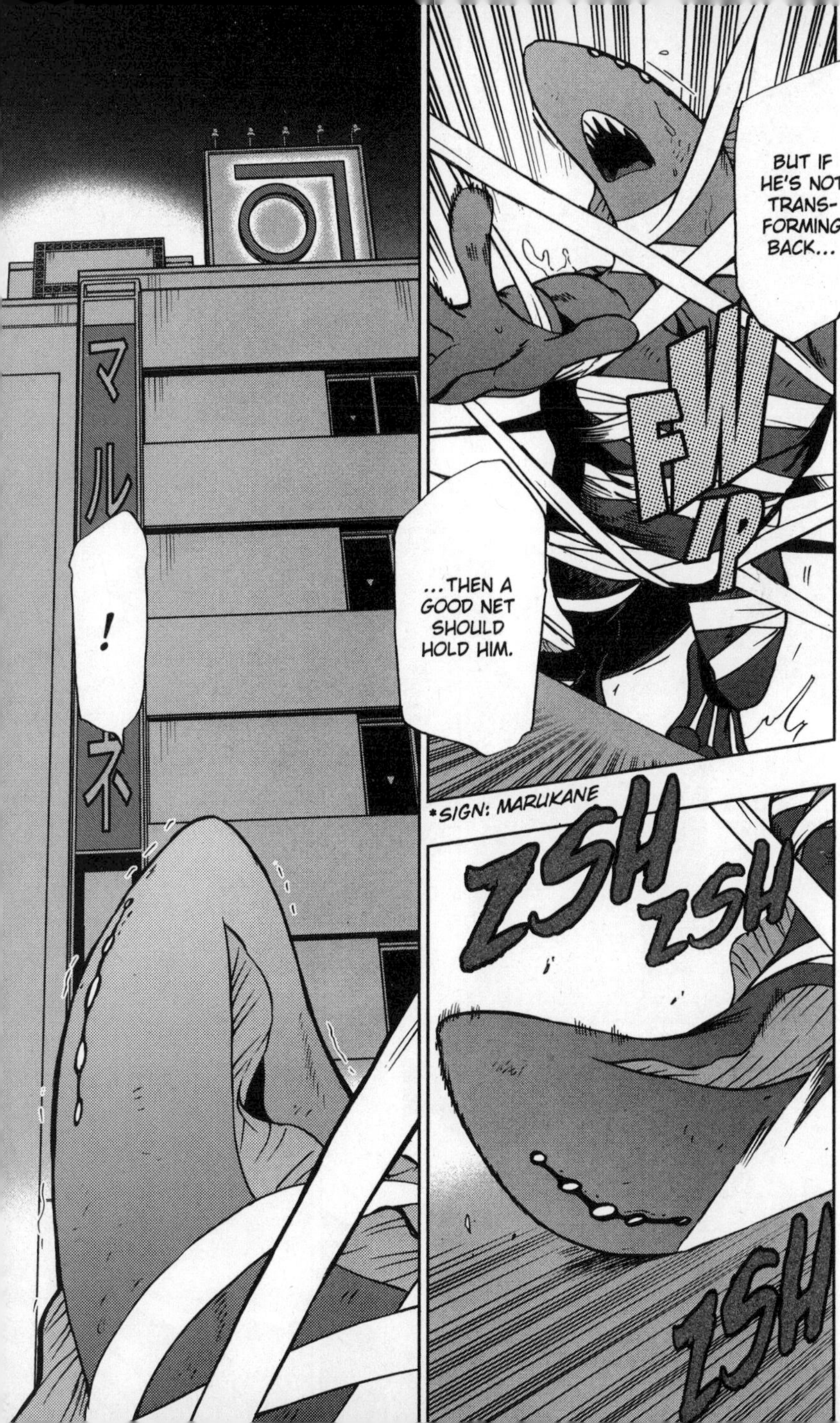
BUT IF HE'S NOT TRANS-FORMING BACK...
FWIP
...THEN A GOOD NET SHOULD HOLD HIM.
ZSH ZSH
ZSH
!
*SIGN: MARUKANE

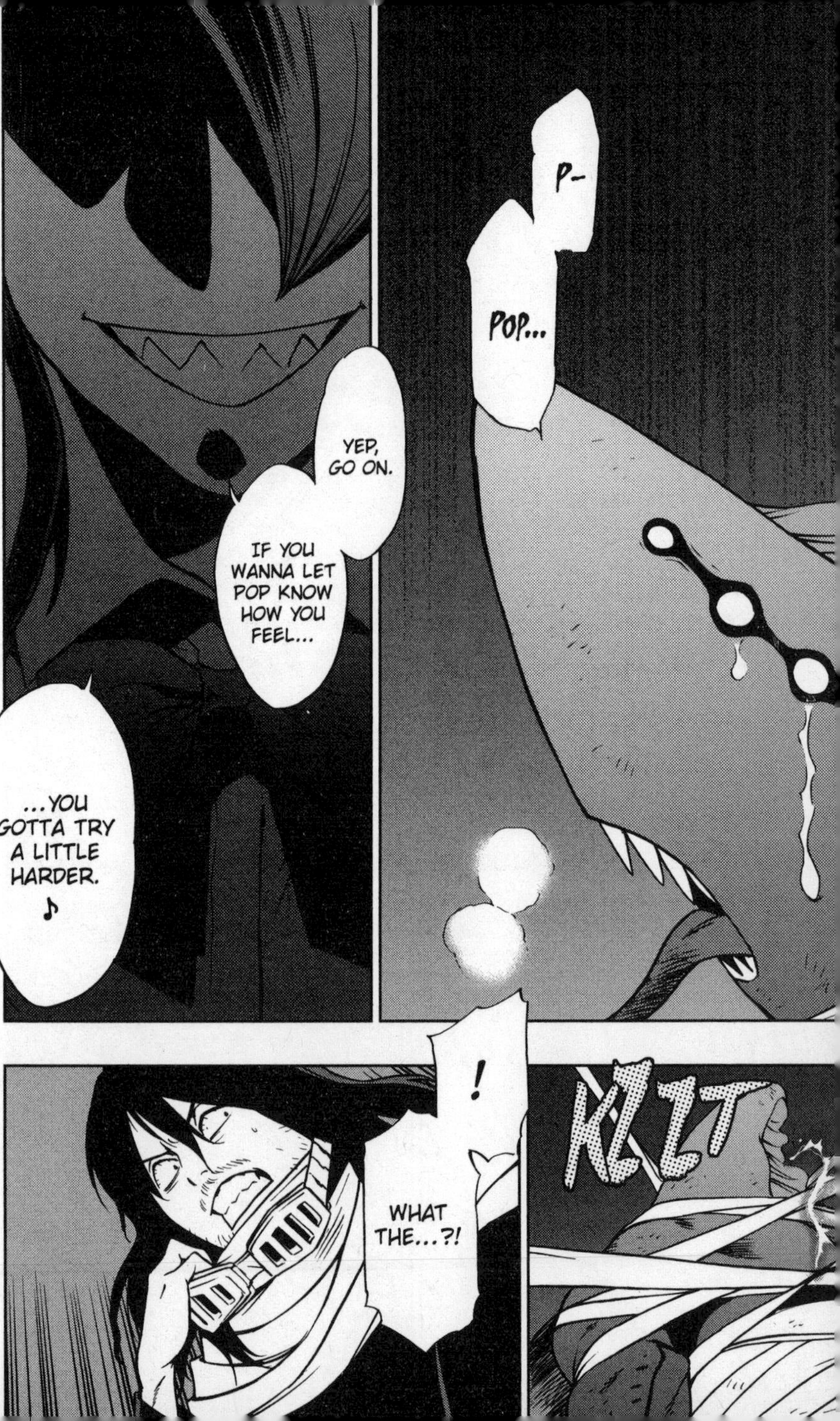
P-
POP...
YEP, GO ON.
IF YOU WANNA LET POP KNOW HOW YOU FEEL...
...YOU GOTTA TRY A LITTLE HARDER. ♪
KZZT
!
WHAT THE...?!

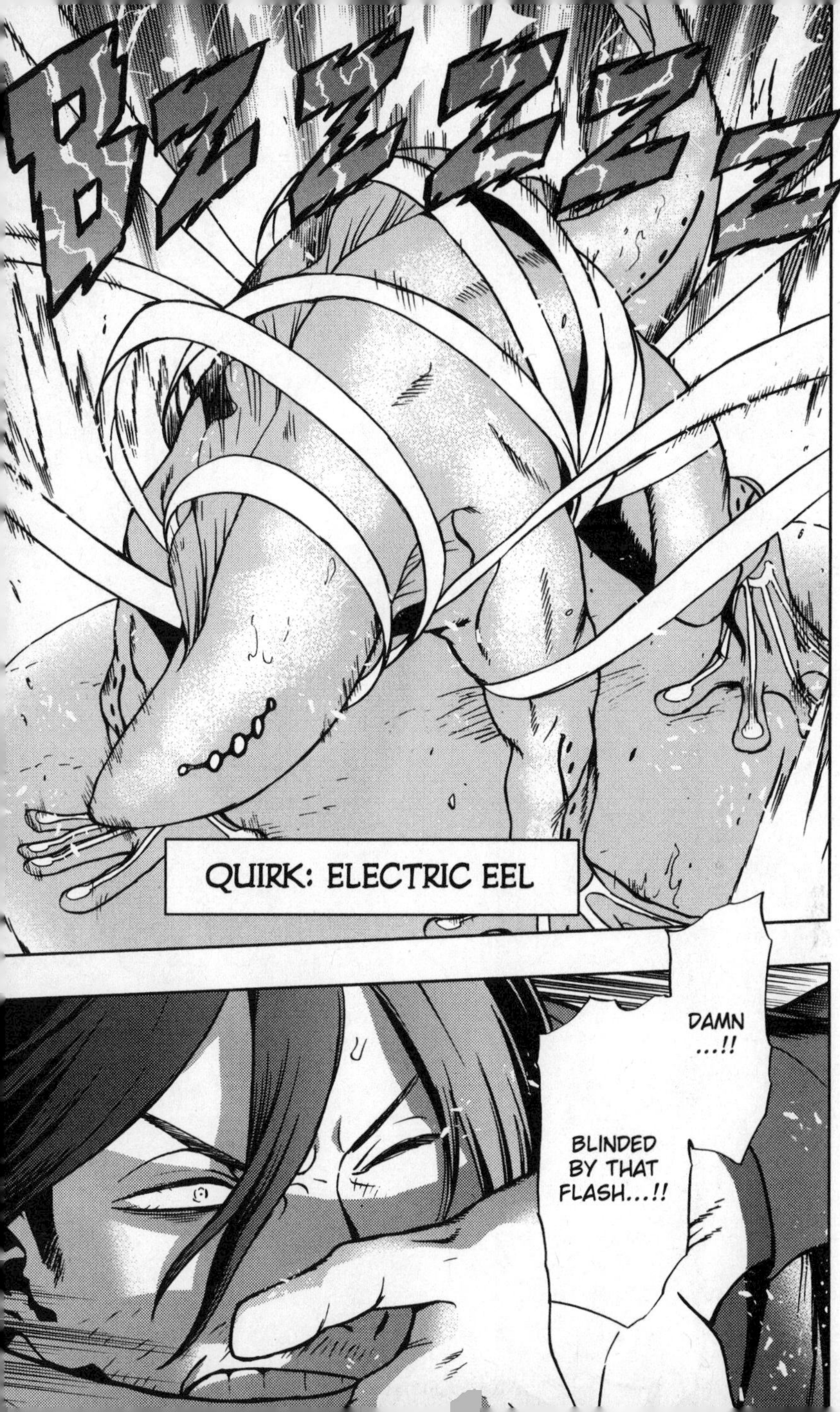
QUIRK: ELECTRIC EEL
DAMN ...!!
BLINDED BY THAT FLASH...!!

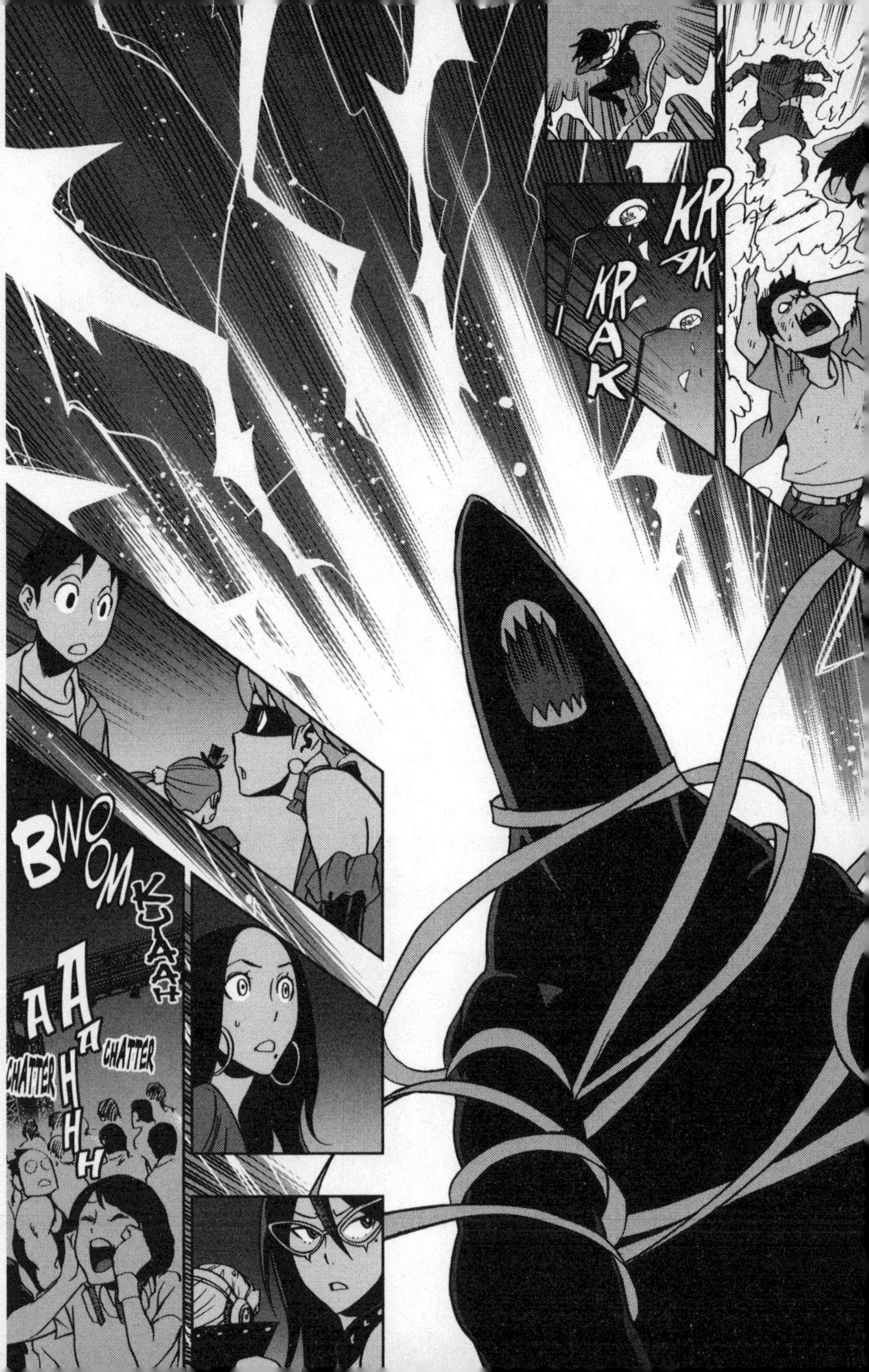
KRAK
KRAK
BWOOM
KYAAH
AAAHHHH
CHATTER
CHATTER

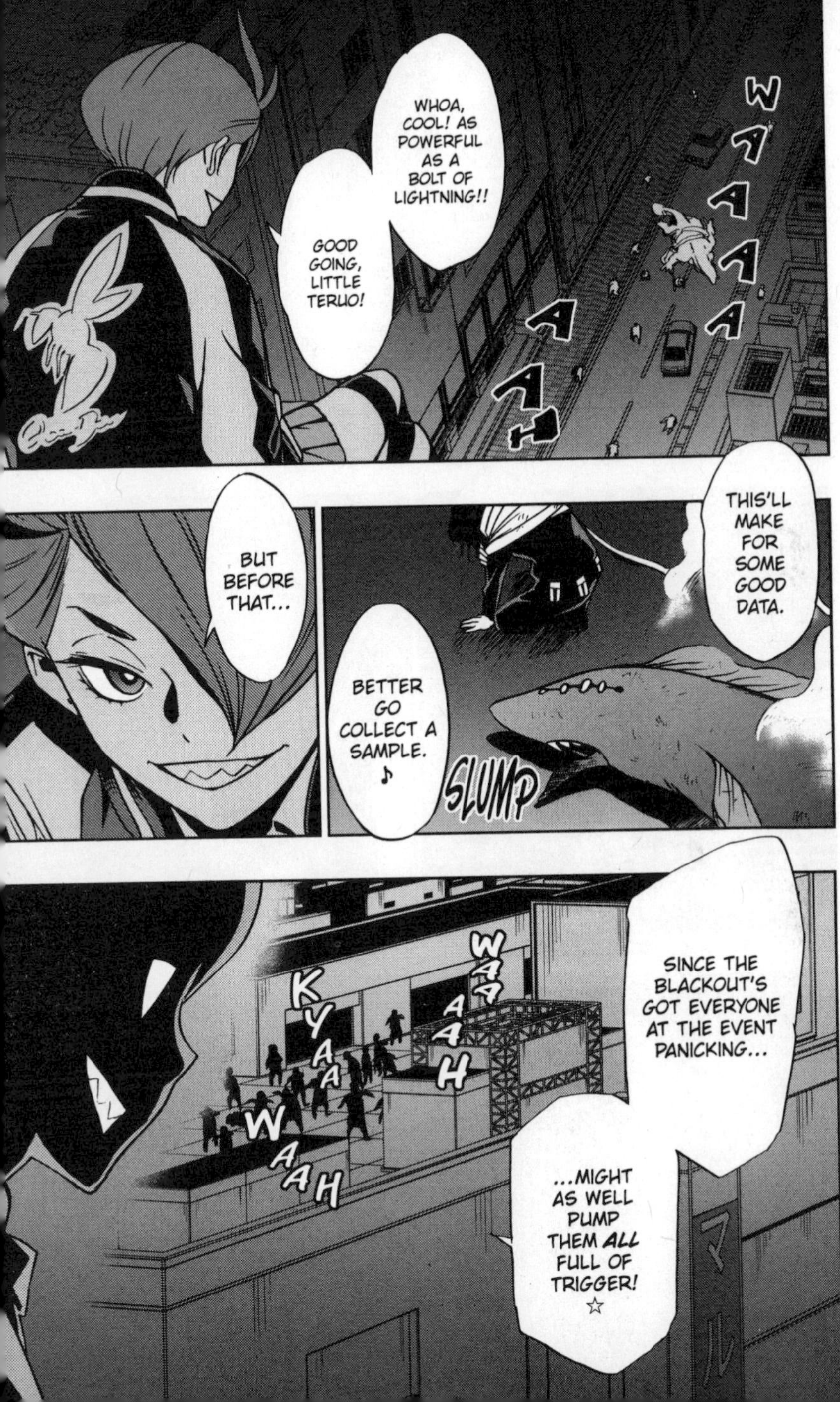
WHOA, COOL! AS POWERFUL AS A BOLT OF LIGHTNING!!
GOOD GOING, LITTLE TERUO!
WAAAAAAAH
THIS'LL MAKE FOR SOME GOOD DATA.
BETTER GO COLLECT A SAMPLE. ♪
SLUMP
BUT BEFORE THAT...
SINCE THE BLACKOUT'S GOT EVERYONE AT THE EVENT PANICKING...
...MIGHT AS WELL PUMP THEM ALL FULL OF TRIGGER! ☆
WAAAH
KYAAA
WAAH

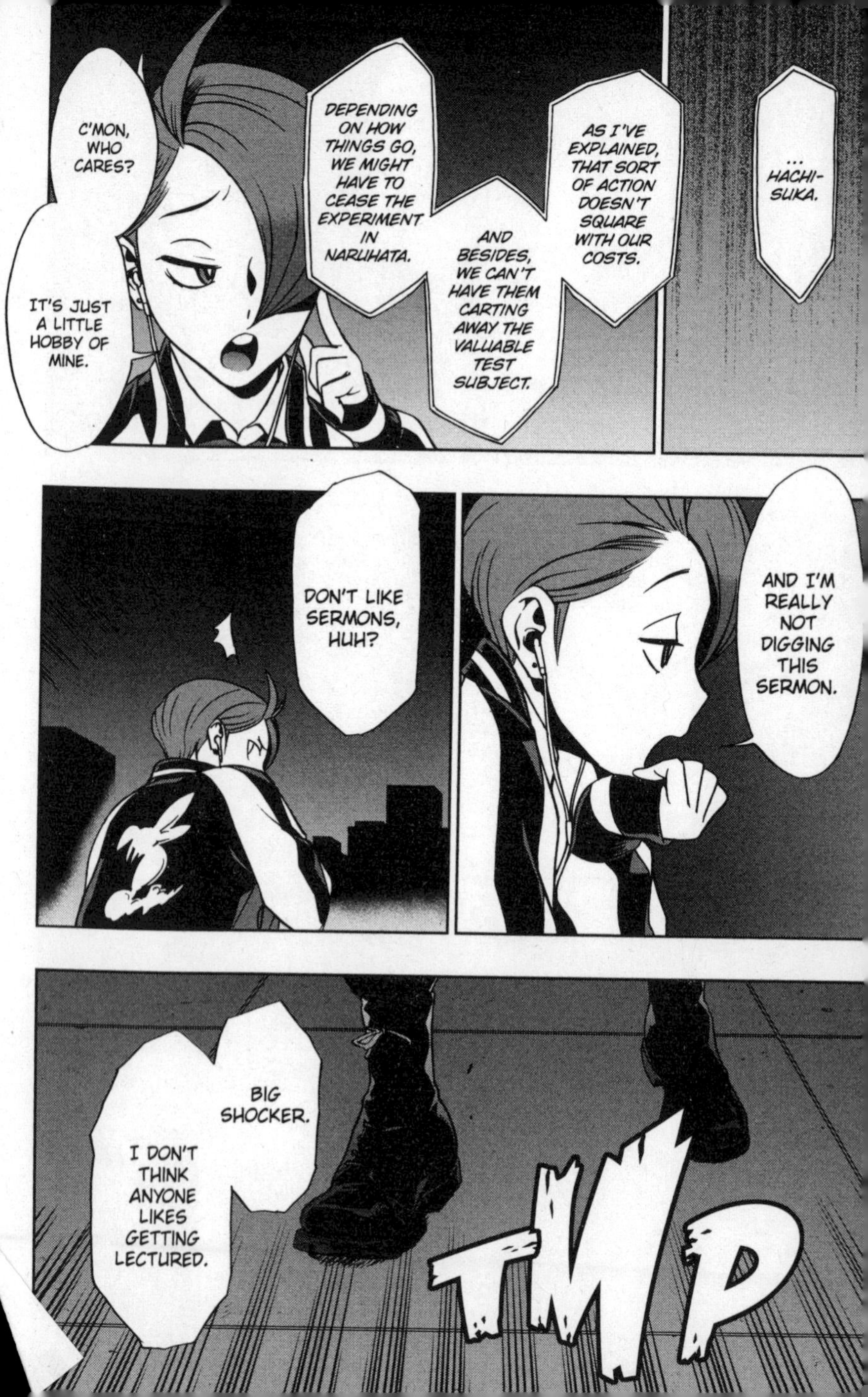
... HACHI-SUKA.
AS I'VE EXPLAINED, THAT SORT OF ACTION DOESN'T SQUARE WITH OUR COSTS.
DEPENDING ON HOW THINGS GO, WE MIGHT HAVE TO CEASE THE EXPERIMENT IN NARUHATA.
AND BESIDES, WE CAN'T HAVE THEM CARTING AWAY THE VALUABLE TEST SUBJECT.
C'MON, WHO CARES?
IT'S JUST A LITTLE HOBBY OF MINE.
AND I'M REALLY NOT DIGGING THIS SERMON.
DON'T LIKE SERMONS, HUH?
BIG SHOCKER.
I DON'T THINK ANYONE LIKES GETTING LECTURED.
TMP

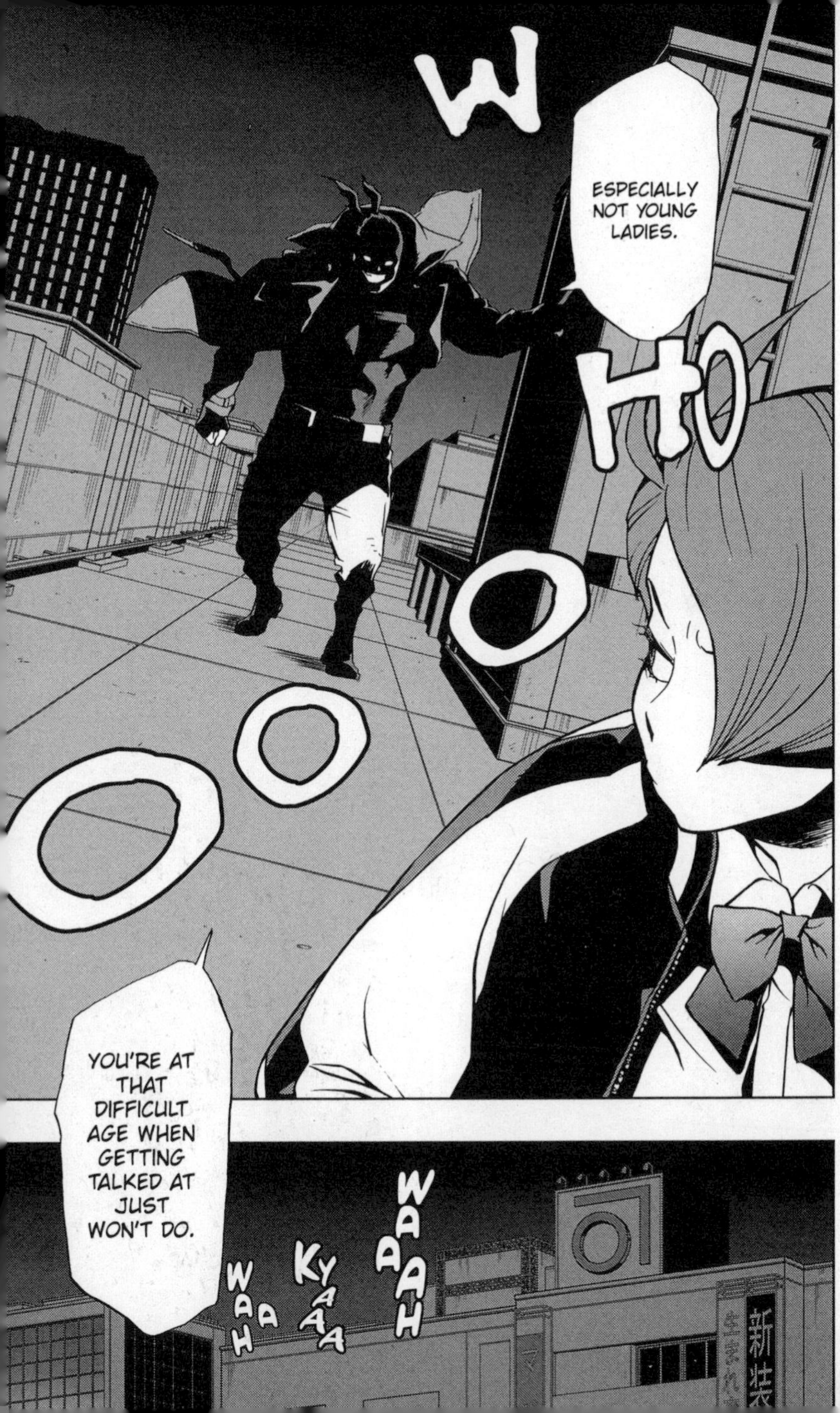
WHOOOO
ESPECIALLY NOT YOUNG LADIES.
YOU'RE AT THAT DIFFICULT AGE WHEN GETTING TALKED AT JUST WON'T DO.
WAAAH
KYAAAA
WAAH
新装

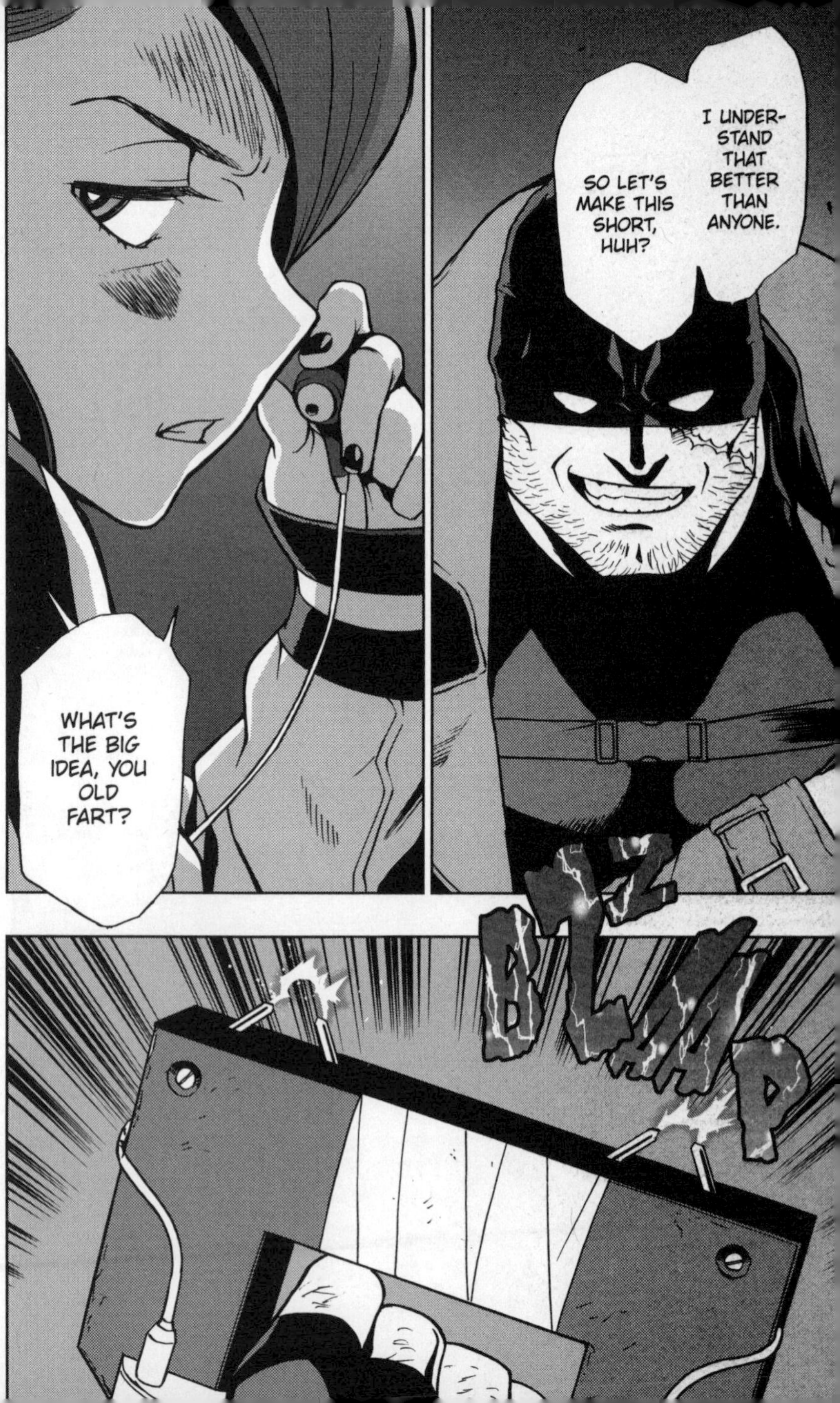
I UNDER-STAND THAT BETTER THAN ANYONE.
SO LET'S MAKE THIS SHORT, HUH?
WHAT'S THE BIG IDEA, YOU OLD FART?

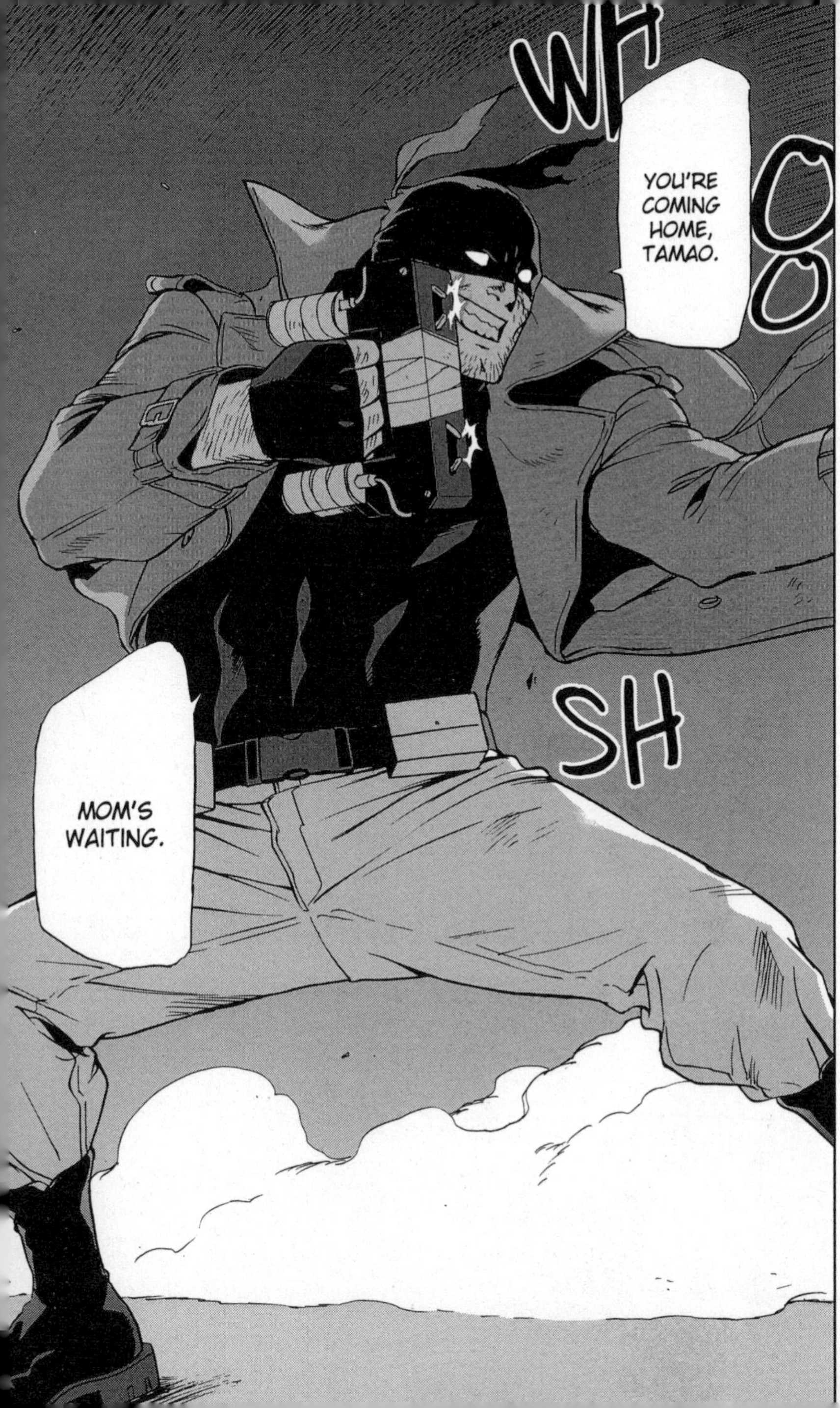
YOU'RE COMING HOME, TAMAO.
WHOOSH
MOM'S WAITING.

ELECTRIC EEL VILLAIN / TERUO UNAGISAWA

THE ROUGH DESIGN

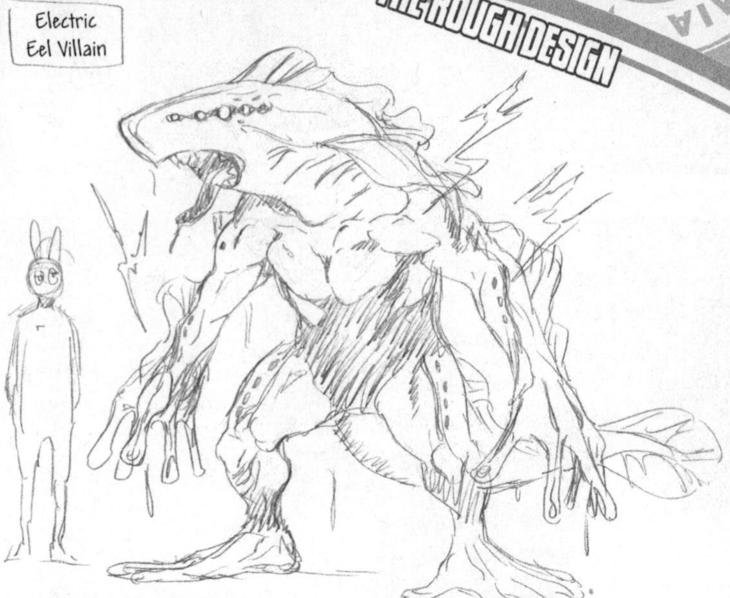
Electric
Eel Villain

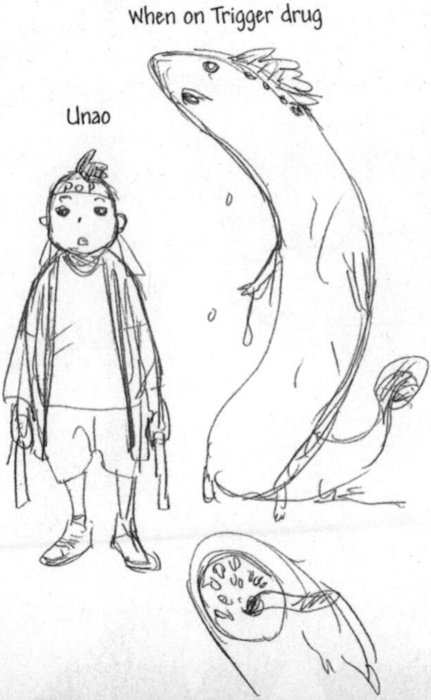
When on Trigger drug
Unao

BEHIND THE SCENES

Little Teruo went missing back in volume 1, and now he's back with a bang. Clearly, strengthening the Eel Quirk results in Electric Eel. I also wanted his very body structure to undergo massive changes and get a big power-up…

—Furuhashi

When designing villains, my drive to make them visually distinct is always at odds with my desire to make them fun to draw. (LOL)

—Betten

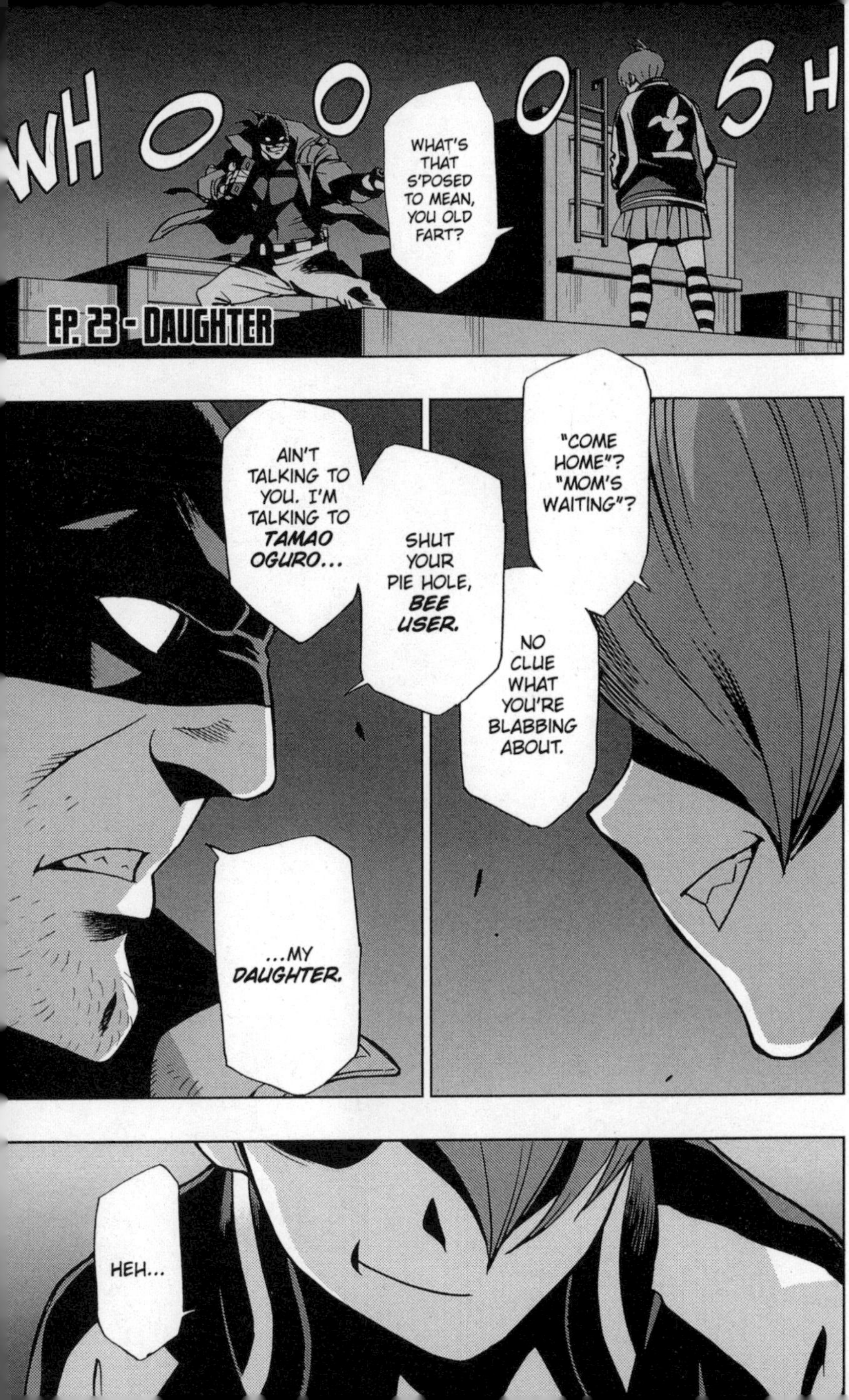
WHOOOOSH
WHAT'S THAT S'POSED TO MEAN, YOU OLD FART?
EP. 23 - DAUGHTER
"COME HOME"? "MOM'S WAITING"?
NO CLUE WHAT YOU'RE BLABBING ABOUT.
SHUT YOUR PIE HOLE, ***BEE USER.***
AIN'T TALKING TO YOU. I'M TALKING TO ***TAMAO OGURO...***
...MY ***DAUGHTER.***
HEH...

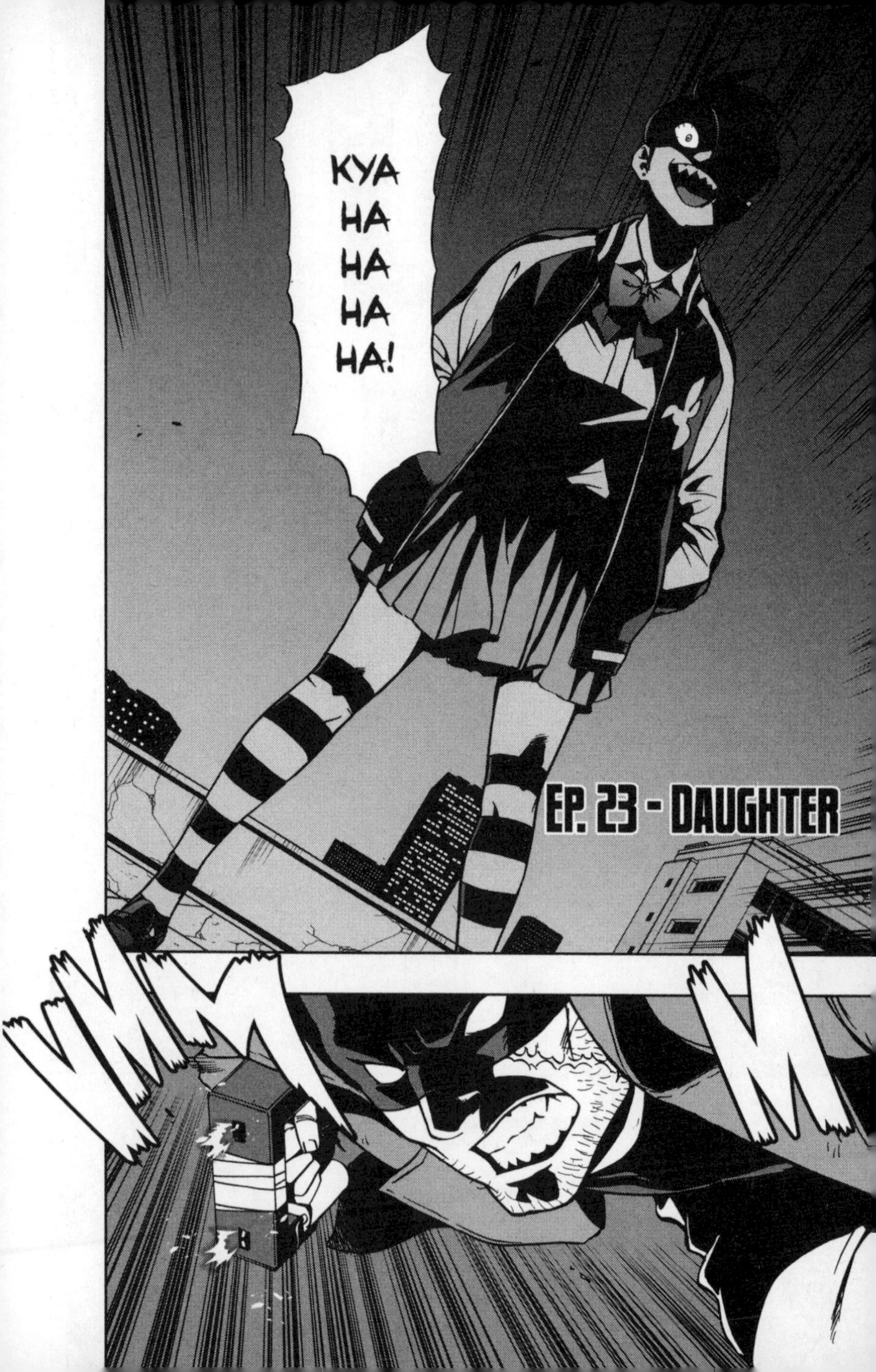
KYA HA HA HA HA!
EP. 23 - DAUGHTER
VMMM

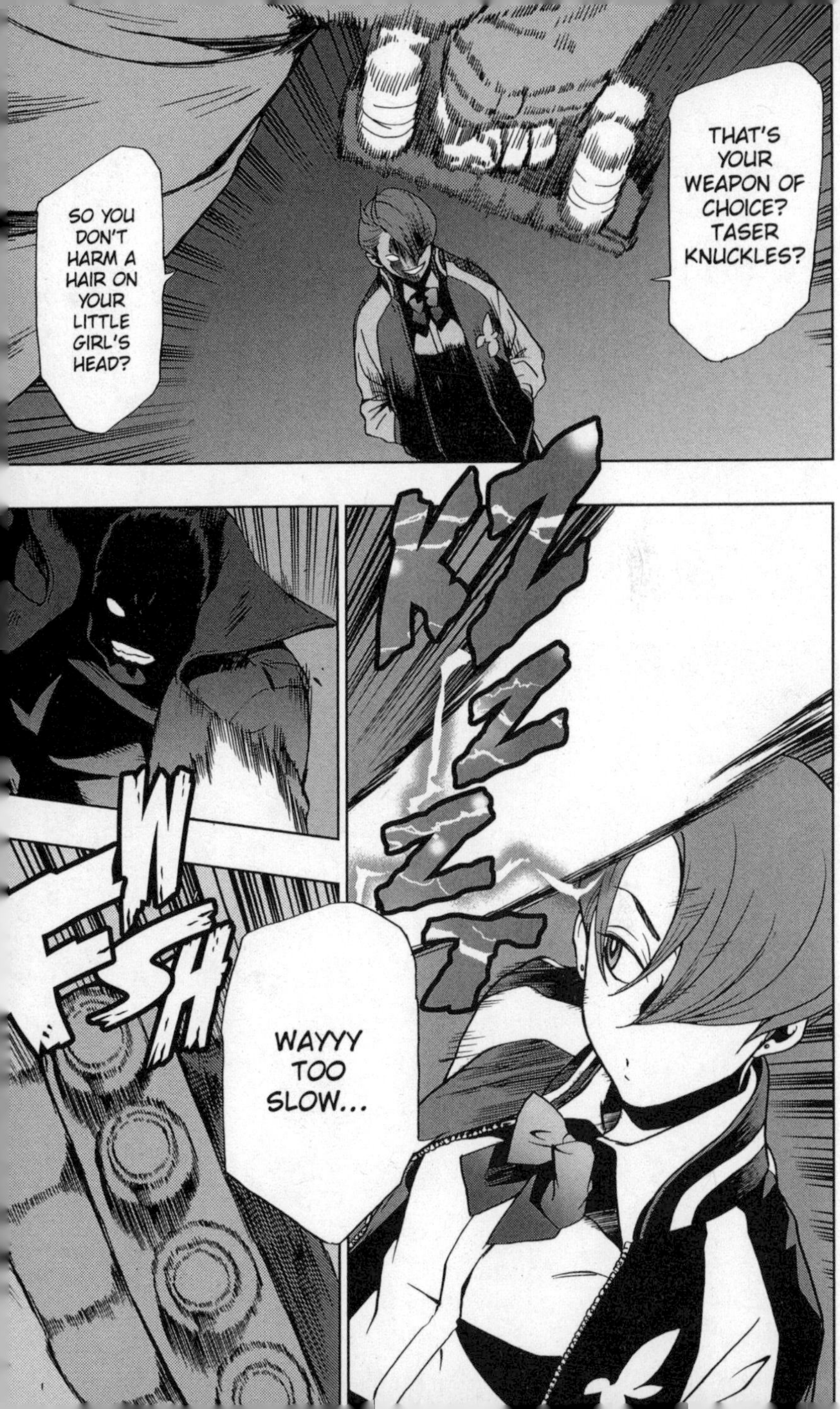
THAT'S YOUR WEAPON OF CHOICE? TASER KNUCKLES?
SO YOU DON'T HARM A HAIR ON YOUR LITTLE GIRL'S HEAD?
KZZZT
WAYYY TOO SLOW...
WFSH

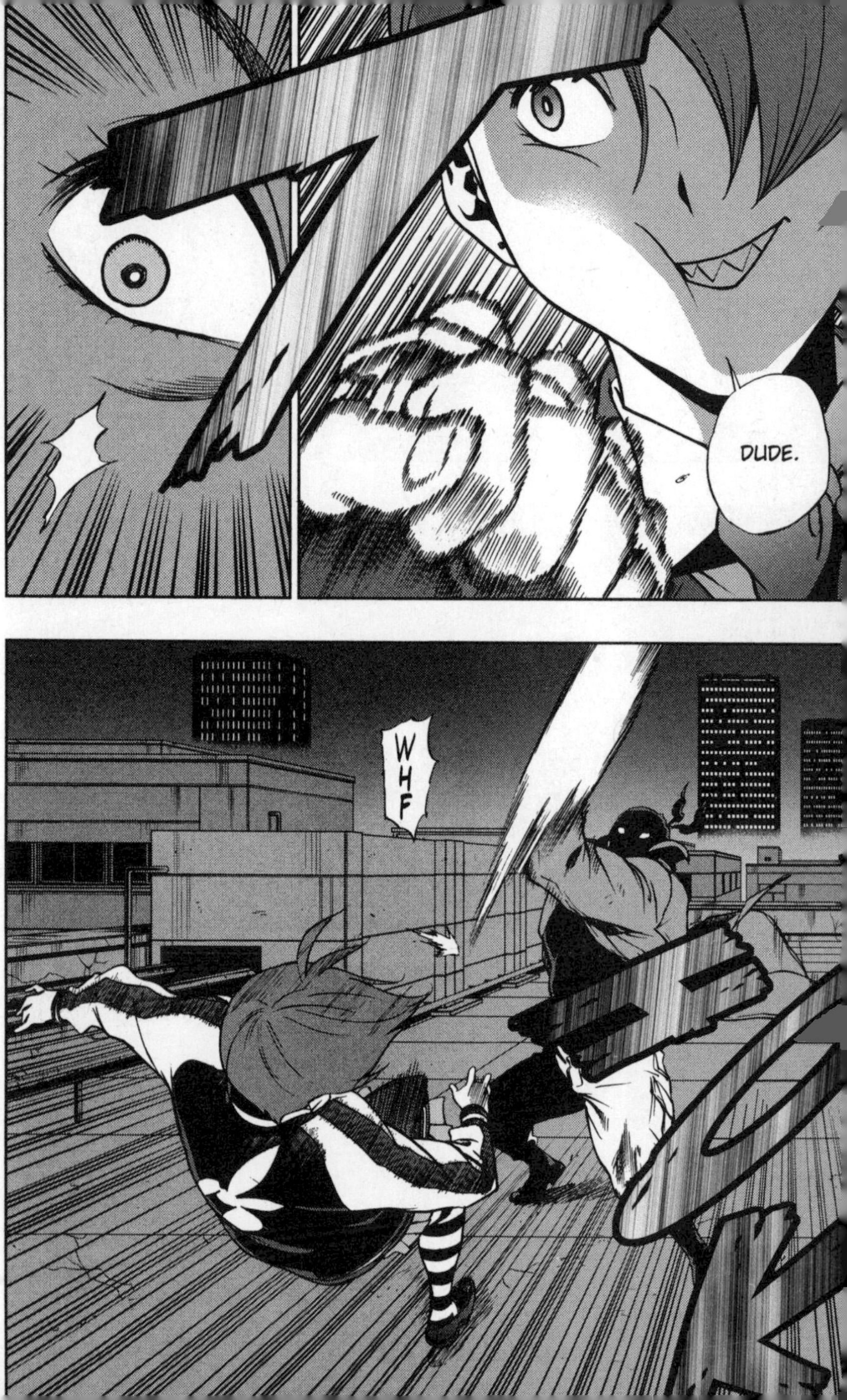
DUDE.
WHF

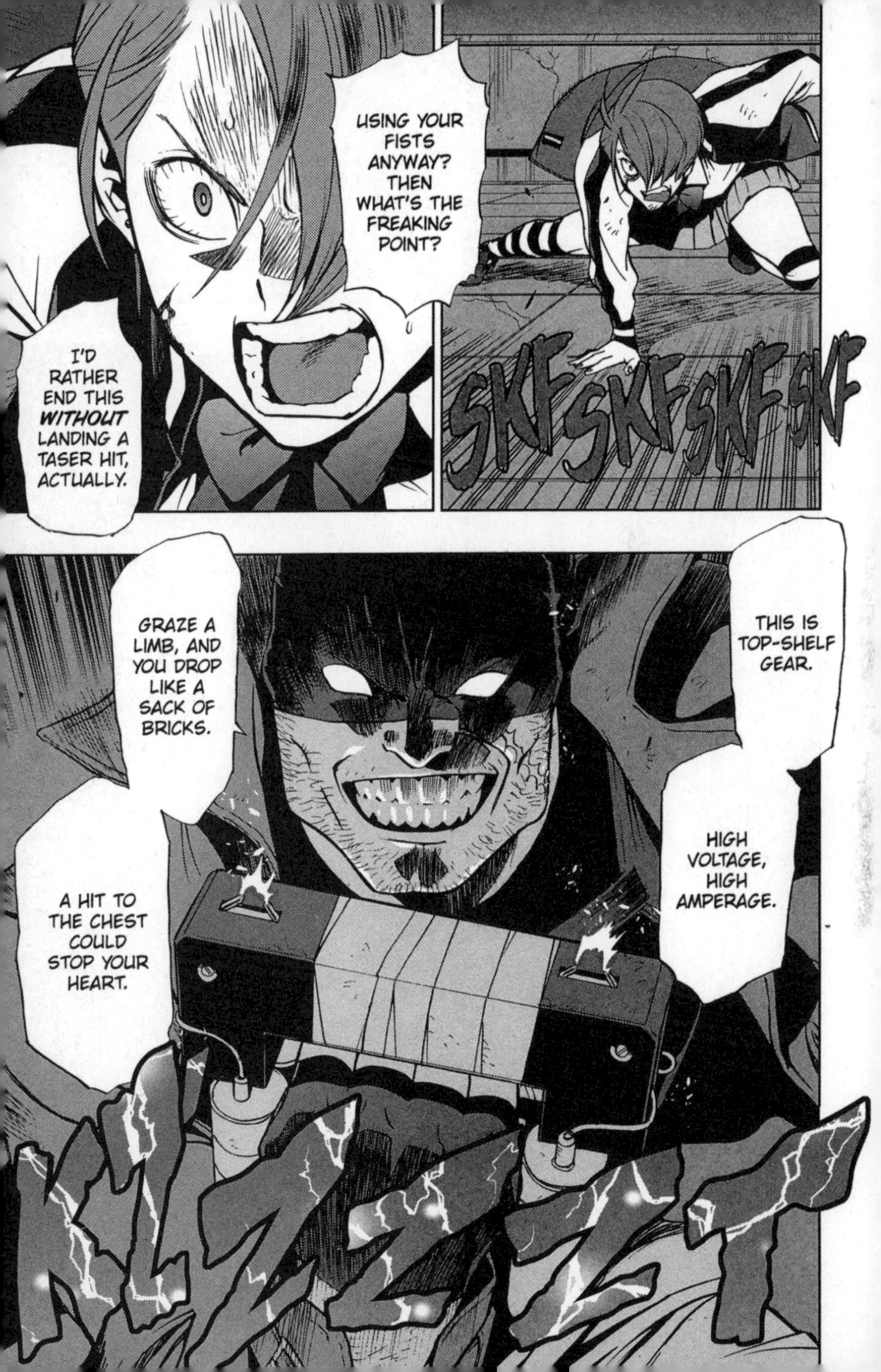
USING YOUR FISTS ANYWAY? THEN WHAT'S THE FREAKING POINT?
SKF SKF SKF SKF
I'D RATHER END THIS ***WITHOUT*** LANDING A TASER HIT, ACTUALLY.
THIS IS TOP-SHELF GEAR.
GRAZE A LIMB, AND YOU DROP LIKE A SACK OF BRICKS.
HIGH VOLTAGE, HIGH AMPERAGE.
A HIT TO THE CHEST COULD STOP YOUR HEART.

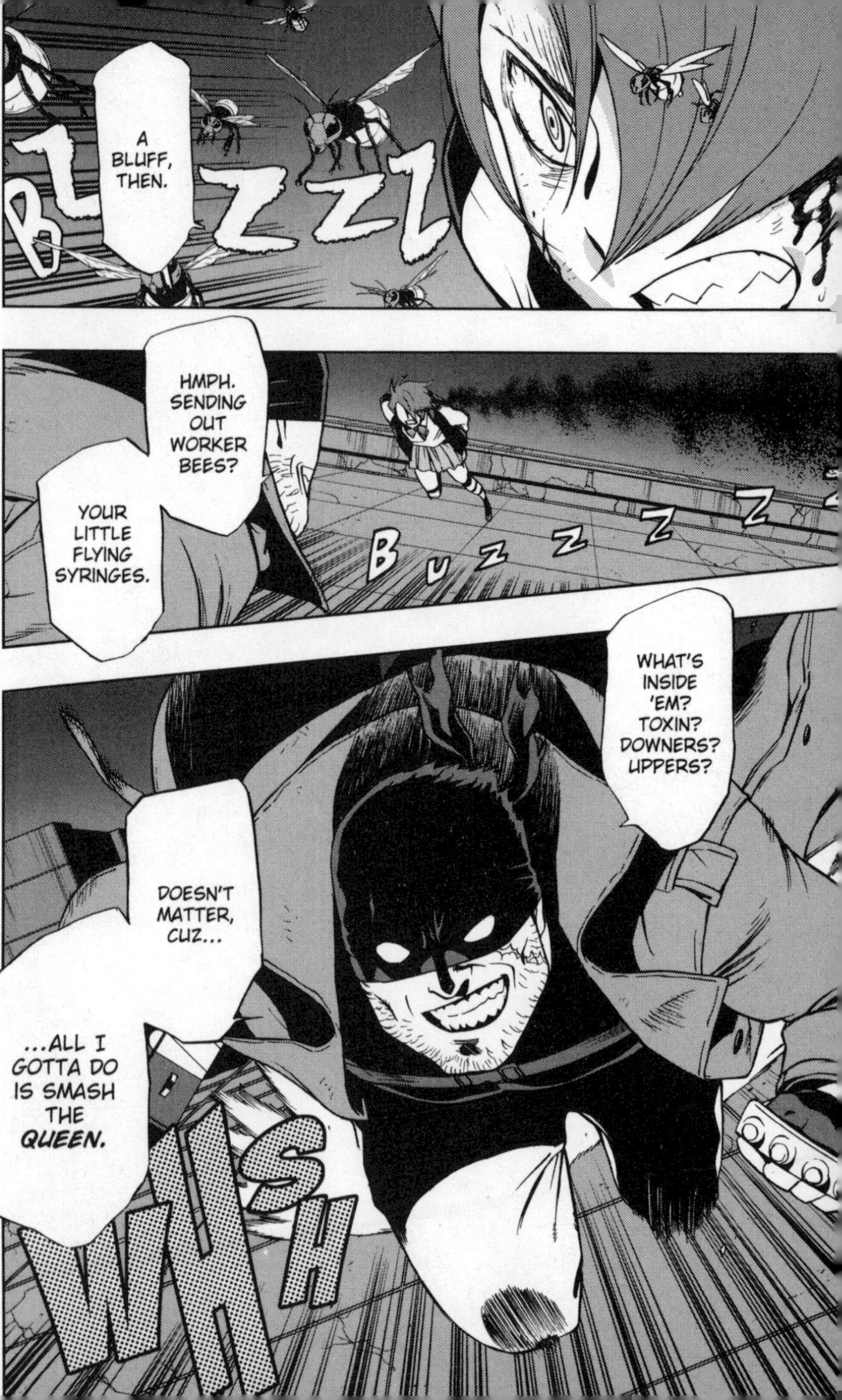
A BLUFF, THEN.
BZZZ
HMPH. SENDING OUT WORKER BEES?
YOUR LITTLE FLYING SYRINGES.
BUZZZZ
WHAT'S INSIDE 'EM? TOXIN? DOWNERS? UPPERS?
DOESN'T MATTER, CUZ...
...ALL I GOTTA DO IS SMASH THE *QUEEN.*
WHSH

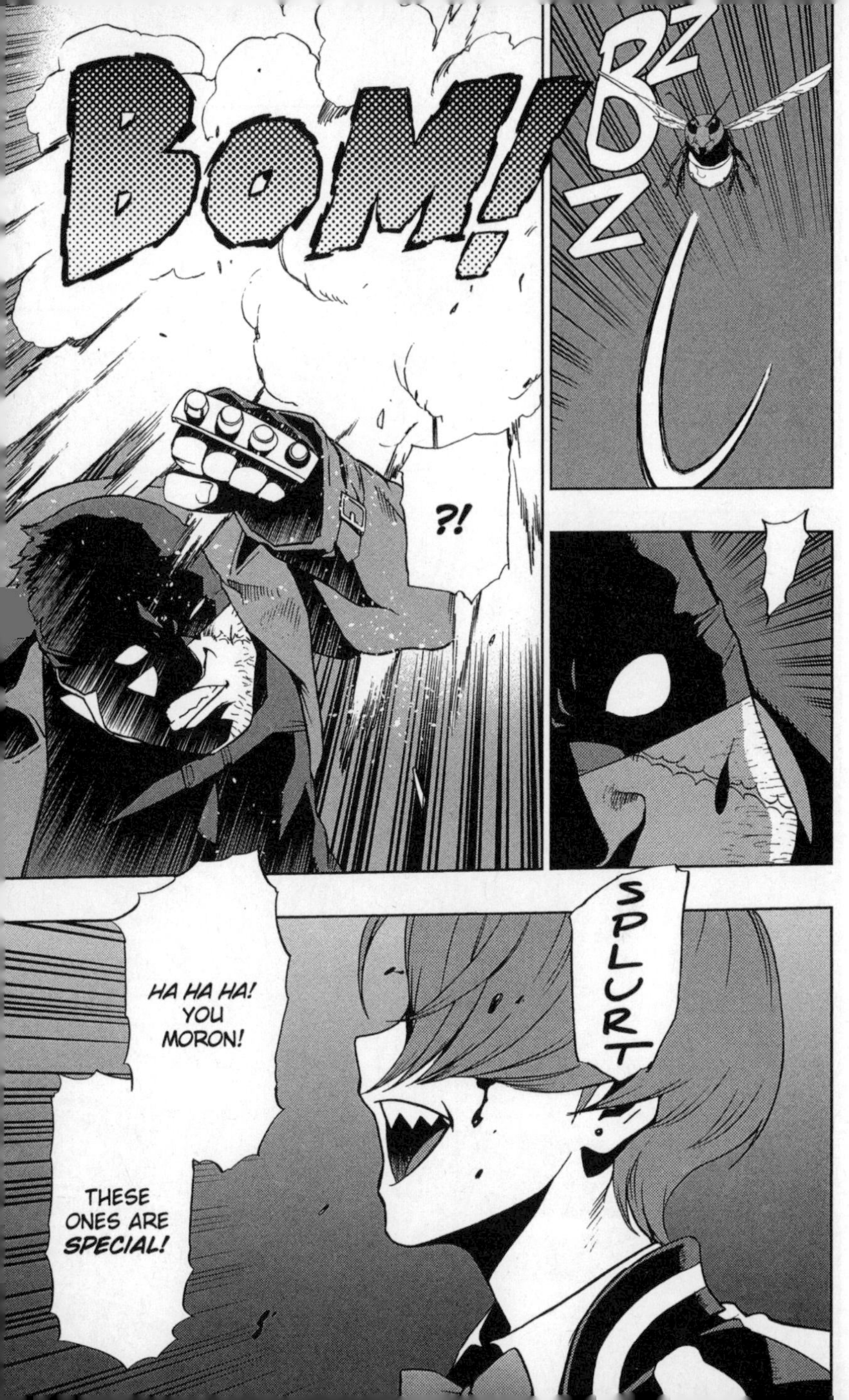
BZZ
BOM!
?!
SPLURT
HA HA HA! YOU MORON!
THESE ONES ARE SPECIAL!

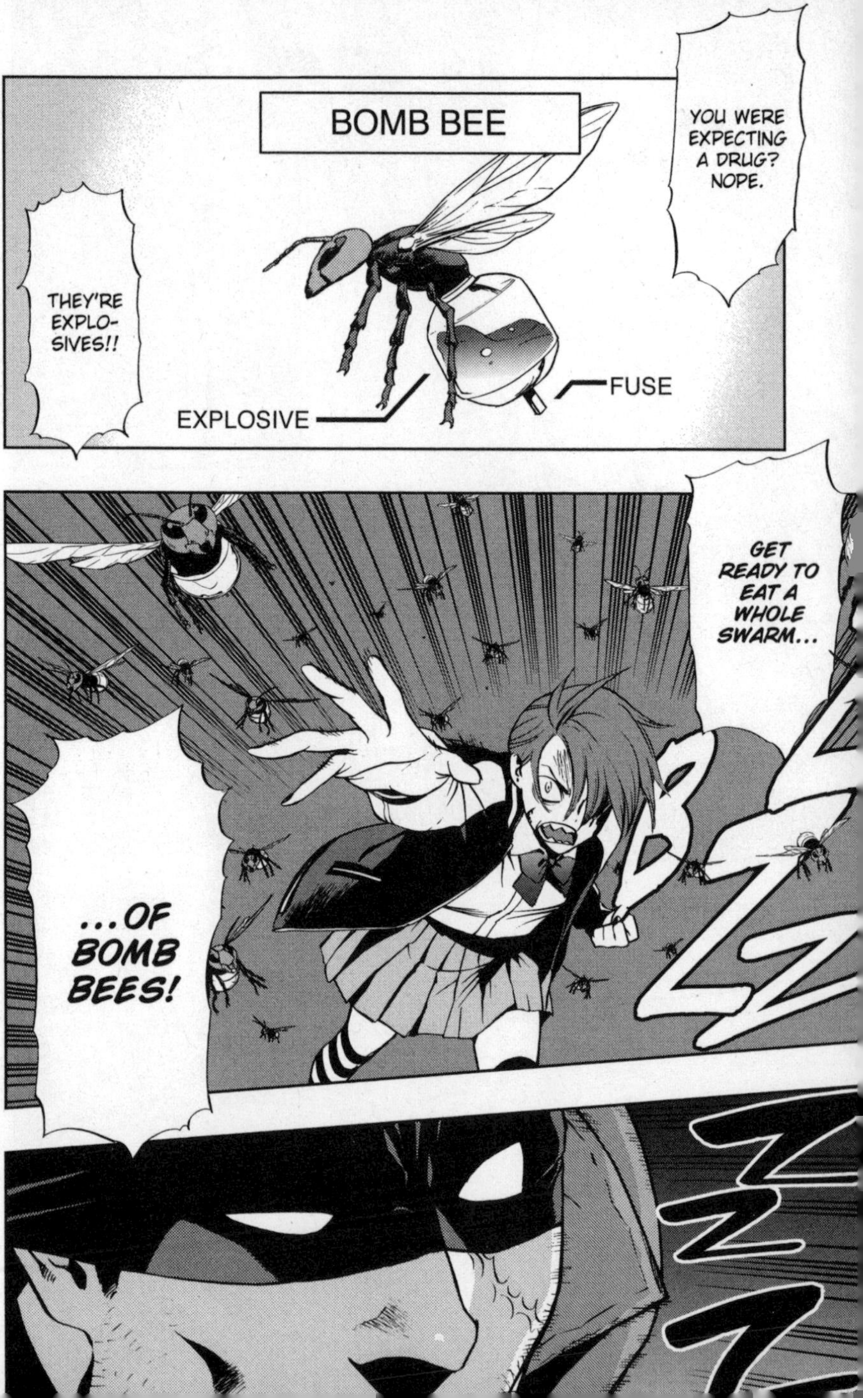
YOU WERE EXPECTING A DRUG? NOPE.
BOMB BEE
FUSE
THEY'RE EXPLO-SIVES!!
EXPLOSIVE
GET READY TO EAT A WHOLE SWARM...
...OF BOMB BEES!

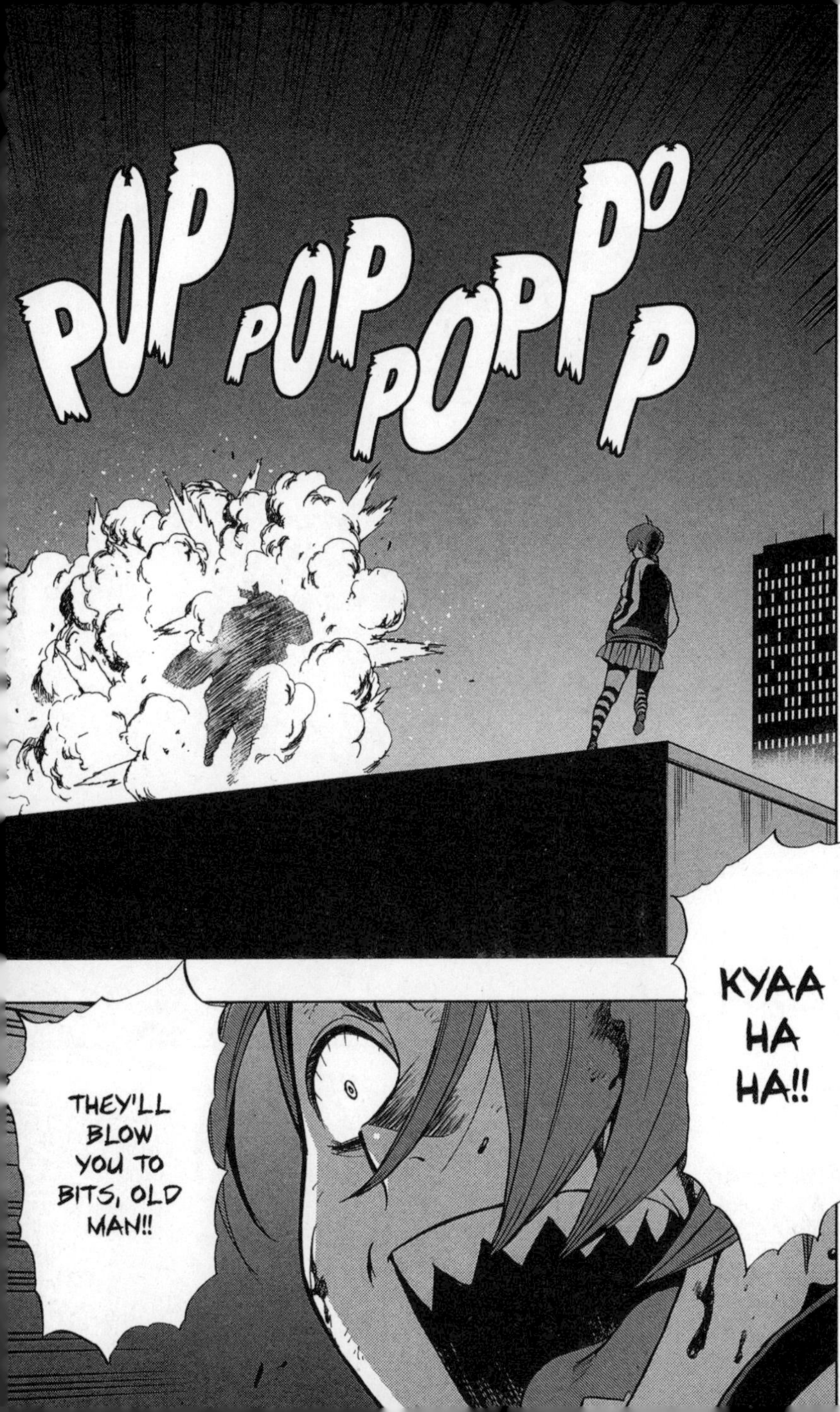
POP POP POP POP
KYAA HA HA!!
THEY'LL BLOW YOU TO BITS, OLD MAN!!

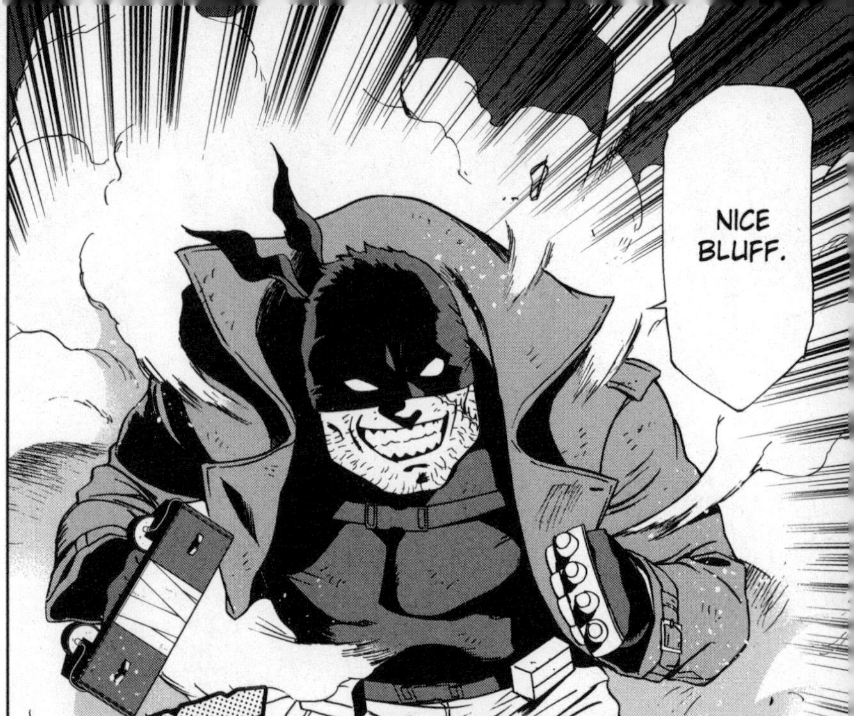
NICE BLUFF.
STOMP
?!
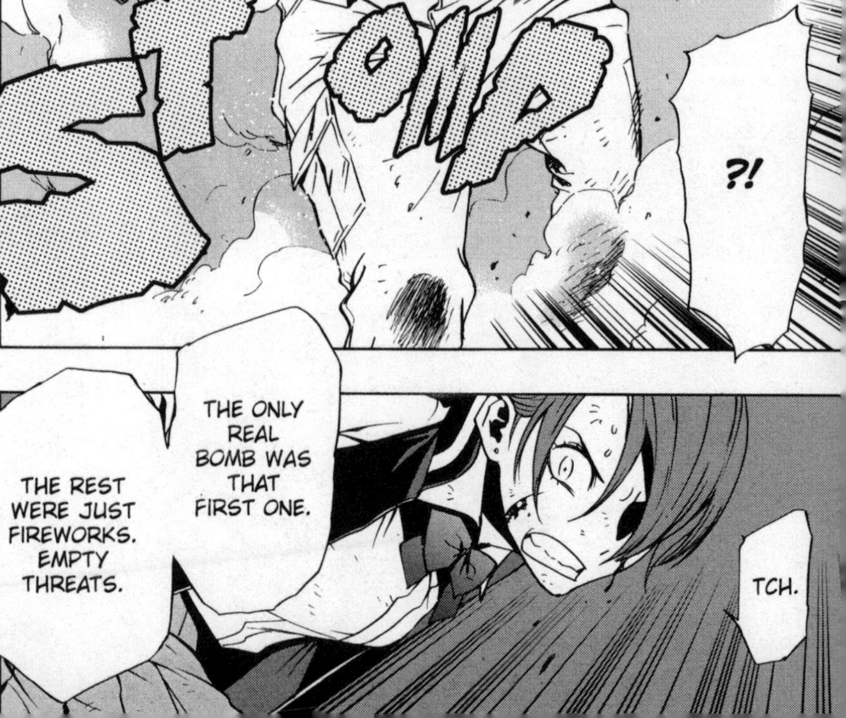
THE ONLY REAL BOMB WAS THAT FIRST ONE.
THE REST WERE JUST FIREWORKS. EMPTY THREATS.
TCH.

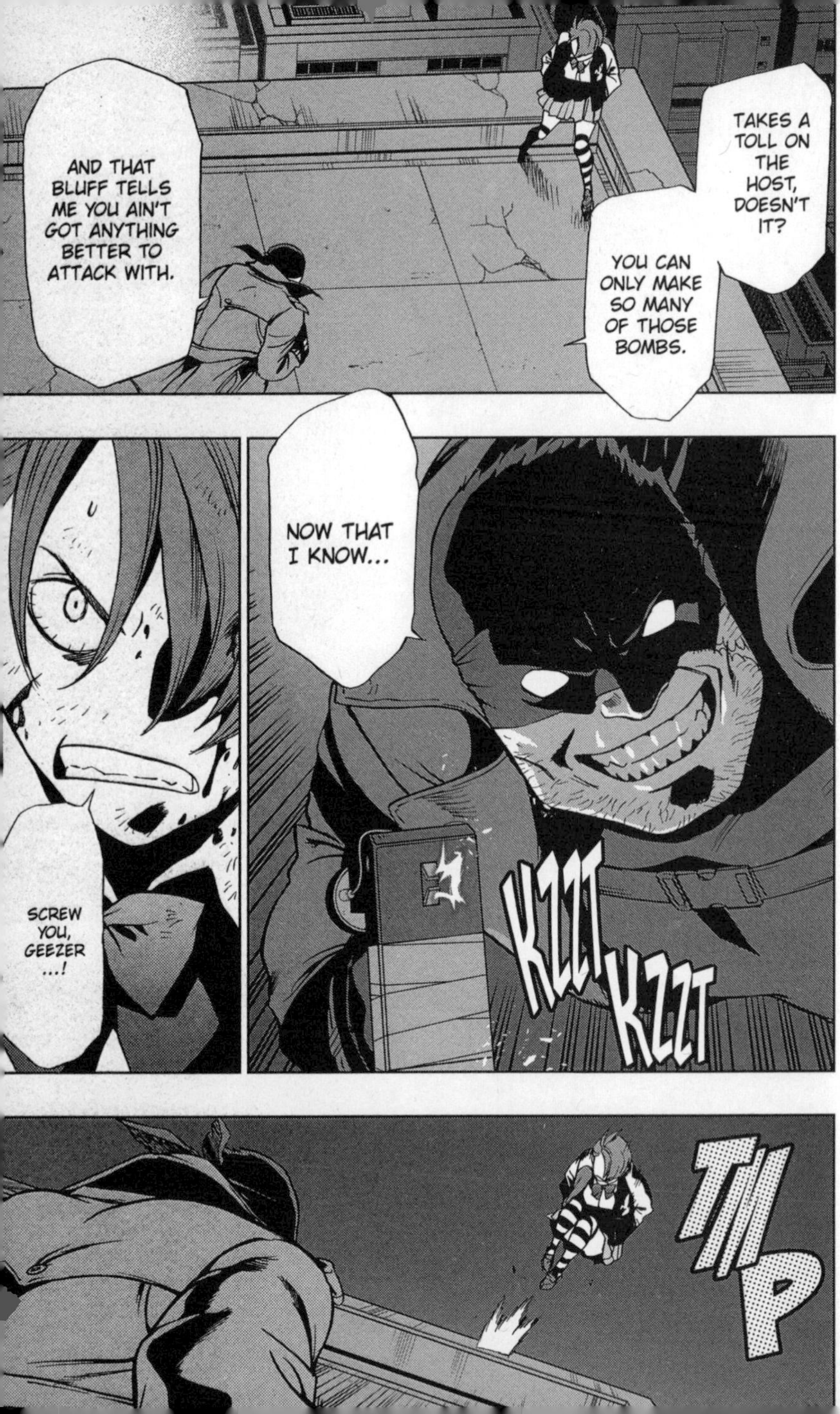
TAKES A TOLL ON THE HOST, DOESN'T IT?
YOU CAN ONLY MAKE SO MANY OF THOSE BOMBS.
AND THAT BLUFF TELLS ME YOU AIN'T GOT ANYTHING BETTER TO ATTACK WITH.
NOW THAT I KNOW...
KZZT KZZT
SCREW YOU, GEEZER ...!
THP

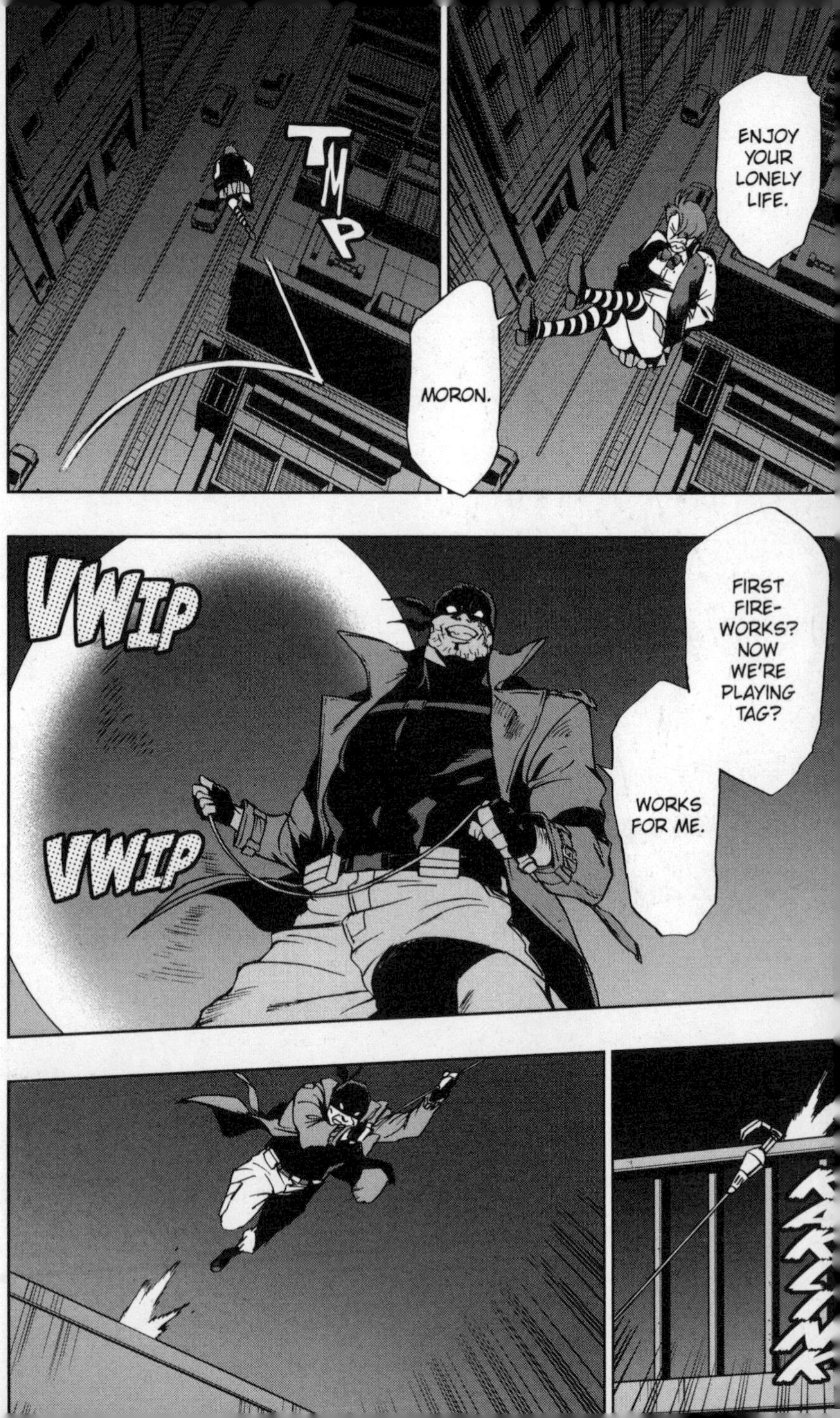
ENJOY YOUR LONELY LIFE.
MORON.
TMP
FIRST FIRE-WORKS? NOW WE'RE PLAYING TAG?
WORKS FOR ME.
VWIP
VWIP

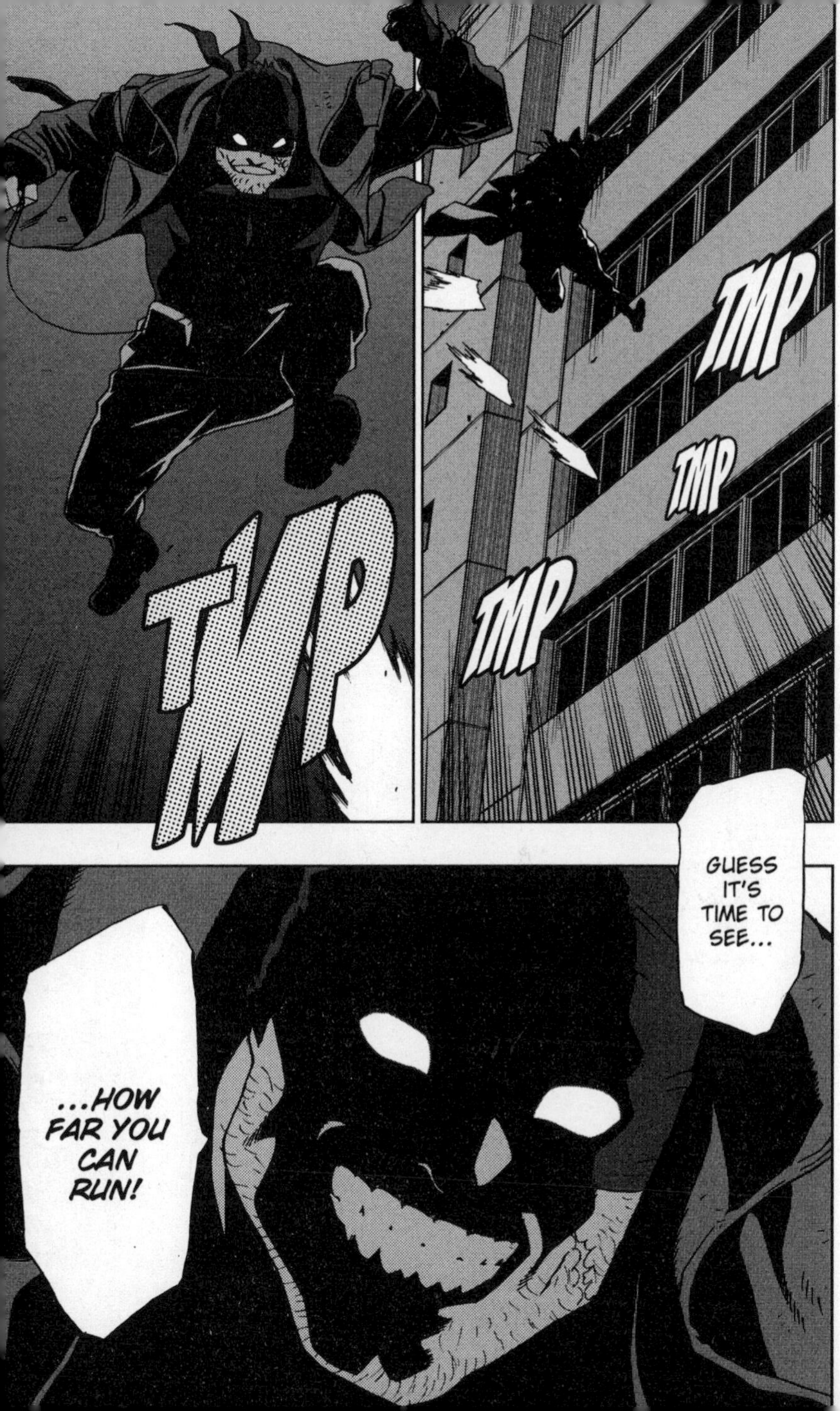
TMP
TMP
TMP
TMP
GUESS IT'S TIME TO SEE...
...HOW FAR YOU CAN RUN!

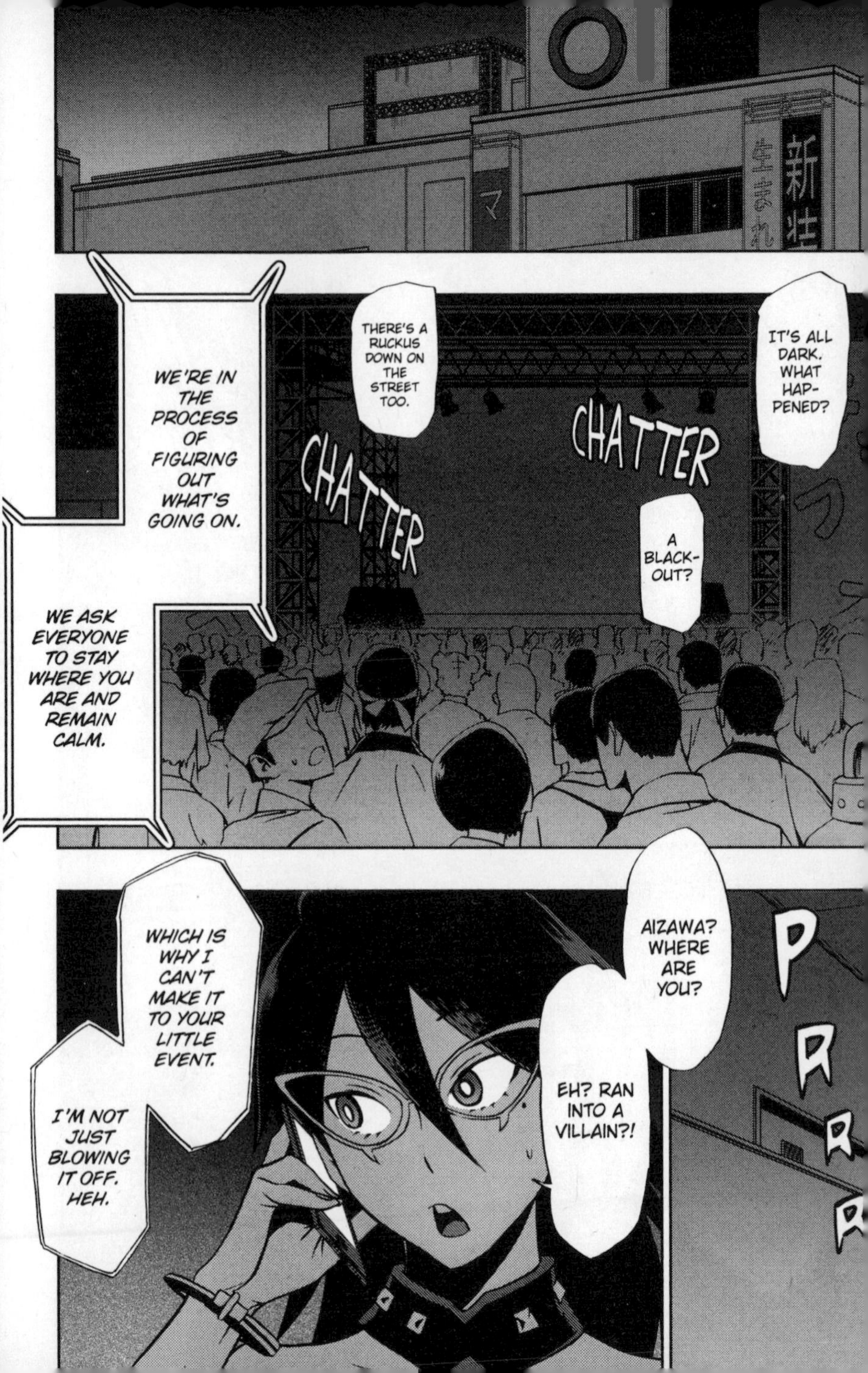
IT'S ALL DARK. WHAT HAP-PENED?
CHATTER
THERE'S A RUCKUS DOWN ON THE STREET TOO.
A BLACK-OUT?
CHATTER
WE'RE IN THE PROCESS OF FIGURING OUT WHAT'S GOING ON.
WE ASK EVERYONE TO STAY WHERE YOU ARE AND REMAIN CALM.
PRRR
AIZAWA? WHERE ARE YOU?
EH? RAN INTO A VILLAIN?!
WHICH IS WHY I CAN'T MAKE IT TO YOUR LITTLE EVENT.
I'M NOT JUST BLOWING IT OFF. HEH.

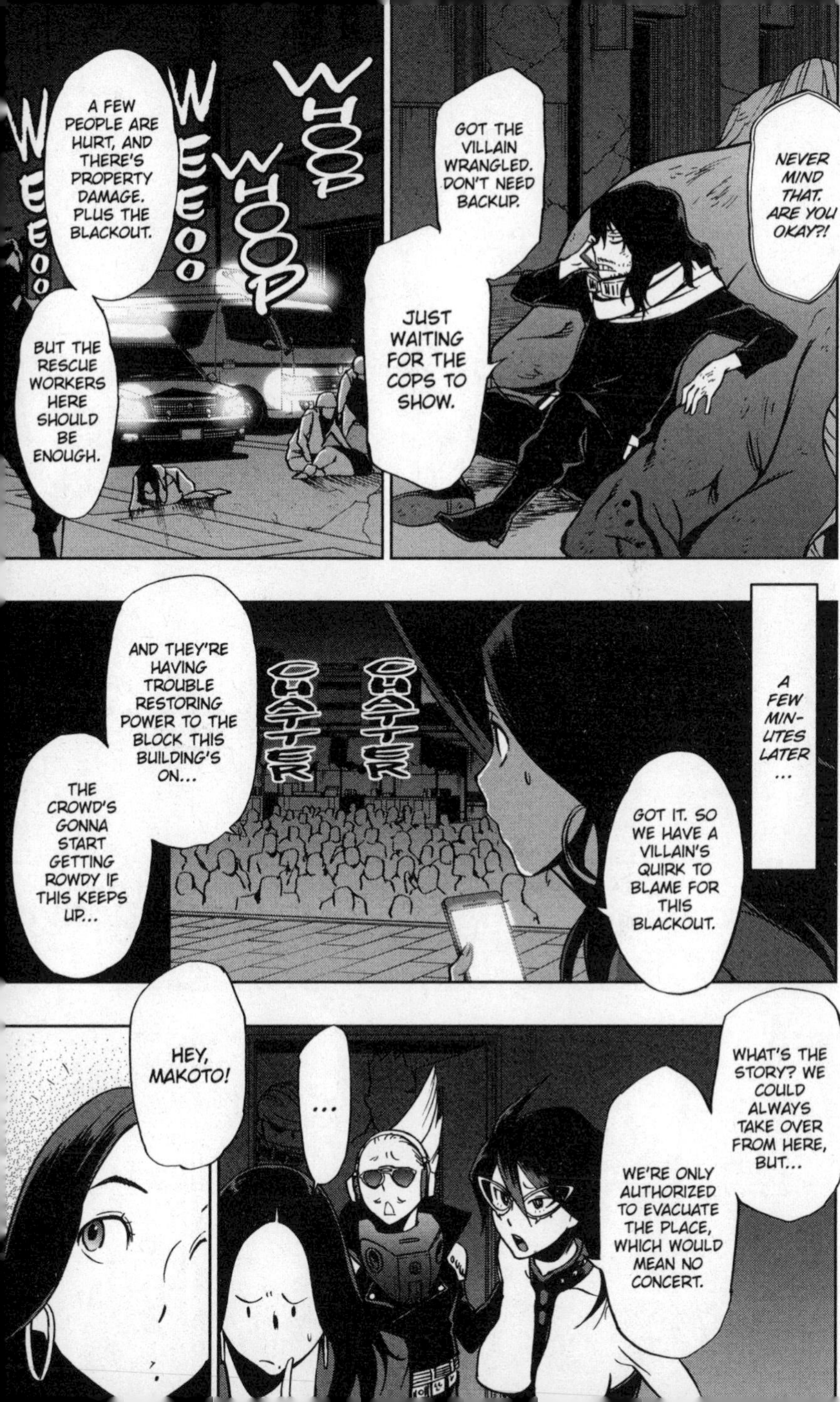
NEVER MIND THAT. ARE YOU OKAY?!
GOT THE VILLAIN WRANGLED. DON'T NEED BACKUP.
JUST WAITING FOR THE COPS TO SHOW.
WHOOP WHOOP
WEEOO WEEOO
A FEW PEOPLE ARE HURT, AND THERE'S PROPERTY DAMAGE. PLUS THE BLACKOUT.
BUT THE RESCUE WORKERS HERE SHOULD BE ENOUGH.
A FEW MIN-UTES LATER...
GOT IT. SO WE HAVE A VILLAIN'S QUIRK TO BLAME FOR THIS BLACKOUT.
CHATTER CHATTER
AND THEY'RE HAVING TROUBLE RESTORING POWER TO THE BLOCK THIS BUILDING'S ON...
THE CROWD'S GONNA START GETTING ROWDY IF THIS KEEPS UP...
WHAT'S THE STORY? WE COULD ALWAYS TAKE OVER FROM HERE, BUT...
WE'RE ONLY AUTHORIZED TO EVACUATE THE PLACE, WHICH WOULD MEAN NO CONCERT.
...
HEY, MAKOTO!

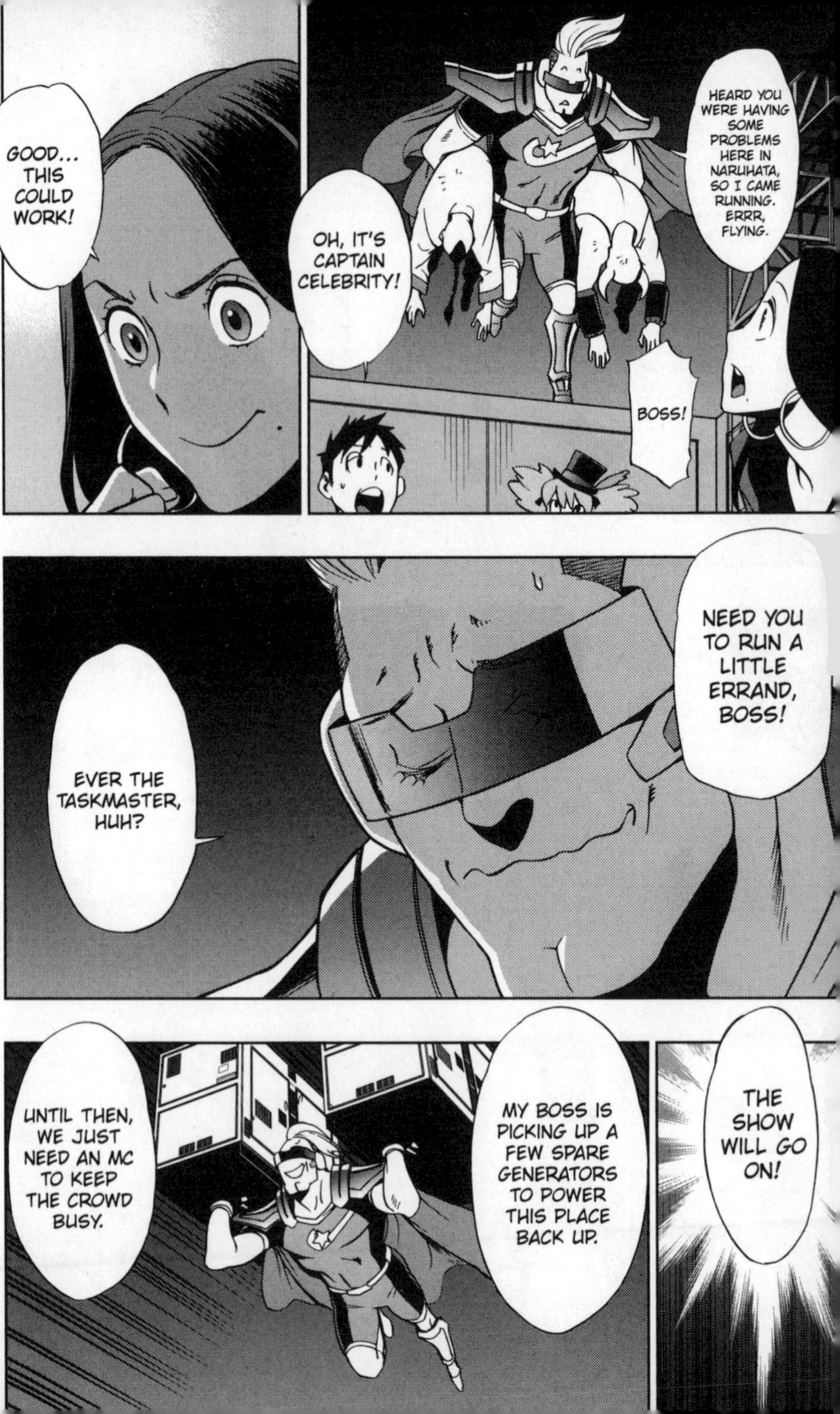
HEARD YOU WERE HAVING SOME PROBLEMS HERE IN NARUHATA, SO I CAME RUNNING. ERRR, FLYING.
OH, IT'S CAPTAIN CELEBRITY!
BOSS!
GOOD... THIS COULD WORK!
NEED YOU TO RUN A LITTLE ERRAND, BOSS!
EVER THE TASKMASTER, HUH?
THE SHOW WILL GO ON!
MY BOSS IS PICKING UP A FEW SPARE GENERATORS TO POWER THIS PLACE BACK UP.
UNTIL THEN, WE JUST NEED AN MC TO KEEP THE CROWD BUSY.

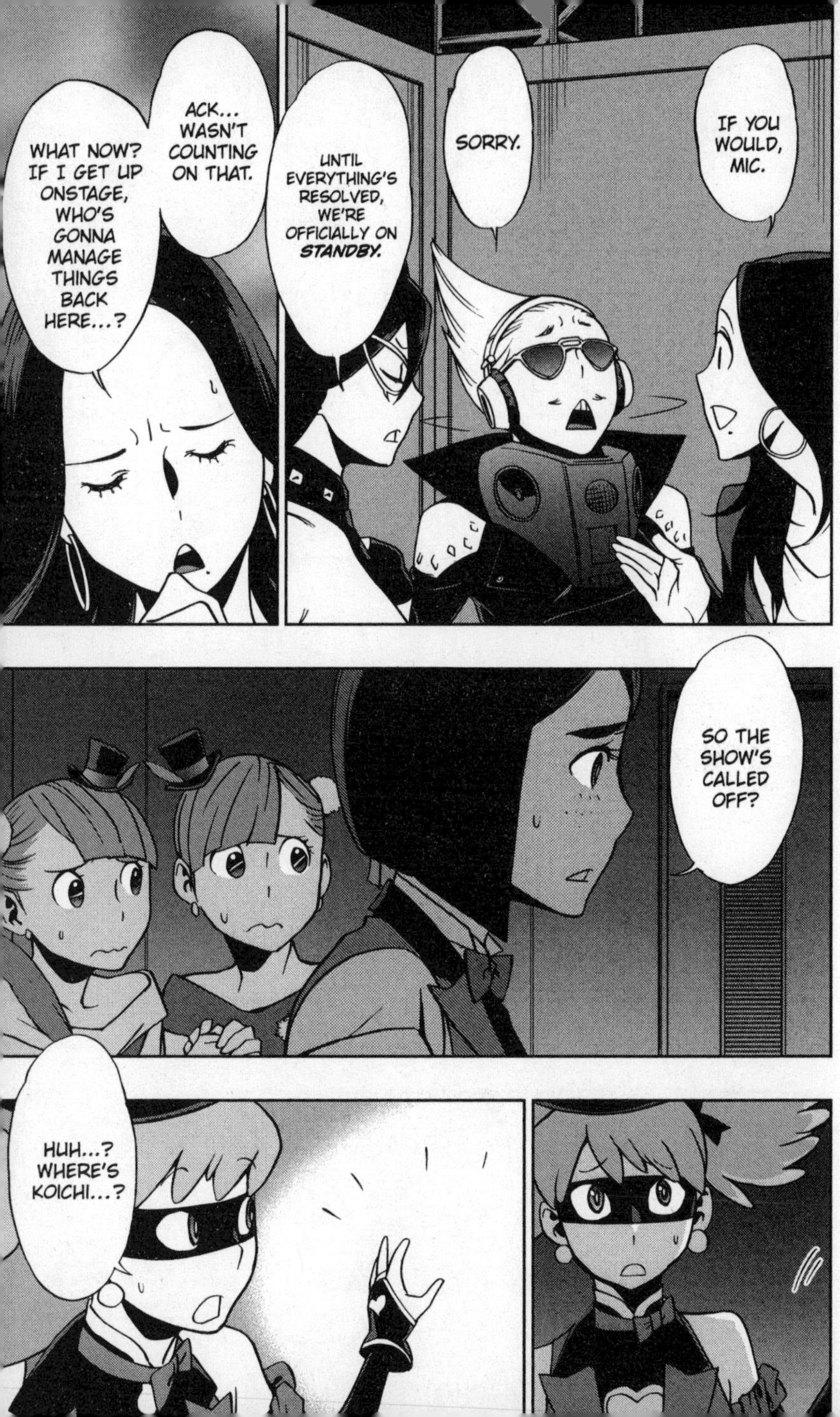
IF YOU WOULD, MIC.
SORRY.
UNTIL EVERYTHING'S RESOLVED, WE'RE OFFICIALLY ON *STANDBY.*
ACK... WASN'T COUNTING ON THAT.
WHAT NOW? IF I GET UP ONSTAGE, WHO'S GONNA MANAGE THINGS BACK HERE...?
SO THE SHOW'S CALLED OFF?
HUH...? WHERE'S KOICHI...?

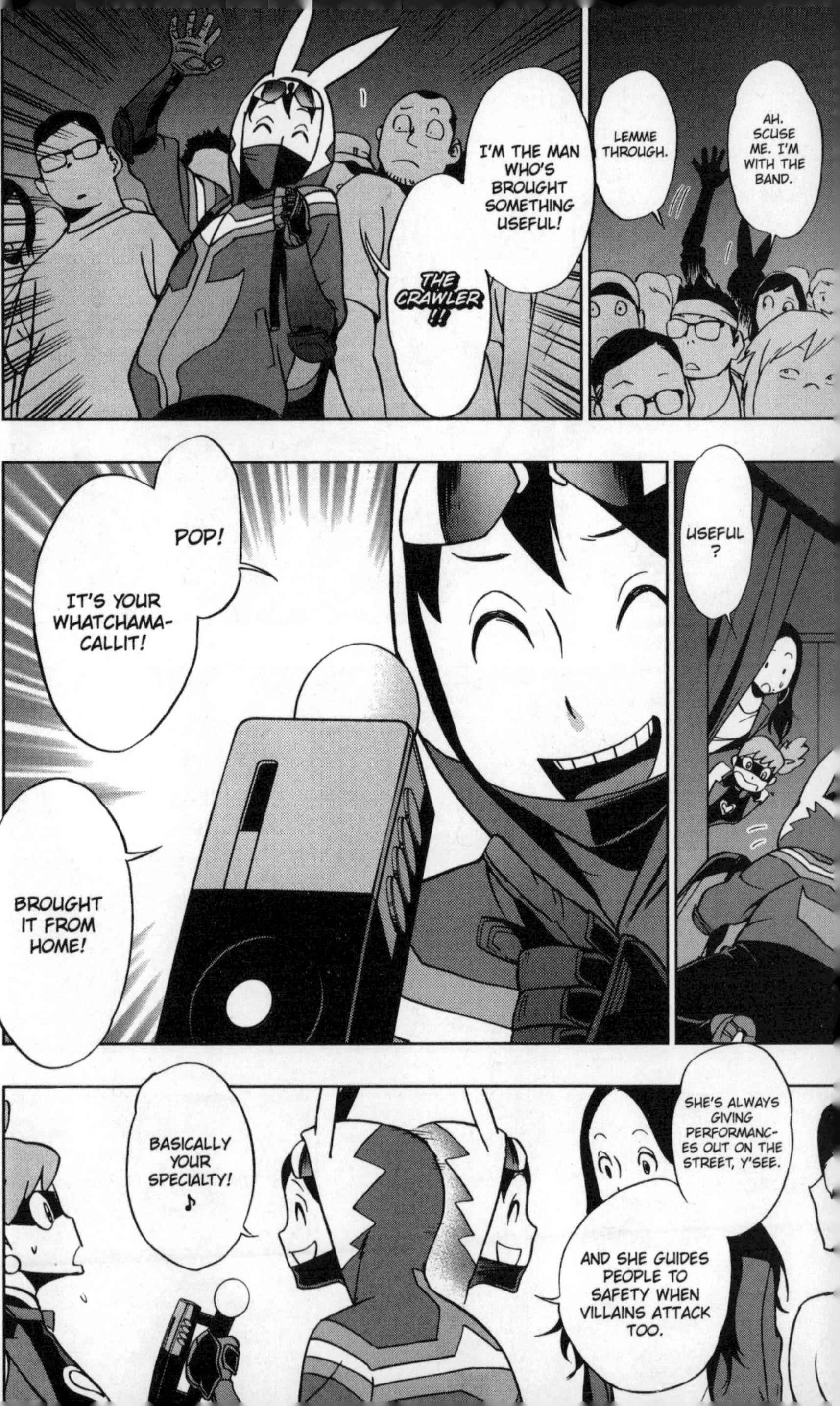
AH. SCUSE ME. I'M WITH THE BAND.
LEMME THROUGH.
I'M THE MAN WHO'S BROUGHT SOMETHING USEFUL!
THE CRAWLER!!
USEFUL?
POP!
IT'S YOUR WHATCHAMA-CALLIT!
BROUGHT IT FROM HOME!
SHE'S ALWAYS GIVING PERFORMANC-ES OUT ON THE STREET, Y'SEE.
AND SHE GUIDES PEOPLE TO SAFETY WHEN VILLAINS ATTACK TOO.
BASICALLY YOUR SPECIALTY! ♪

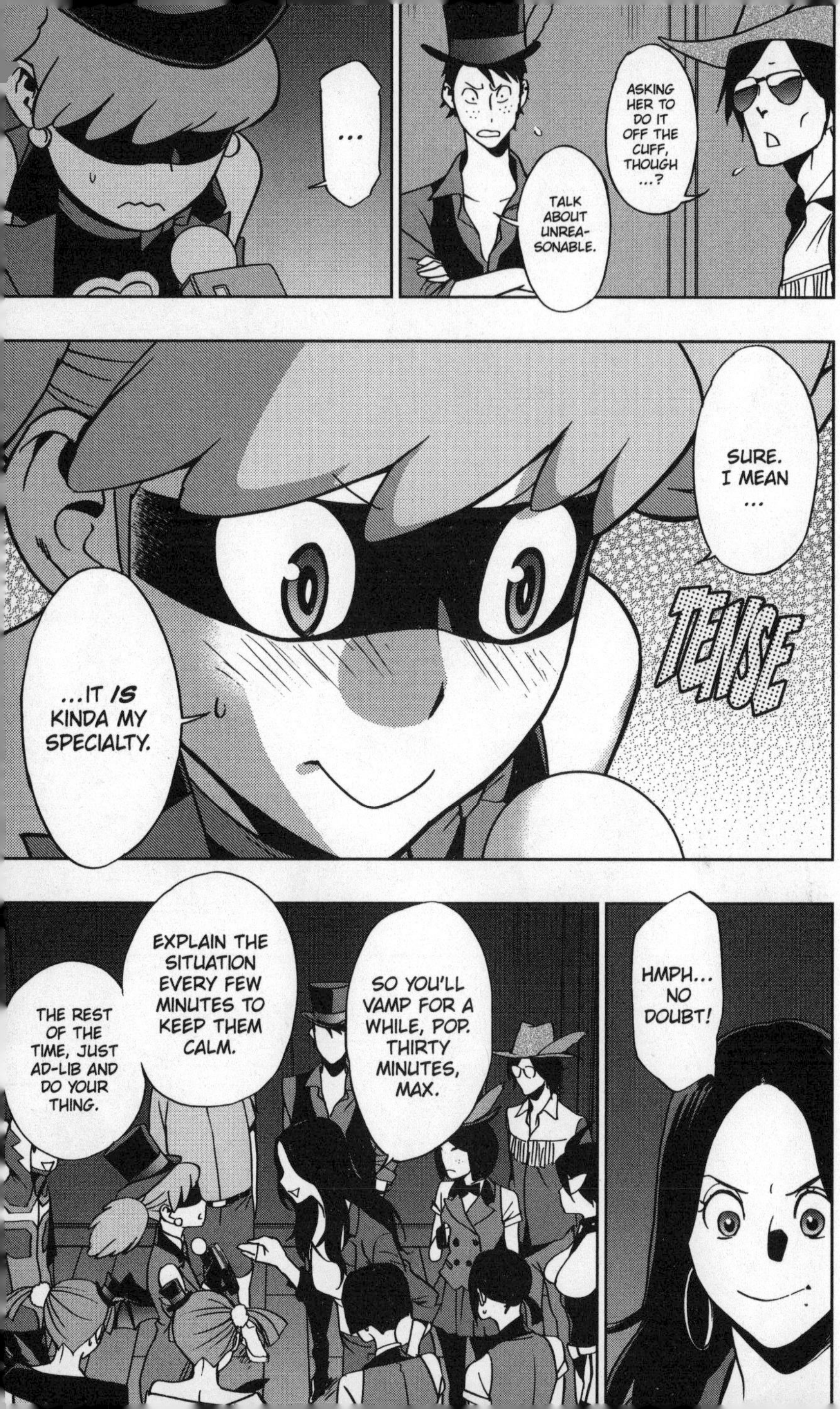
ASKING HER TO DO IT OFF THE CUFF, THOUGH ...?
TALK ABOUT UNREA-SONABLE.
...
SURE. I MEAN ...
TENSE
...IT *IS* KINDA MY SPECIALTY.
HMPH... NO DOUBT!
SO YOU'LL VAMP FOR A WHILE, POP. THIRTY MINUTES, MAX.
EXPLAIN THE SITUATION EVERY FEW MINUTES TO KEEP THEM CALM.
THE REST OF THE TIME, JUST AD-LIB AND DO YOUR THING.

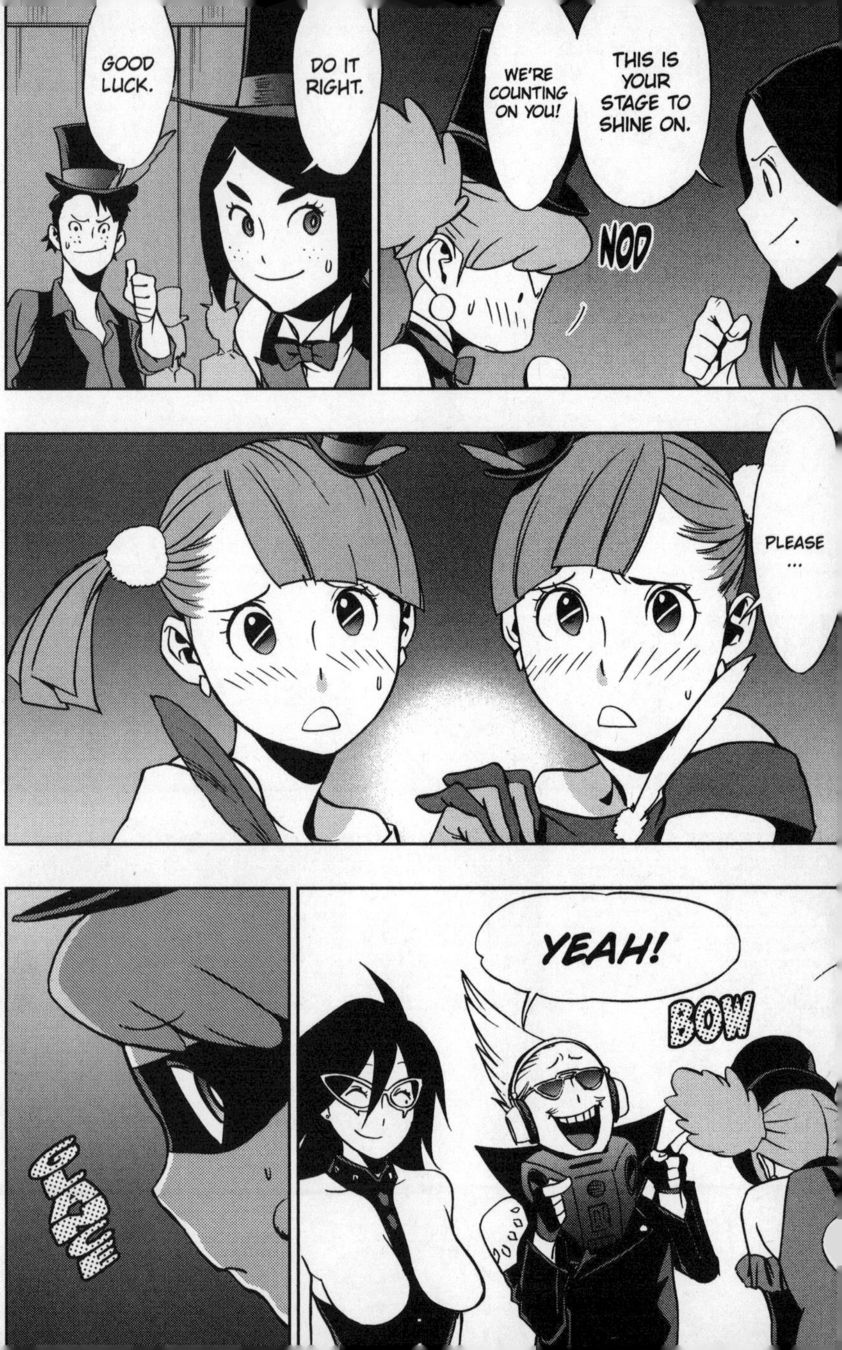
THIS IS YOUR STAGE TO SHINE ON.
WE'RE COUNTING ON YOU!
NOD
DO IT RIGHT.
GOOD LUCK.
PLEASE ...
YEAH!
BOW
GLARE

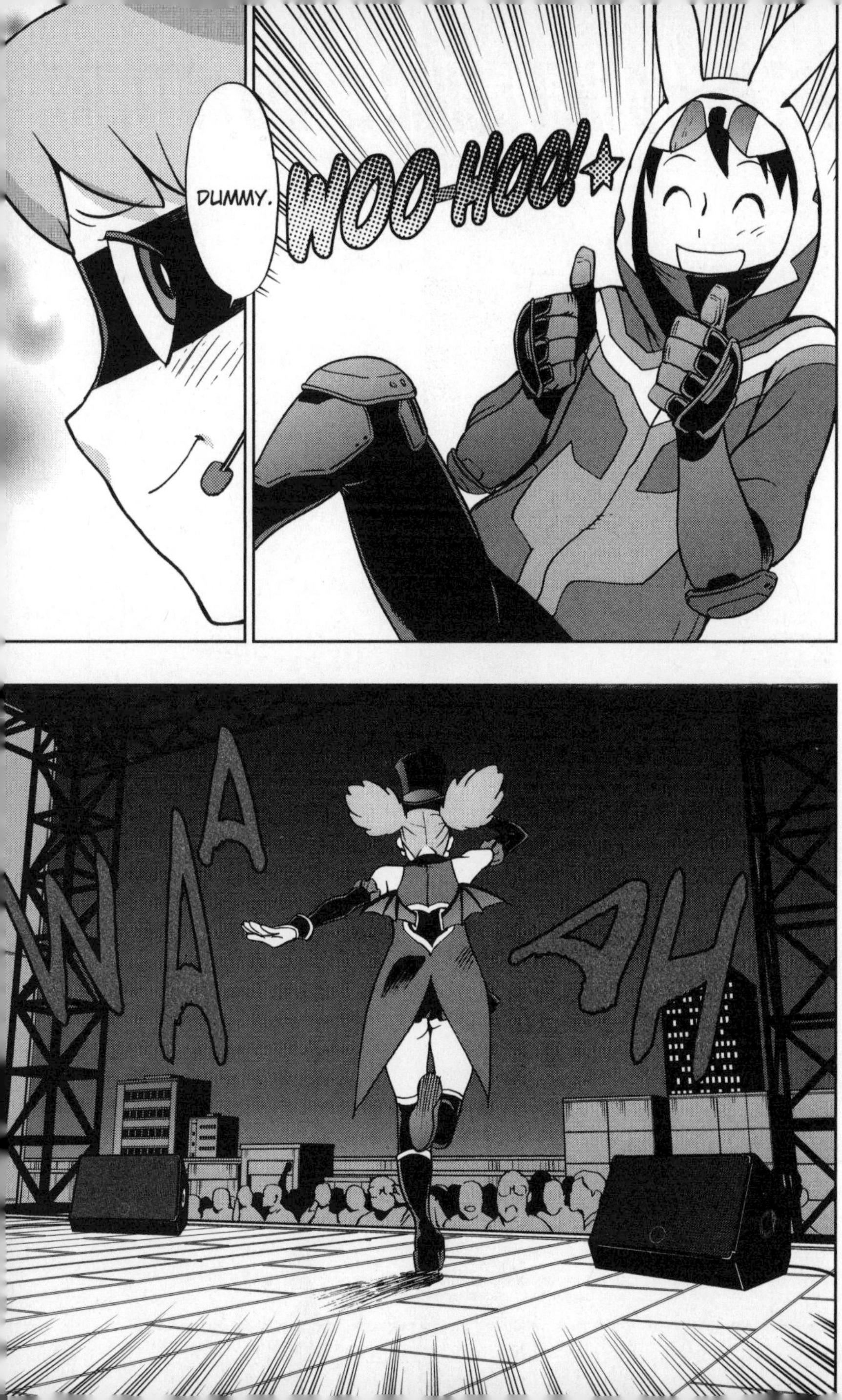
WOO-HOO!☆
DUMMY.
WAAAH

EAST HIGH DANCE SQUAD & MAD HATTERS

THE ROUGH DESIGN

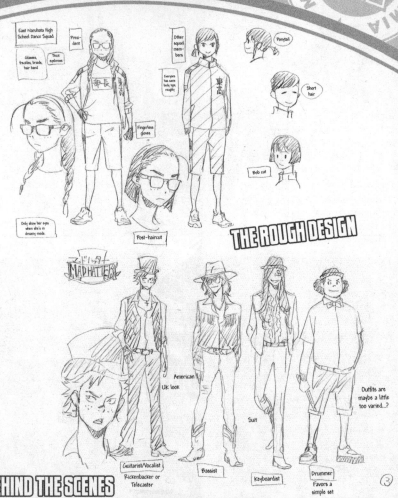

East Naruhata High School Dance Squad
President
Glasses, freckles, braids, hair band
Thick eyebrows
Only show her eyes when she's in dreamy mode.
Post-haircut
Fingerless gloves
Other squad members
Everyone has same body type, roughly
Ponytail
Short hair
Bob cut
MADHATTER
UK look
American
Suit
Outfits are maybe a little too varied...?
Guitarist/Vocalist
Rickenbacker or Telecaster
Bassist
Keyboardist
Drummer
Favors a simple set
③

BEHIND THE SCENES

The ensemble members who all burst onto the scene in chapter 21. There are a lot of characters here (four in each group), but only the squad president and the guitarist actually get fleshed out, with the others just sort of being there. Actually, though, I put a lot of thought into the band members.

—Furuhashi

I remember it being tough to come up with these designs all at once.

Dance squads are kind of totalitarian, right? So none of them stand out too much. Rock bands emphasize idiosyncrasy, though? Those were my thoughts as I struggled with these designs. I ended up going with my first impressions.

Only the dance squad president had those specific design points, which gives me an idea about Furuhashi-san's preferences. (LOL)

—Betten

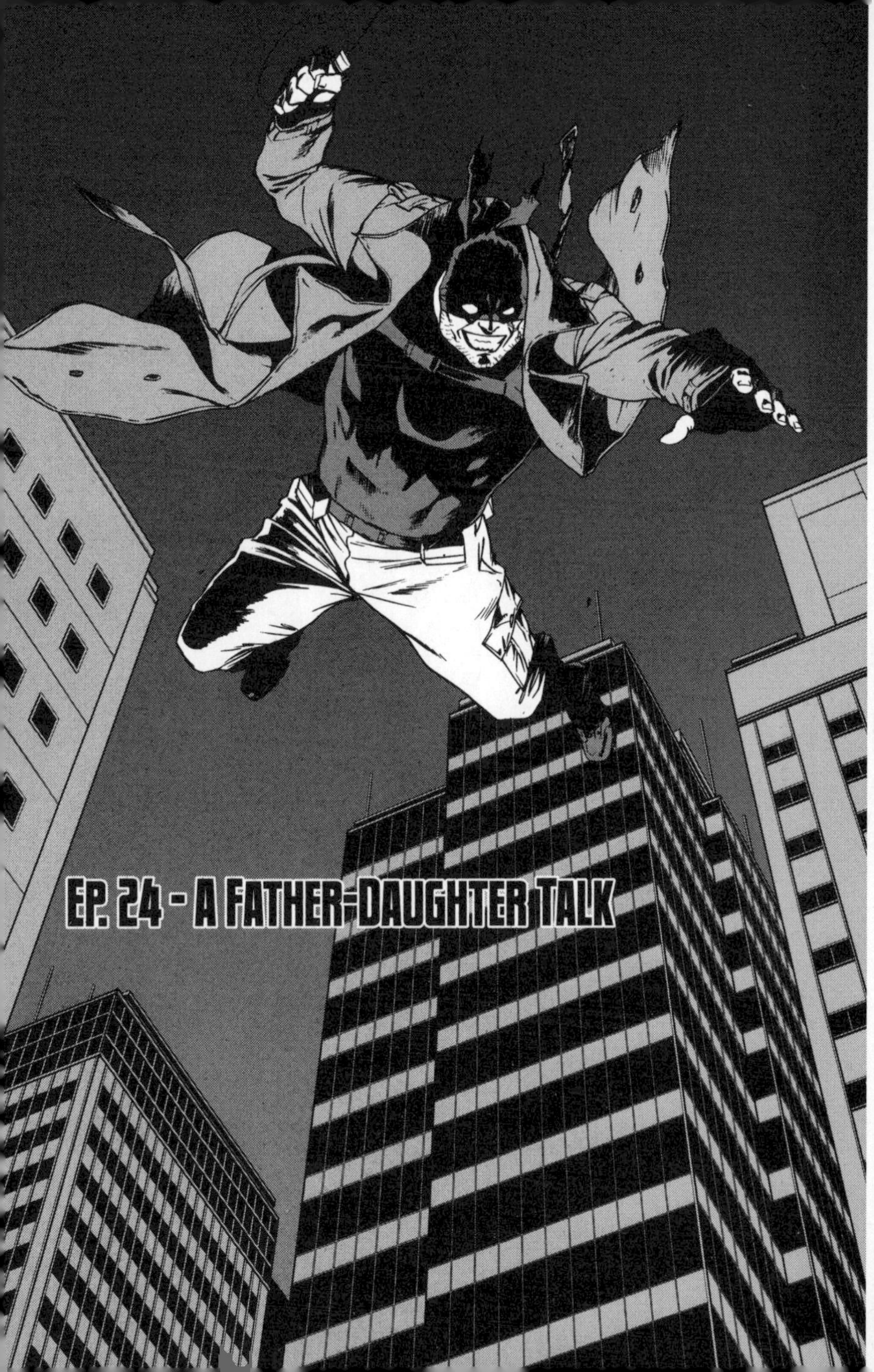
EP. 24 - A FATHER-DAUGHTER TALK

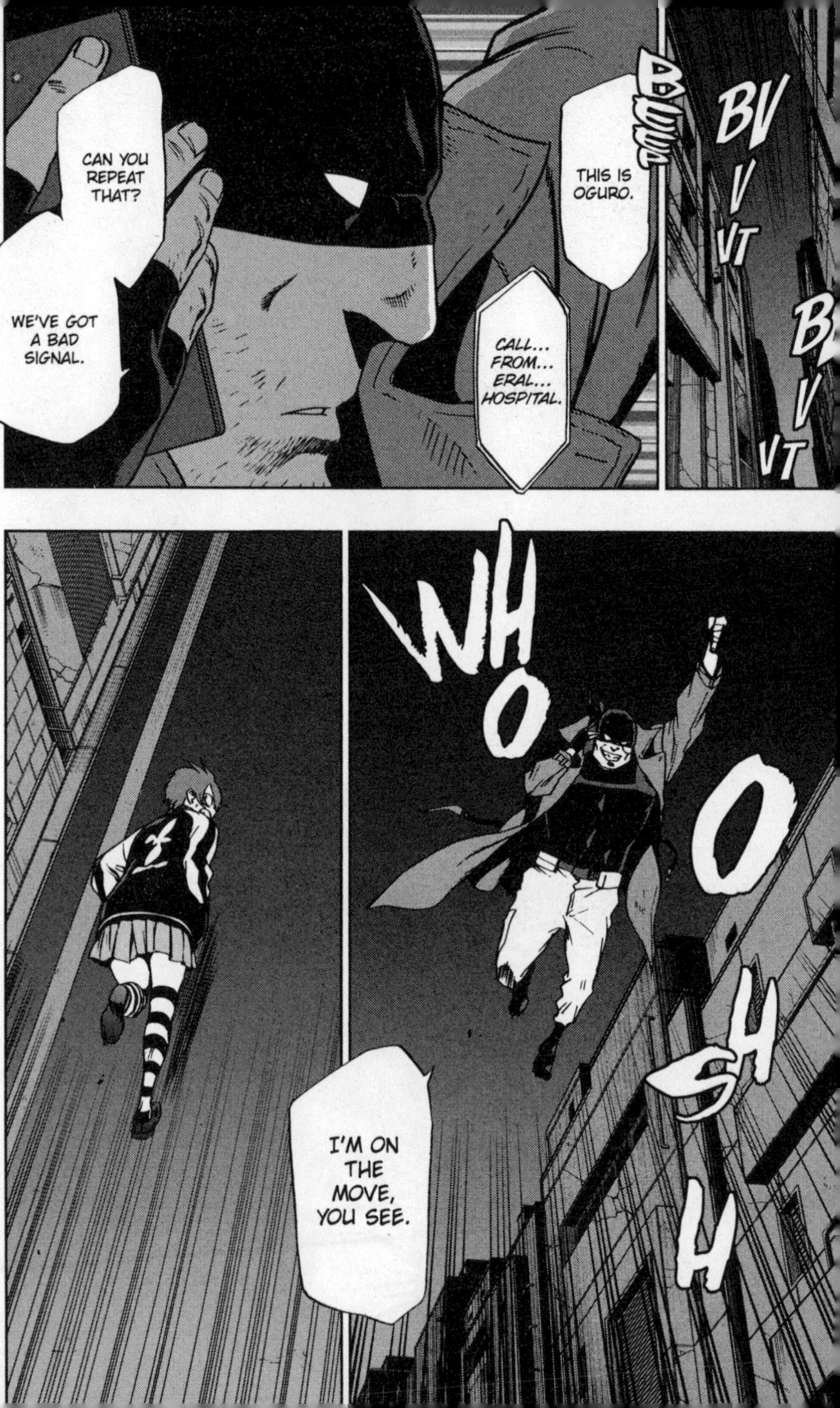
BVVVT
BVVVT
THIS IS OGURO.
CALL... FROM... ERAL... HOSPITAL.
CAN YOU REPEAT THAT?
WE'VE GOT A BAD SIGNAL.
WHOOOSHH
I'M ON THE MOVE, YOU SEE.

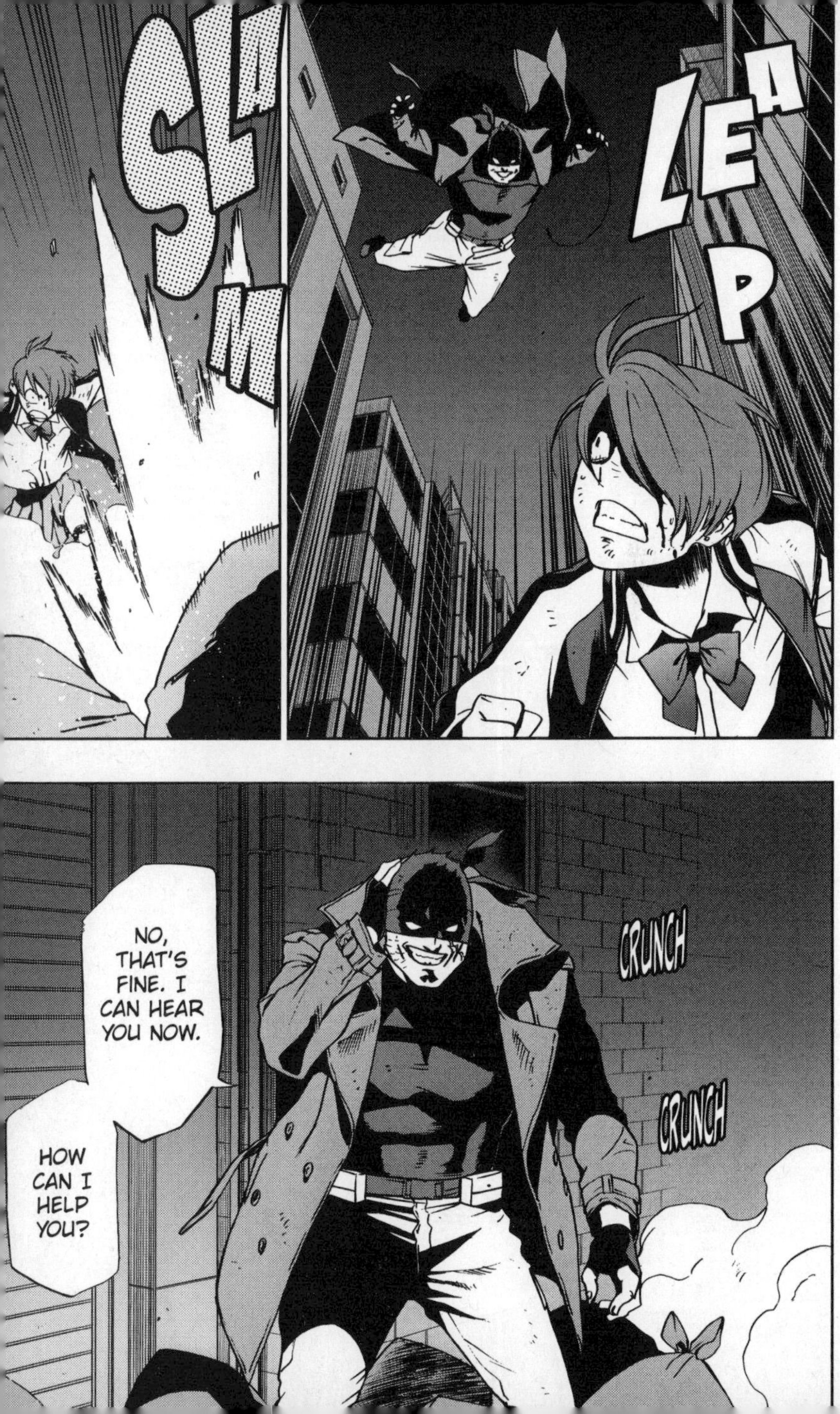
LEAP
SLAM
CRUNCH
NO, THAT'S FINE. I CAN HEAR YOU NOW.
CRUNCH
HOW CAN I HELP YOU?

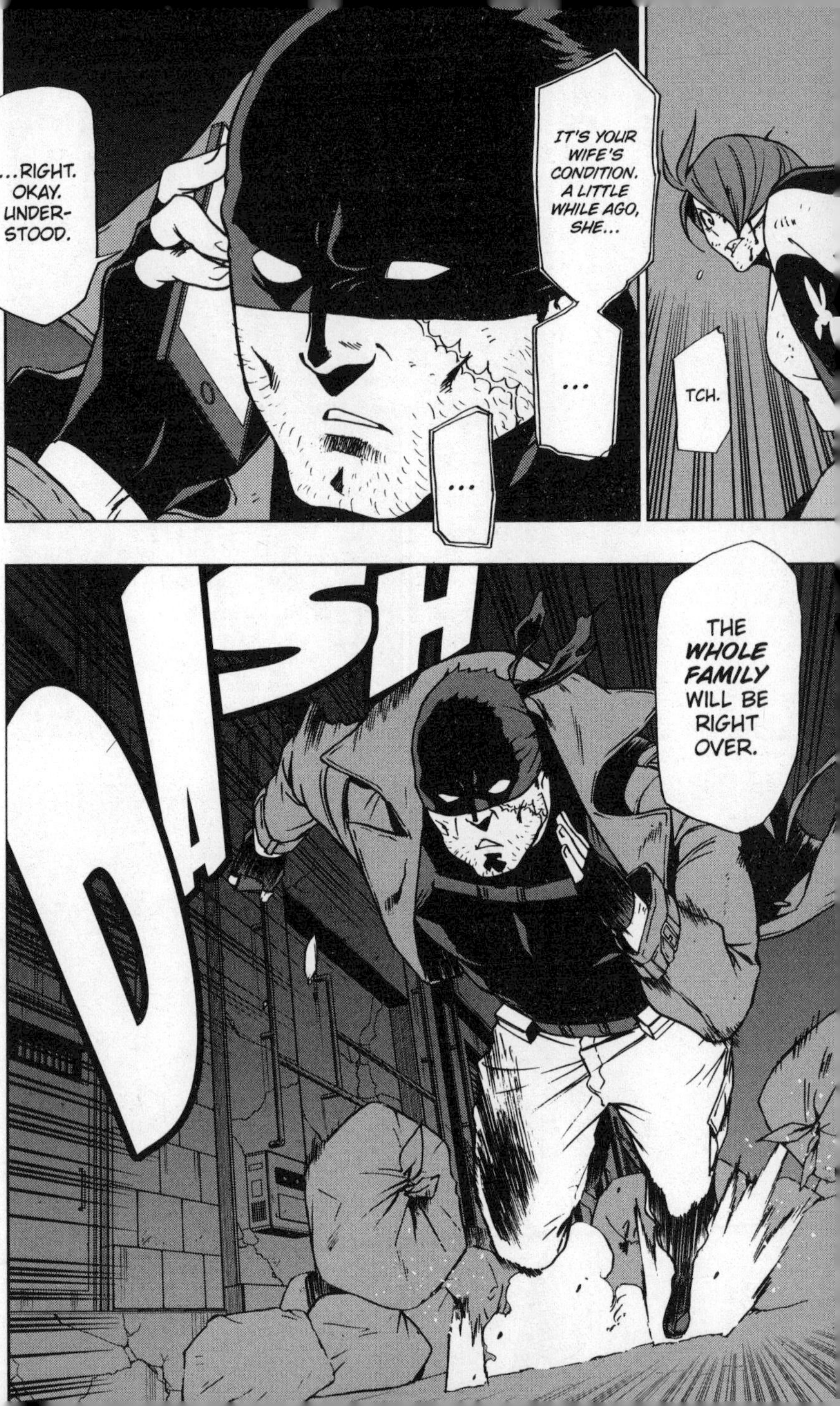
TCH.
IT'S YOUR WIFE'S CONDITION. A LITTLE WHILE AGO, SHE...
...
...
...RIGHT. OKAY. UNDER-STOOD.
THE WHOLE FAMILY WILL BE RIGHT OVER.
DASH

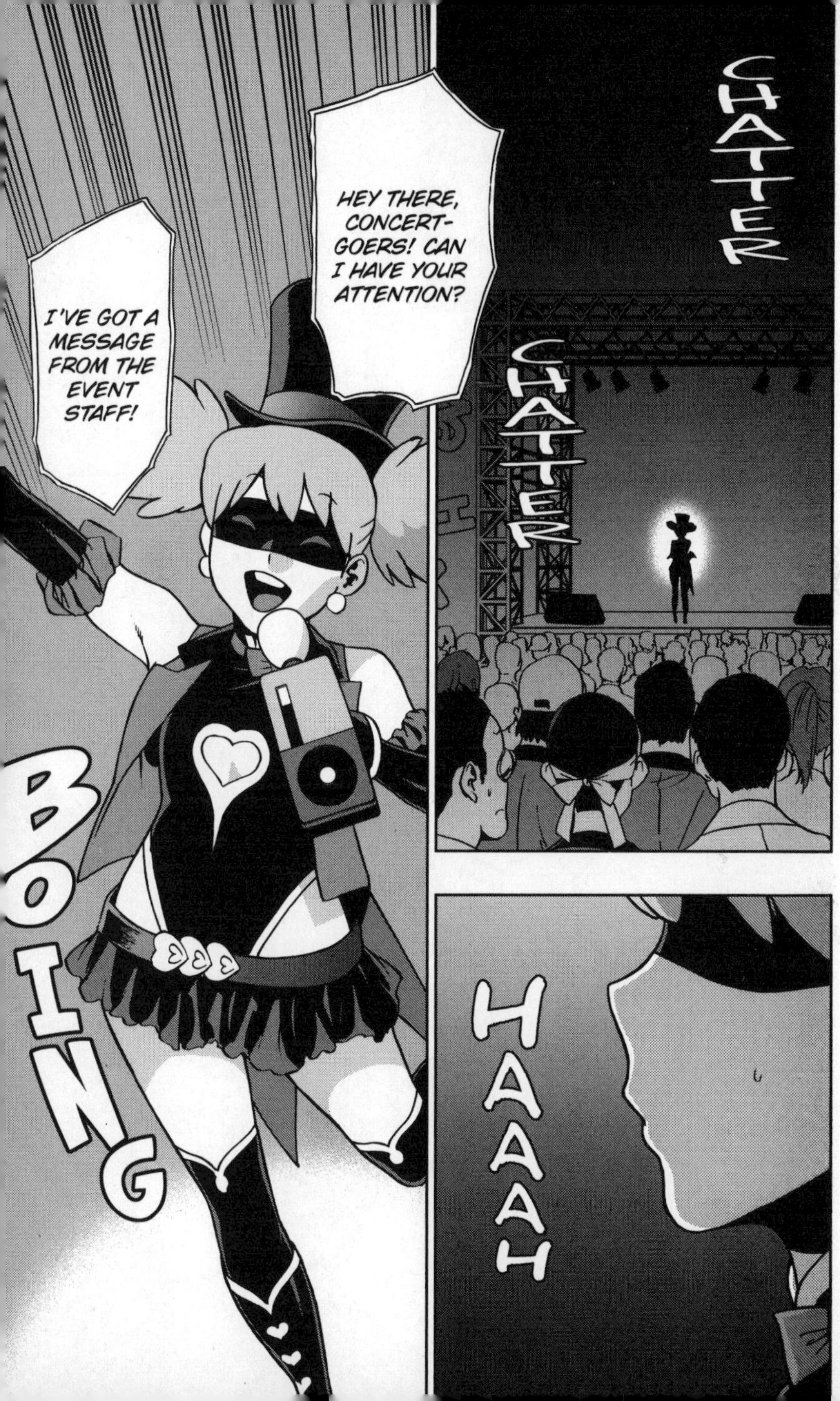
CHATTER
CHATTER
HAAAH
HEY THERE, CONCERT-GOERS! CAN I HAVE YOUR ATTENTION?
I'VE GOT A MESSAGE FROM THE EVENT STAFF!
BOING

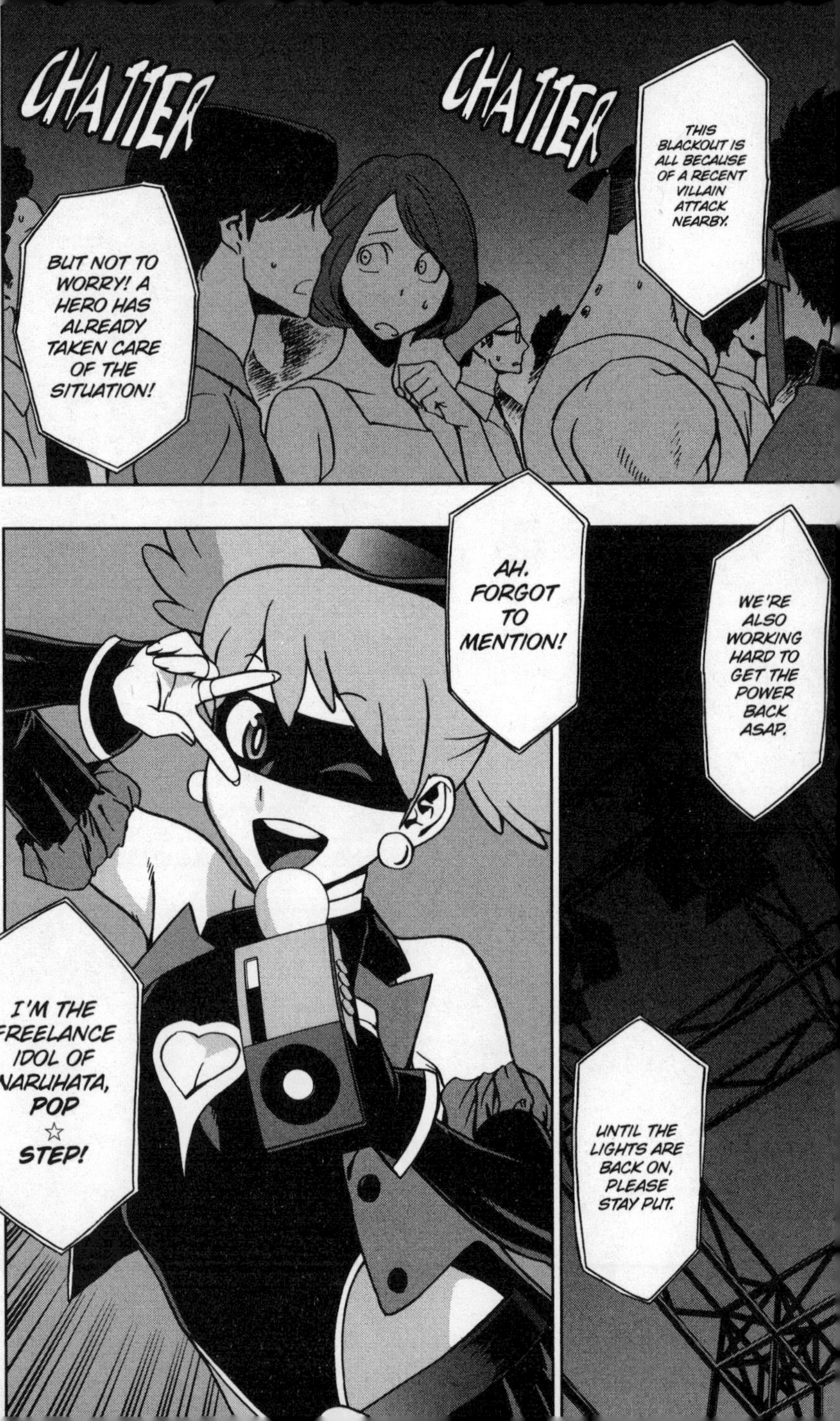
CHATTER
CHATTER
THIS BLACKOUT IS ALL BECAUSE OF A RECENT VILLAIN ATTACK NEARBY.
BUT NOT TO WORRY! A HERO HAS ALREADY TAKEN CARE OF THE SITUATION!
WE'RE ALSO WORKING HARD TO GET THE POWER BACK ASAP.
UNTIL THE LIGHTS ARE BACK ON, PLEASE STAY PUT.
AH. FORGOT TO MENTION!
I'M THE FREELANCE IDOL OF NARUHATA, POP ☆ STEP!

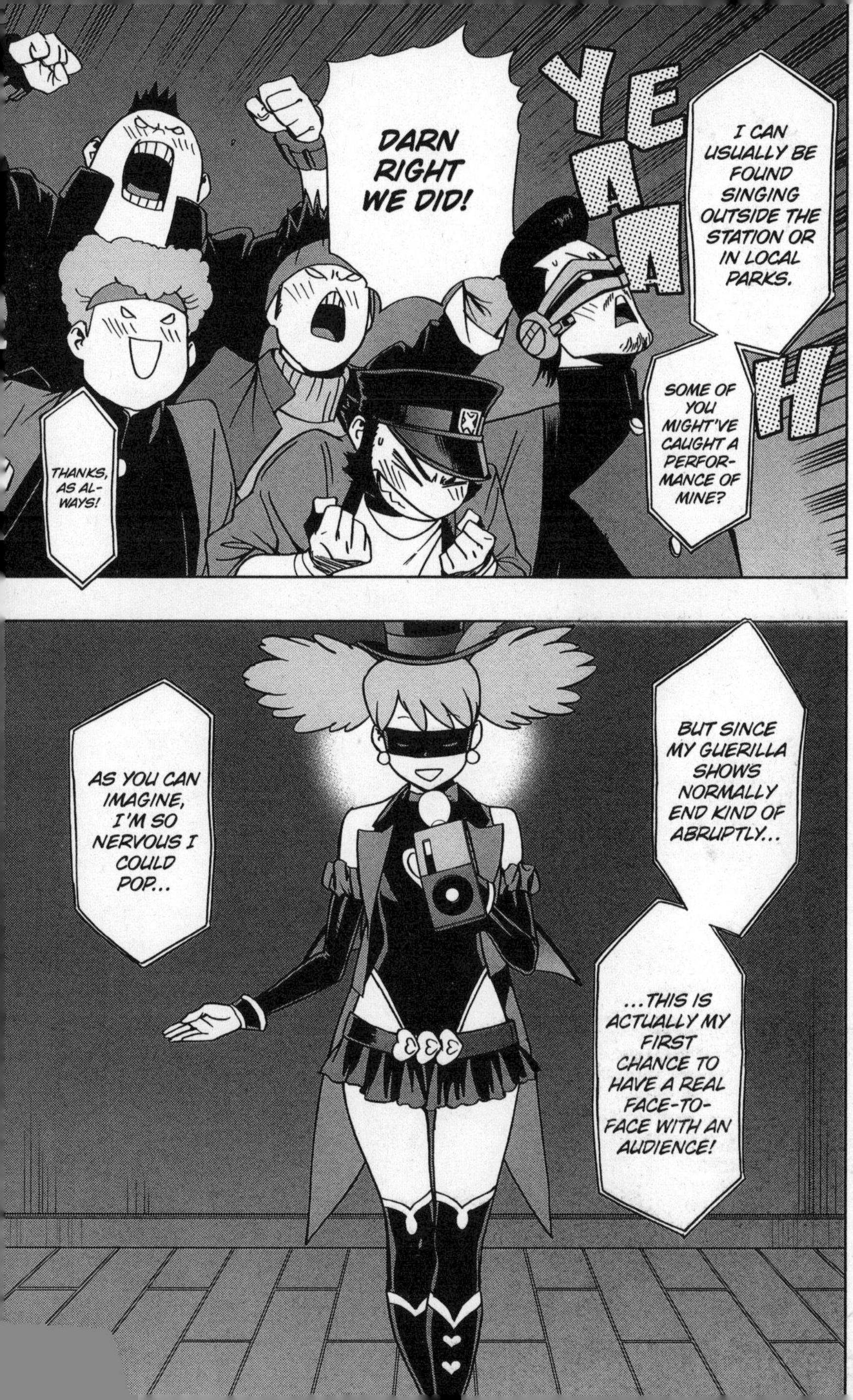
I CAN USUALLY BE FOUND SINGING OUTSIDE THE STATION OR IN LOCAL PARKS.
SOME OF YOU MIGHT'VE CAUGHT A PERFOR-MANCE OF MINE?
DARN RIGHT WE DID!
YEAAAH
THANKS, AS AL-WAYS!
BUT SINCE MY GUERILLA SHOWS NORMALLY END KIND OF ABRUPTLY...
...THIS IS ACTUALLY MY FIRST CHANCE TO HAVE A REAL FACE-TO-FACE WITH AN AUDIENCE!
AS YOU CAN IMAGINE, I'M SO NERVOUS I COULD POP...

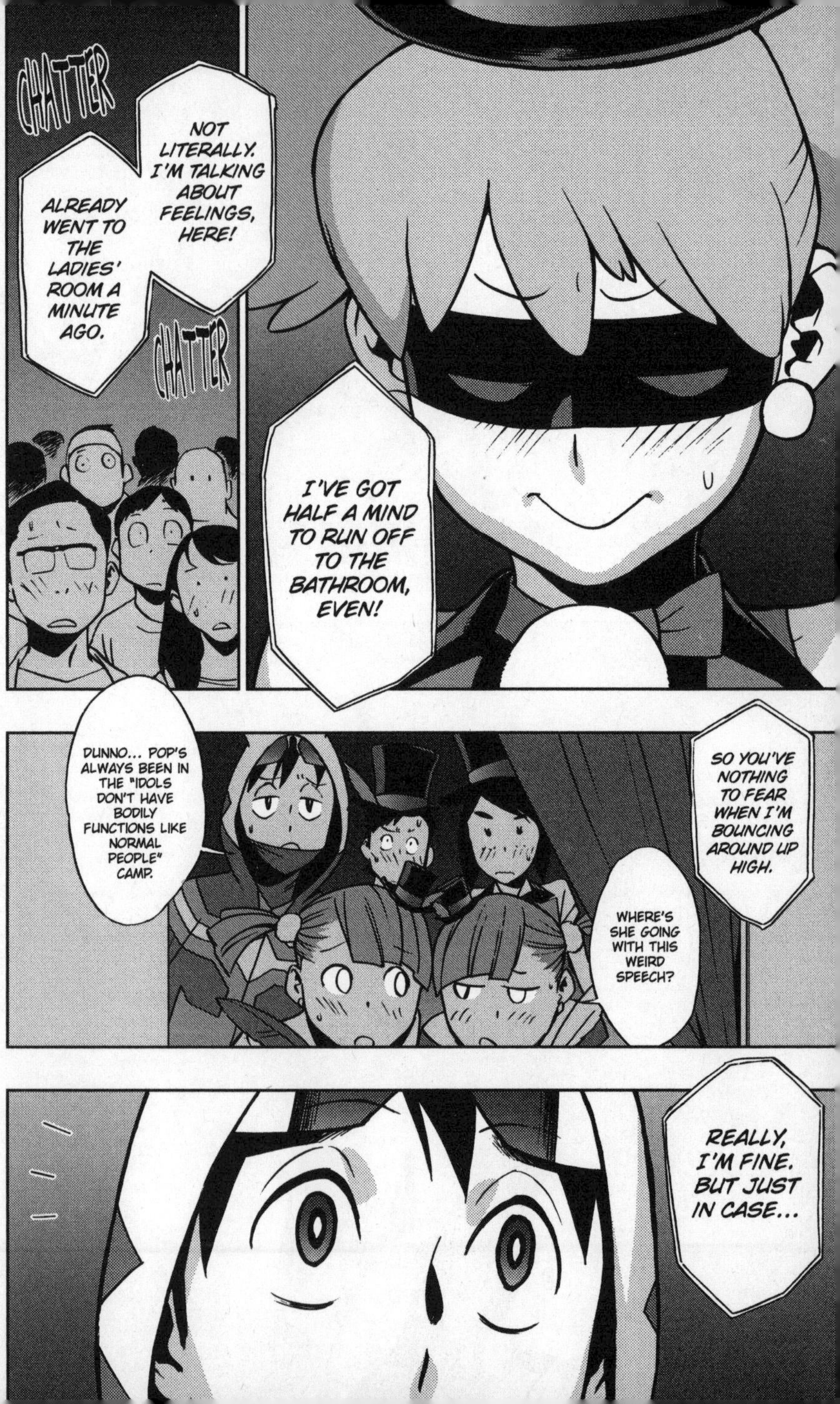
I'VE GOT HALF A MIND TO RUN OFF TO THE BATHROOM, EVEN!
CHATTER
ALREADY WENT TO THE LADIES' ROOM A MINUTE AGO.
NOT LITERALLY. I'M TALKING ABOUT FEELINGS, HERE!
CHATTER
SO YOU'VE NOTHING TO FEAR WHEN I'M BOUNCING AROUND UP HIGH.
WHERE'S SHE GOING WITH THIS WEIRD SPEECH?
DUNNO... POP'S ALWAYS BEEN IN THE "IDOLS DON'T HAVE BODILY FUNCTIONS LIKE NORMAL PEOPLE" CAMP.
REALLY, I'M FINE. BUT JUST IN CASE...

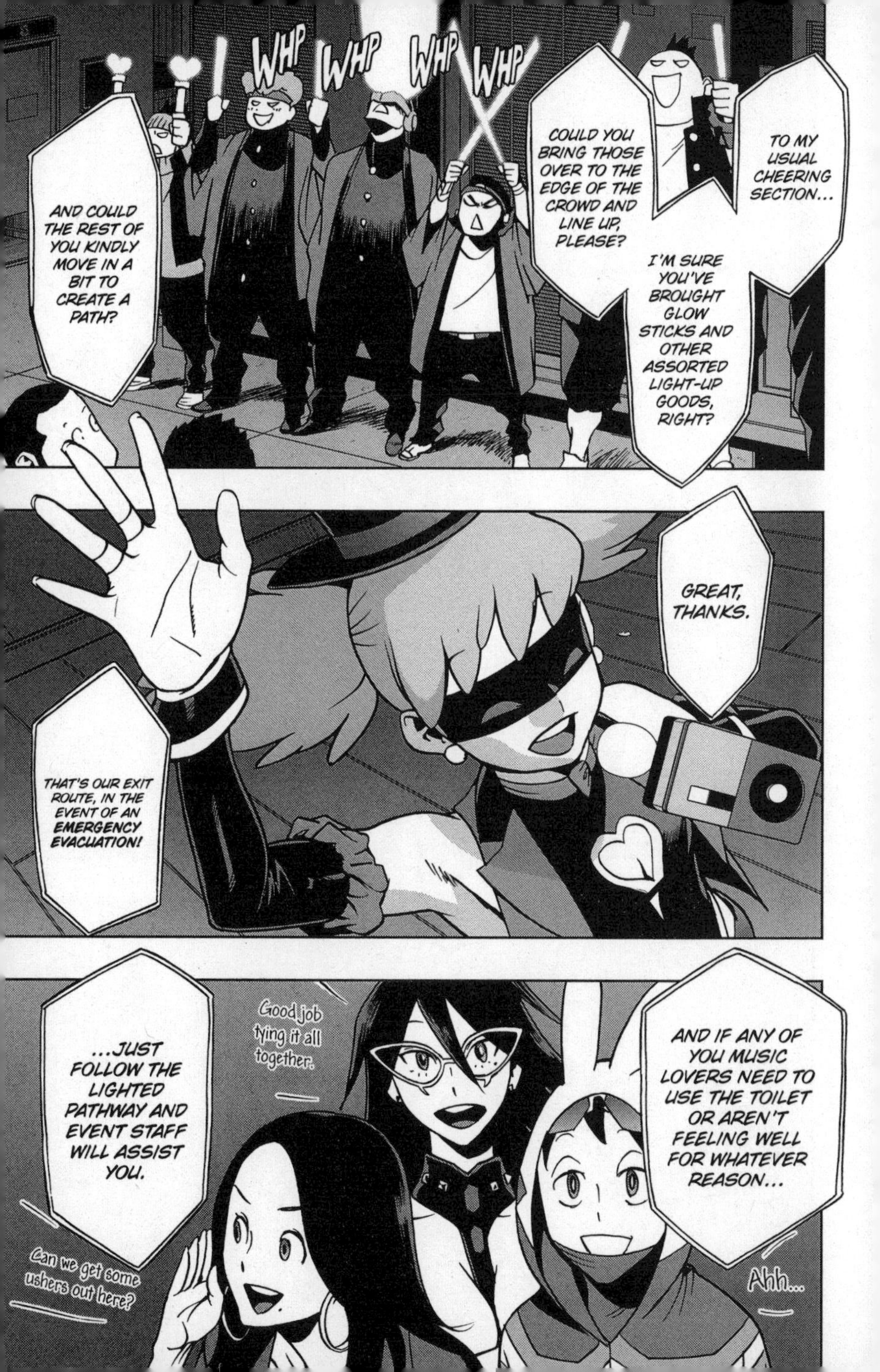
WHP WHP WHP WHP
TO MY USUAL CHEERING SECTION...
I'M SURE YOU'VE BROUGHT GLOW STICKS AND OTHER ASSORTED LIGHT-UP GOODS, RIGHT?
COULD YOU BRING THOSE OVER TO THE EDGE OF THE CROWD AND LINE UP, PLEASE?
AND COULD THE REST OF YOU KINDLY MOVE IN A BIT TO CREATE A PATH?
GREAT, THANKS.
THAT'S OUR EXIT ROUTE, IN THE EVENT OF AN EMERGENCY EVACUATION!
AND IF ANY OF YOU MUSIC LOVERS NEED TO USE THE TOILET OR AREN'T FEELING WELL FOR WHATEVER REASON...
Ahh...
Good job tying it all together.
...JUST FOLLOW THE LIGHTED PATHWAY AND EVENT STAFF WILL ASSIST YOU.
Can we get some ushers out here?

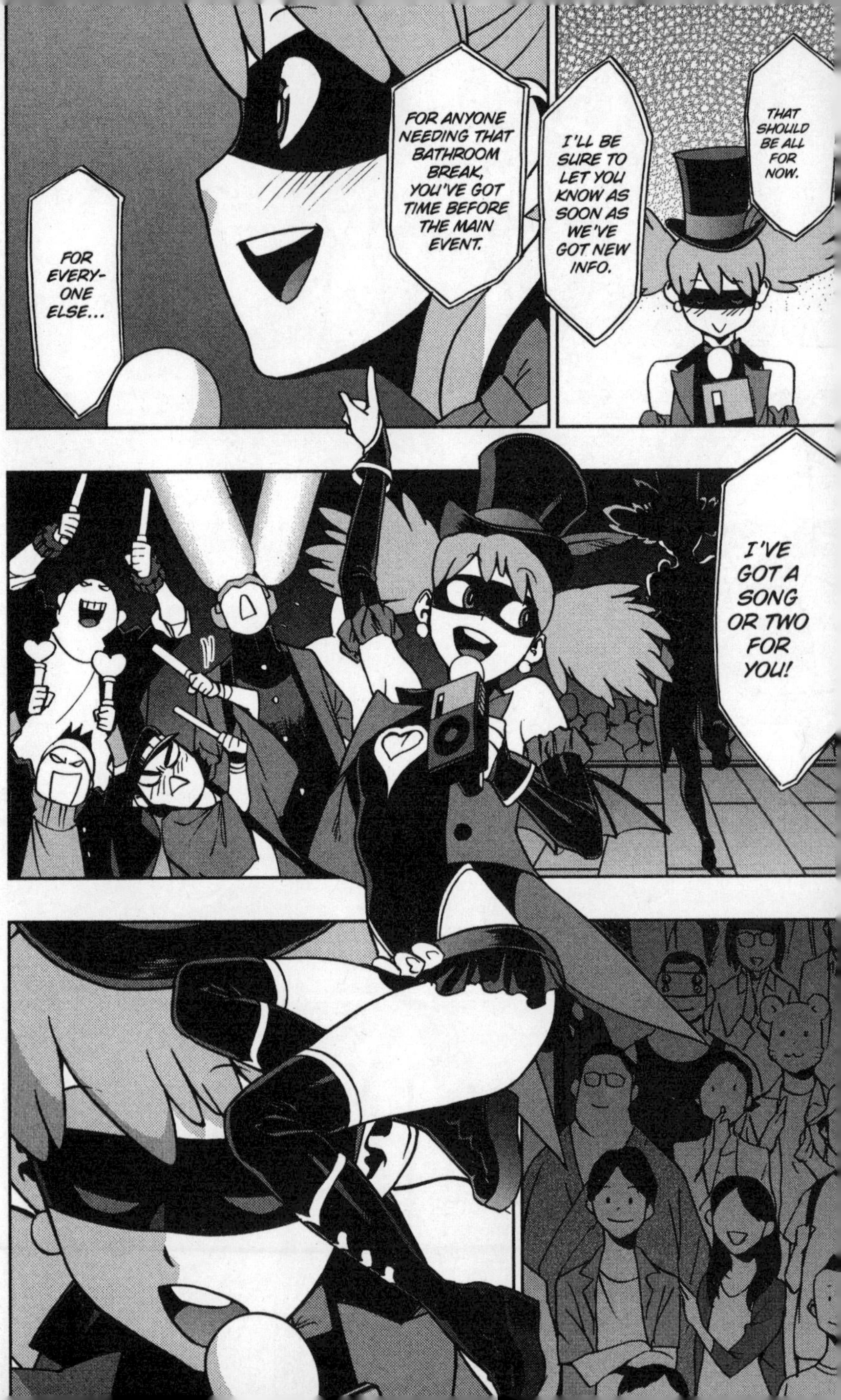
THAT SHOULD BE ALL FOR NOW.
I'LL BE SURE TO LET YOU KNOW AS SOON AS WE'VE GOT NEW INFO.
FOR ANYONE NEEDING THAT BATHROOM BREAK, YOU'VE GOT TIME BEFORE THE MAIN EVENT.
FOR EVERY-ONE ELSE...
I'VE GOT A SONG OR TWO FOR YOU!

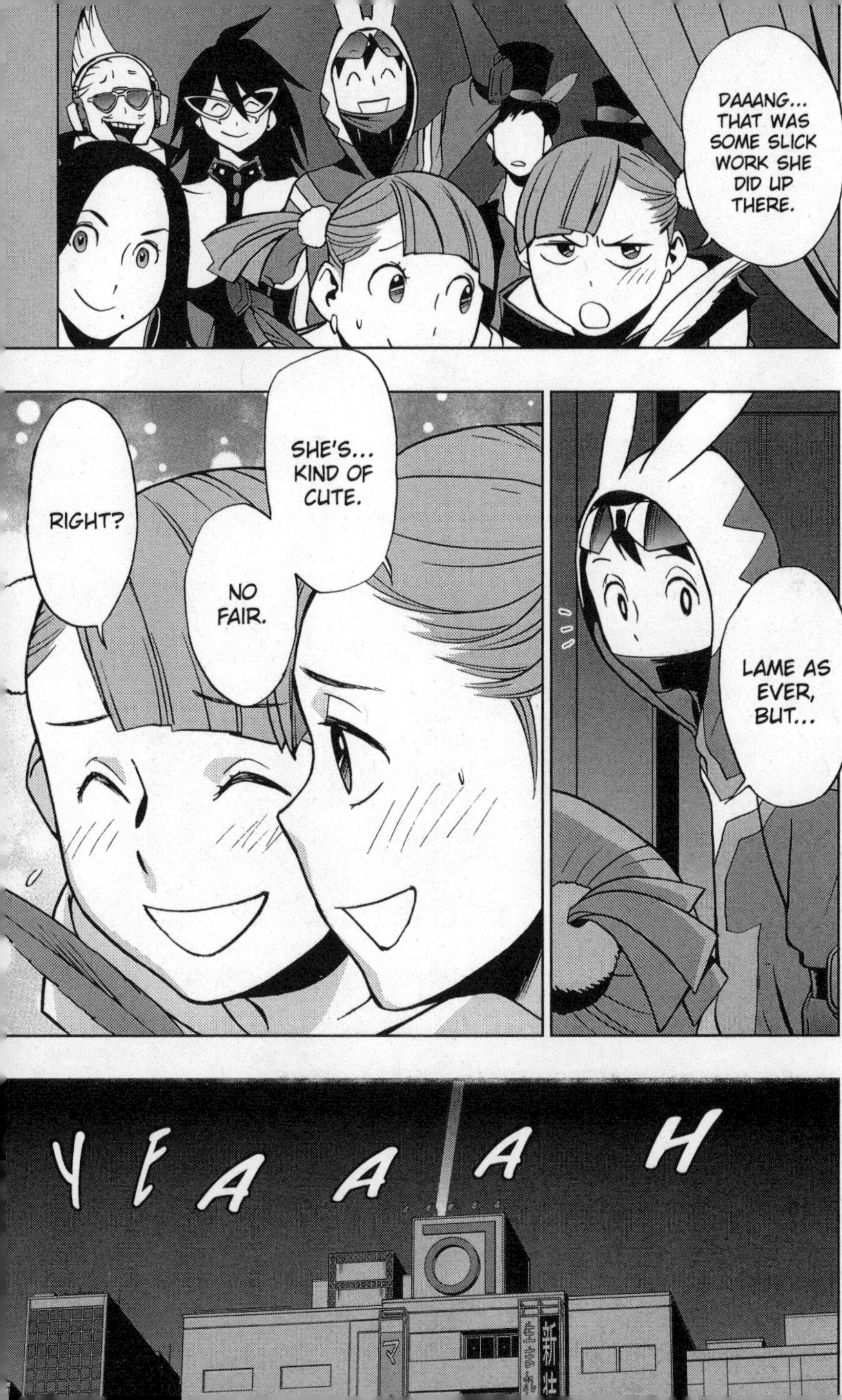
DAAANG... THAT WAS SOME SLICK WORK SHE DID UP THERE.
LAME AS EVER, BUT...
SHE'S... KIND OF CUTE.
NO FAIR.
RIGHT?
YEAAAH

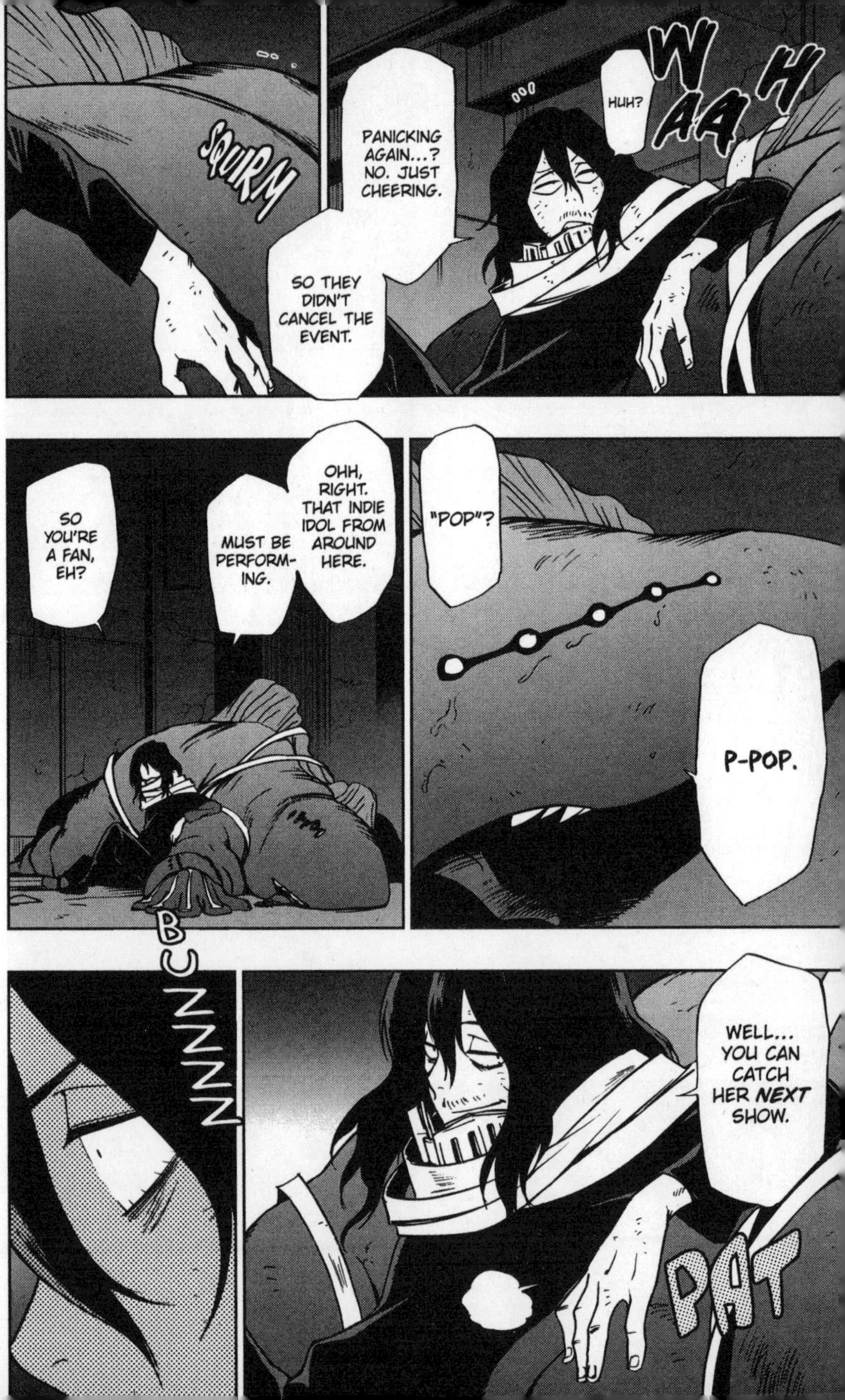
WHAAH
HUH?
PANICKING AGAIN...? NO. JUST CHEERING.
SO THEY DIDN'T CANCEL THE EVENT.
SQUIRM
"POP"?
P-POP.
OHH, RIGHT. THAT INDIE IDOL FROM AROUND HERE.
MUST BE PERFORMING.
SO YOU'RE A FAN, EH?
BUZZZZ
WELL... YOU CAN CATCH HER *NEXT* SHOW.
PAT

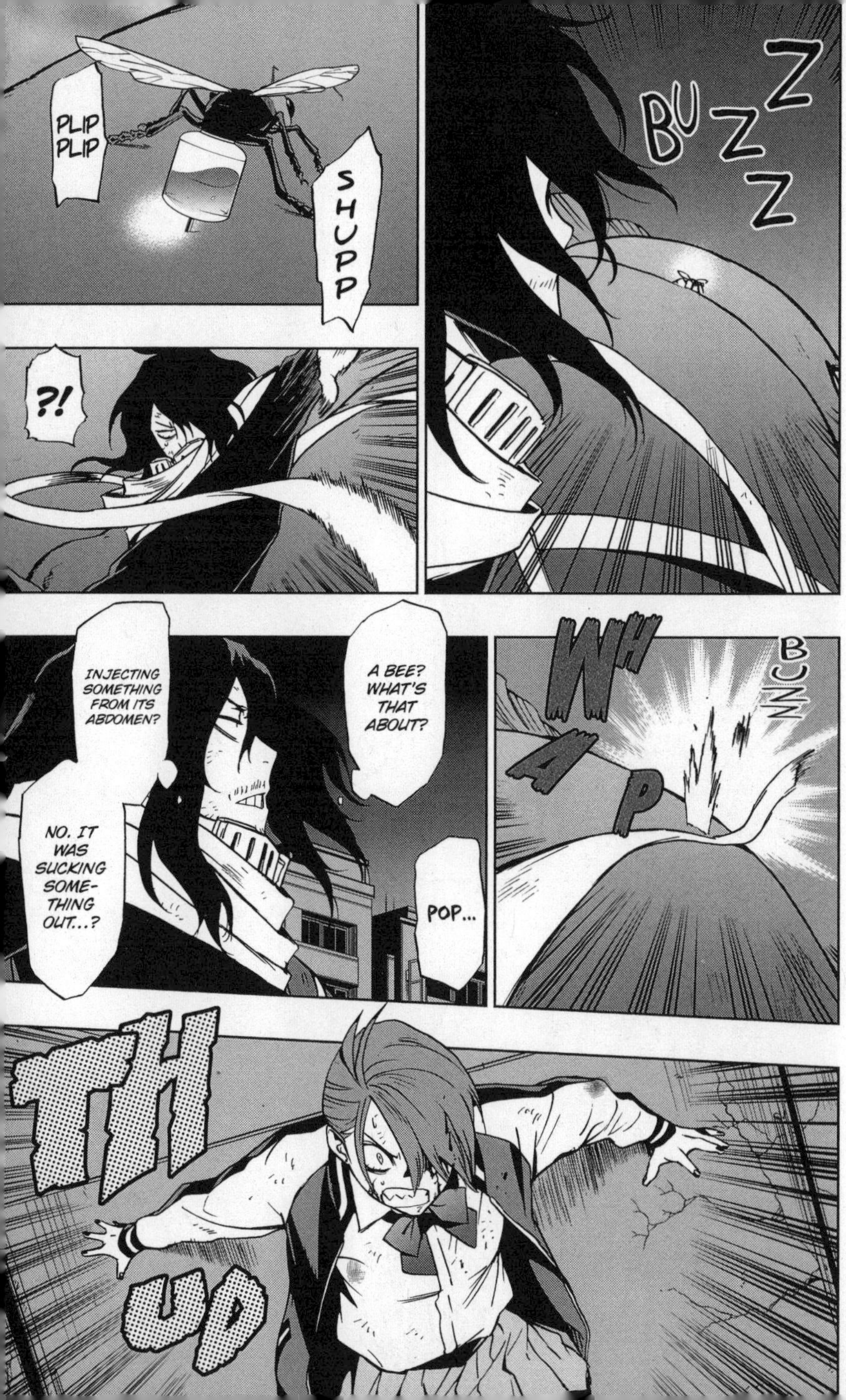
BUZZZ
PLIP PLIP
SHUPP
?!
WHAP
BUZZ
A BEE? WHAT'S THAT ABOUT?
INJECTING SOMETHING FROM ITS ABDOMEN?
NO. IT WAS SUCKING SOME-THING OUT...?
POP...
THUD

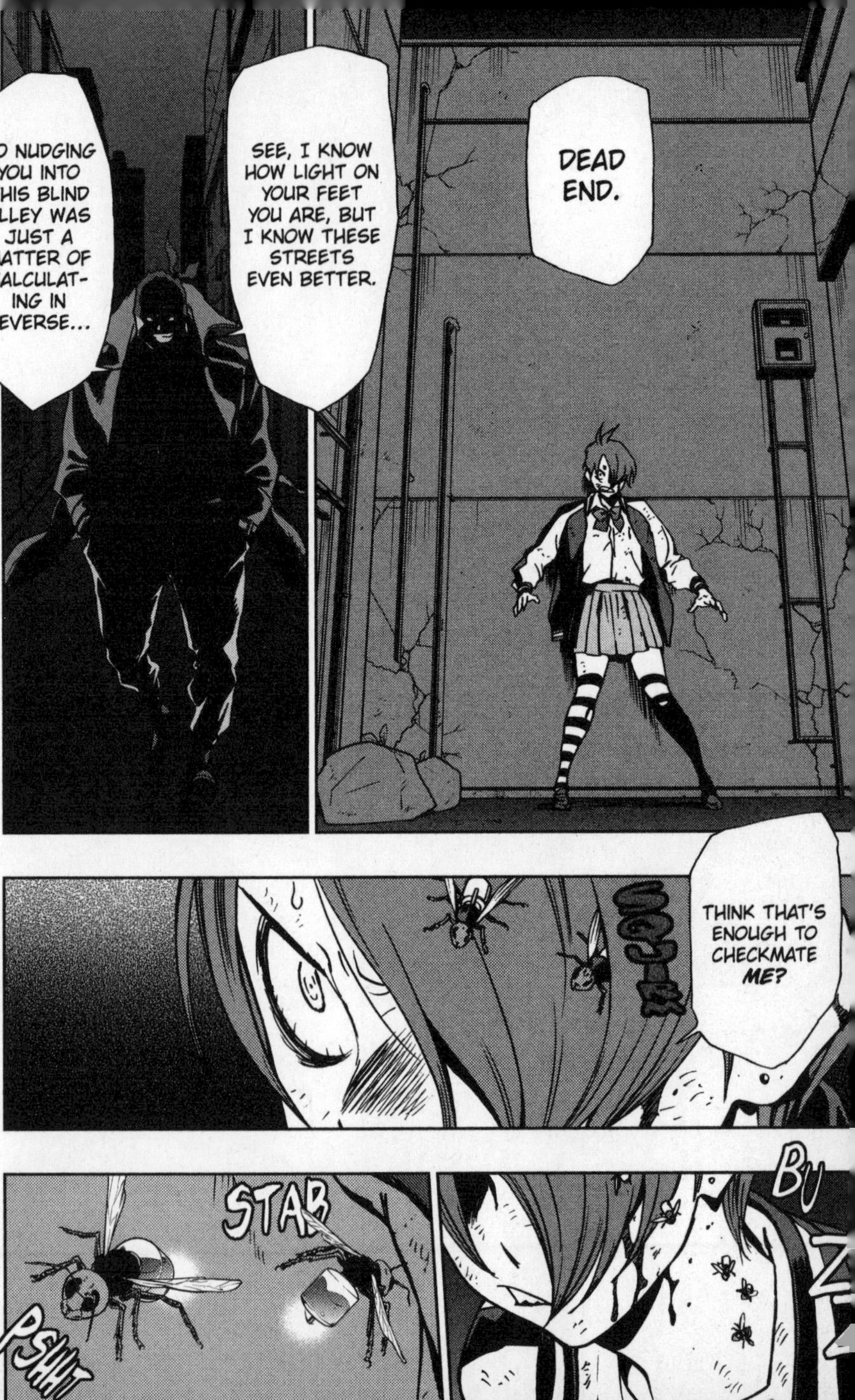
DEAD END.
SEE, I KNOW HOW LIGHT ON YOUR FEET YOU ARE, BUT I KNOW THESE STREETS EVEN BETTER.
SO NUDGING YOU INTO THIS BLIND ALLEY WAS JUST A MATTER OF CALCULATING IN REVERSE...
THINK THAT'S ENOUGH TO CHECKMATE ME?
BUZZ
STAB
PSHHT

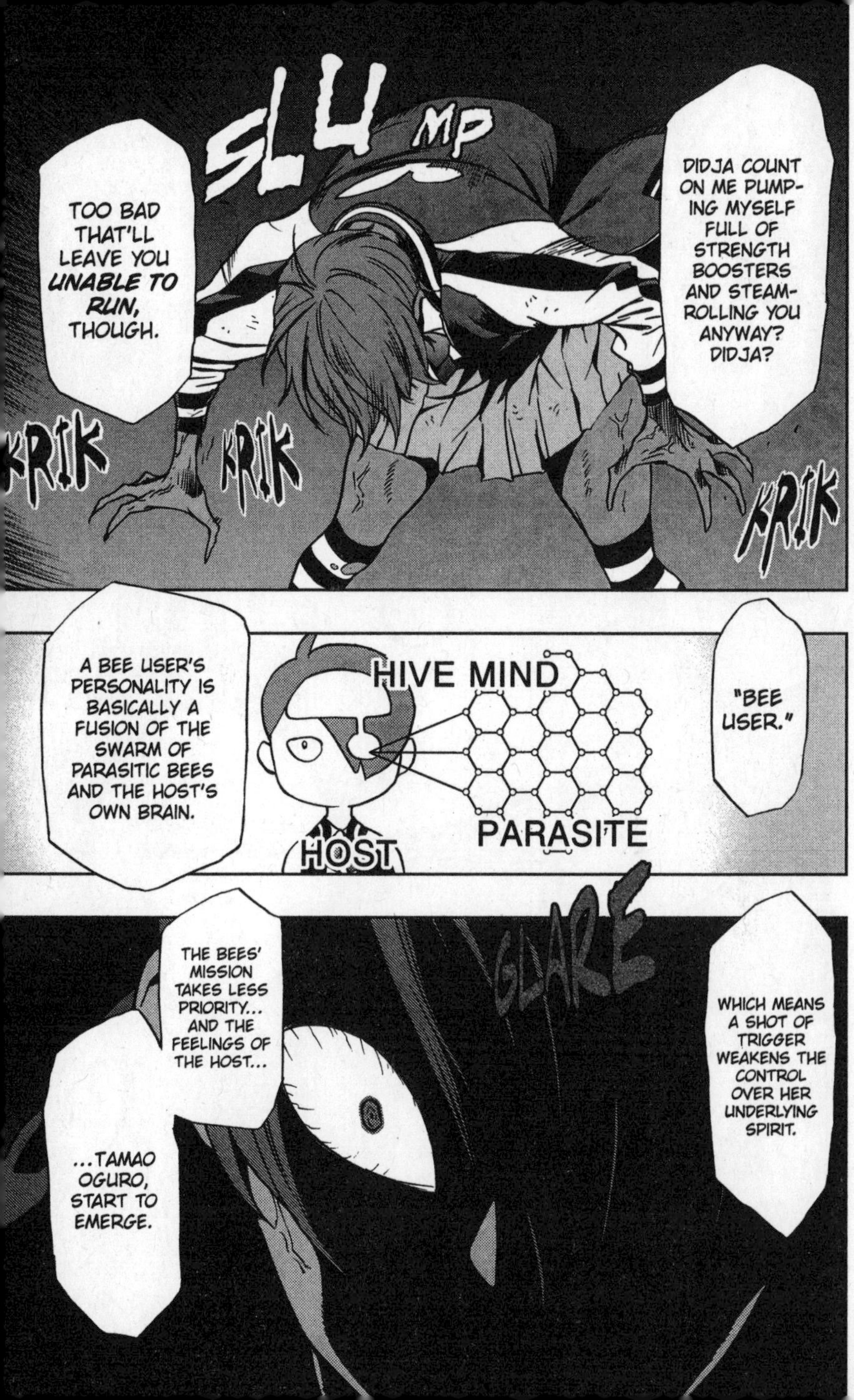
DIDJA COUNT ON ME PUMPING MYSELF FULL OF STRENGTH BOOSTERS AND STEAMROLLING YOU ANYWAY? DIDJA?
SLUMP
TOO BAD THAT'LL LEAVE YOU *UNABLE TO RUN,* THOUGH.
KRIK
KRIK
KRIK
"BEE USER."
HIVE MIND
PARASITE
HOST
A BEE USER'S PERSONALITY IS BASICALLY A FUSION OF THE SWARM OF PARASITIC BEES AND THE HOST'S OWN BRAIN.
WHICH MEANS A SHOT OF TRIGGER WEAKENS THE CONTROL OVER HER UNDERLYING SPIRIT.
GLARE
THE BEES' MISSION TAKES LESS PRIORITY... AND THE FEELINGS OF THE HOST...
...TAMAO OGURO, START TO EMERGE.

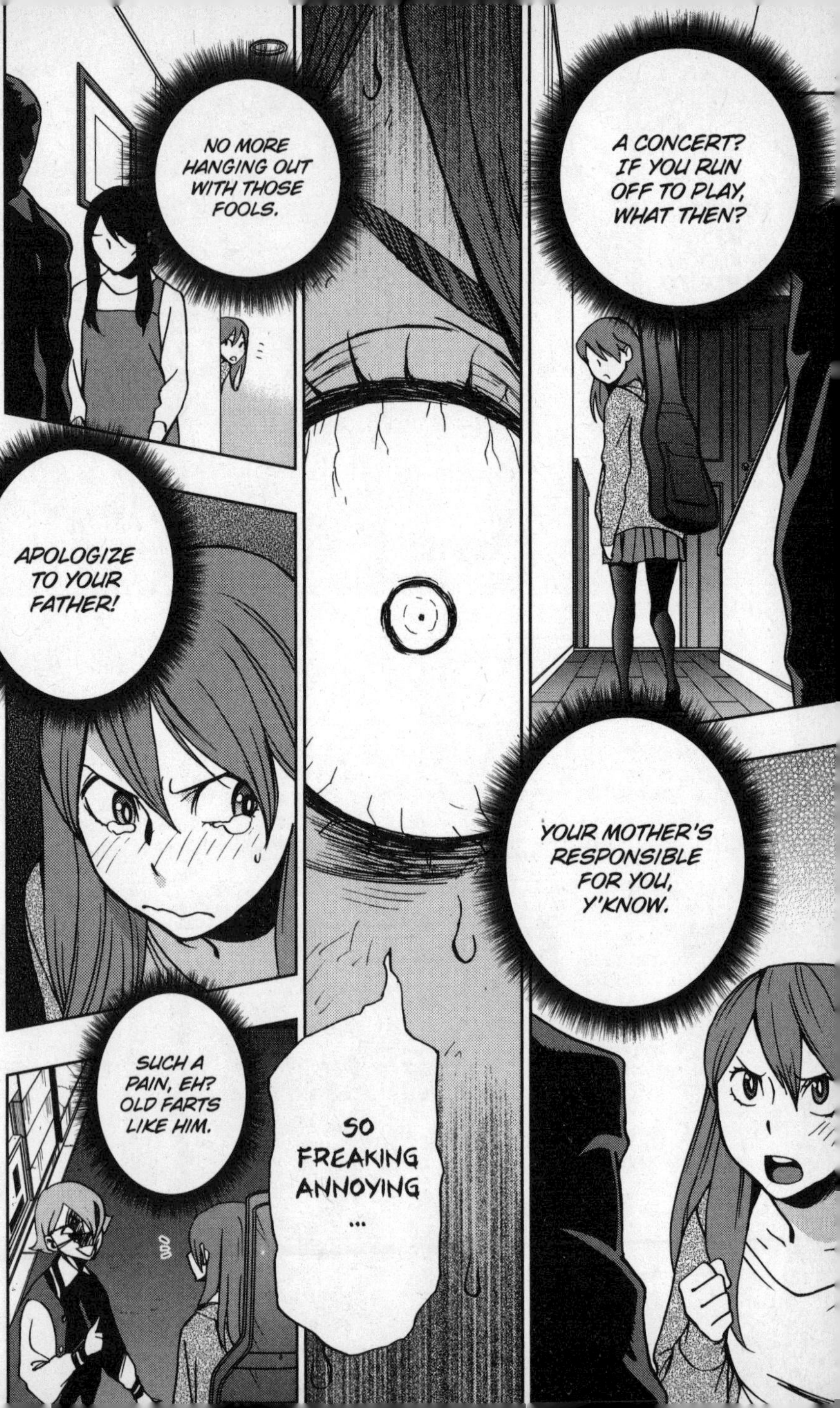
A CONCERT? IF YOU RUN OFF TO PLAY, WHAT THEN?
YOUR MOTHER'S RESPONSIBLE FOR YOU, Y'KNOW.
SO FREAKING ANNOYING ...
NO MORE HANGING OUT WITH THOSE FOOLS.
APOLOGIZE TO YOUR FATHER!
SUCH A PAIN, EH? OLD FARTS LIKE HIM.

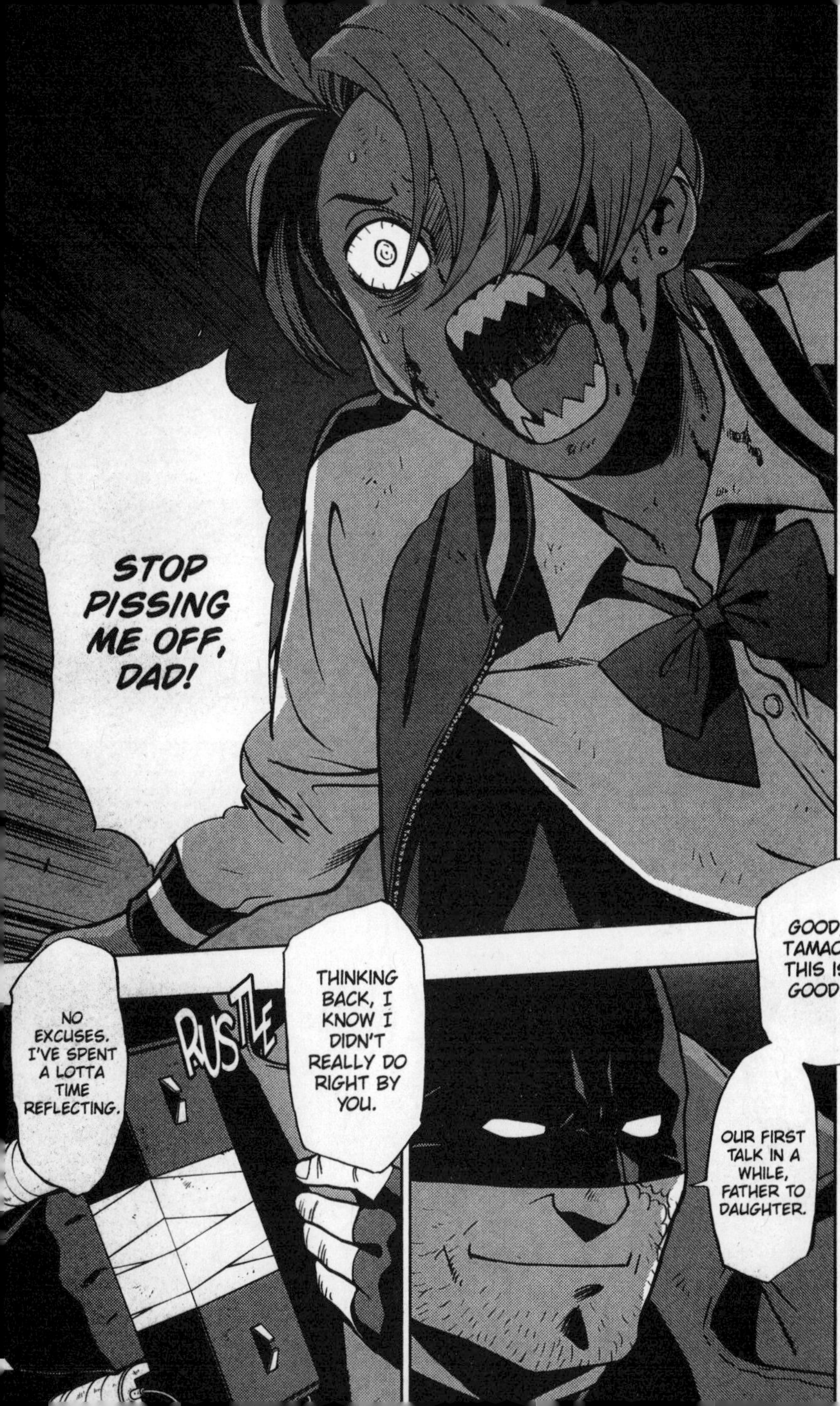
STOP PISSING ME OFF, DAD!
GOOD, TAMAO. THIS IS GOOD.
OUR FIRST TALK IN A WHILE, FATHER TO DAUGHTER.
THINKING BACK, I KNOW I DIDN'T REALLY DO RIGHT BY YOU.
RUSTLE
NO EXCUSES. I'VE SPENT A LOTTA TIME REFLECTING.

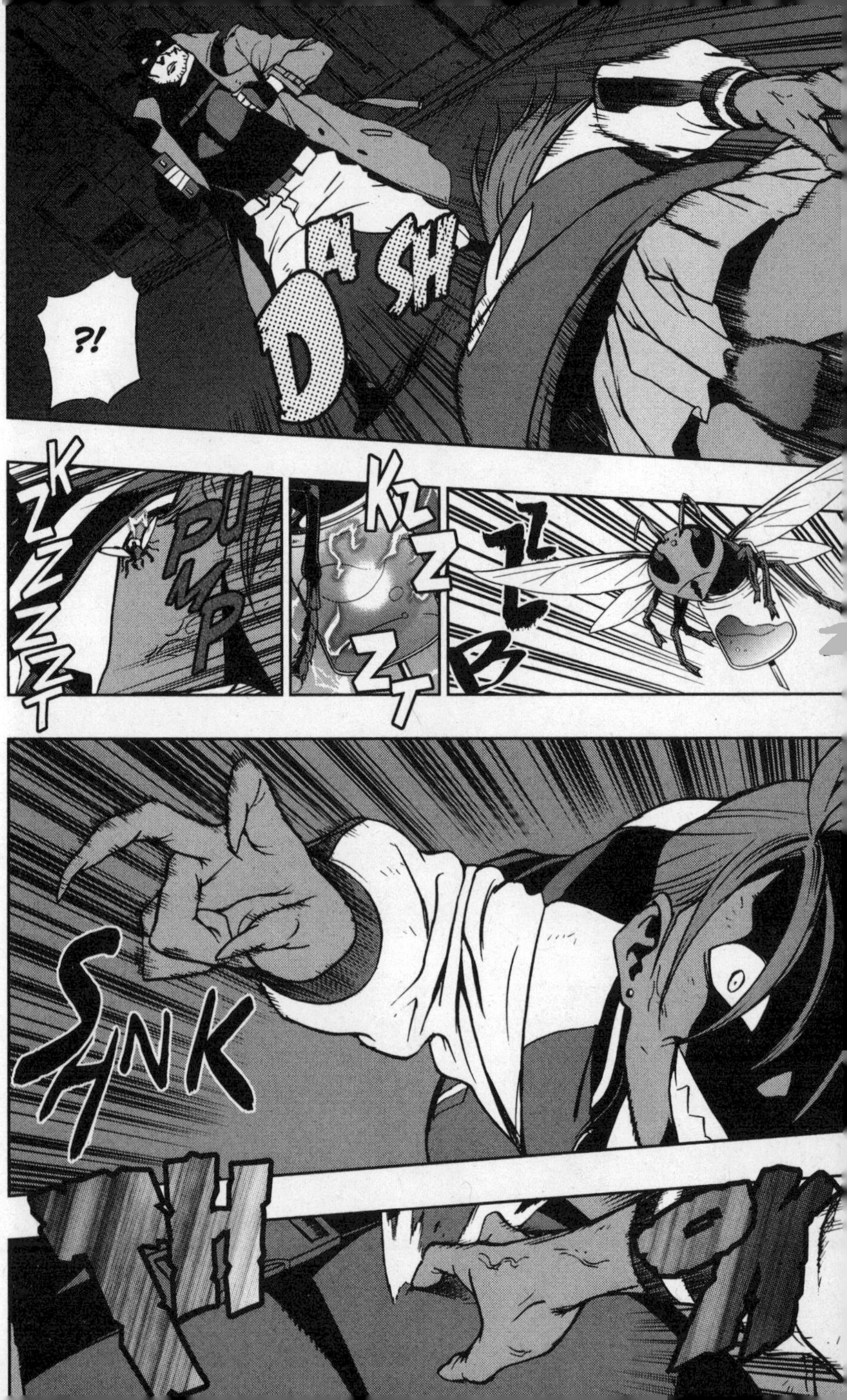
DASH
?!
BZZZ
KZZZT
PUMP
KZZZZZT
SHNK

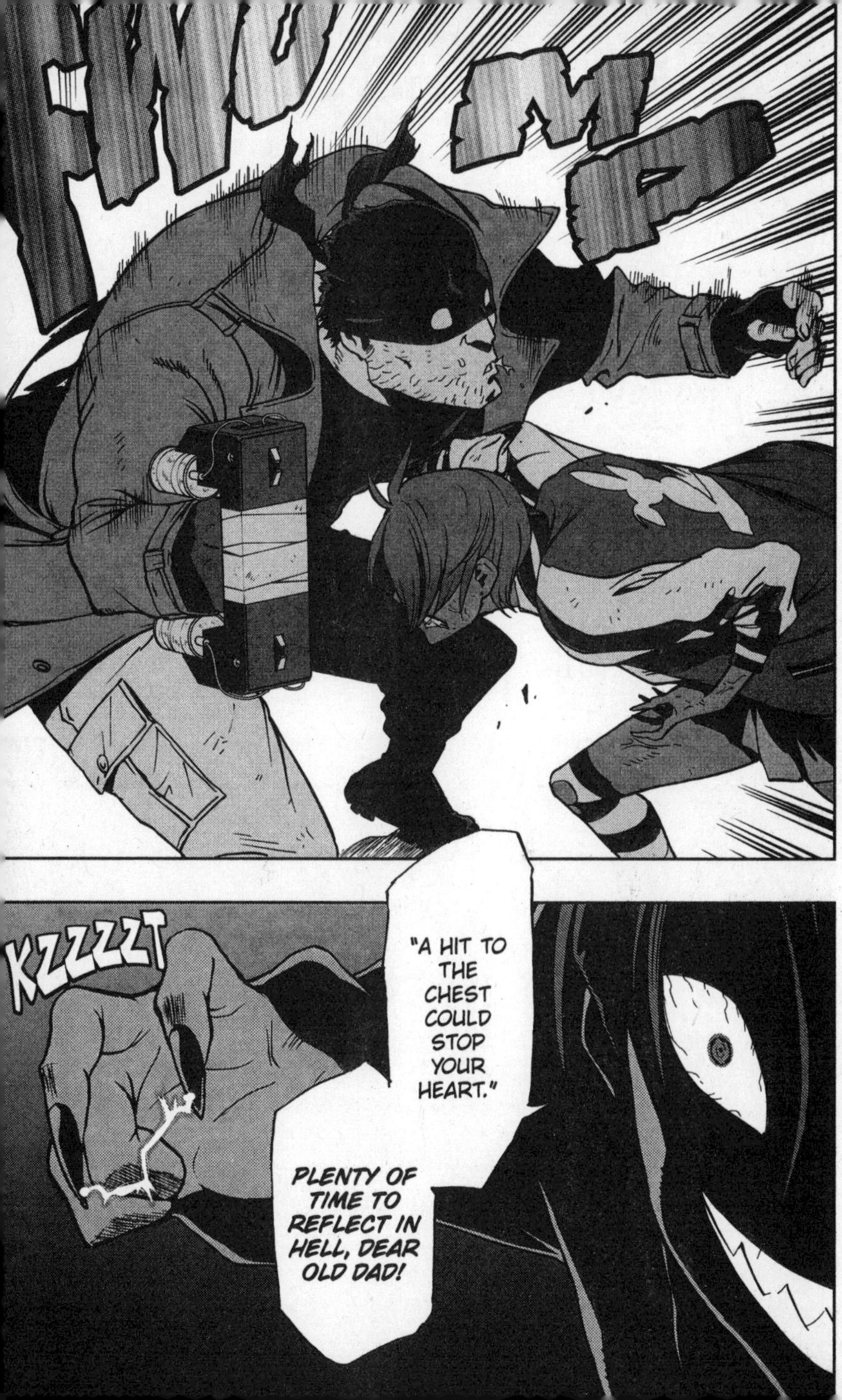
"A HIT TO THE CHEST COULD STOP YOUR HEART."
PLENTY OF TIME TO REFLECT IN HELL, DEAR OLD DAD!
KZZZZT

FEATHERHATS STAGE COSTUMES

THE ROUGH DESIGN

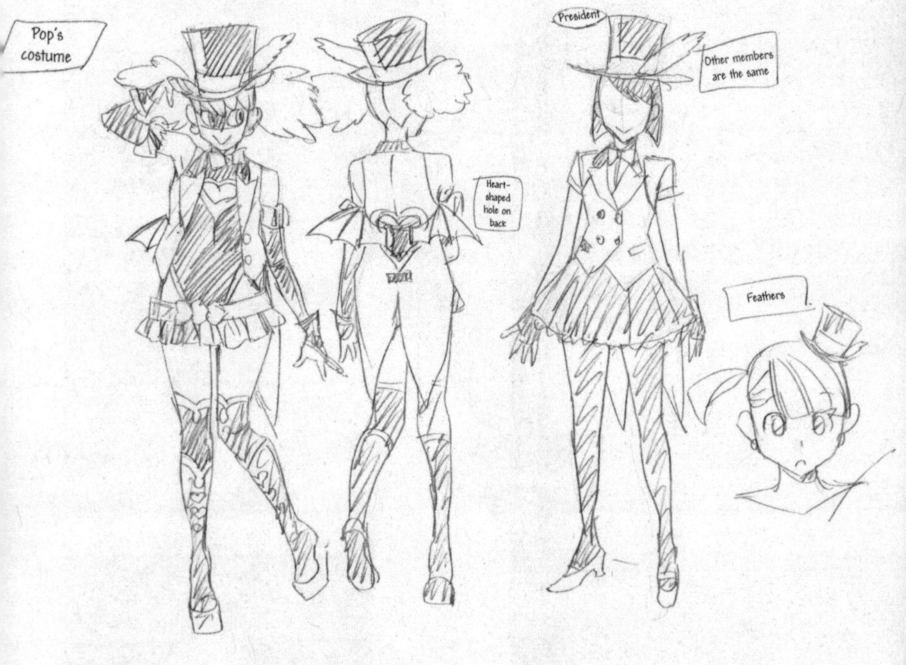

Pop's costume
Heart-shaped hole on back
President
Other members are the same
Feathers

BEHIND THE SCENES

Pop, the twins, the dance squad and the band come together to form the FeatherHATS, and these are their costumes. Each member basically gets his or her original costume, in addition to the hat with a feather on it.

The band members just got a feather on their preexisting hats. How slapdash! (LOL)

—Furuhashi

Given my tight schedule, I mostly just made minor adjustments while working on the actual draft (hah).

Out of all of this, the decision to have Pop's wings coming out of the heart-shaped hole is what I'm most proud of.

—Betten

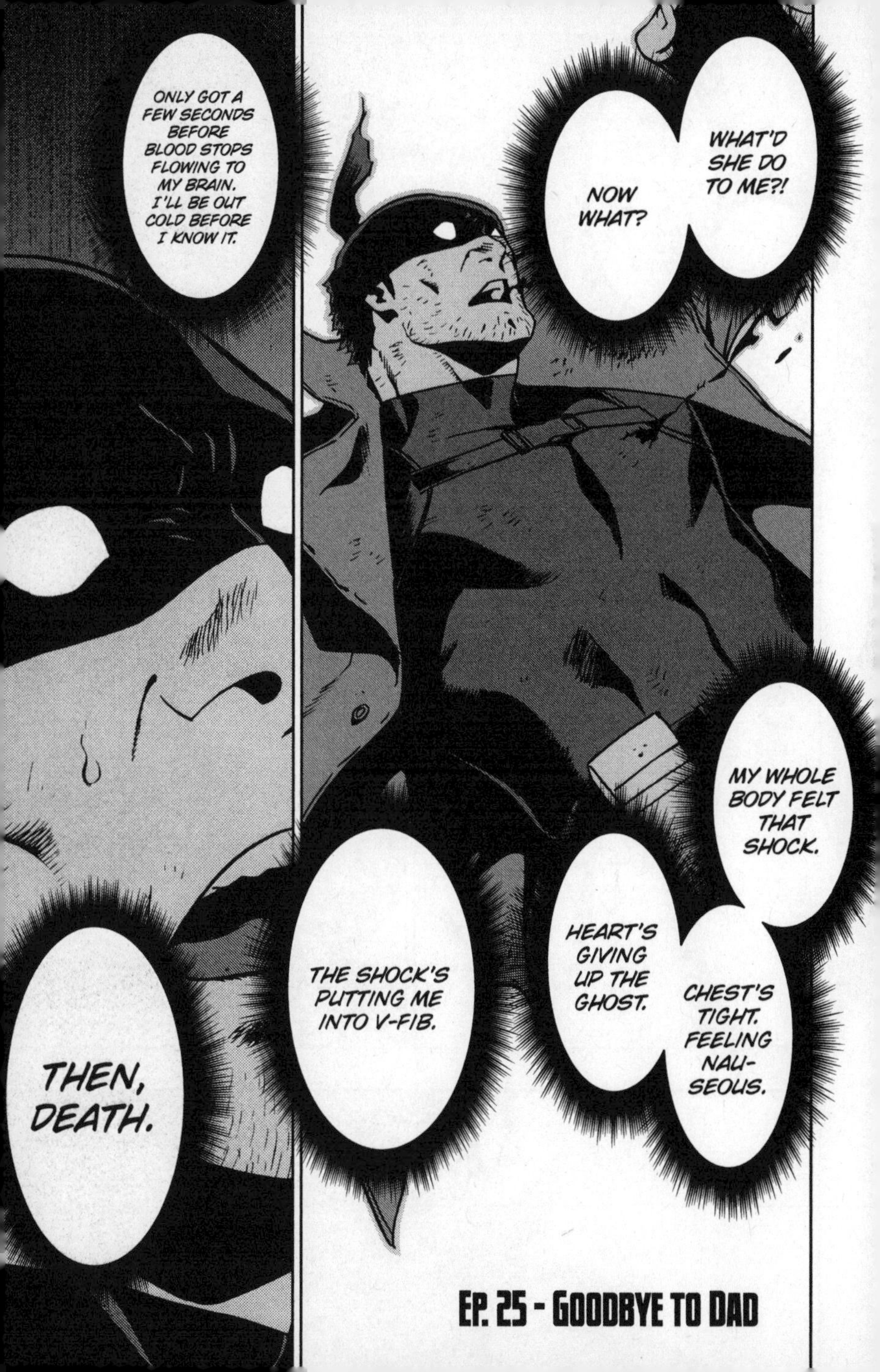
WHAT'D SHE DO TO ME?!
NOW WHAT?
MY WHOLE BODY FELT THAT SHOCK.
CHEST'S TIGHT. FEELING NAU-SEOUS.
HEART'S GIVING UP THE GHOST.
THE SHOCK'S PUTTING ME INTO V-FIB.
EP. 25 - GOODBYE TO DAD
ONLY GOT A FEW SECONDS BEFORE BLOOD STOPS FLOWING TO MY BRAIN. I'LL BE OUT COLD BEFORE I KNOW IT.
THEN, DEATH.

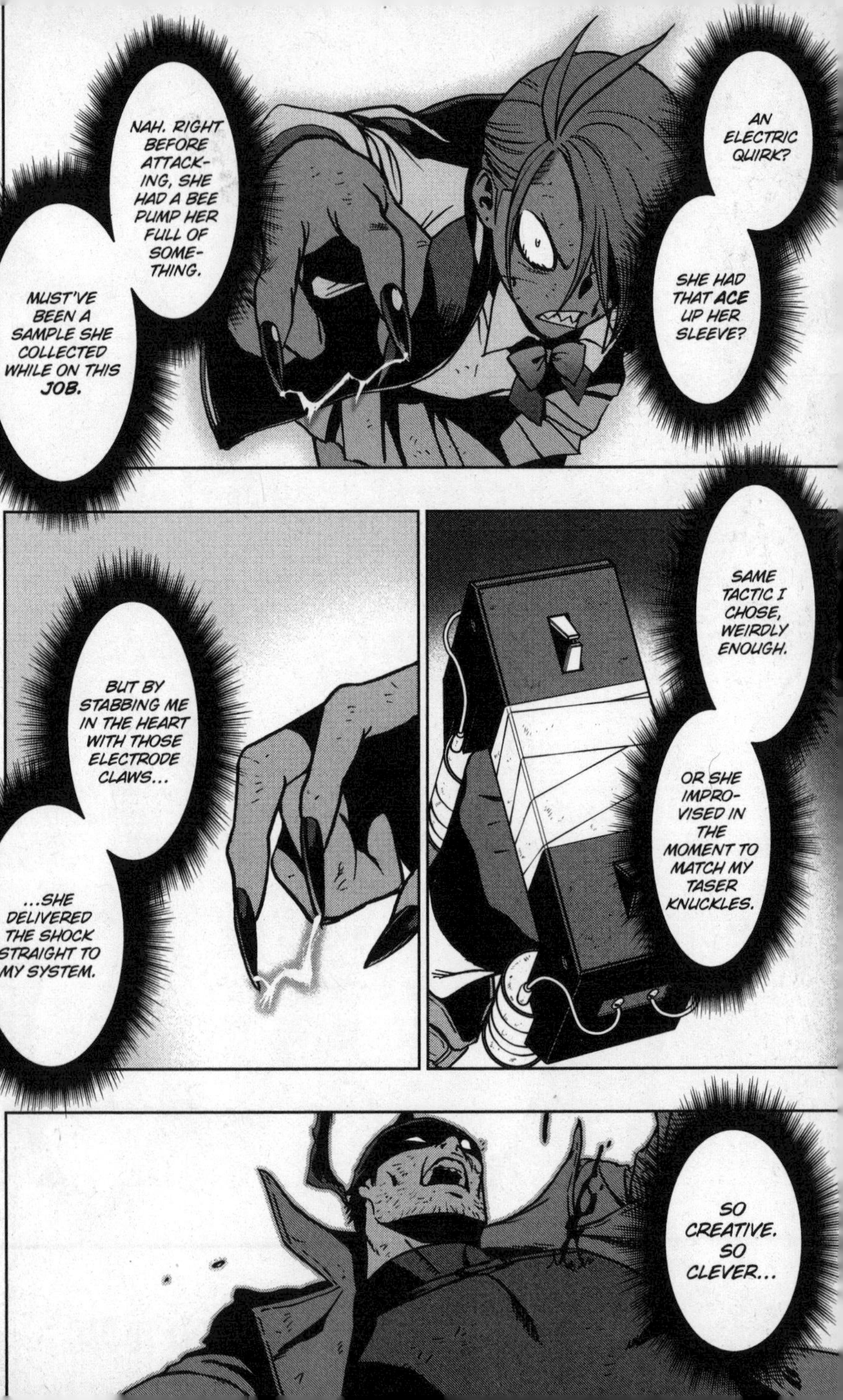
AN ELECTRIC QUIRK?
SHE HAD THAT ACE UP HER SLEEVE?
NAH. RIGHT BEFORE ATTACK-ING, SHE HAD A BEE PUMP HER FULL OF SOME-THING.
MUST'VE BEEN A SAMPLE SHE COLLECTED WHILE ON THIS JOB.
SAME TACTIC I CHOSE, WEIRDLY ENOUGH.
OR SHE IMPRO-VISED IN THE MOMENT TO MATCH MY TASER KNUCKLES.
BUT BY STABBING ME IN THE HEART WITH THOSE ELECTRODE CLAWS...
...SHE DELIVERED THE SHOCK STRAIGHT TO MY SYSTEM.
SO CREATIVE. SO CLEVER...

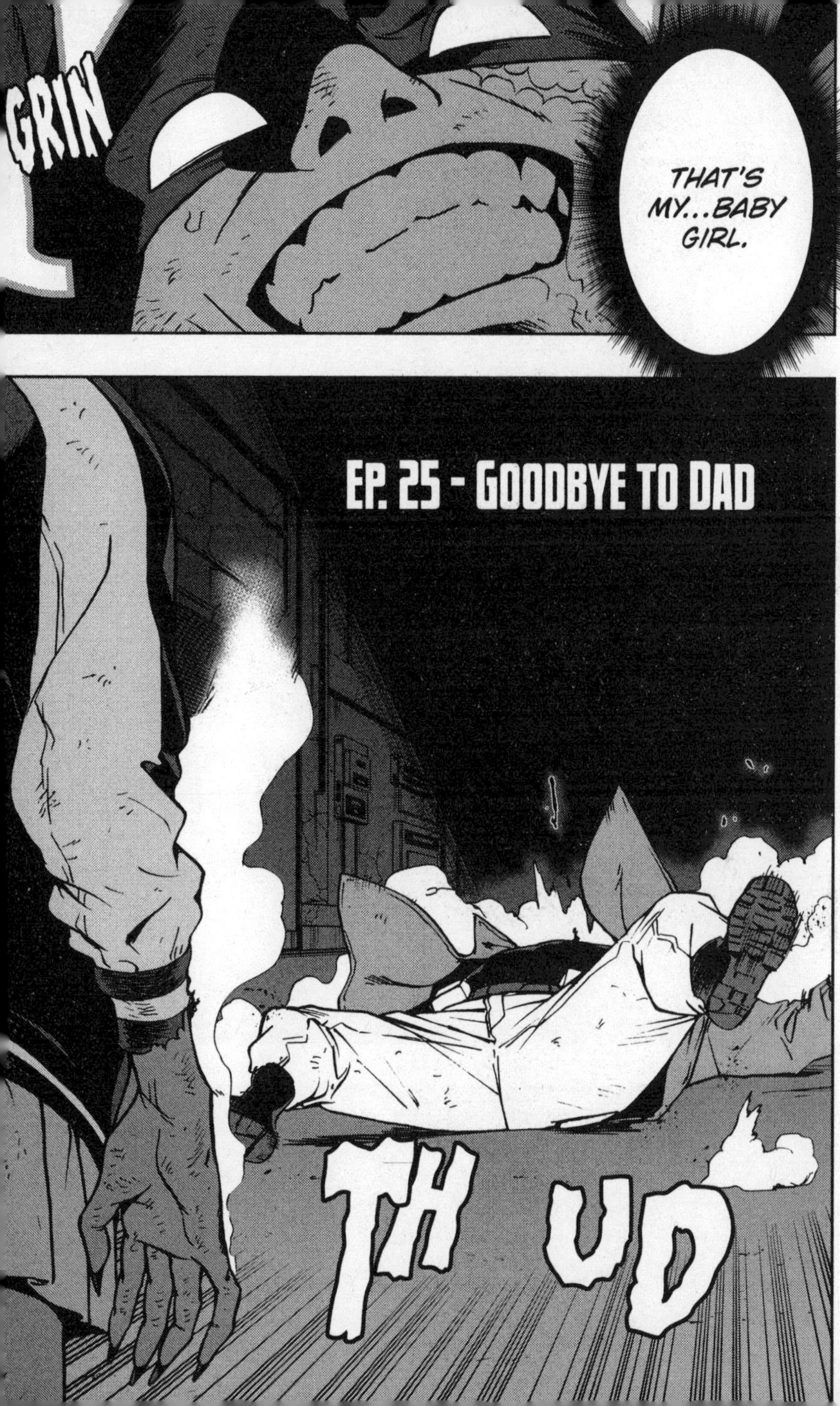
THAT'S MY...BABY GIRL.
GRIN
EP. 25 - GOODBYE TO DAD
TH UD

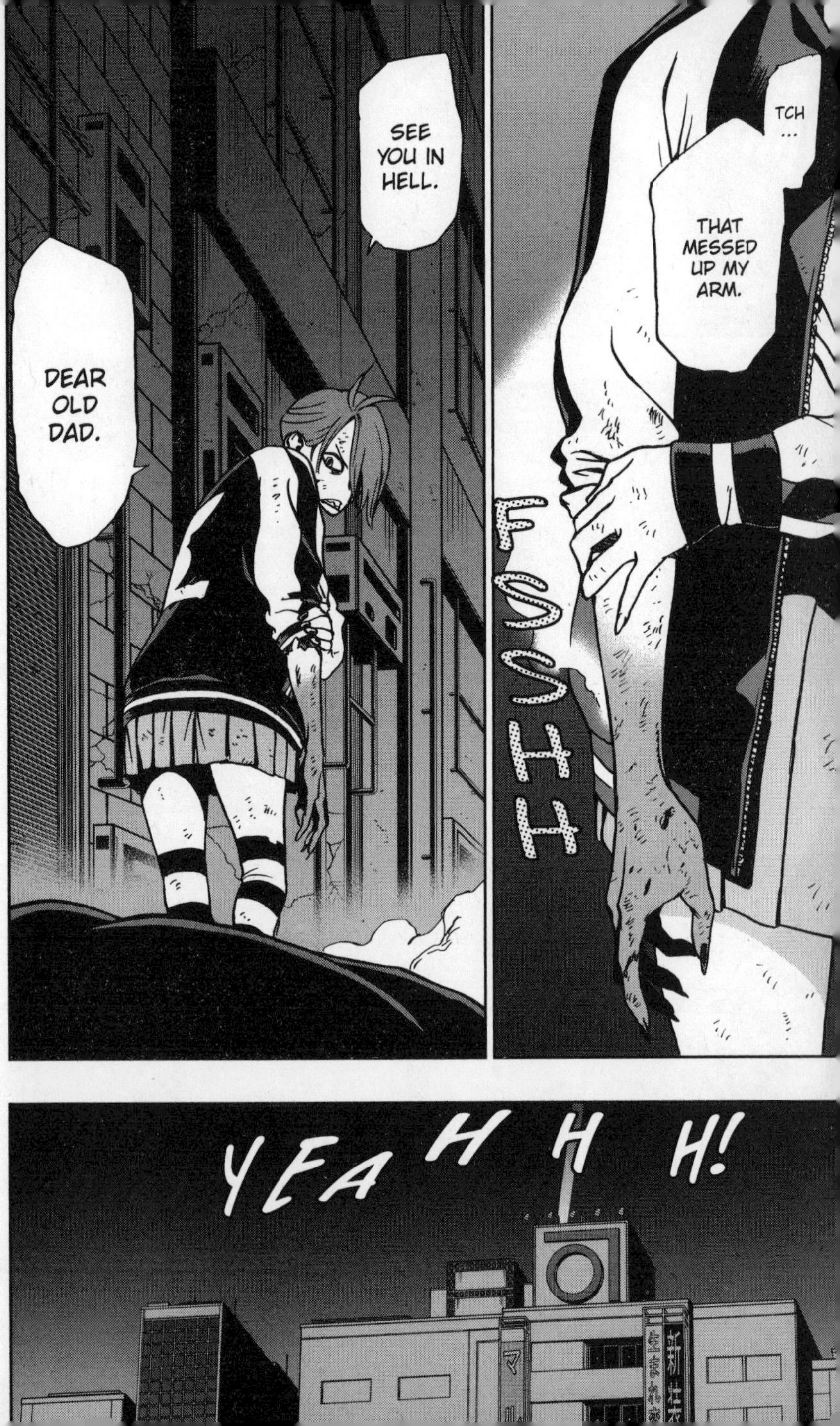
TCH...
THAT MESSED UP MY ARM.
FSSHHH
SEE YOU IN HELL.
DEAR OLD DAD.
YEAHHH!

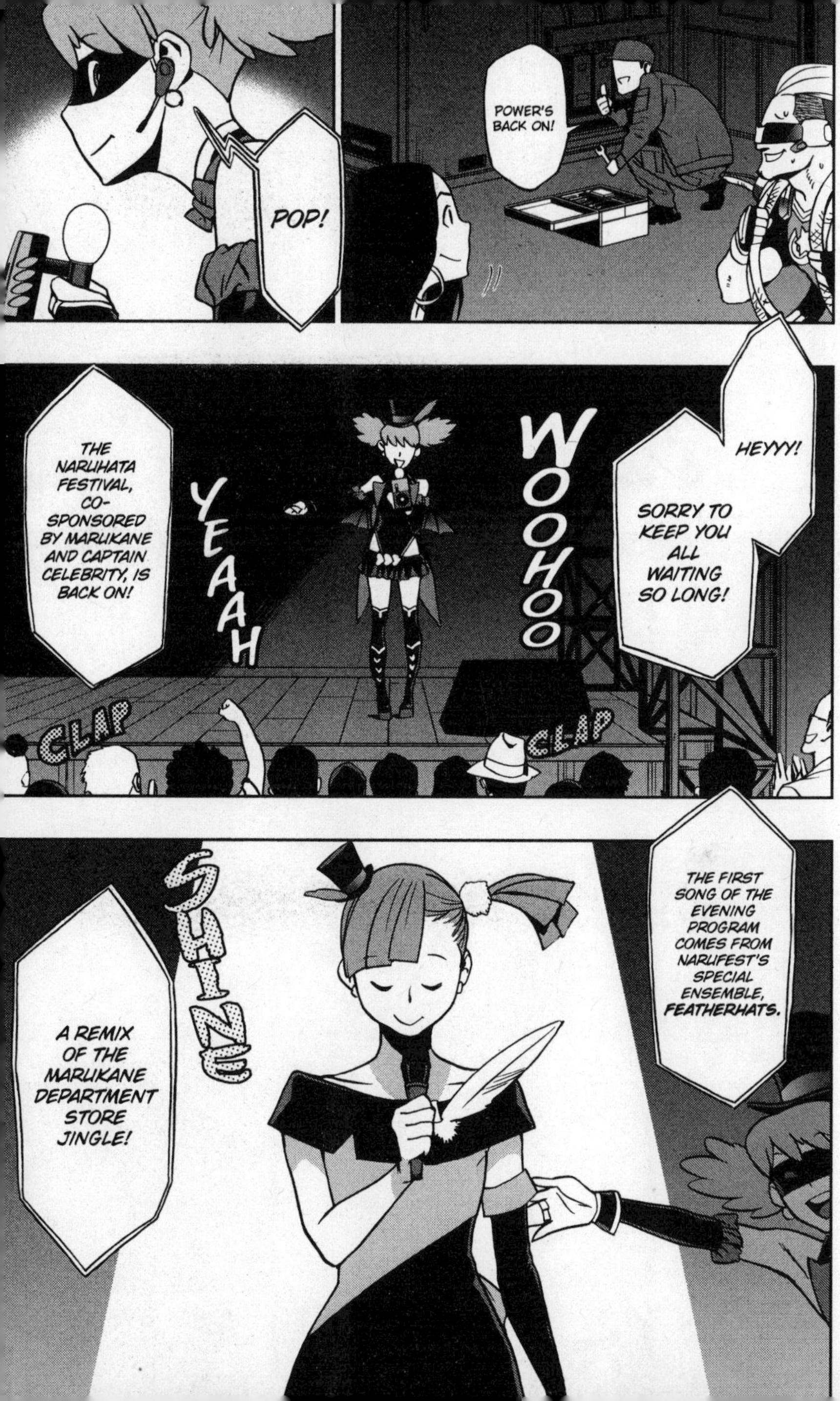
POWER'S BACK ON!
POP!
HEYYY!
SORRY TO KEEP YOU ALL WAITING SO LONG!
WOOHOO
YEAAH
THE NARUHATA FESTIVAL, CO-SPONSORED BY MARUKANE AND CAPTAIN CELEBRITY, IS BACK ON!
CLAP
CLAP
THE FIRST SONG OF THE EVENING PROGRAM COMES FROM NARUFEST'S SPECIAL ENSEMBLE, **FEATHERHATS.**
SHINE
A REMIX OF THE MARUKANE DEPARTMENT STORE JINGLE!

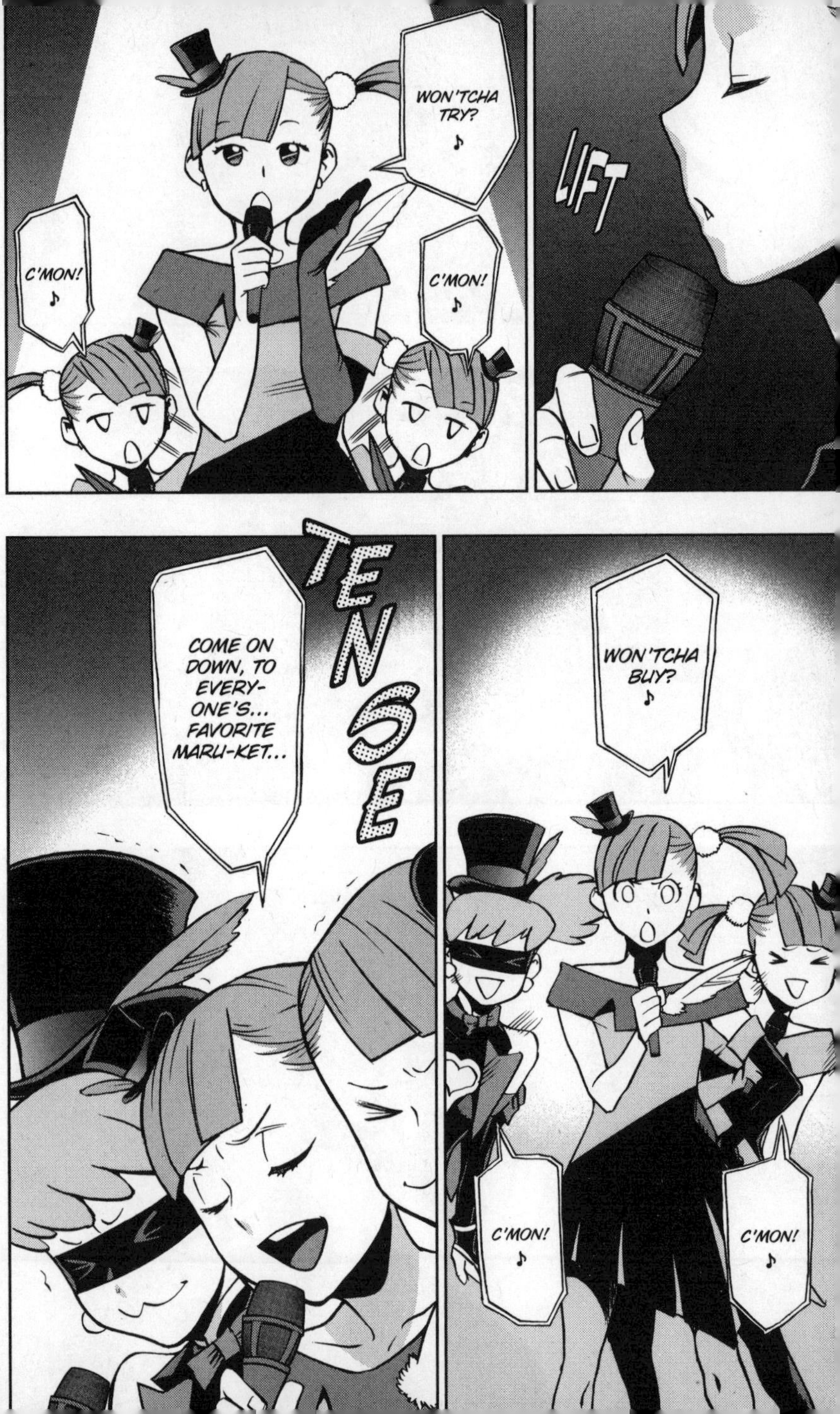
LIFT
WON'TCHA TRY? ♪
C'MON! ♪
C'MON! ♪
WON'TCHA BUY? ♪
C'MON! ♪
C'MON! ♪
TENSE
COME ON DOWN, TO EVERY-ONE'S... FAVORITE MARU-KET...

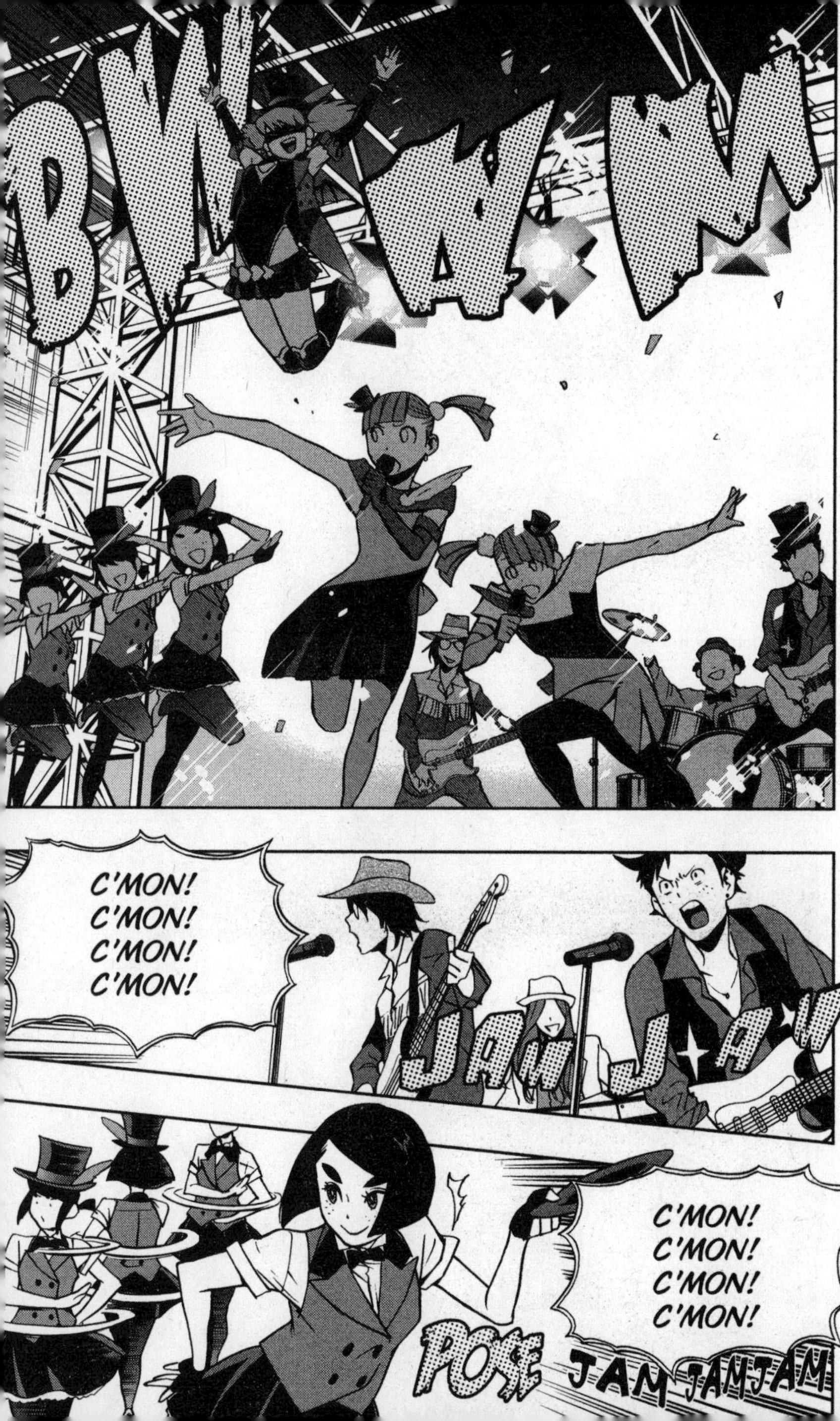
BWAM
C'MON! C'MON! C'MON! C'MON!
JAM JAM!
C'MON! C'MON! C'MON! C'MON!
POSE
JAM JAMJAM

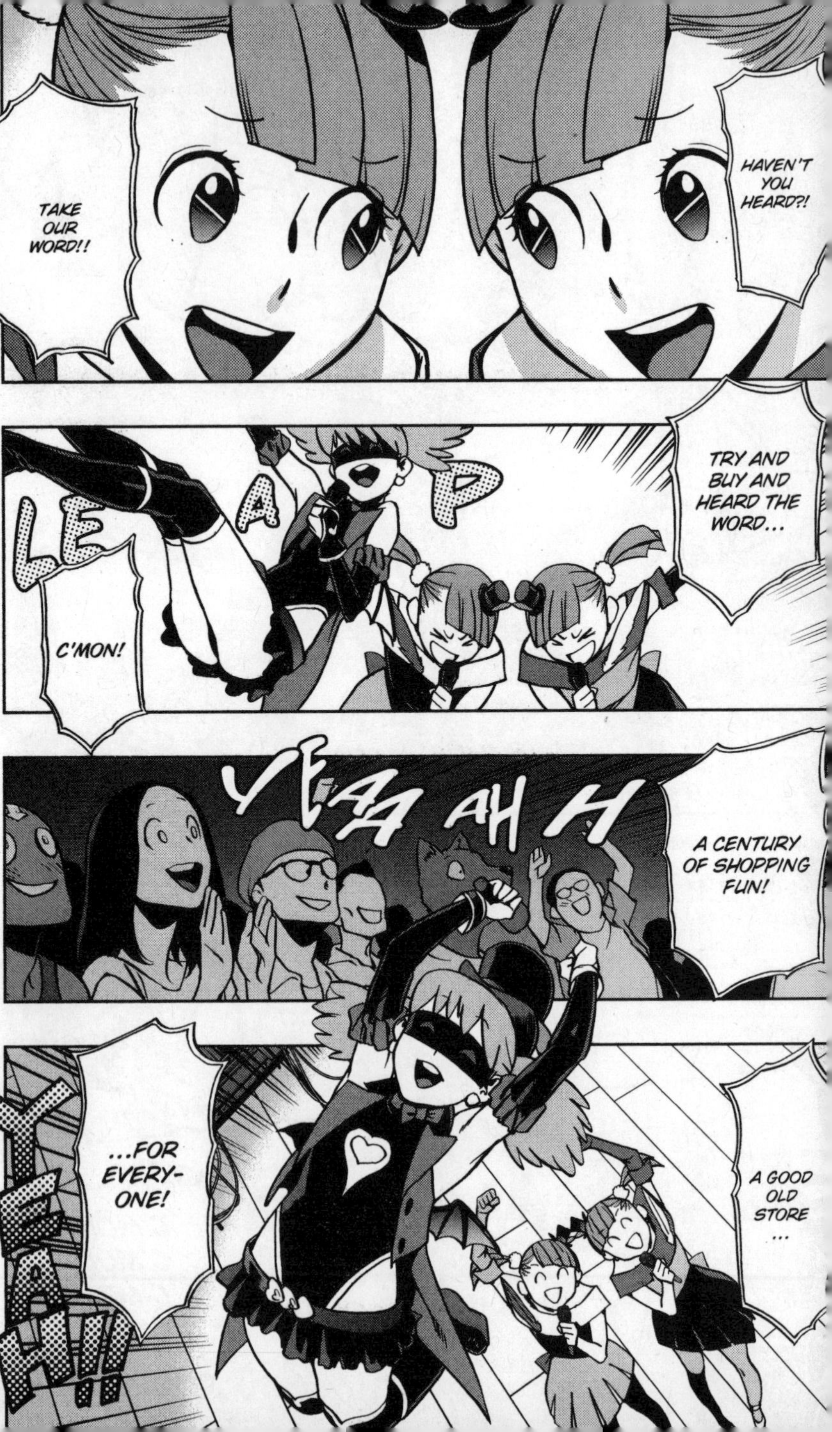
HAVEN'T YOU HEARD?!
TAKE OUR WORD!!
TRY AND BUY AND HEARD THE WORD...
LEAP
C'MON!
A CENTURY OF SHOPPING FUN!
YEAAAHH
A GOOD OLD STORE ...
...FOR EVERY-ONE!
YEAH!!!

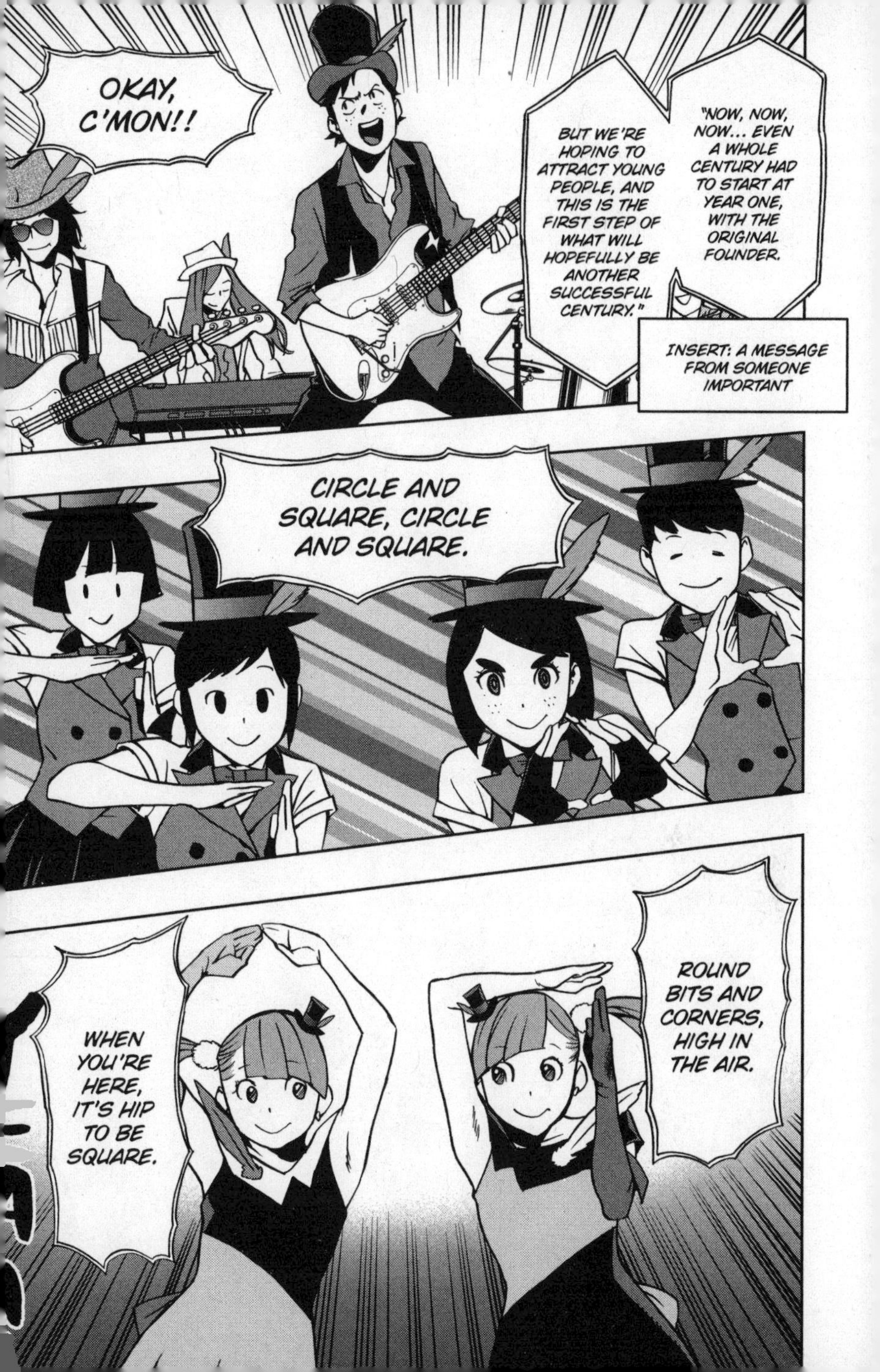
"NOW, NOW, NOW... EVEN A WHOLE CENTURY HAD TO START AT YEAR ONE, WITH THE ORIGINAL FOUNDER.
BUT WE'RE HOPING TO ATTRACT YOUNG PEOPLE, AND THIS IS THE FIRST STEP OF WHAT WILL HOPEFULLY BE ANOTHER SUCCESSFUL CENTURY."
INSERT: A MESSAGE FROM SOMEONE IMPORTANT
OKAY, C'MON!!
CIRCLE AND SQUARE, CIRCLE AND SQUARE.
ROUND BITS AND CORNERS, HIGH IN THE AIR.
WHEN YOU'RE HERE, IT'S HIP TO BE SQUARE.

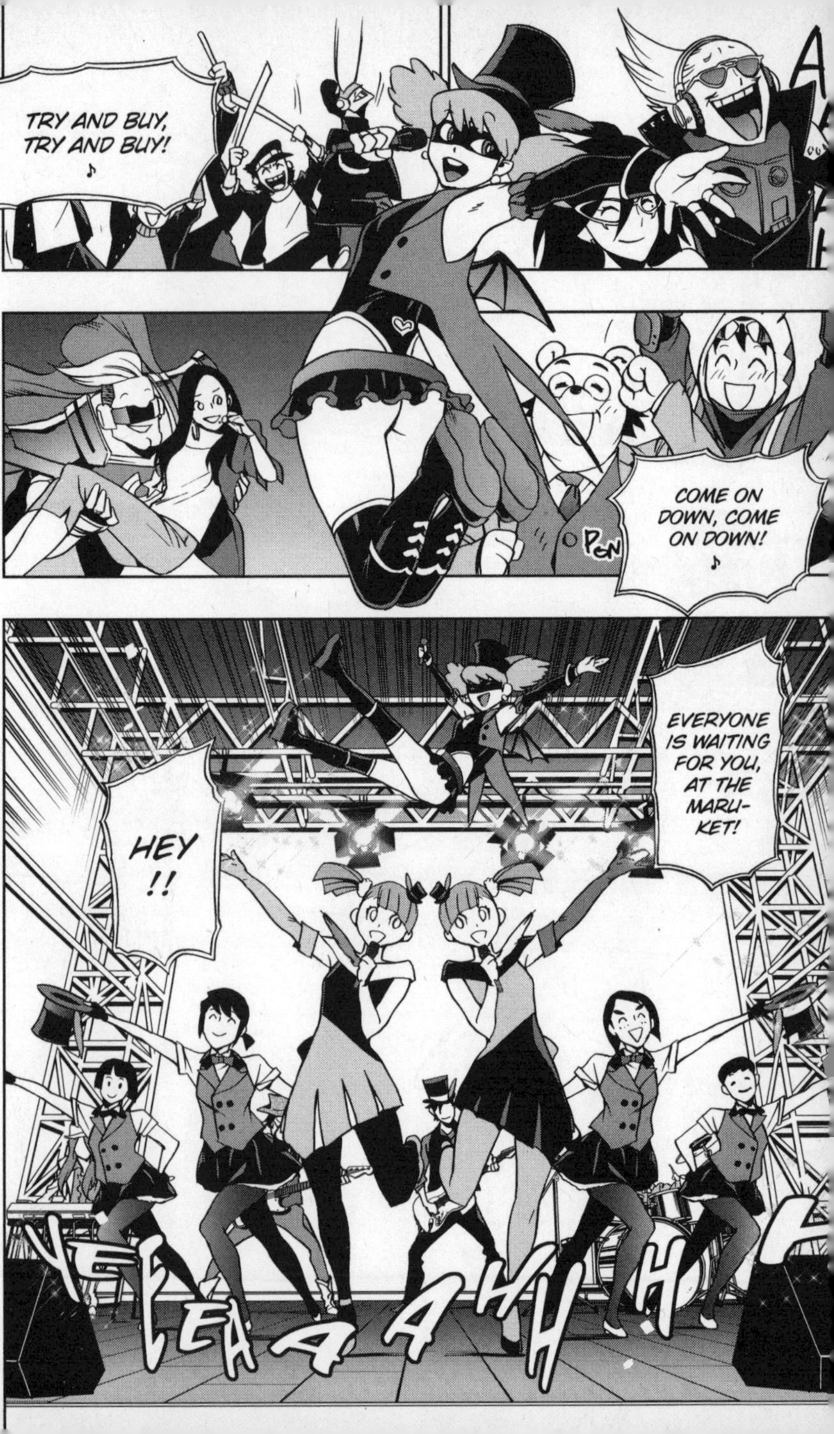
TRY AND BUY, TRY AND BUY! ♪
COME ON DOWN, COME ON DOWN! ♪
PON
EVERYONE IS WAITING FOR YOU, AT THE MARU-KET!
HEY !!
YEEEAAAHHHH

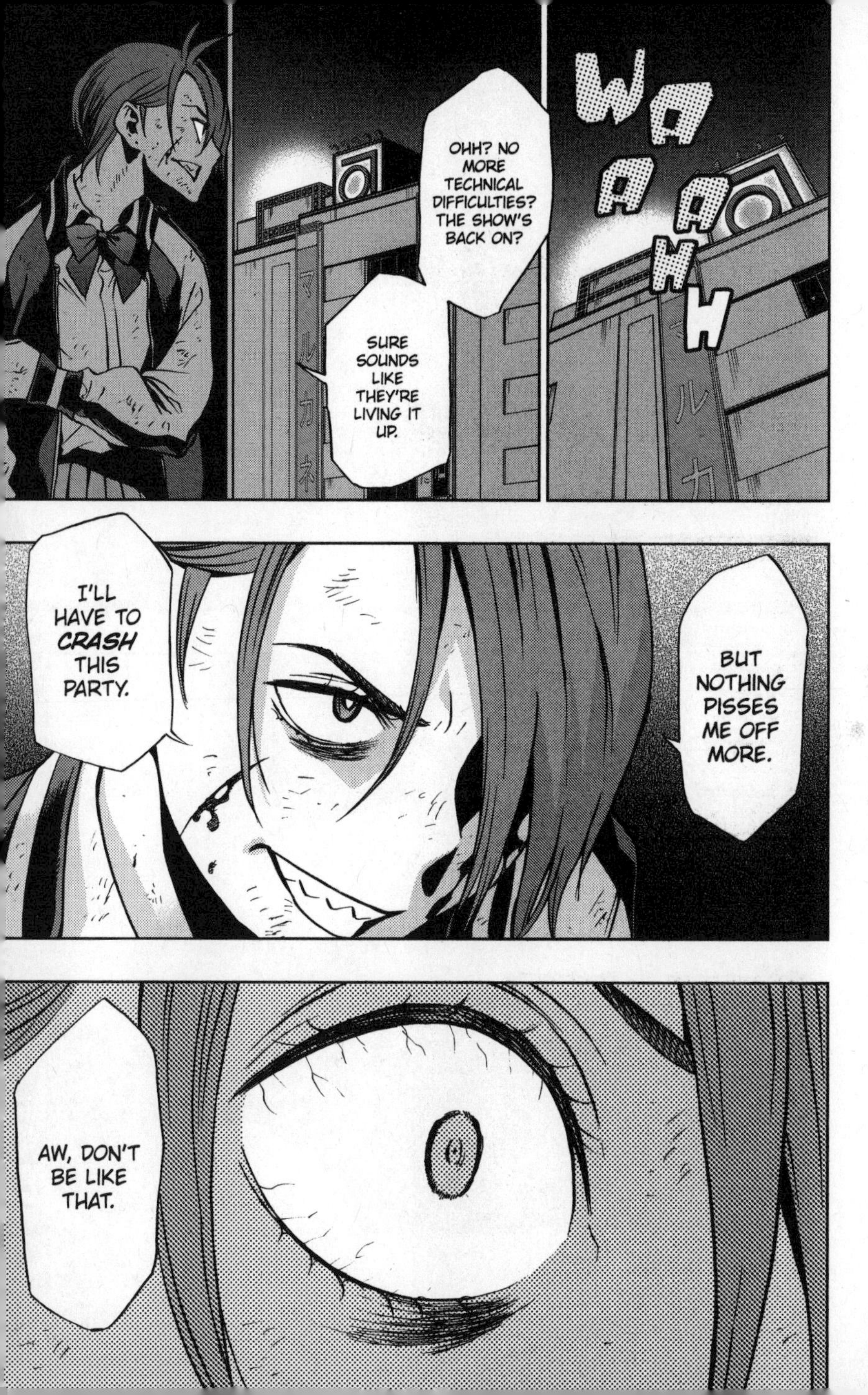
WAAAHH
OHH? NO MORE TECHNICAL DIFFICULTIES? THE SHOW'S BACK ON?
SURE SOUNDS LIKE THEY'RE LIVING IT UP.
BUT NOTHING PISSES ME OFF MORE.
I'LL HAVE TO *CRASH* THIS PARTY.
AW, DON'T BE LIKE THAT.

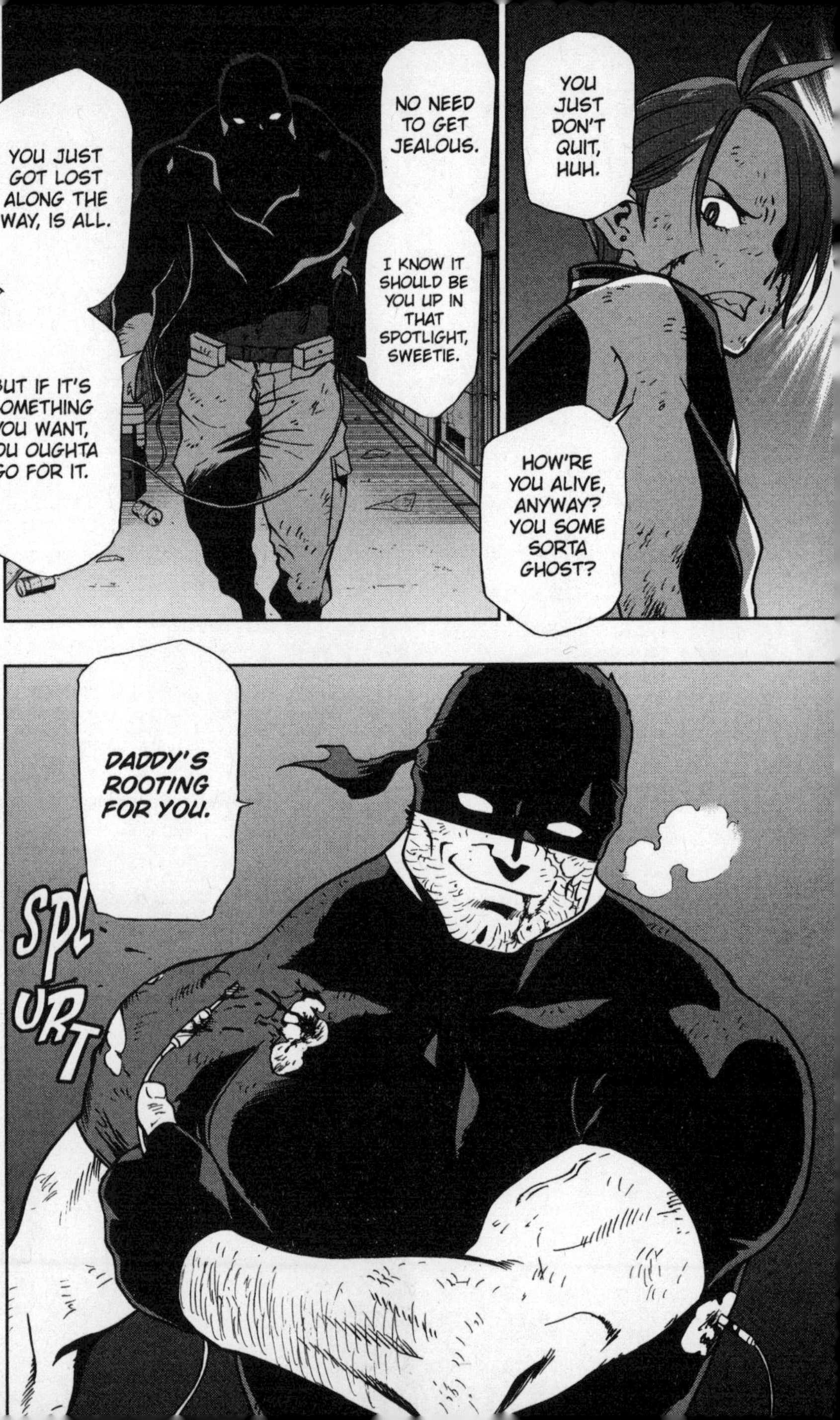
YOU JUST DON'T QUIT, HUH.
HOW'RE YOU ALIVE, ANYWAY? YOU SOME SORTA GHOST?
NO NEED TO GET JEALOUS.
I KNOW IT SHOULD BE YOU UP IN THAT SPOTLIGHT, SWEETIE.
YOU JUST GOT LOST ALONG THE WAY, IS ALL.
BUT IF IT'S SOMETHING YOU WANT, YOU OUGHTA GO FOR IT.
DADDY'S ROOTING FOR YOU.
SPLURT

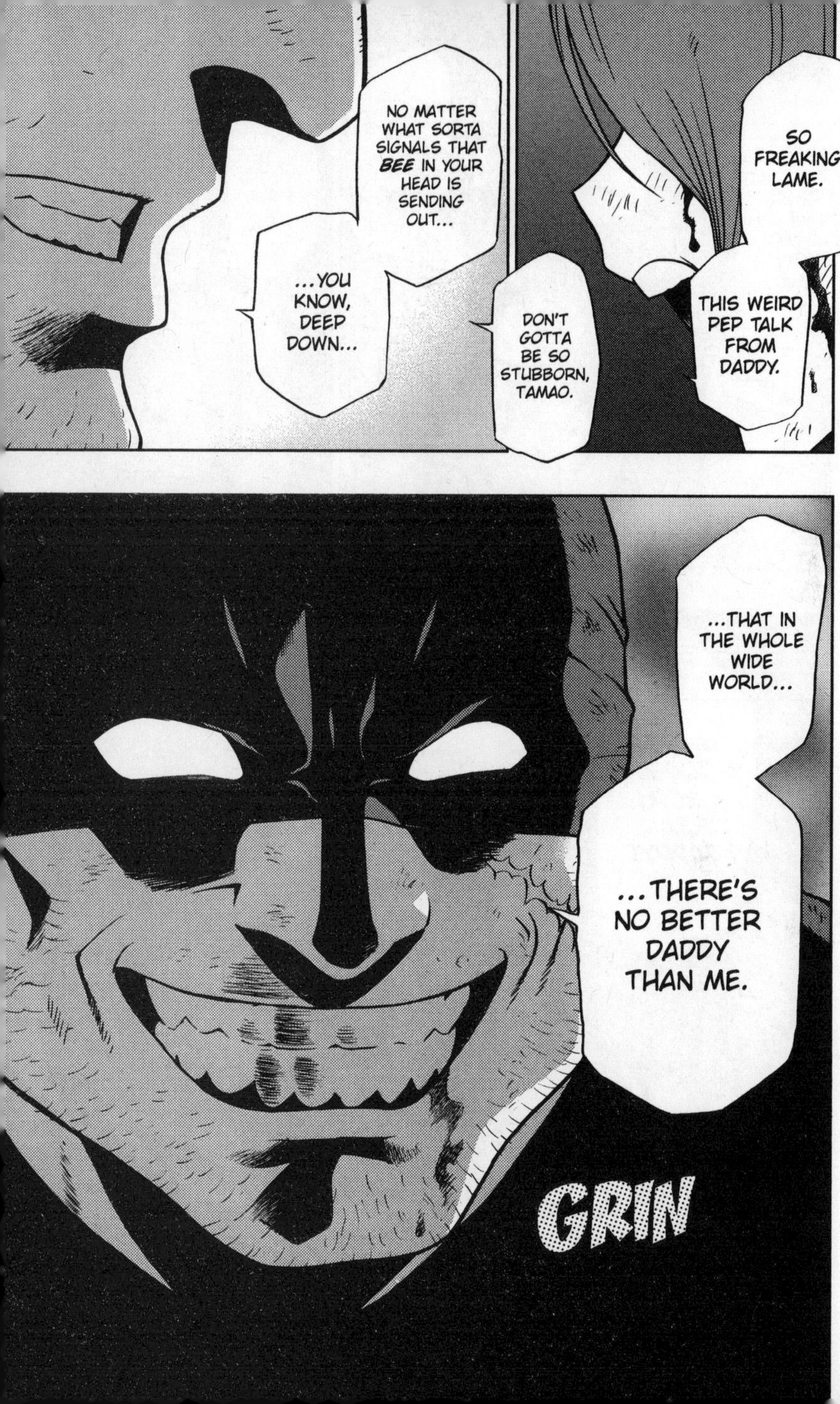
SO FREAKING LAME.
THIS WEIRD PEP TALK FROM DADDY.
DON'T GOTTA BE SO STUBBORN, TAMAO.
NO MATTER WHAT SORTA SIGNALS THAT *BEE* IN YOUR HEAD IS SENDING OUT...
...YOU KNOW, DEEP DOWN...
...THAT IN THE WHOLE WIDE WORLD...
...THERE'S NO BETTER DADDY THAN ME.
GRIN

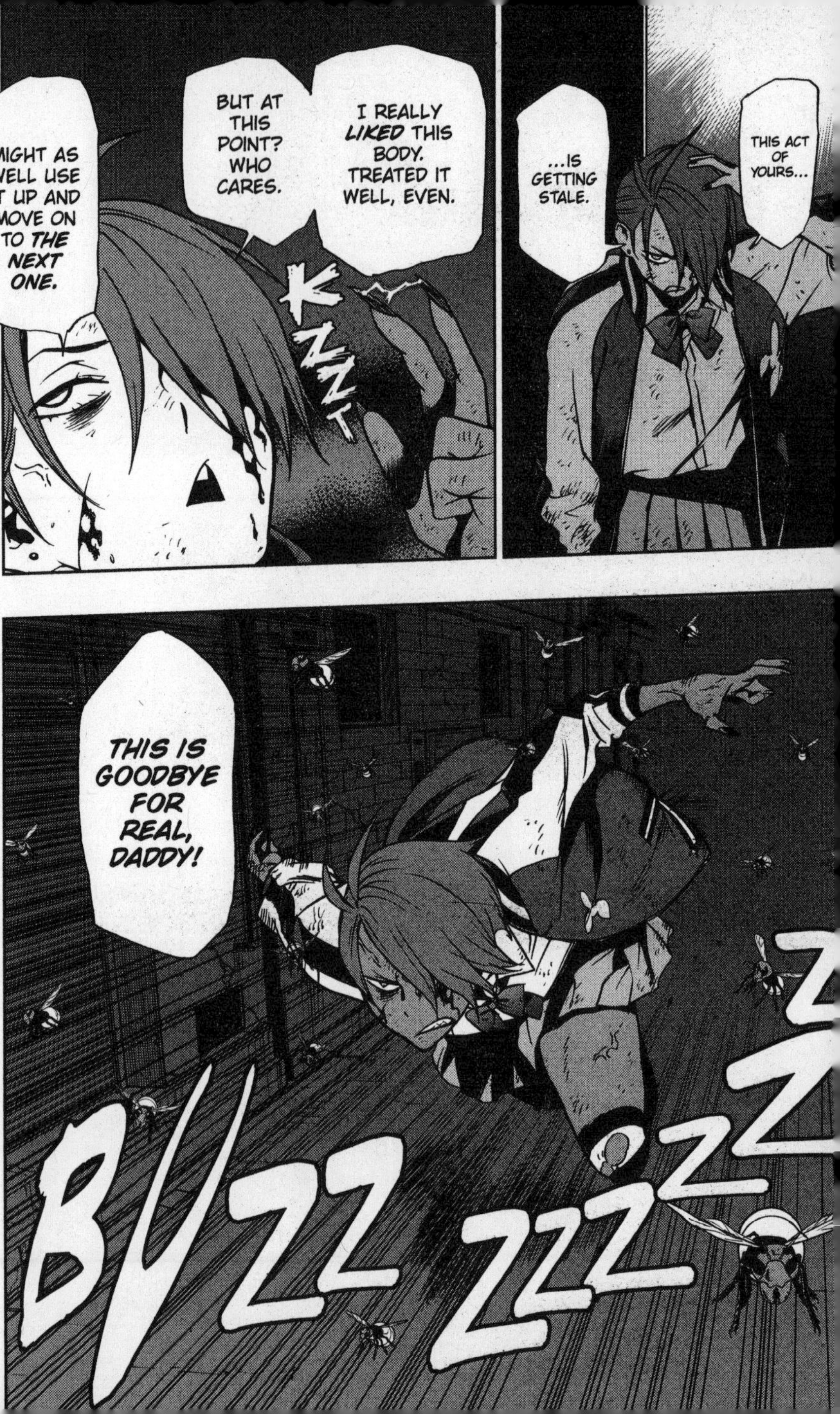
THIS ACT OF YOURS...
...IS GETTING STALE.
I REALLY *LIKED* THIS BODY. TREATED IT WELL, EVEN.
BUT AT THIS POINT? WHO CARES.
MIGHT AS WELL USE IT UP AND MOVE ON TO *THE NEXT ONE.*
KZZT
THIS IS GOODBYE FOR REAL, DADDY!
BUZZ ZZZZZ

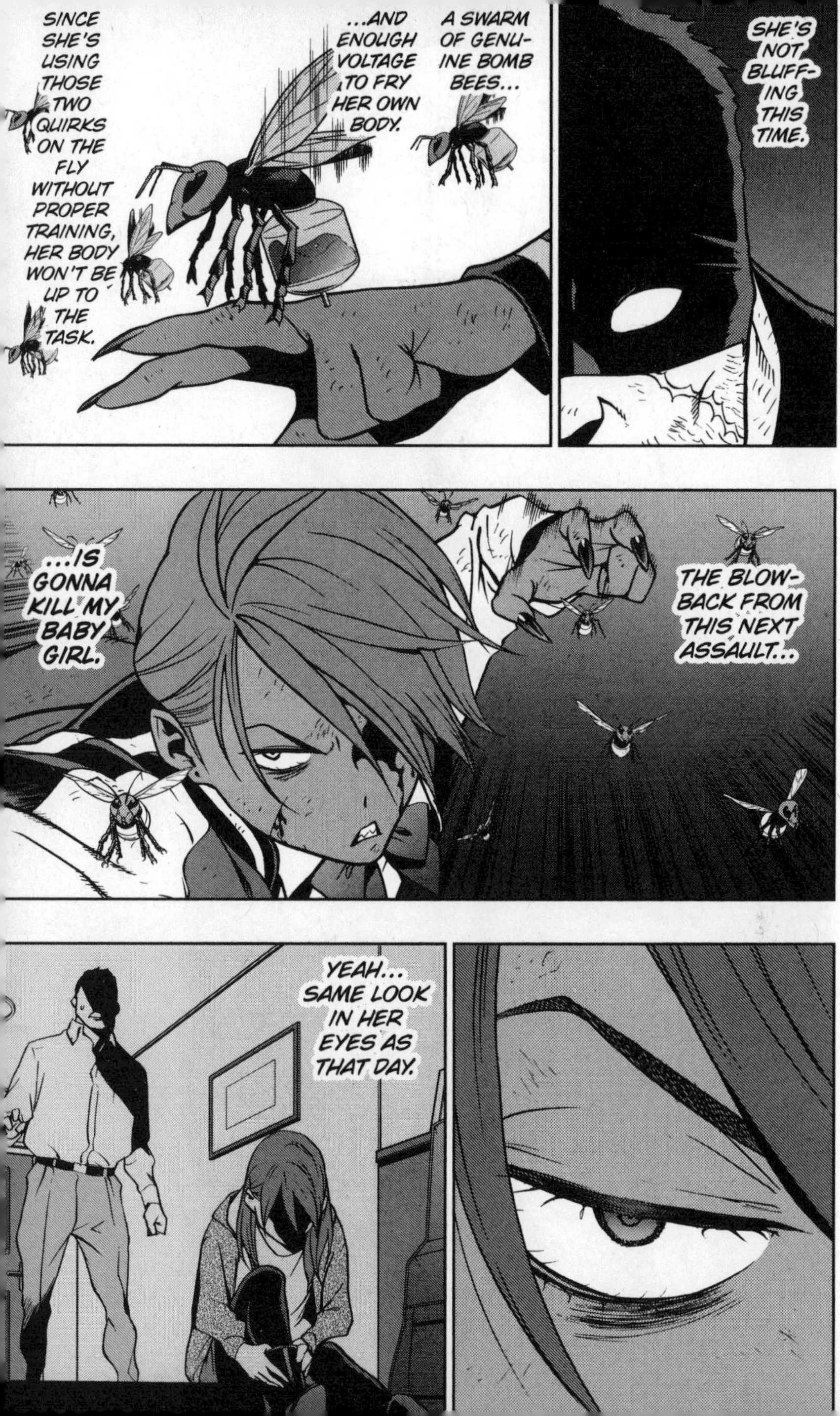
SHE'S NOT BLUFFING THIS TIME.
A SWARM OF GENUINE BOMB BEES...
...AND ENOUGH VOLTAGE TO FRY HER OWN BODY.
SINCE SHE'S USING THOSE TWO QUIRKS ON THE FLY WITHOUT PROPER TRAINING, HER BODY WON'T BE UP TO THE TASK.
THE BLOWBACK FROM THIS NEXT ASSAULT...
...IS GONNA KILL MY BABY GIRL.
YEAH... SAME LOOK IN HER EYES AS THAT DAY.

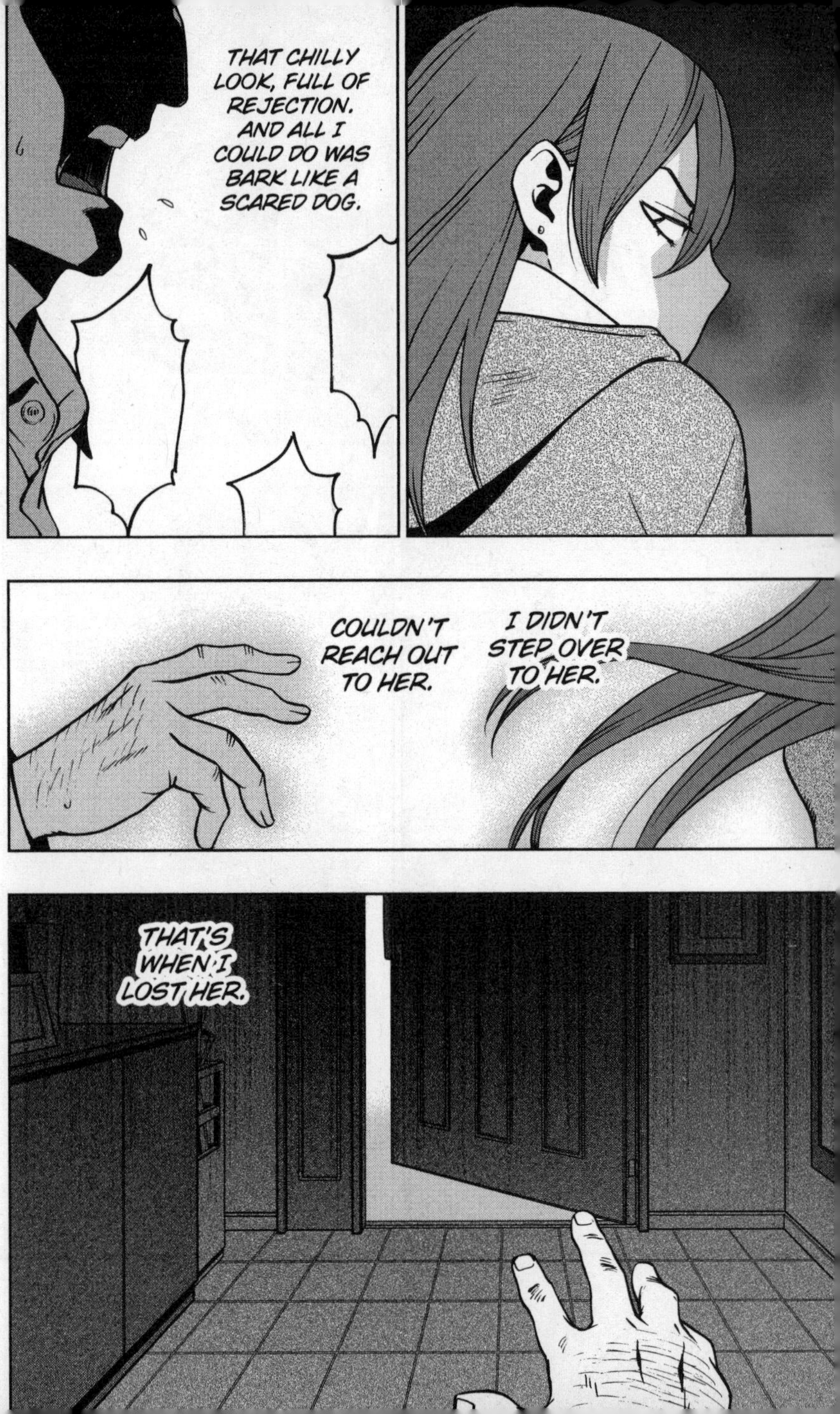
THAT CHILLY LOOK, FULL OF REJECTION. AND ALL I COULD DO WAS BARK LIKE A SCARED DOG.
I DIDN'T STEP OVER TO HER.
COULDN'T REACH OUT TO HER.
THAT'S WHEN I LOST HER.

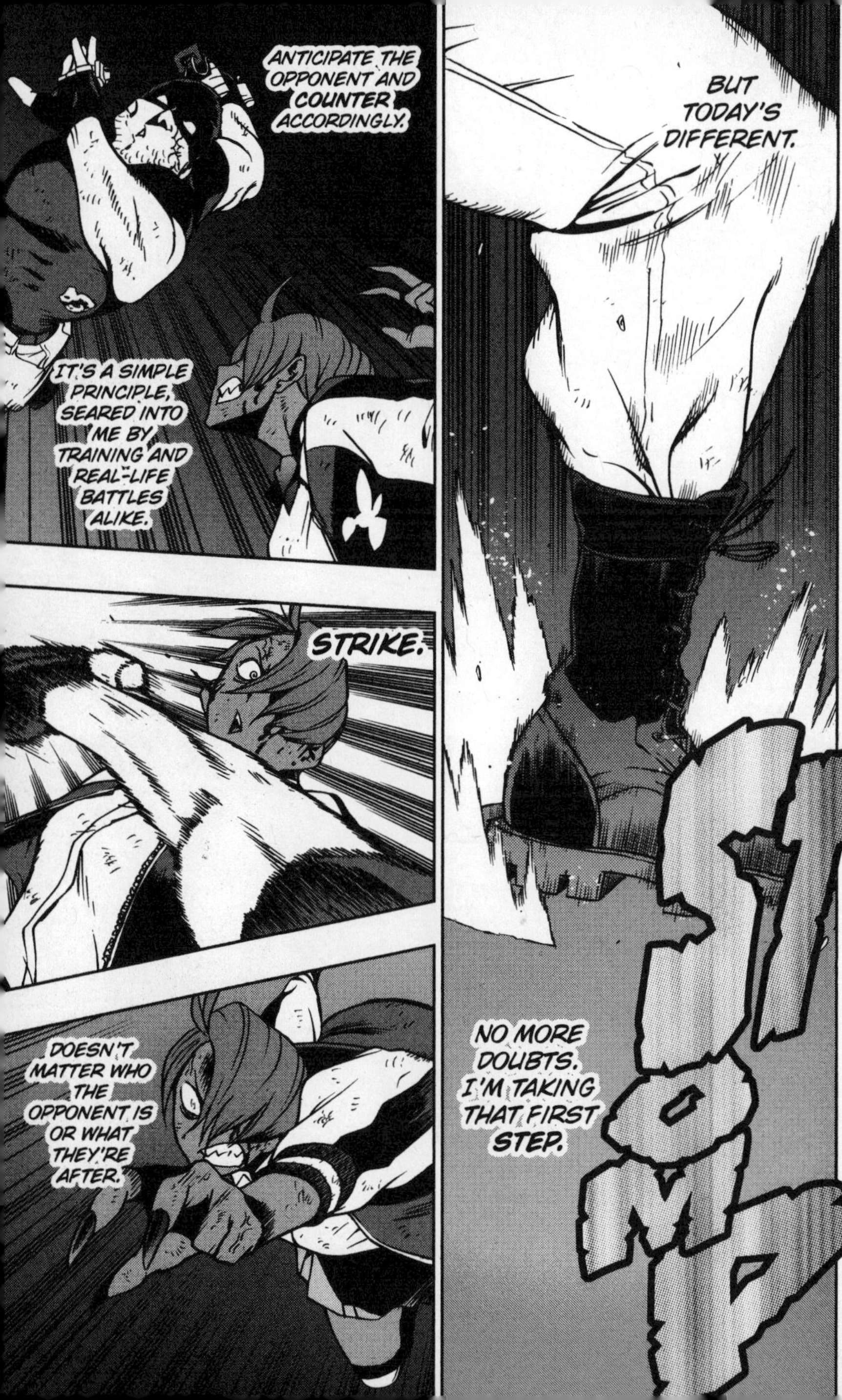
ANTICIPATE THE OPPONENT AND COUNTER ACCORDINGLY.
IT'S A SIMPLE PRINCIPLE, SEARED INTO ME BY TRAINING AND REAL-LIFE BATTLES ALIKE.
STRIKE.
DOESN'T MATTER WHO THE OPPONENT IS OR WHAT THEY'RE AFTER.
BUT TODAY'S DIFFERENT.
NO MORE DOUBTS. I'M TAKING THAT FIRST STEP.
STOMP

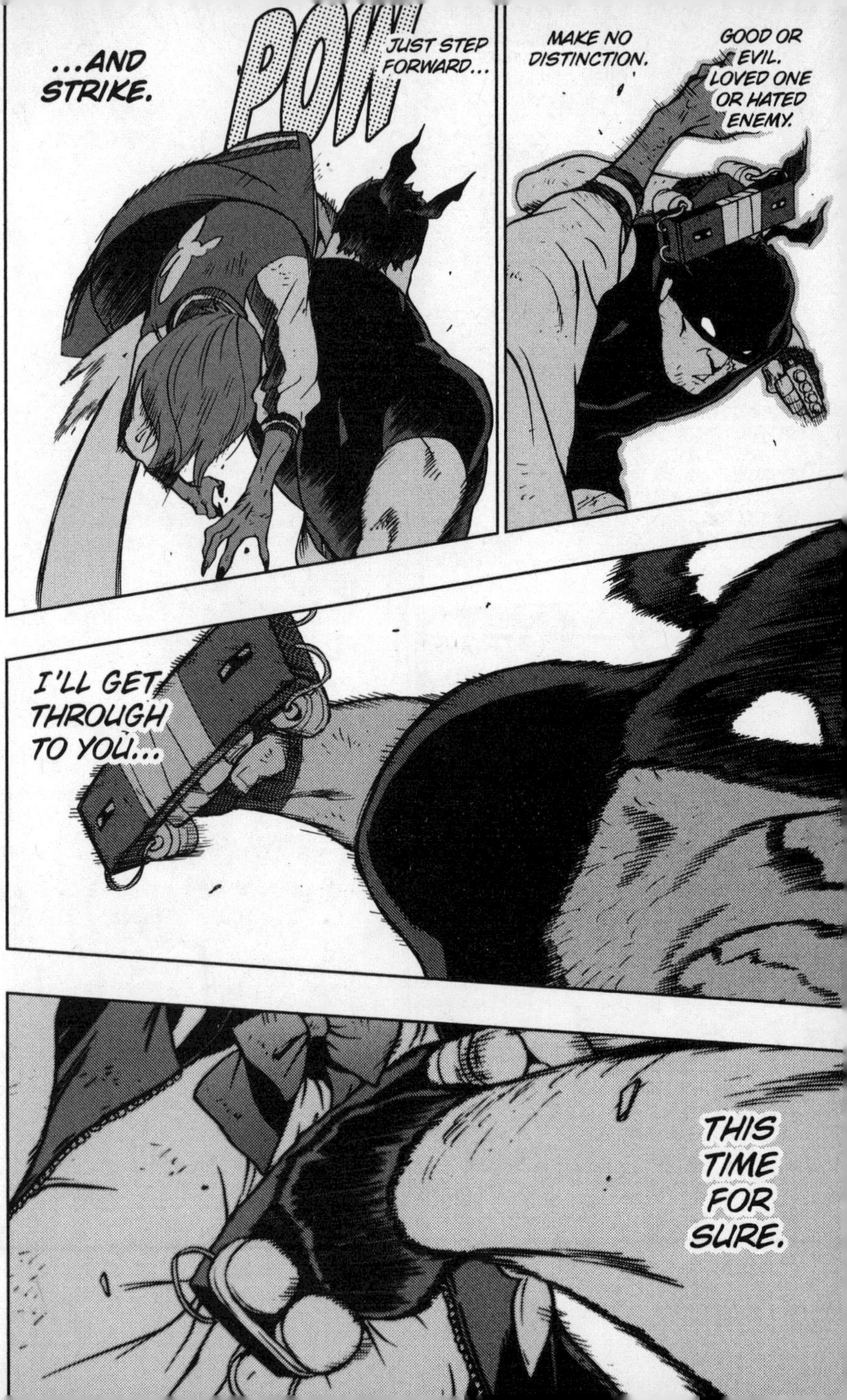
GOOD OR EVIL. LOVED ONE OR HATED ENEMY.
MAKE NO DISTINCTION.
JUST STEP FORWARD...
POW
...AND STRIKE.
I'LL GET THROUGH TO YOU...
THIS TIME FOR SURE.

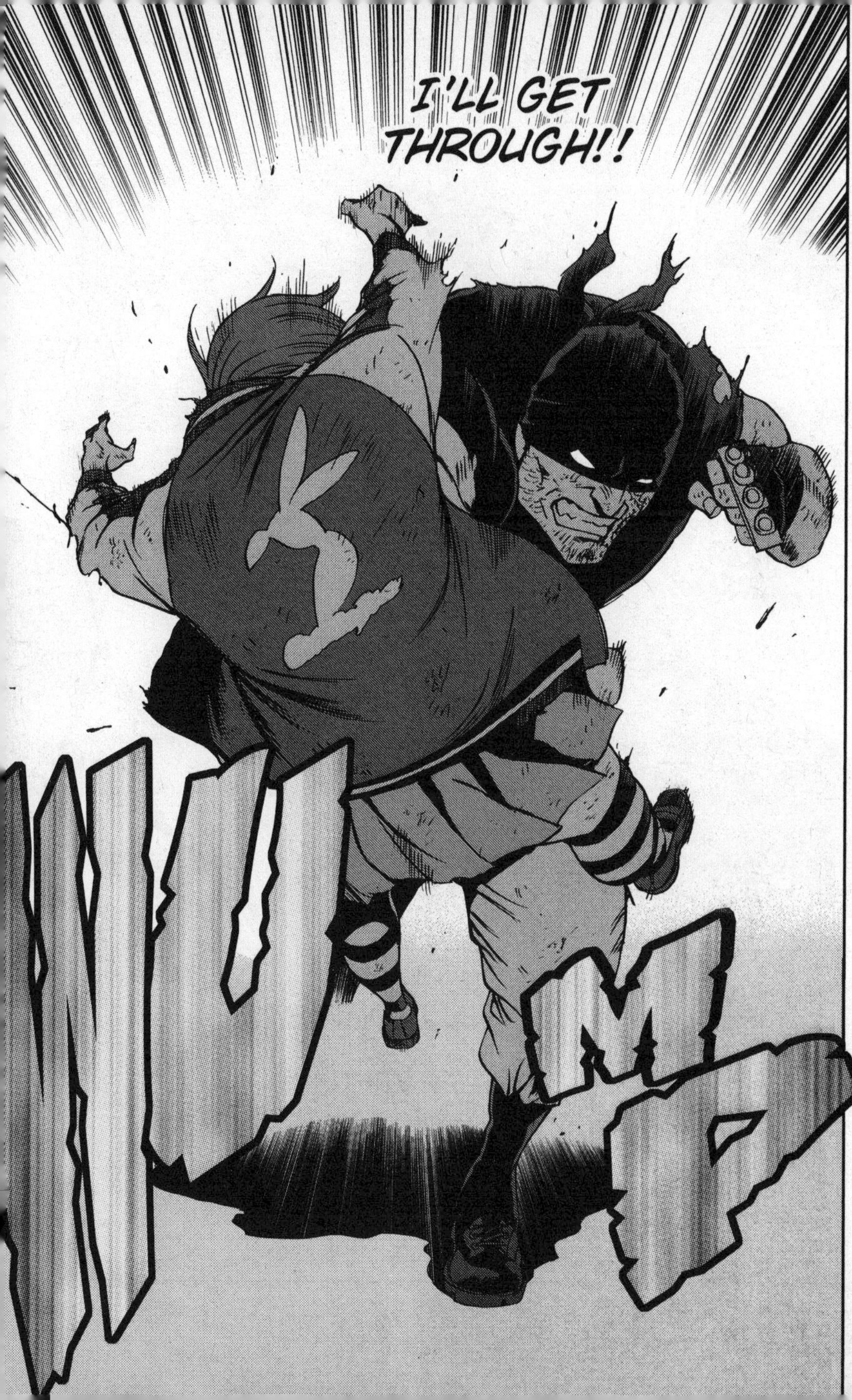
I'LL GET THROUGH!!
WUMP

CONGRATULATIONS ON VOLUME 4!
KNUCKLEDUSTER REALLY IS THE GREATEST!!

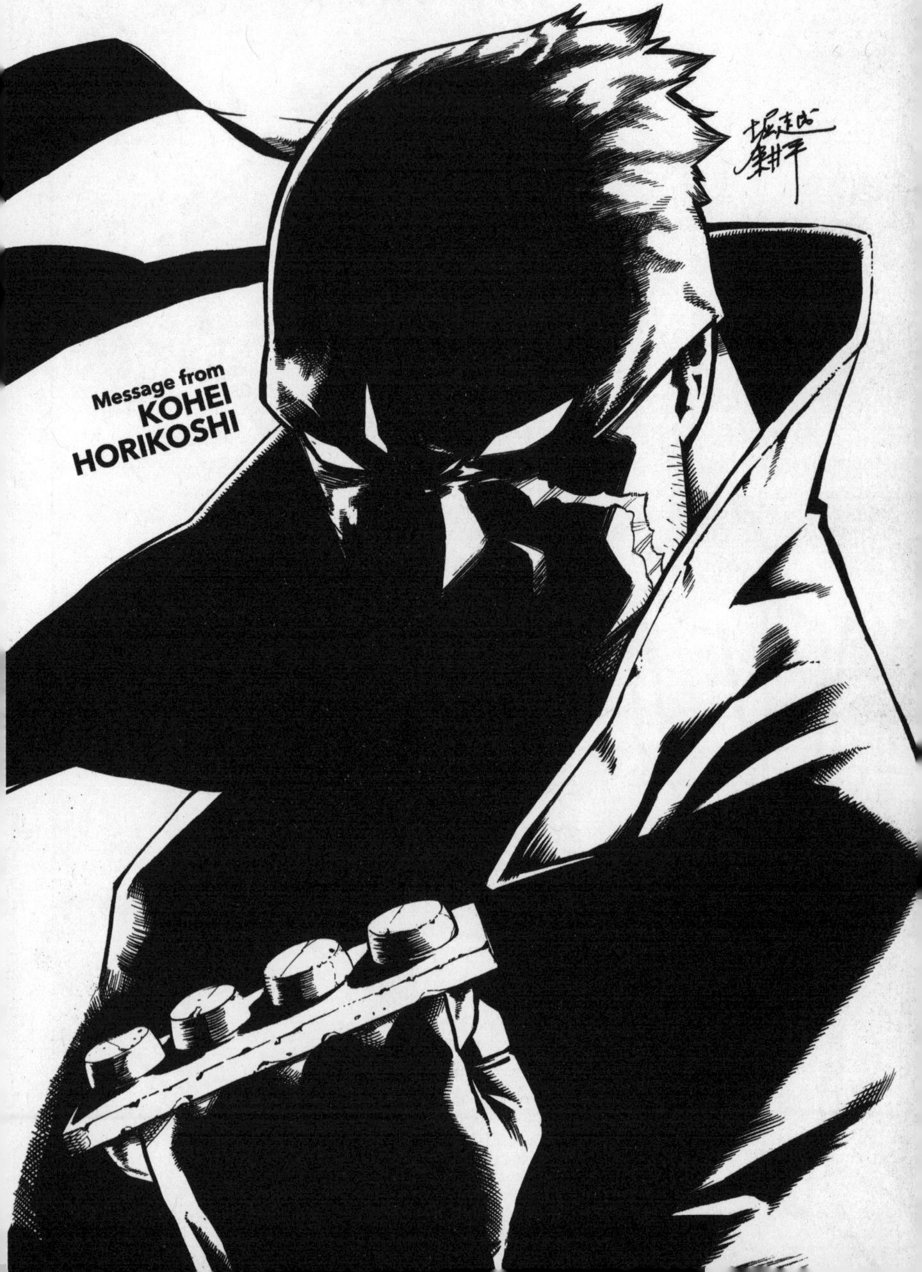
Message from
KOHEI
HORIKOSHI

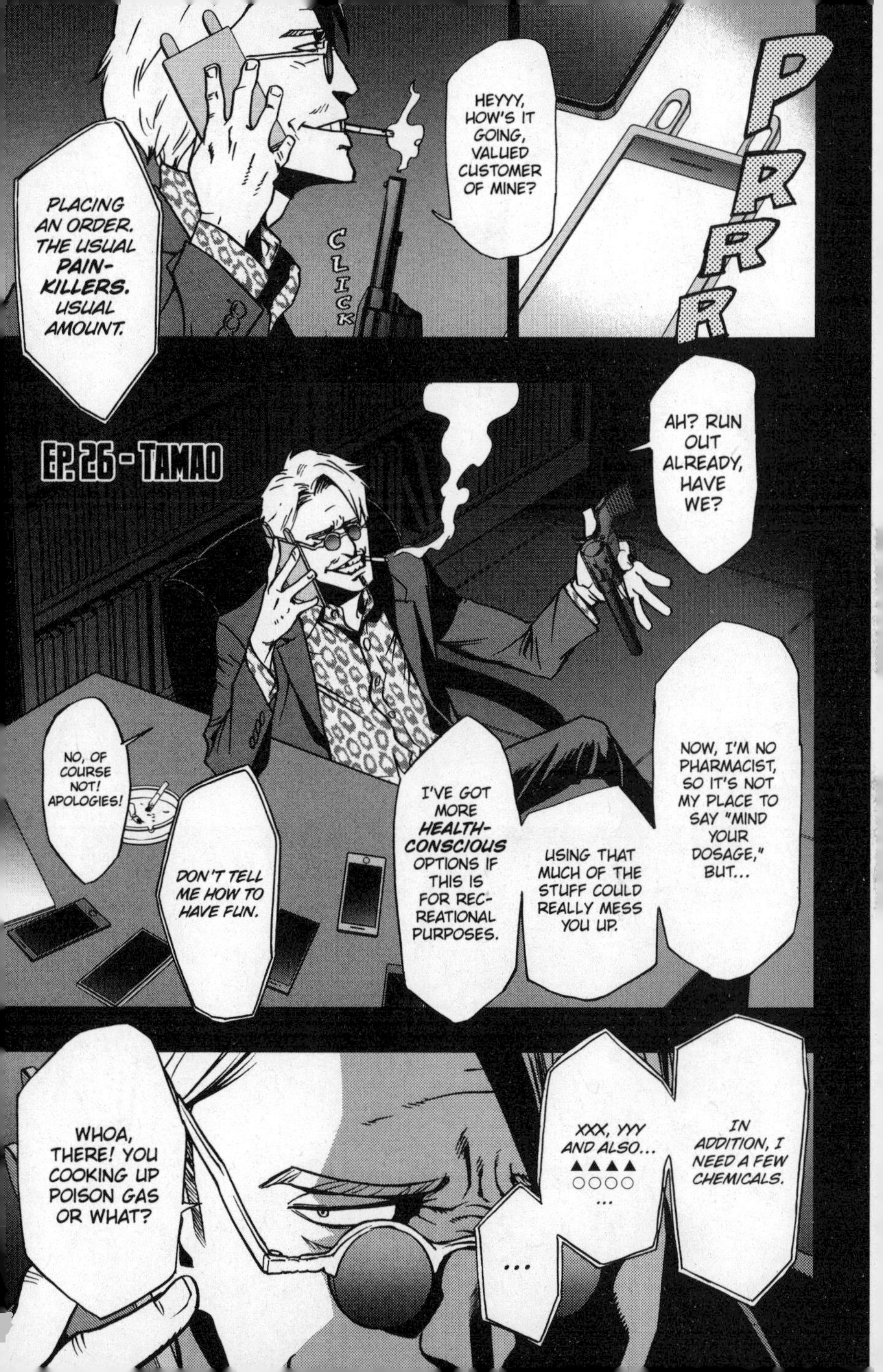
PRRR
HEYYY, HOW'S IT GOING, VALUED CUSTOMER OF MINE?
CLICK
PLACING AN ORDER. THE USUAL **PAIN-KILLERS.** USUAL AMOUNT.
AH? RUN OUT ALREADY, HAVE WE?
EP. 26 - TAMAO
NOW, I'M NO PHARMACIST, SO IT'S NOT MY PLACE TO SAY "MIND YOUR DOSAGE," BUT...
USING THAT MUCH OF THE STUFF COULD REALLY MESS YOU UP.
I'VE GOT MORE ***HEALTH-CONSCIOUS*** OPTIONS IF THIS IS FOR REC-REATIONAL PURPOSES.
NO, OF COURSE NOT! APOLOGIES!
DON'T TELL ME HOW TO HAVE FUN.
IN ADDITION, I NEED A FEW CHEMICALS.
XXX, YYY AND ALSO... ▲▲▲▲ ○○○○ ...
...
WHOA, THERE! YOU COOKING UP POISON GAS OR WHAT?

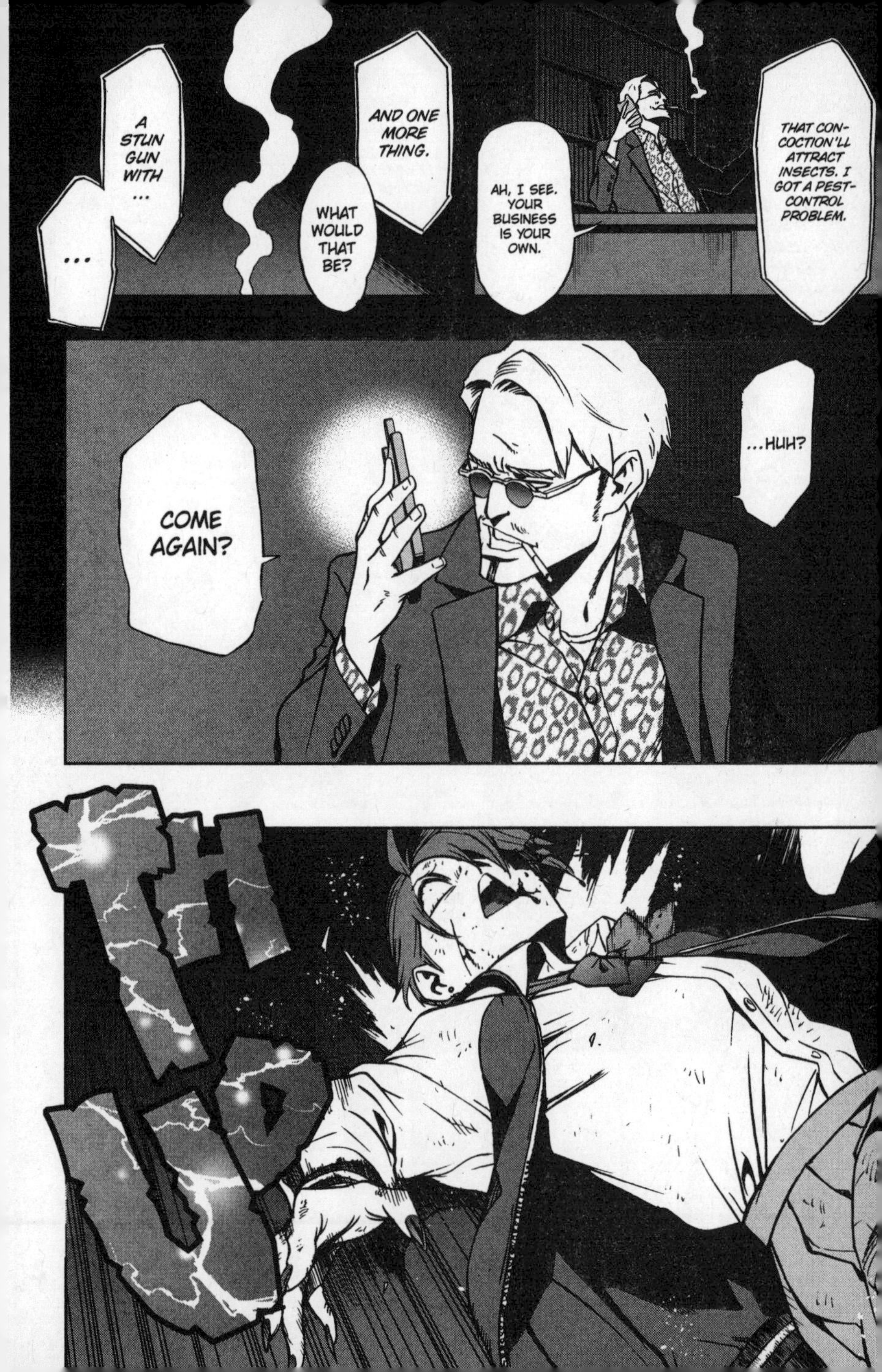
THAT CONCOCTION'LL ATTRACT INSECTS. I GOT A PEST-CONTROL PROBLEM.
AH, I SEE. YOUR BUSINESS IS YOUR OWN.
AND ONE MORE THING.
WHAT WOULD THAT BE?
A STUN GUN WITH ...
...
...HUH?
COME AGAIN?
THUD

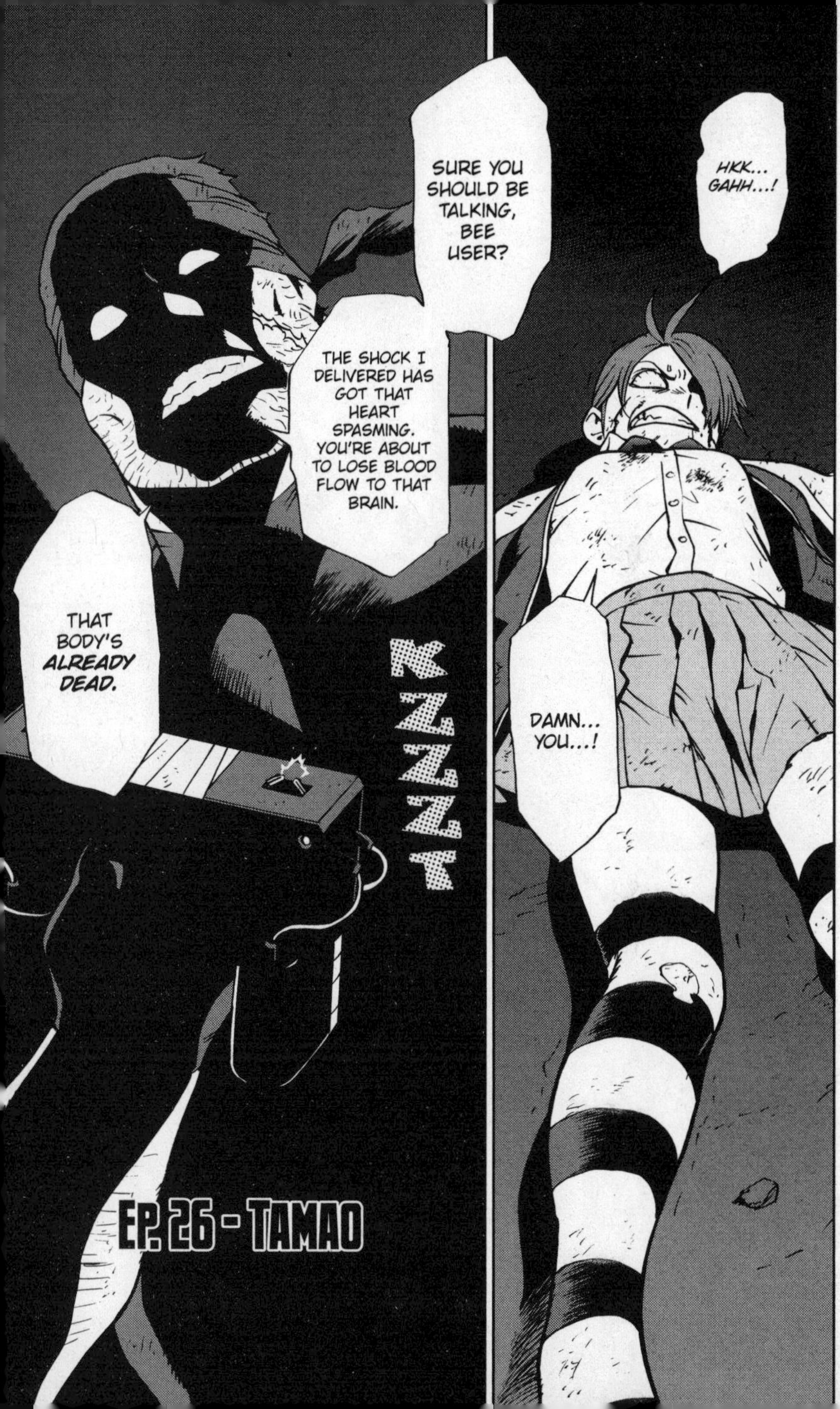
HKK... GAHH...!
DAMN... YOU...!
SURE YOU SHOULD BE TALKING, BEE USER?
THE SHOCK I DELIVERED HAS GOT THAT HEART SPASMING. YOU'RE ABOUT TO LOSE BLOOD FLOW TO THAT BRAIN.
THAT BODY'S ALREADY DEAD.
KZZZT
EP. 26 - TAMAO

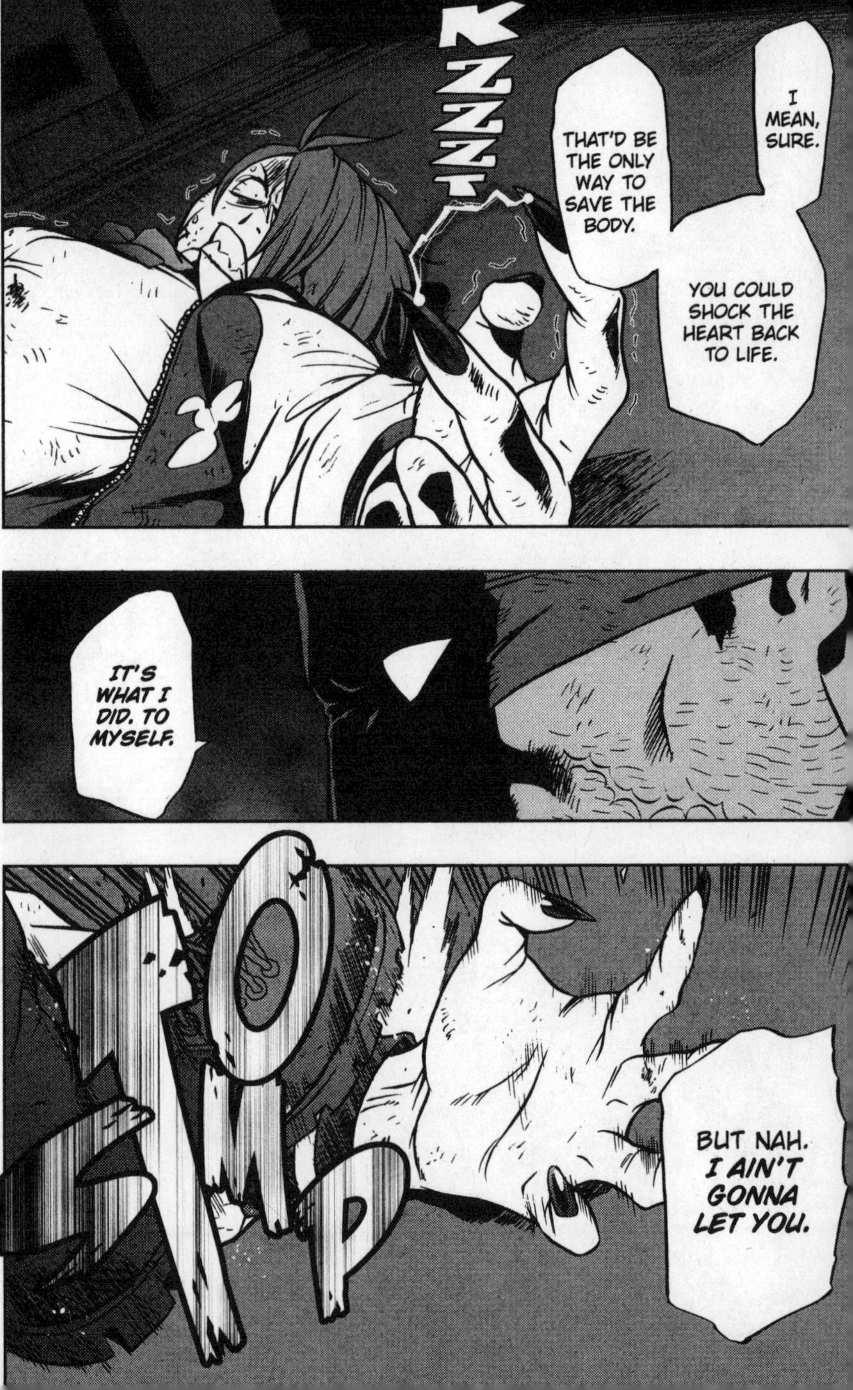
KZZZT
I MEAN, SURE.
YOU COULD SHOCK THE HEART BACK TO LIFE.
THAT'D BE THE ONLY WAY TO SAVE THE BODY.
IT'S WHAT I DID. TO MYSELF.
BUT NAH. I AIN'T GONNA LET YOU.

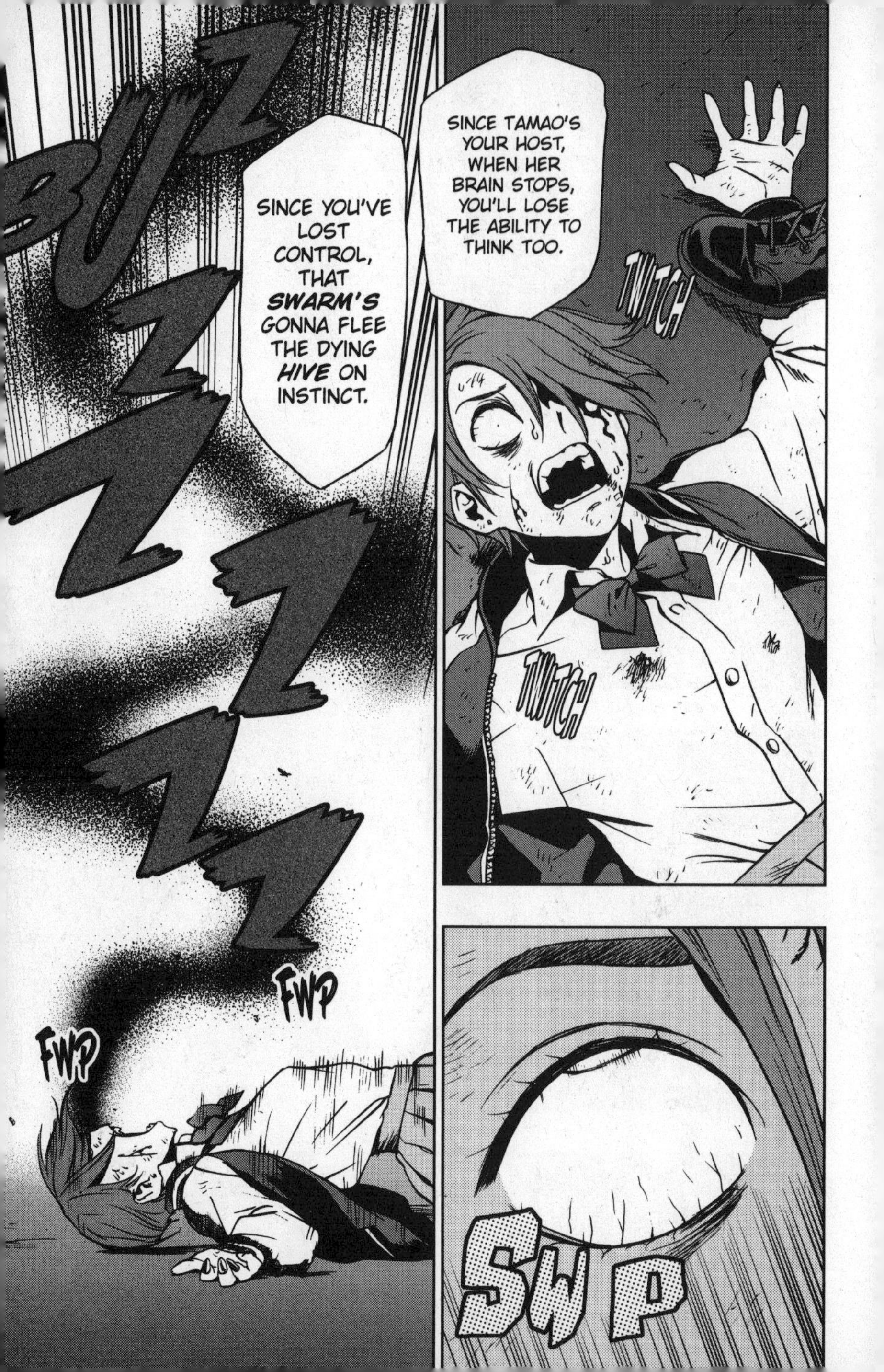
SINCE TAMAO'S YOUR HOST, WHEN HER BRAIN STOPS, YOU'LL LOSE THE ABILITY TO THINK TOO.
TWITCH
TWITCH
SWP
BUZZZZZZ
SINCE YOU'VE LOST CONTROL, THAT SWARM'S GONNA FLEE THE DYING HIVE ON INSTINCT.
FWP
FWP

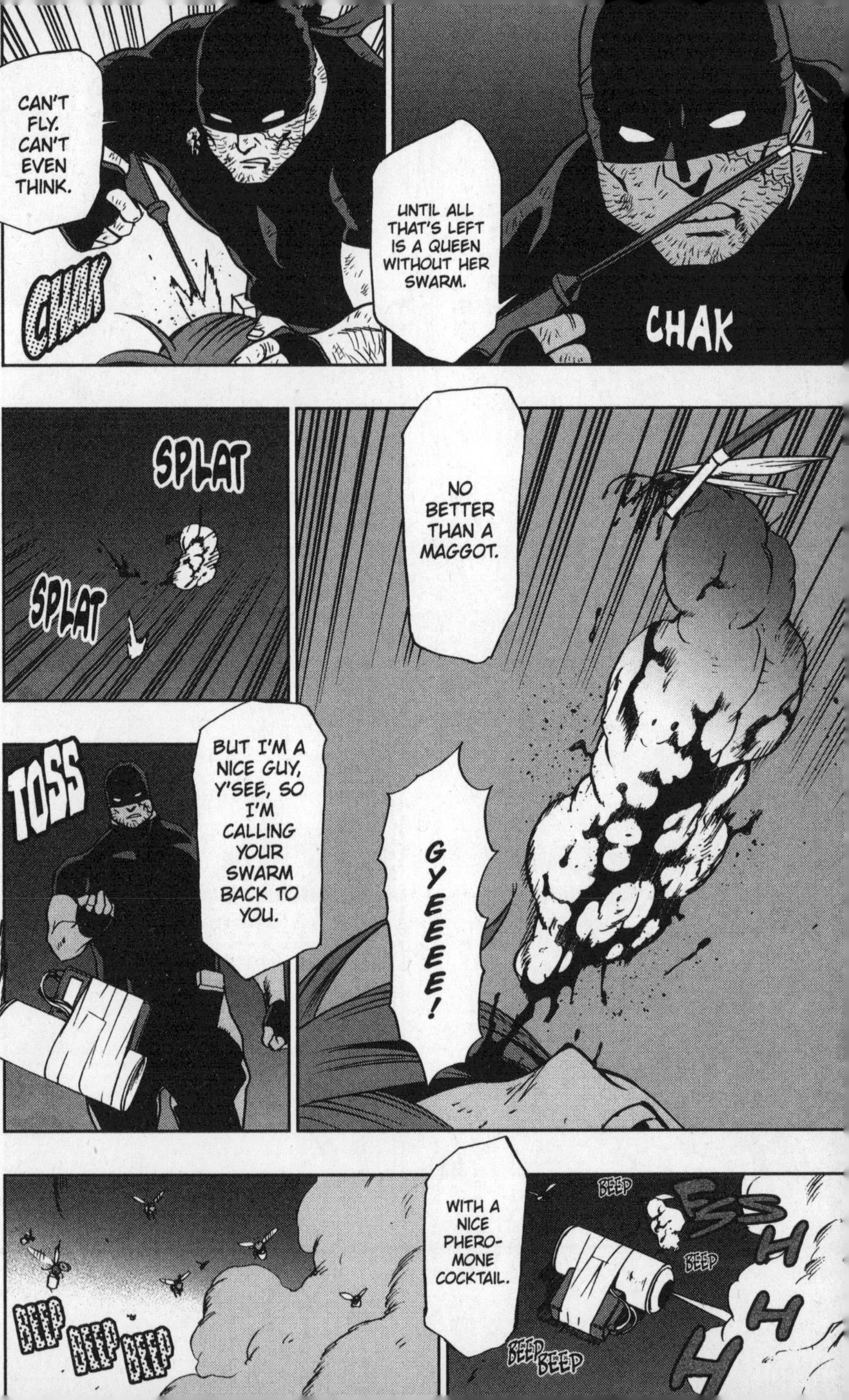
UNTIL ALL THAT'S LEFT IS A QUEEN WITHOUT HER SWARM.
CHAK
CAN'T FLY. CAN'T EVEN THINK.
CHUK
NO BETTER THAN A MAGGOT.
GYEEEEE!
SPLAT
SPLAT
TOSS
BUT I'M A NICE GUY, Y'SEE, SO I'M CALLING YOUR SWARM BACK TO YOU.
WITH A NICE PHERO-MONE COCKTAIL.
BEEP
FSSHHHH
BEEP
BEEP BEEP
BEEP BEEP BEEP

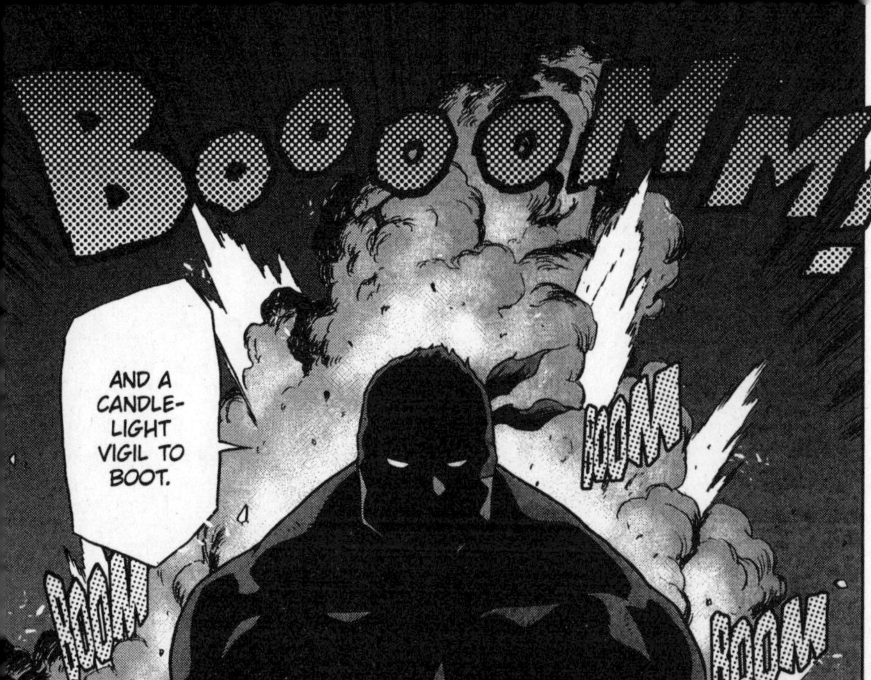
BOOOOOMM!
BOOM
AND A CANDLE-LIGHT VIGIL TO BOOT.
BOOM
BOOM
BOOM
BOOM
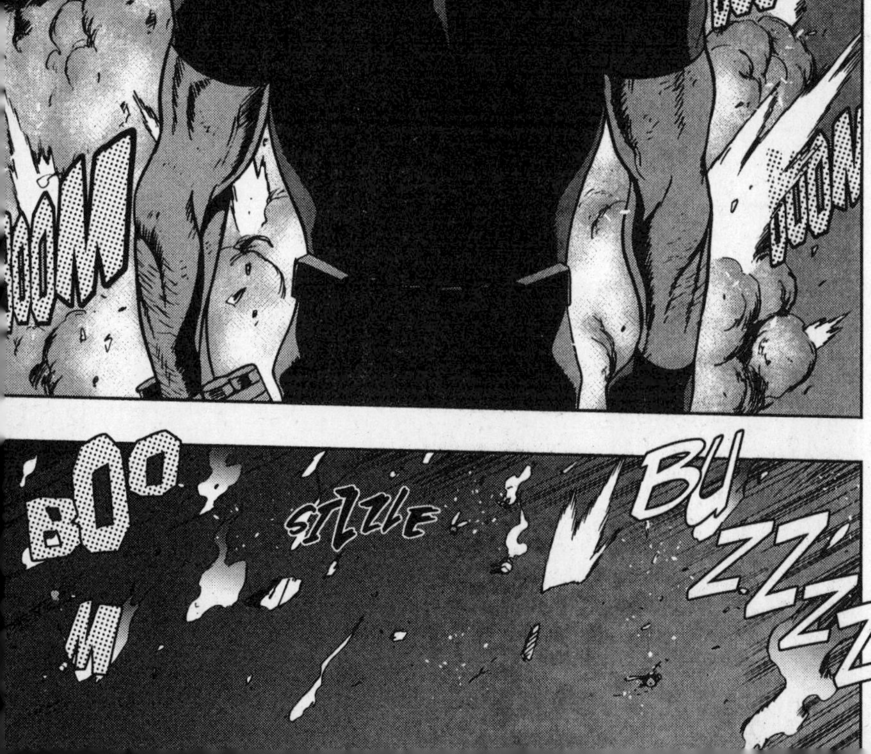
BUZZZZ
SIZZLE
BOOOM

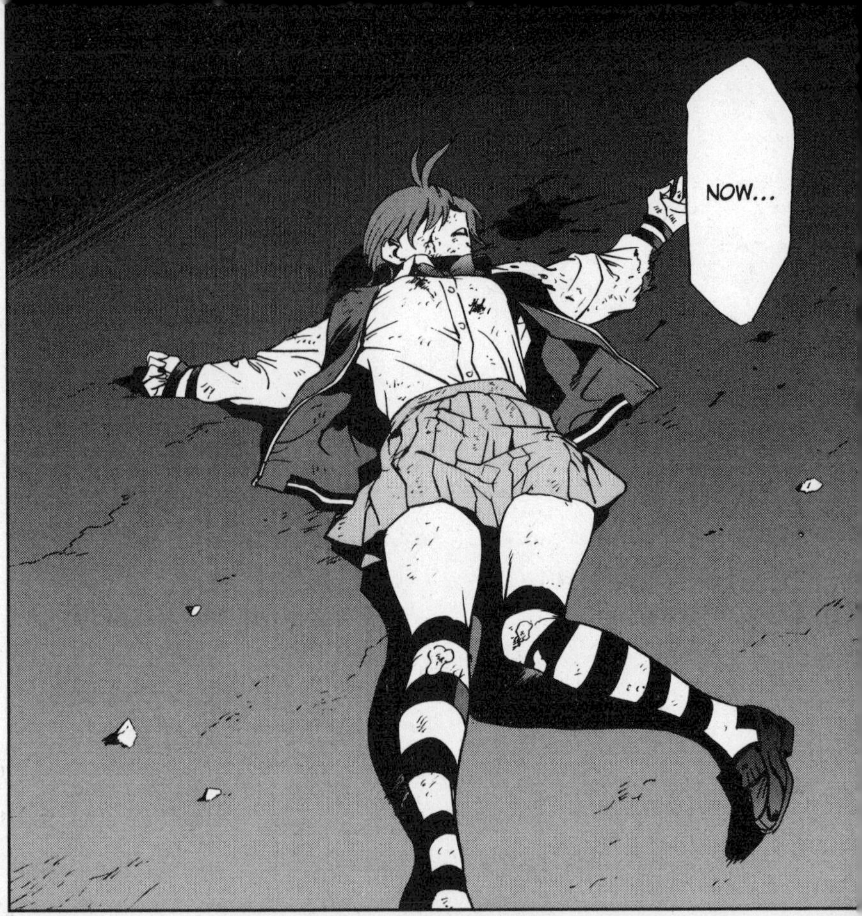
NOW...
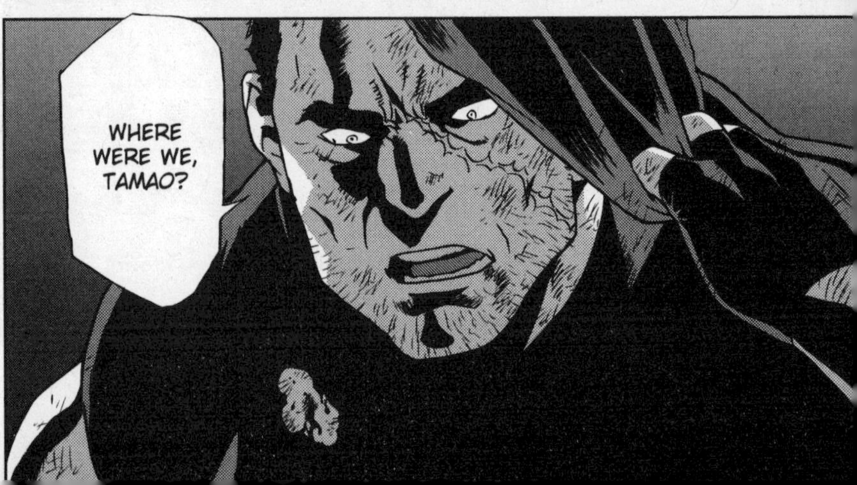
WHERE WERE WE, TAMAO?

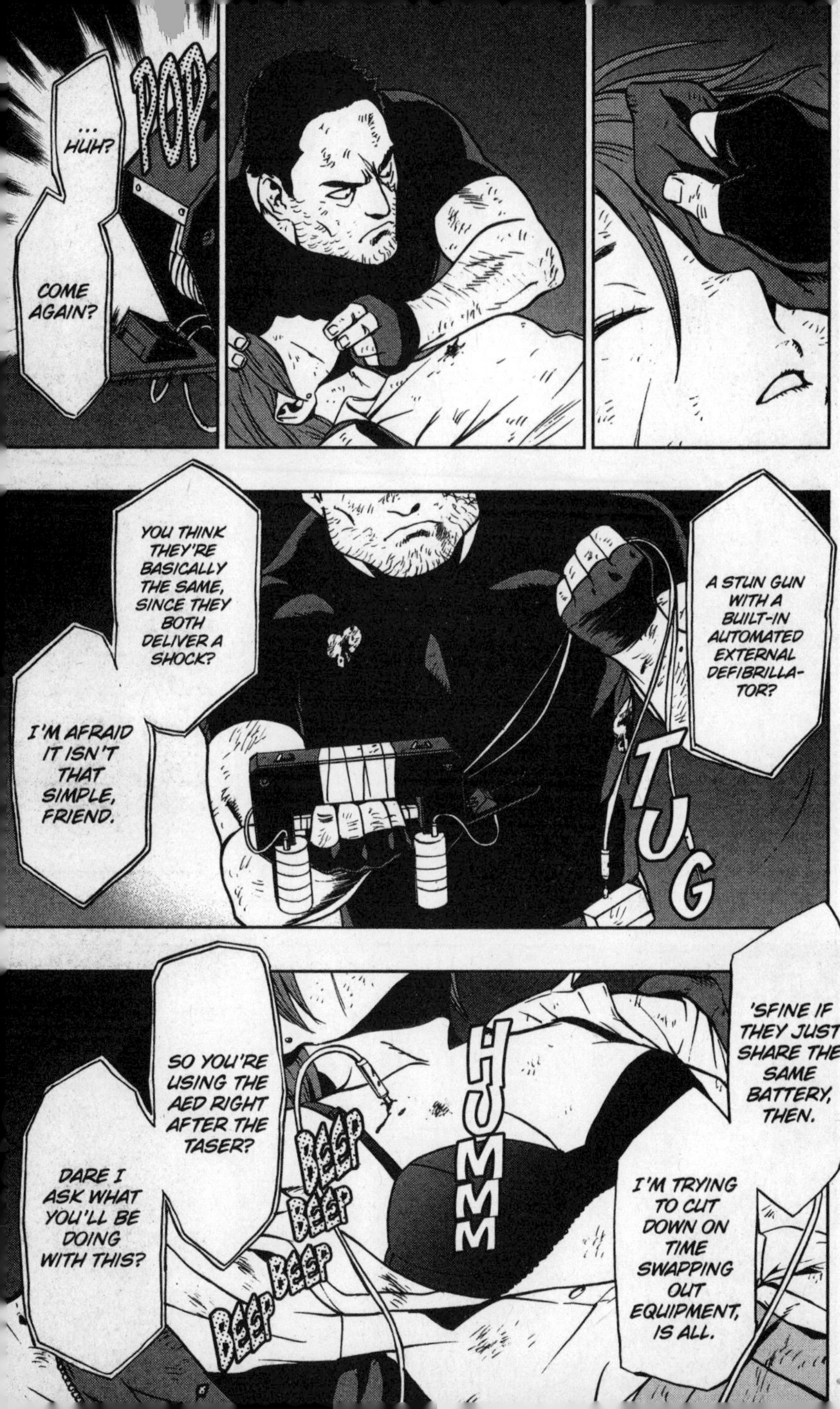
POP
... HUH?
COME AGAIN?
A STUN GUN WITH A BUILT-IN AUTOMATED EXTERNAL DEFIBRILLA-TOR?
TUG
YOU THINK THEY'RE BASICALLY THE SAME, SINCE THEY BOTH DELIVER A SHOCK?
I'M AFRAID IT ISN'T THAT SIMPLE, FRIEND.
'SFINE IF THEY JUST SHARE THE SAME BATTERY, THEN.
I'M TRYING TO CUT DOWN ON TIME SWAPPING OUT EQUIPMENT, IS ALL.
HUMM
SO YOU'RE USING THE AED RIGHT AFTER THE TASER?
BEEP
BEEP
BEEP
BEEP
DARE I ASK WHAT YOU'LL BE DOING WITH THIS?

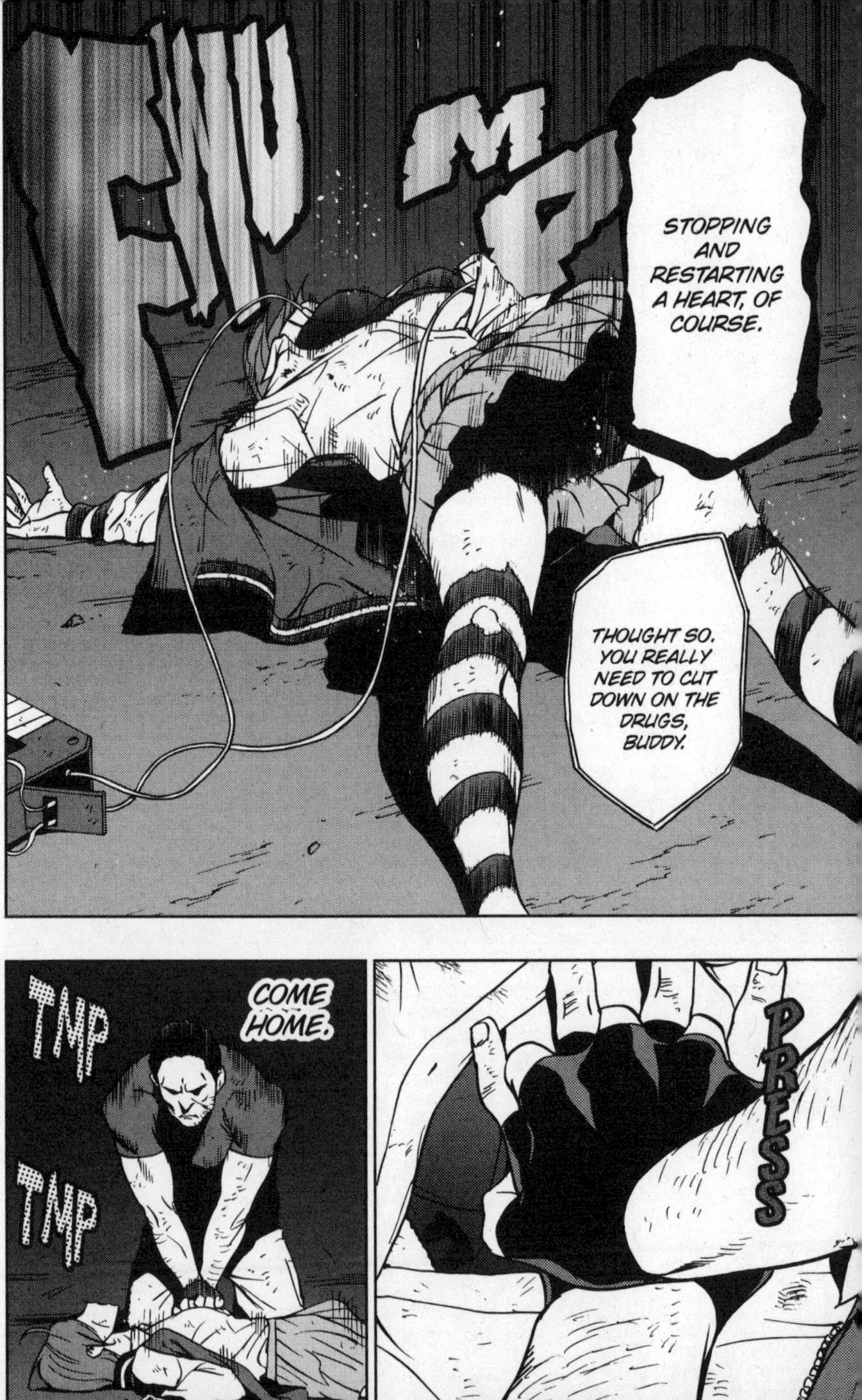
STOPPING AND RESTARTING A HEART, OF COURSE.
THUMP
THOUGHT SO. YOU REALLY NEED TO CUT DOWN ON THE DRUGS, BUDDY.
PRESS
COME HOME.
TMP
TMP

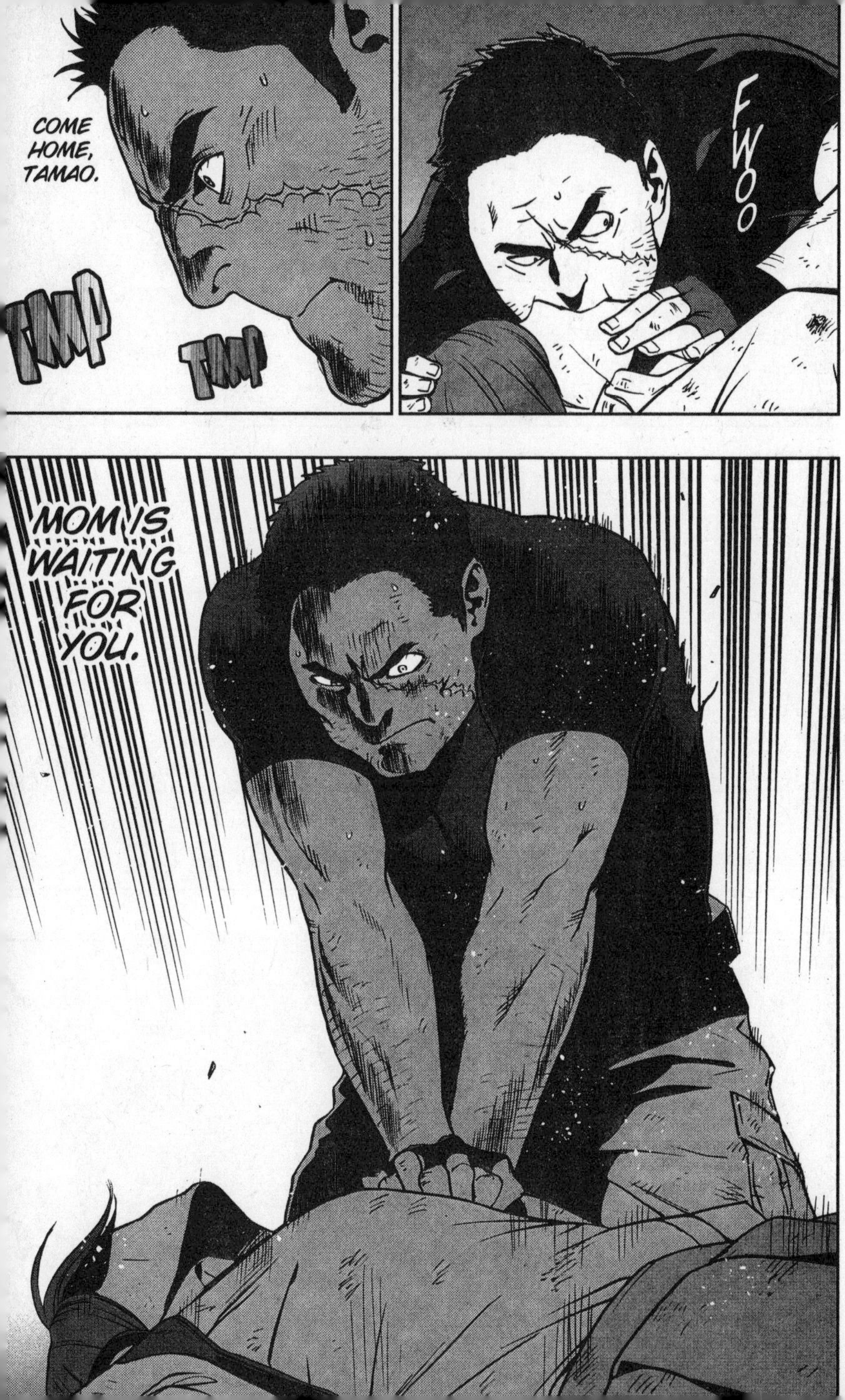
FWOO
COME HOME, TAMAO.
TMP
TMP
MOM IS WAITING FOR YOU.

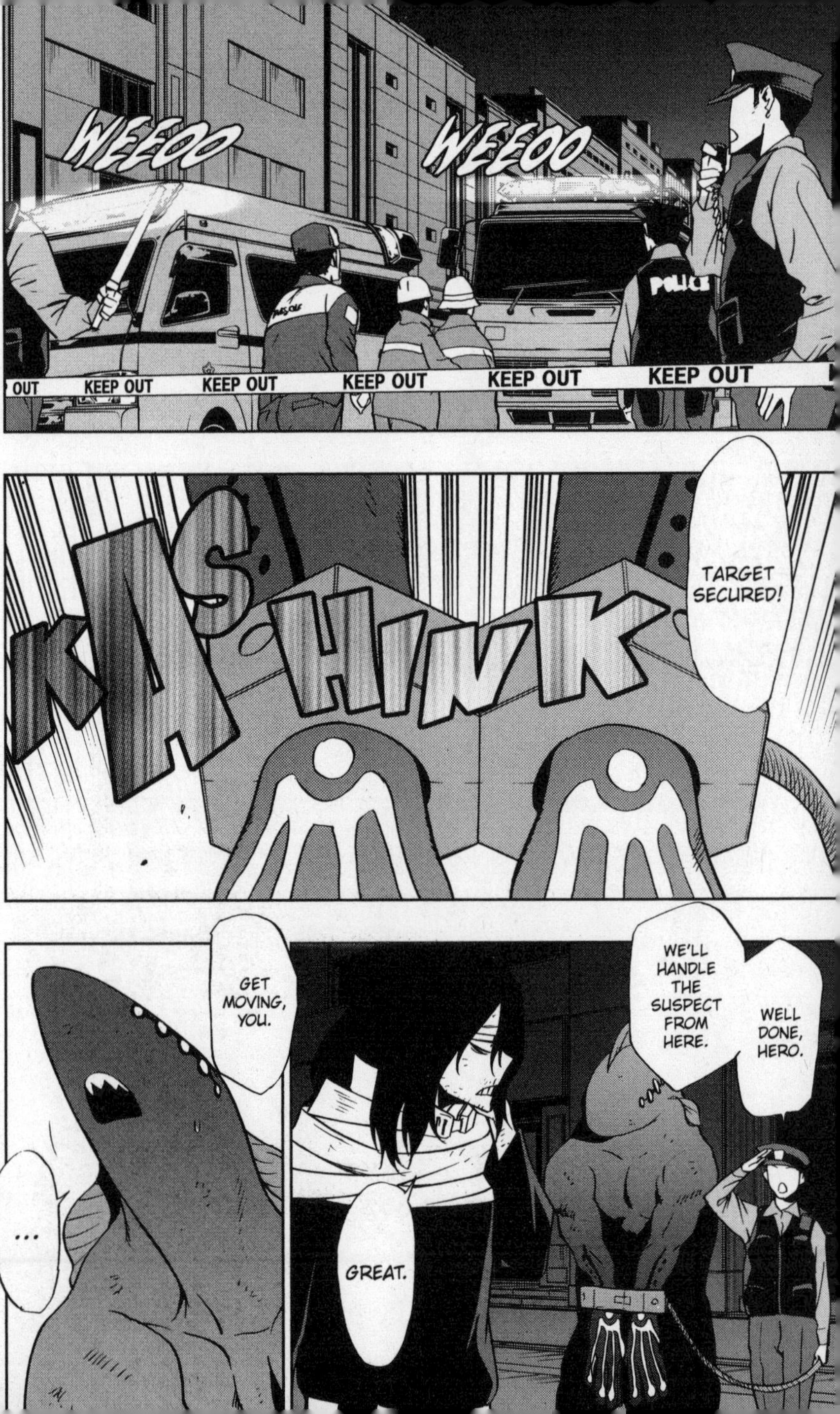
WEEOO
WEEOO
POLICE
KEEP OUT
KEEP OUT
KEEP OUT
KEEP OUT
KEEP OUT
OUT
TARGET SECURED!
KA-SHINK
WELL DONE, HERO.
WE'LL HANDLE THE SUSPECT FROM HERE.
GET MOVING, YOU.
GREAT.
...

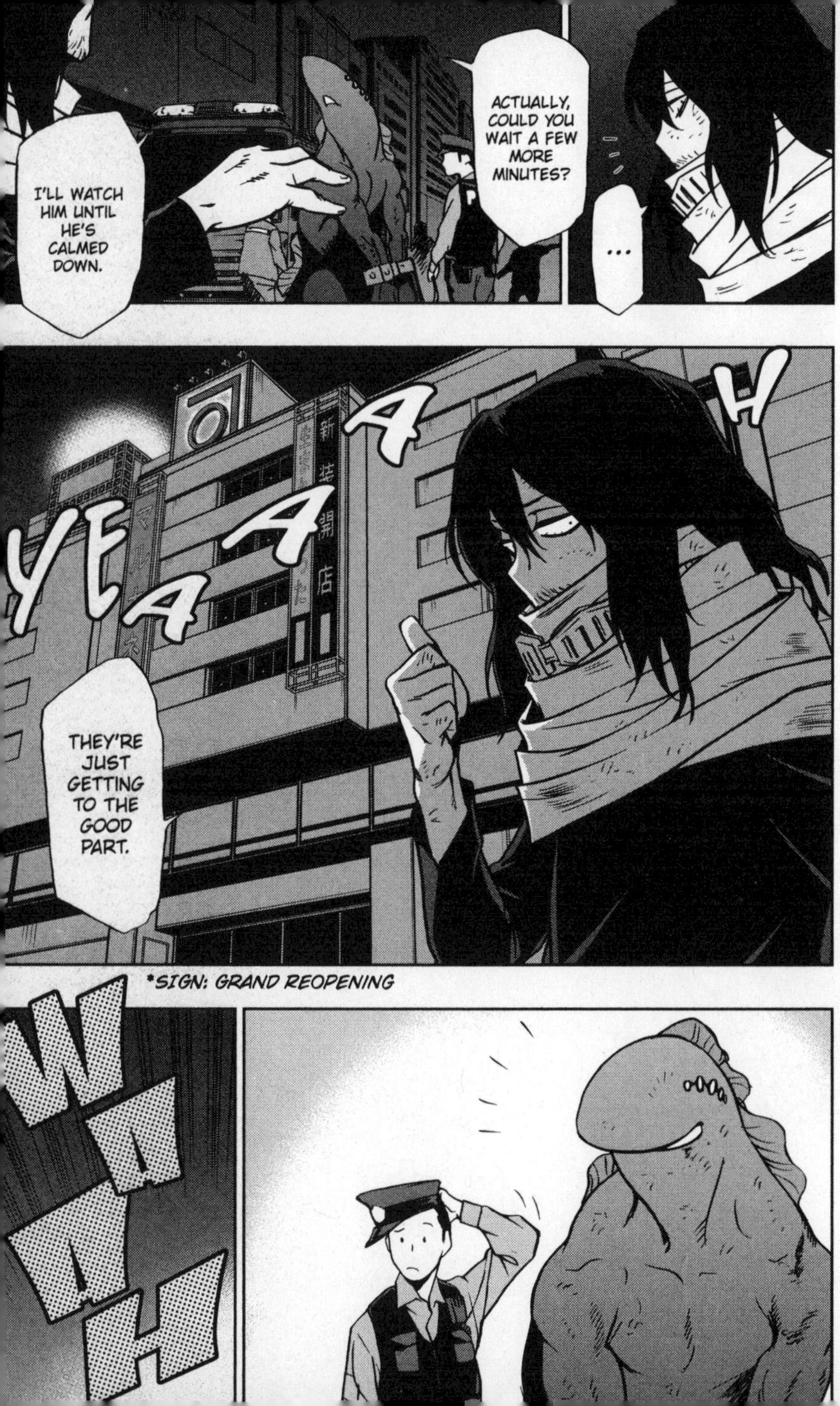
...
ACTUALLY, COULD YOU WAIT A FEW MORE MINUTES?
I'LL WATCH HIM UNTIL HE'S CALMED DOWN.
YEAAAAH
新装開店
THEY'RE JUST GETTING TO THE GOOD PART.
*SIGN: GRAND REOPENING
WHAAAH

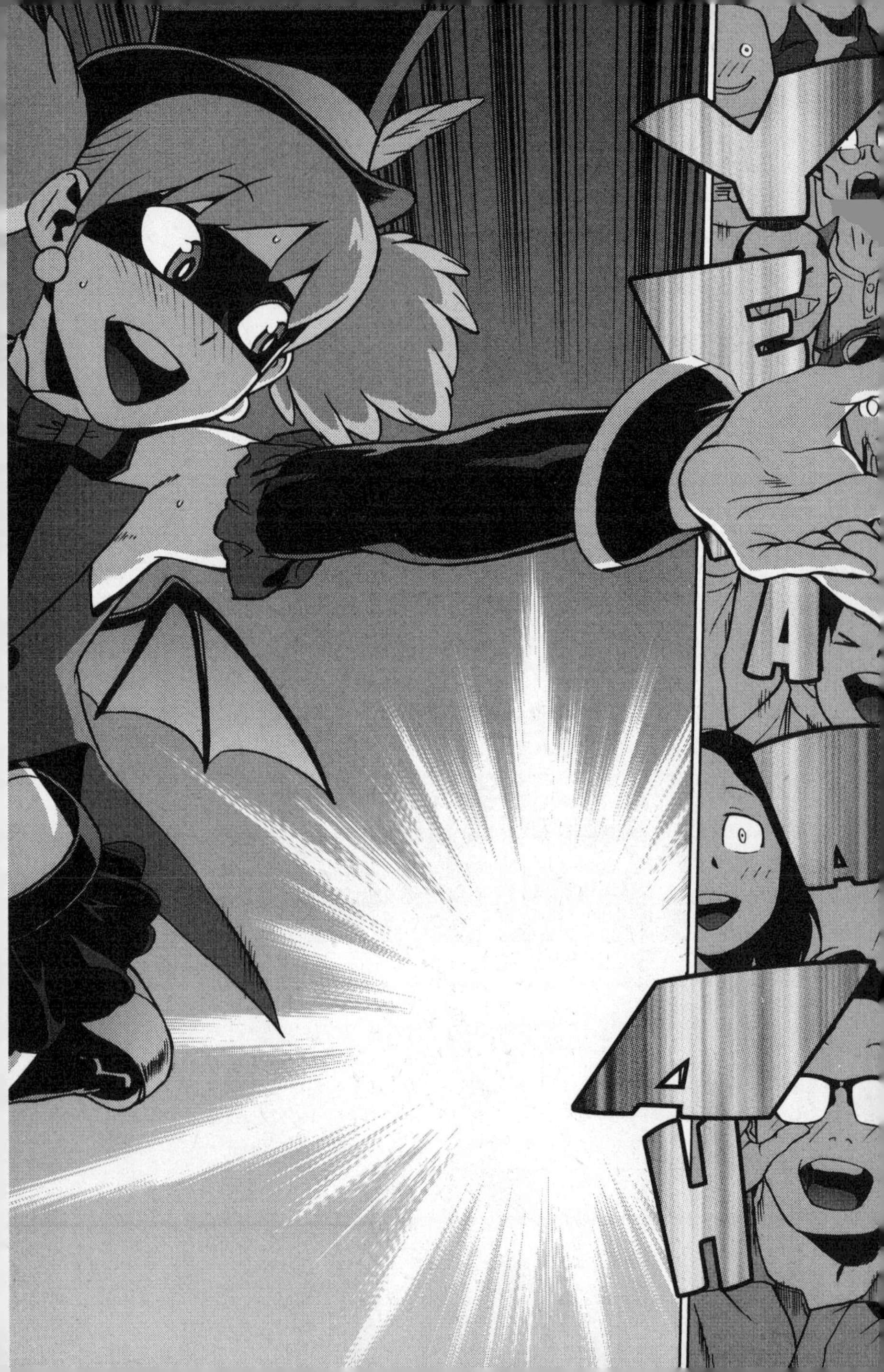
YEAAAH

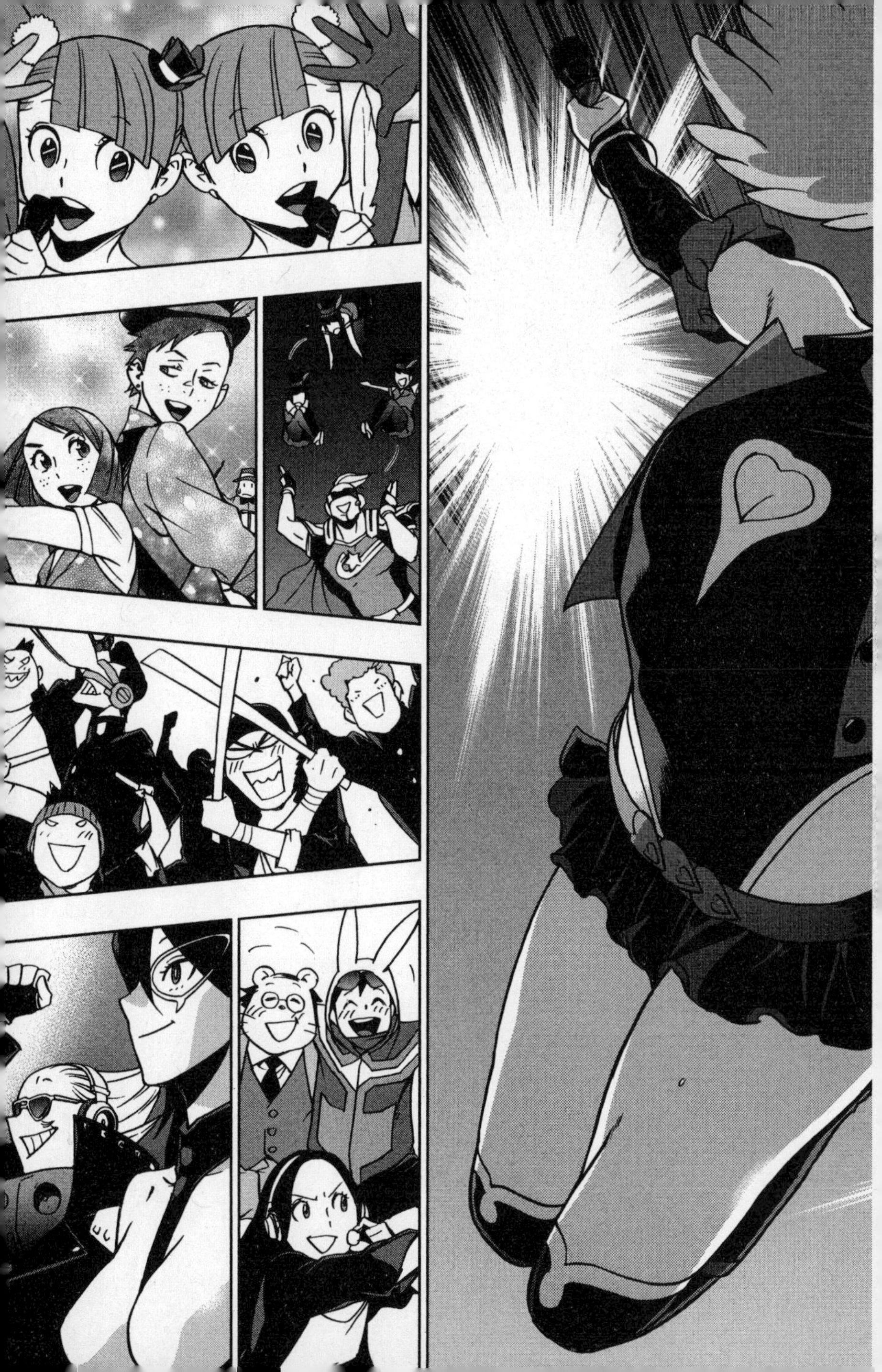

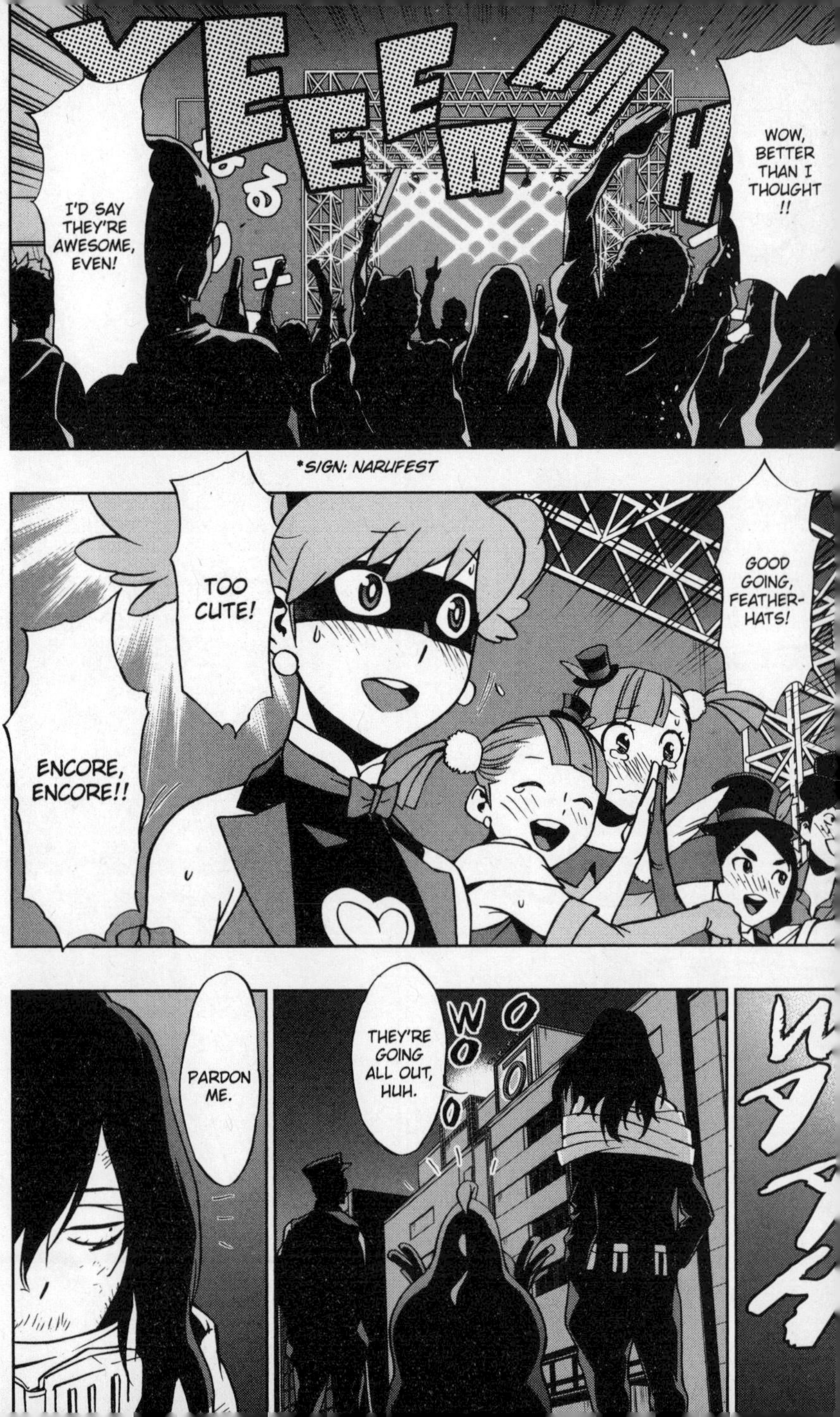
WOW, BETTER THAN I THOUGHT!!
YEEEAAAH
I'D SAY THEY'RE AWESOME, EVEN!
*SIGN: NARUFEST
GOOD GOING, FEATHER-HATS!
TOO CUTE!
ENCORE, ENCORE!!
WOOOO
THEY'RE GOING ALL OUT, HUH.
PARDON ME.

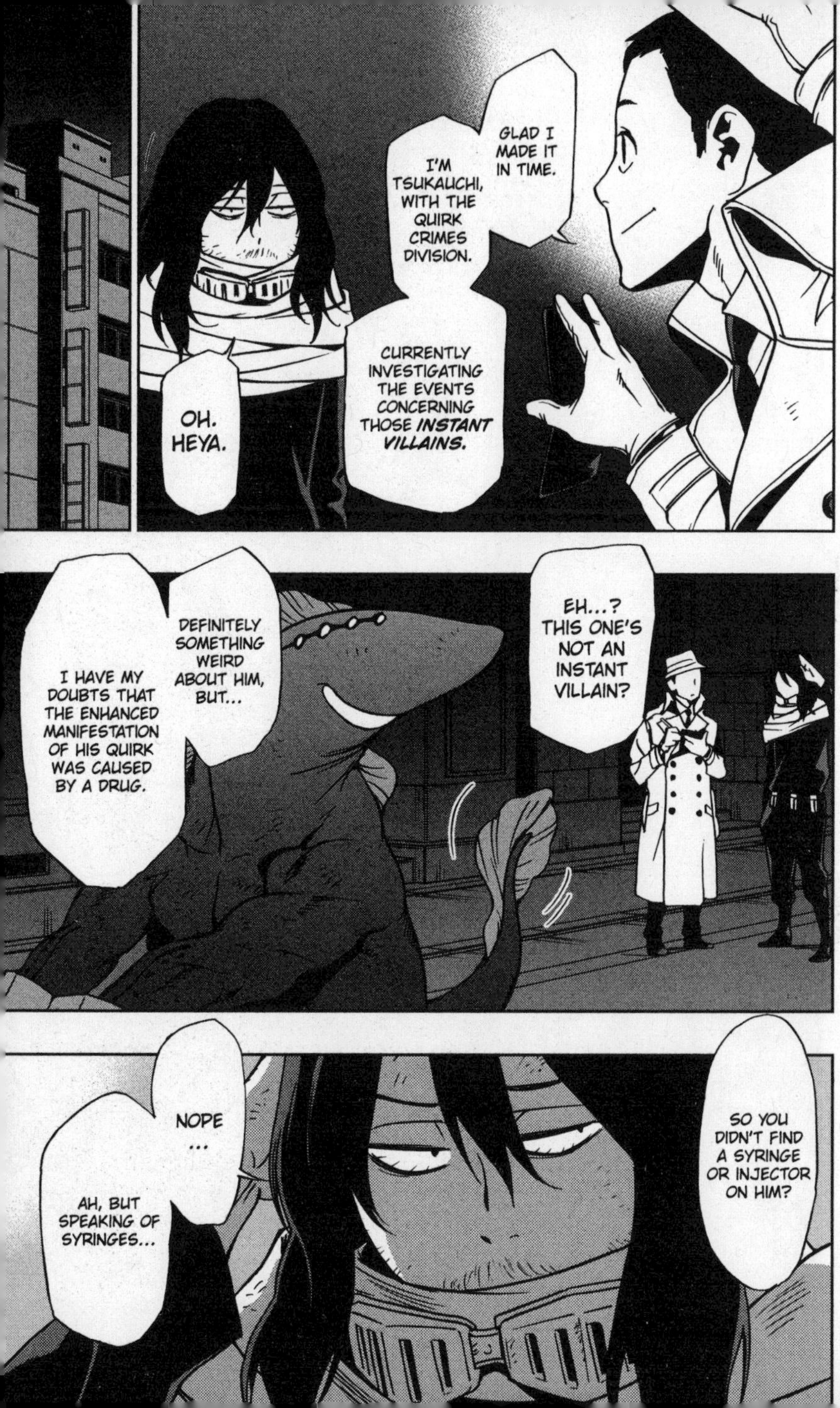
GLAD I MADE IT IN TIME.
I'M TSUKAUCHI, WITH THE QUIRK CRIMES DIVISION.
CURRENTLY INVESTIGATING THE EVENTS CONCERNING THOSE *INSTANT VILLAINS.*
OH. HEYA.
EH...? THIS ONE'S NOT AN INSTANT VILLAIN?
DEFINITELY SOMETHING WEIRD ABOUT HIM, BUT...
I HAVE MY DOUBTS THAT THE ENHANCED MANIFESTATION OF HIS QUIRK WAS CAUSED BY A DRUG.
SO YOU DIDN'T FIND A SYRINGE OR INJECTOR ON HIM?
NOPE ...
AH, BUT SPEAKING OF SYRINGES...

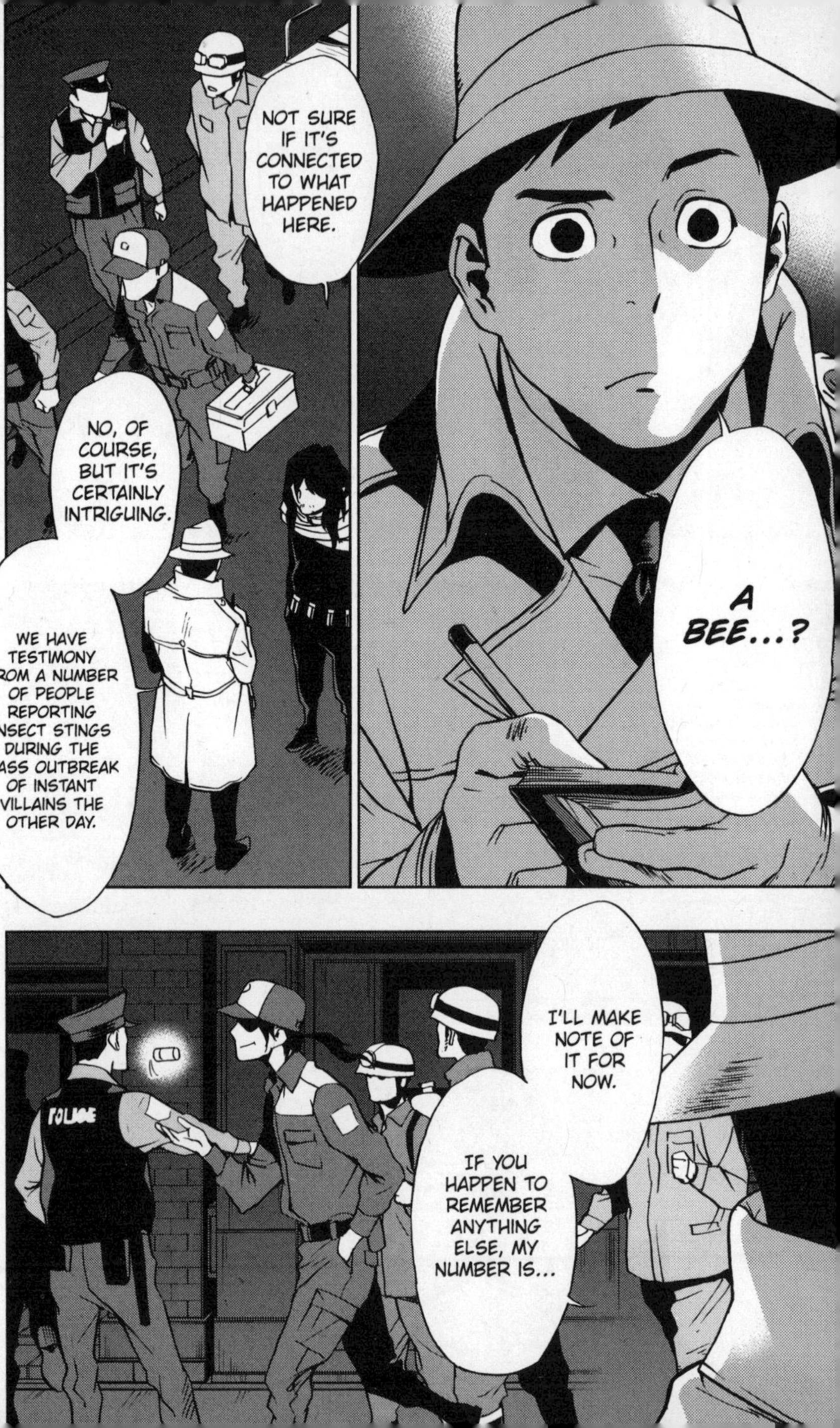
A BEE...?
NOT SURE IF IT'S CONNECTED TO WHAT HAPPENED HERE.
NO, OF COURSE, BUT IT'S CERTAINLY INTRIGUING.
WE HAVE TESTIMONY FROM A NUMBER OF PEOPLE REPORTING INSECT STINGS DURING THE MASS OUTBREAK OF INSTANT VILLAINS THE OTHER DAY.
POLICE
I'LL MAKE NOTE OF IT FOR NOW.
IF YOU HAPPEN TO REMEMBER ANYTHING ELSE, MY NUMBER IS...

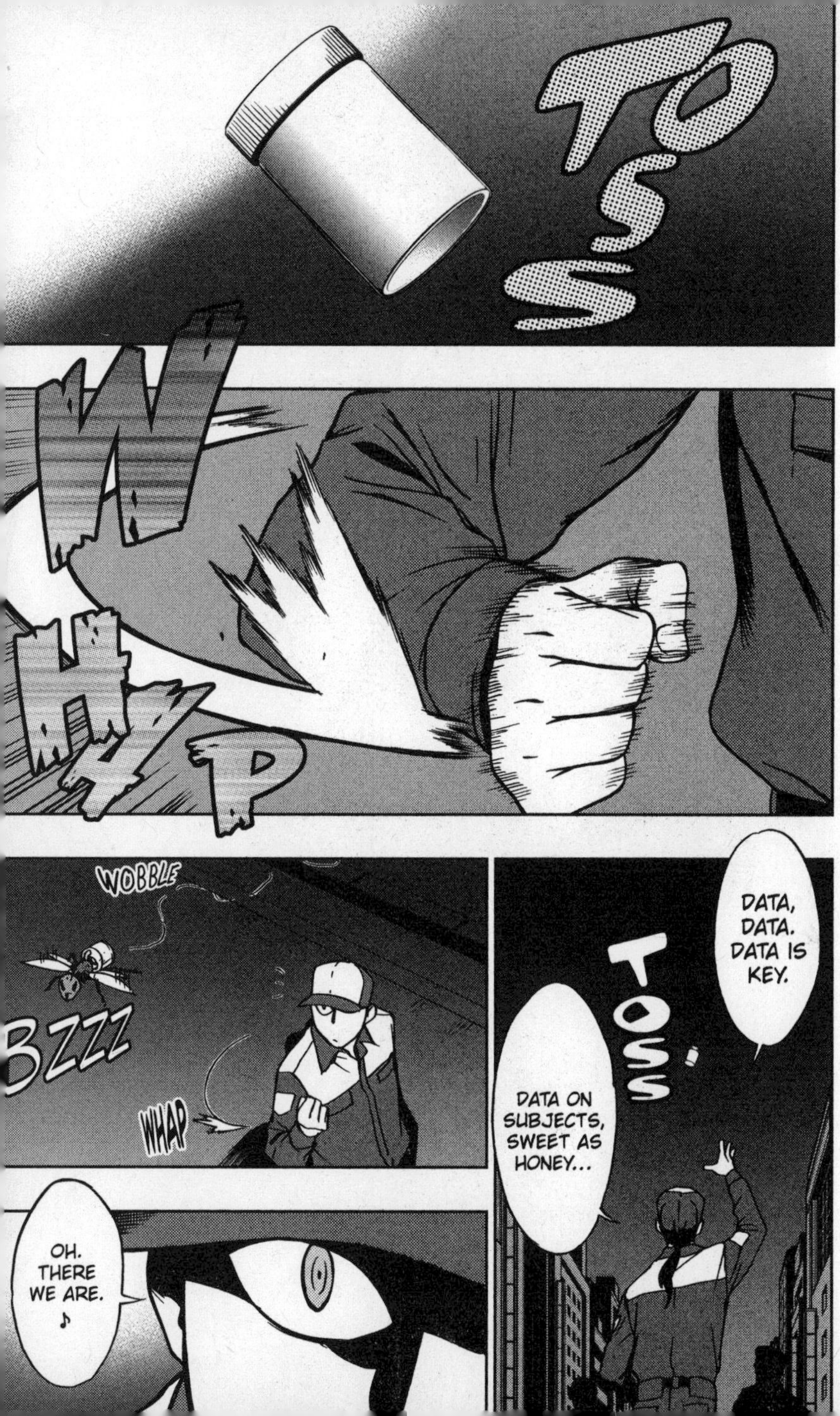
TOSSS
WHAP
DATA, DATA. DATA IS KEY.
TOSS
DATA ON SUBJECTS, SWEET AS HONEY...
WOBBLE
BZZZ
WHAP
OH. THERE WE ARE. ♪

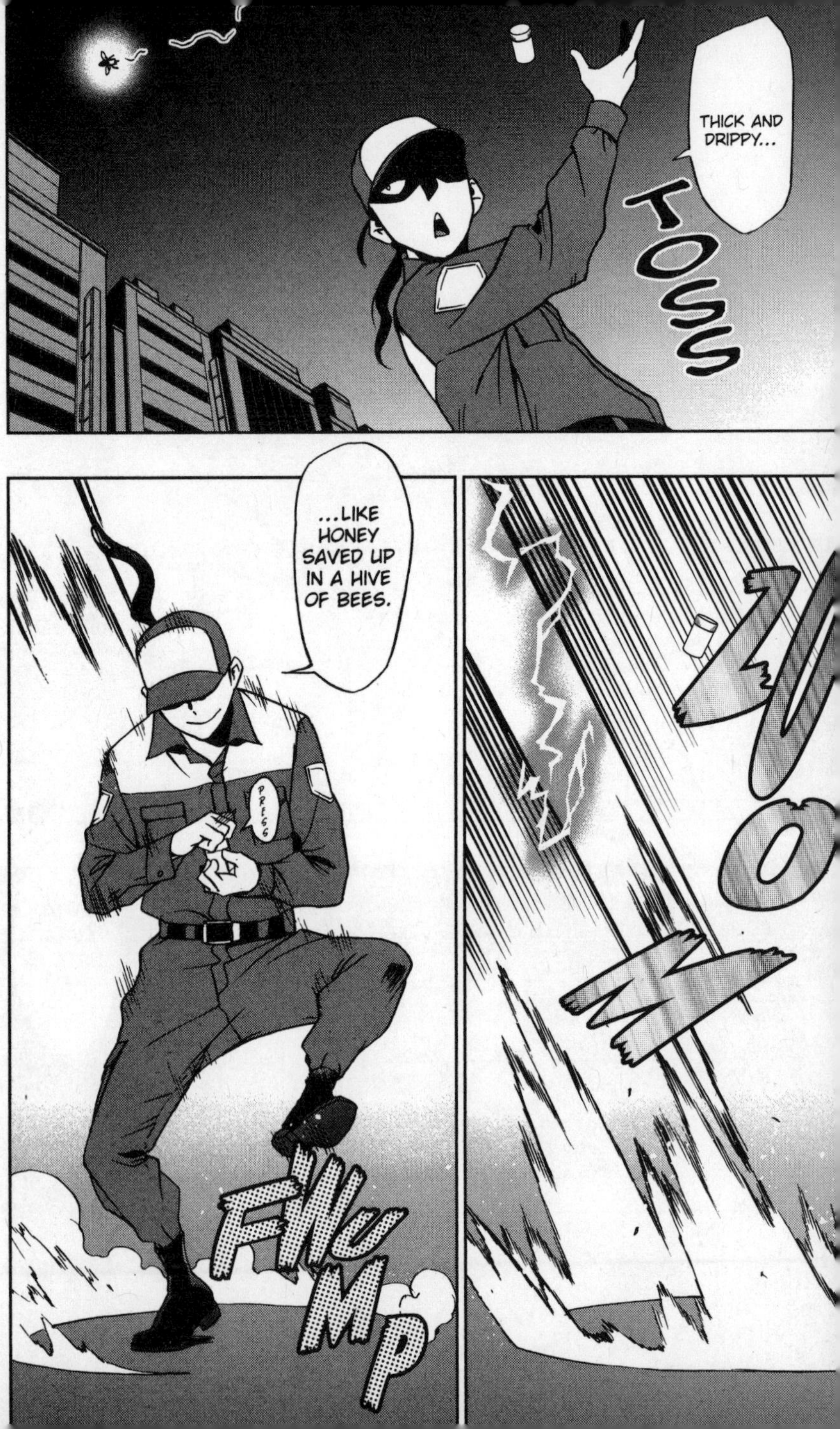
THICK AND DRIPPY...
TOSS
ZOOM
...LIKE HONEY SAVED UP IN A HIVE OF BEES.
PRESS
FWUMP

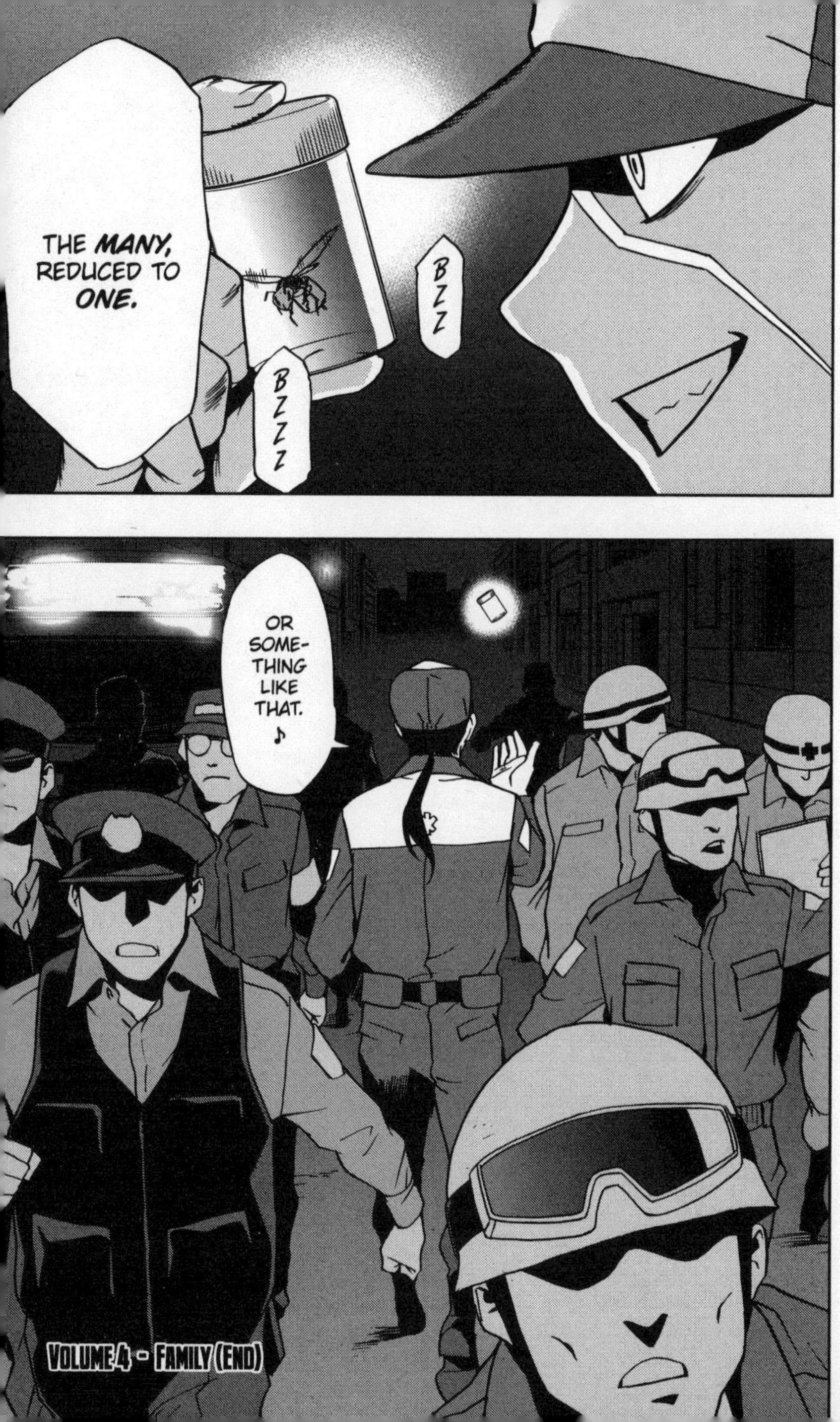
BZZ
THE MANY, REDUCED TO ONE.
BZZZ
OR SOME-THING LIKE THAT. ♪
VOLUME 4 - FAMILY (END)

EXPLANATION

The following Episode Zero ran in *Jump GIGA* 2016, vol. 2. It's a special chapter that's like a movie trailer.

In order to emphasize the connection to *My Hero Academia* as much as possible, we have guest appearances by various pro heroes and U.A. students. However, in the actual continuity, Mt. Lady and Kamui Woods hadn't made their debuts yet, and Deku and friends would've still been in elementary school.

Just think of it as a non-canon feature!

—Furuhashi

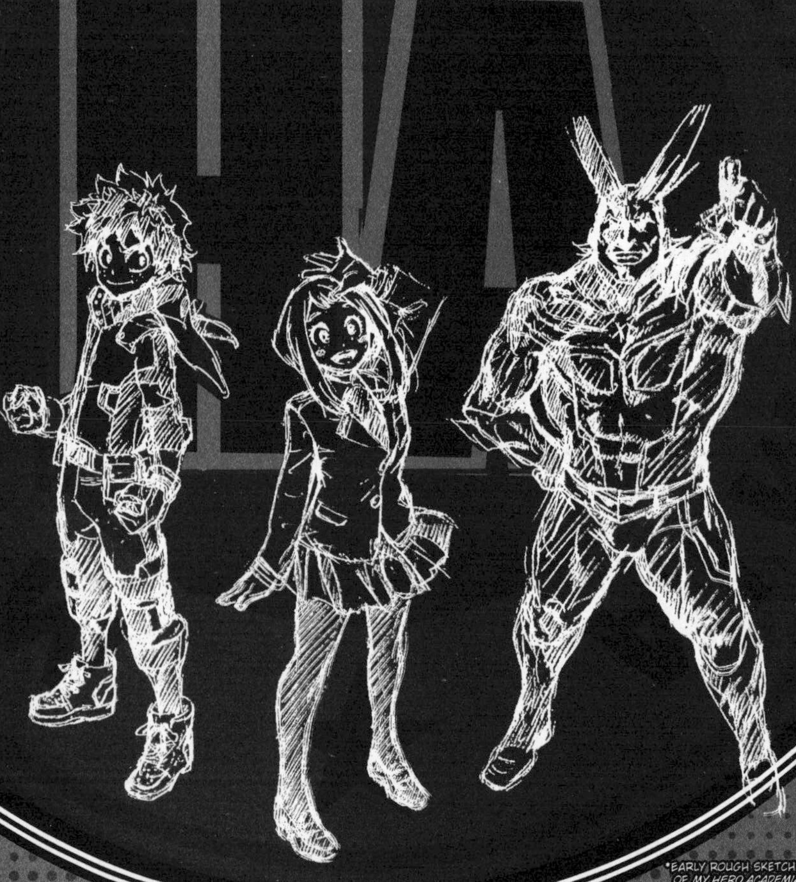

*EARLY ROUGH SKETCHES OF *MY HERO ACADEMIA* CHARACTERS BY BETTEN SENSEI.

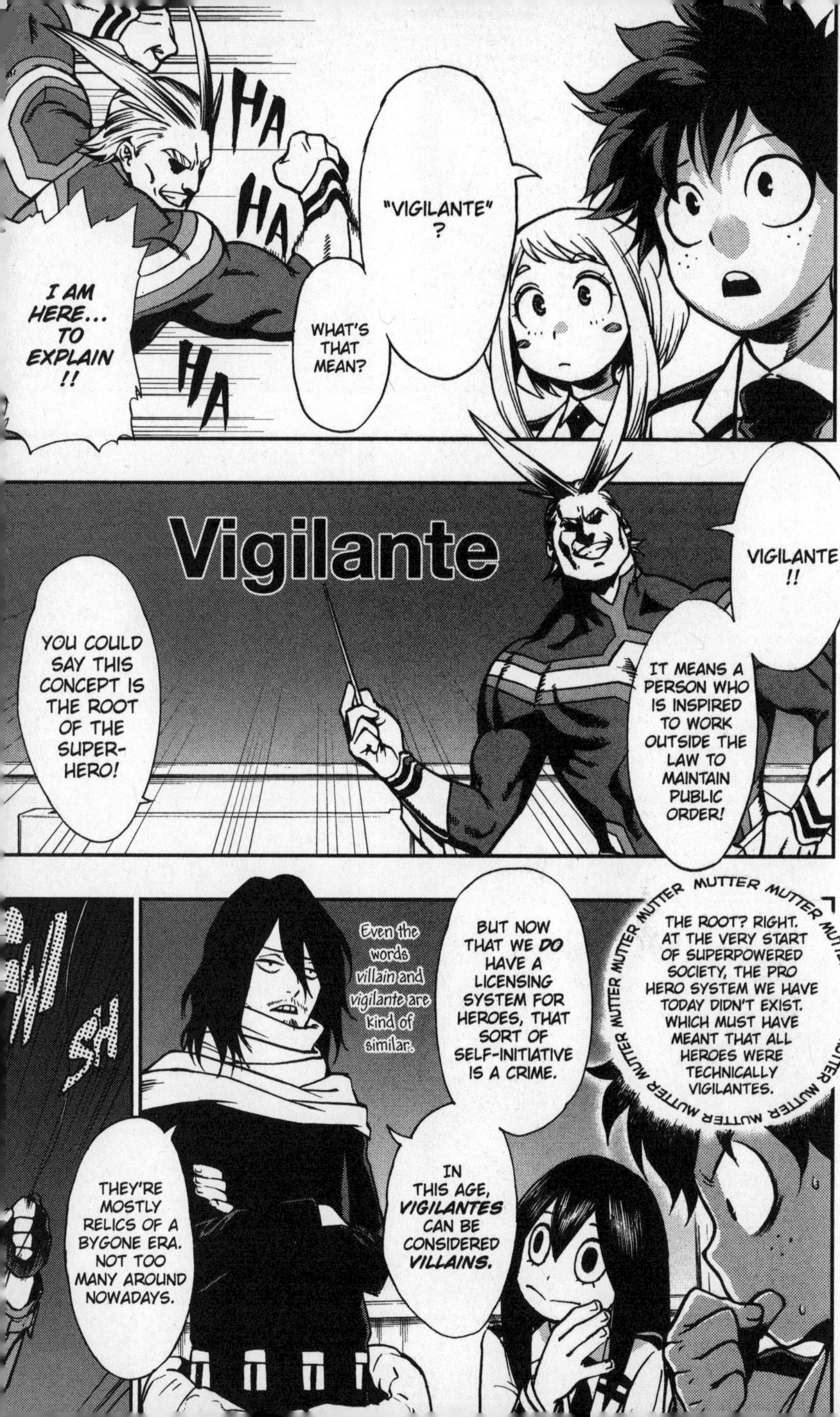
"VIGILANTE"
?
WHAT'S THAT MEAN?
HA HA HA
I AM HERE... TO EXPLAIN !!
VIGILANTE !!
IT MEANS A PERSON WHO IS INSPIRED TO WORK OUTSIDE THE LAW TO MAINTAIN PUBLIC ORDER!
Vigilante
YOU COULD SAY THIS CONCEPT IS THE ROOT OF THE SUPER-HERO!
MUTTER MUTTER MUTTER MUTTER MUTTER MUTTER MUTTER MUTTER
THE ROOT? RIGHT. AT THE VERY START OF SUPERPOWERED SOCIETY, THE PRO HERO SYSTEM WE HAVE TODAY DIDN'T EXIST. WHICH MUST HAVE MEANT THAT ALL HEROES WERE TECHNICALLY VIGILANTES.
BUT NOW THAT WE *DO* HAVE A LICENSING SYSTEM FOR HEROES, THAT SORT OF SELF-INITIATIVE IS A CRIME.
Even the words villain and vigilante are kind of similar.
IN THIS AGE, ***VIGILANTES*** CAN BE CONSIDERED ***VILLAINS.***
THEY'RE MOSTLY RELICS OF A BYGONE ERA. NOT TOO MANY AROUND NOWADAYS.
SH SH

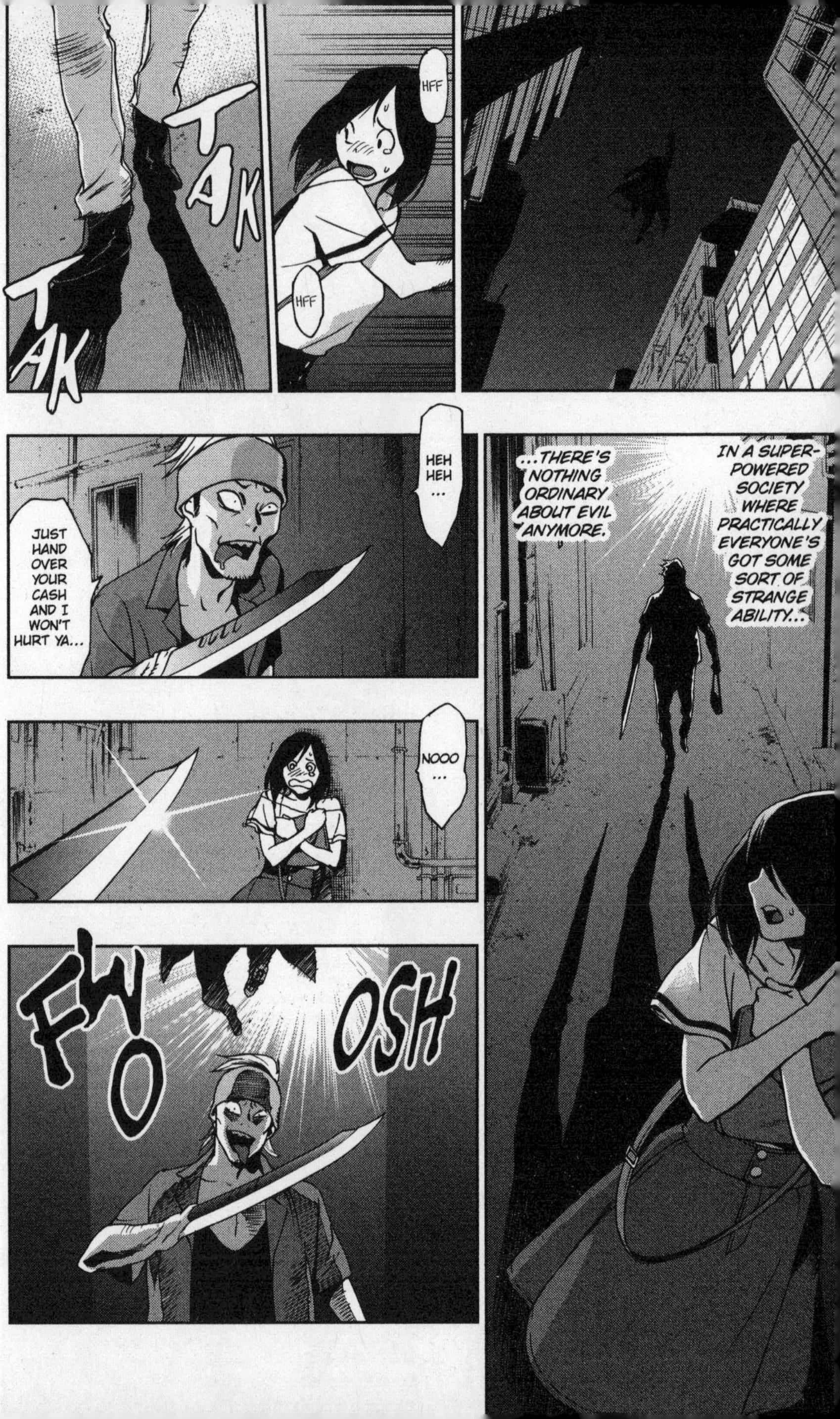
HFF
HFF
TAK
TAK
IN A SUPER-POWERED SOCIETY WHERE PRACTICALLY EVERYONE'S GOT SOME SORT OF STRANGE ABILITY...
...THERE'S NOTHING ORDINARY ABOUT EVIL ANYMORE.
HEH HEH ...
JUST HAND OVER YOUR CASH AND I WON'T HURT YA...
NOOO ...
FWOOSH

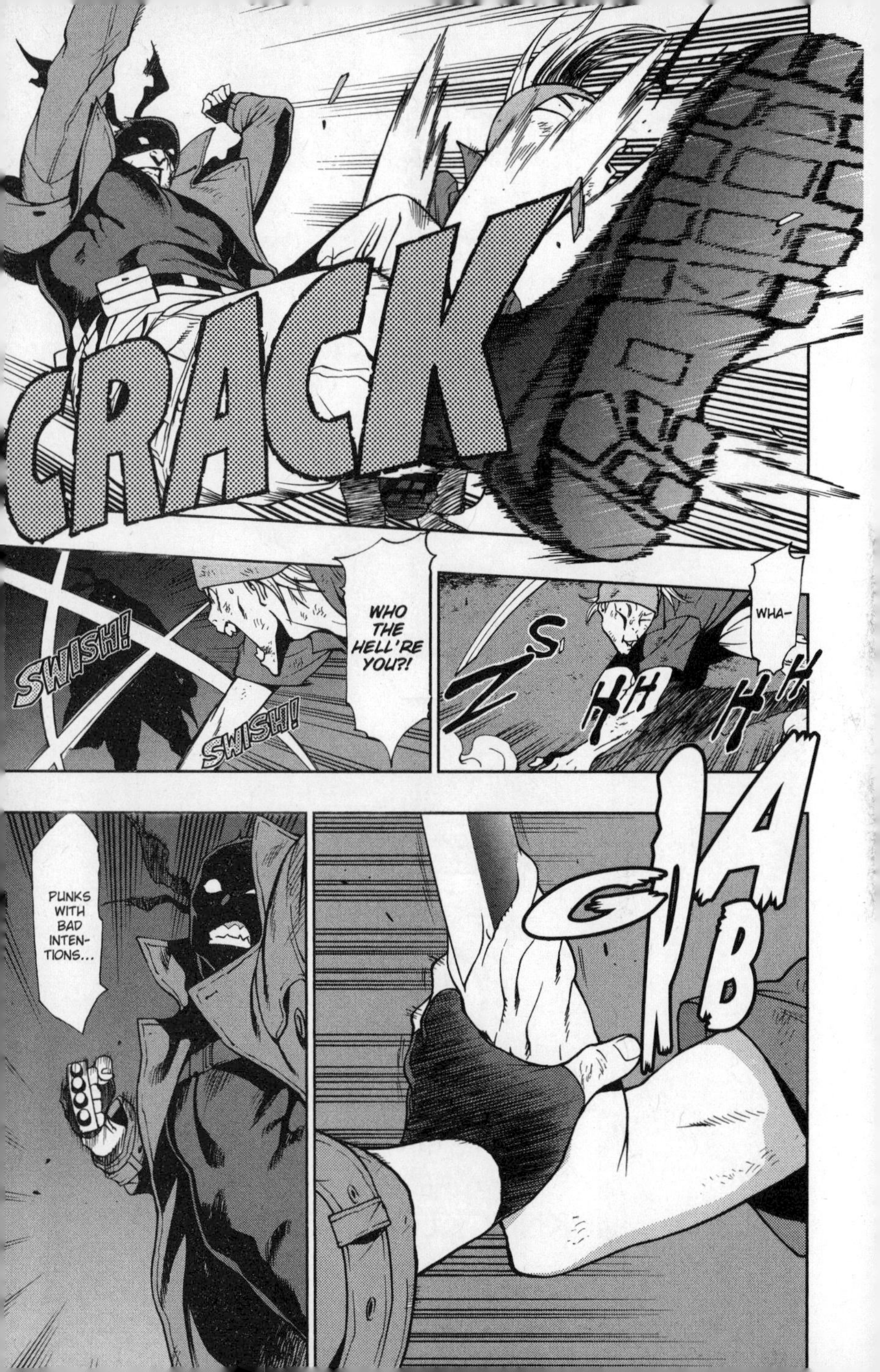
CRACK
WHA-
WHO THE HELL'RE YOU?!
SWISH!
SWISH!
PUNKS WITH BAD INTEN-TIONS...

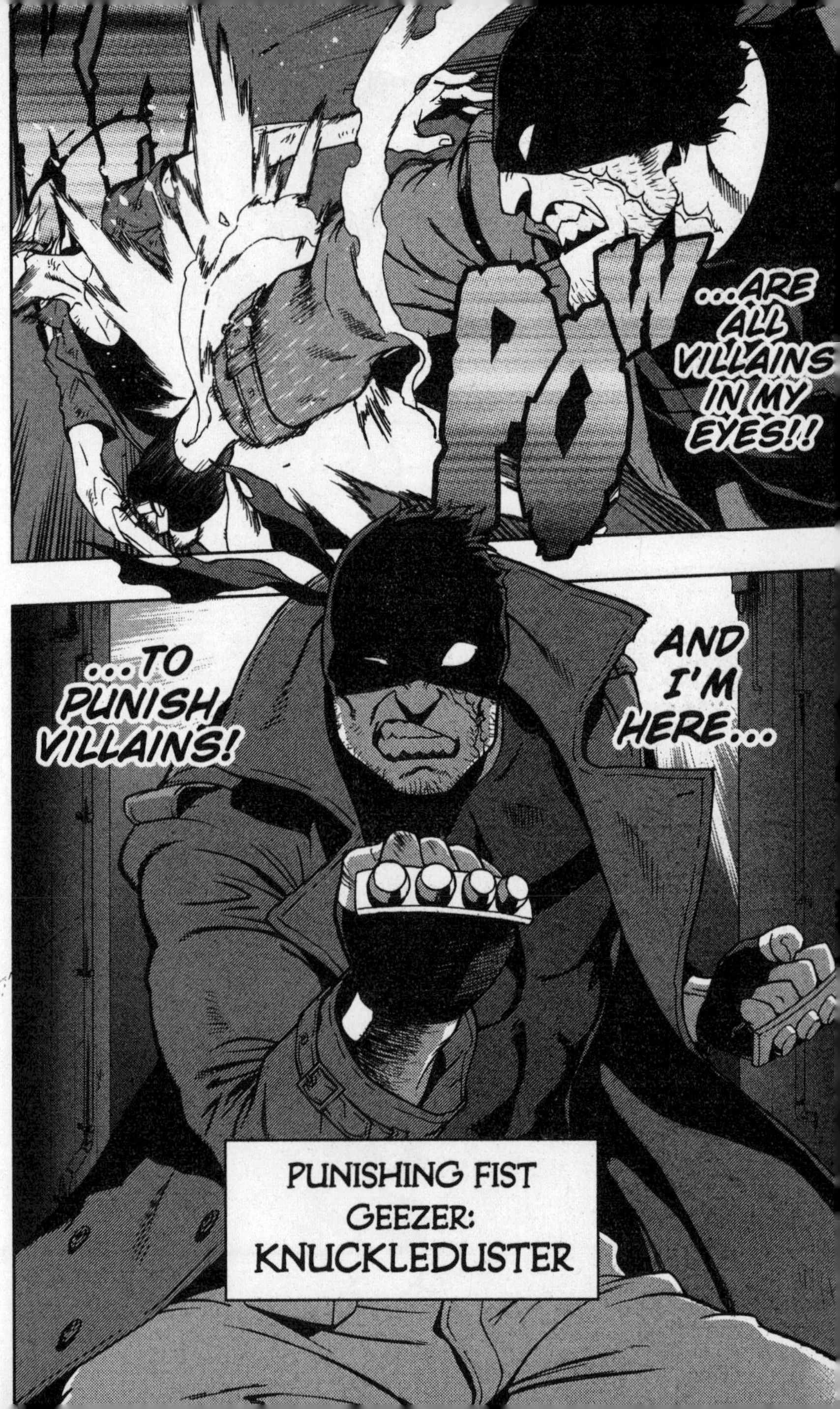
POW
...ARE ALL VILLAINS IN MY EYES!!
AND I'M HERE...
...TO PUNISH VILLAINS!
PUNISHING FIST GEEZER: KNUCKLEDUSTER

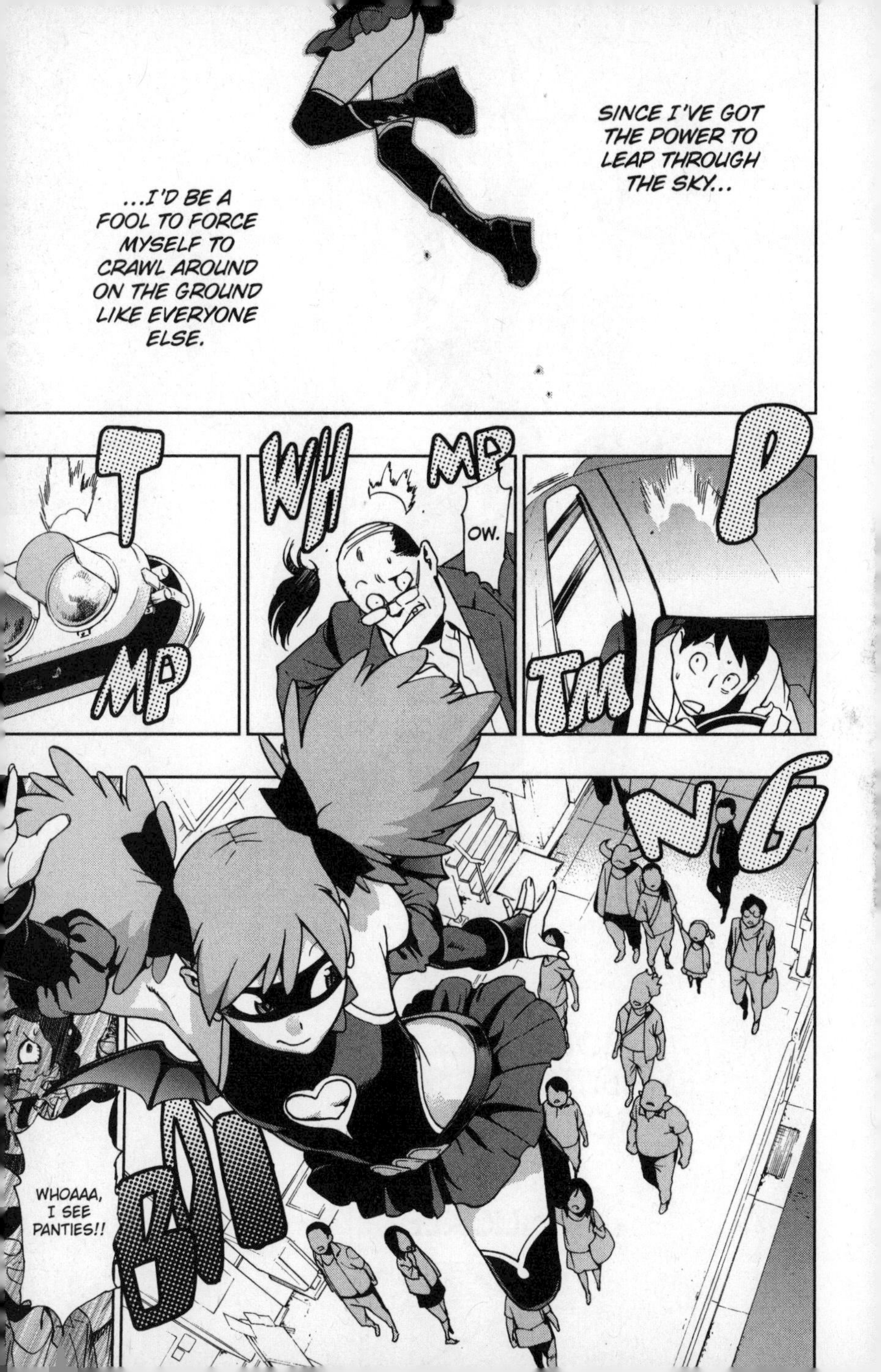
SINCE I'VE GOT THE POWER TO LEAP THROUGH THE SKY...
...I'D BE A FOOL TO FORCE MYSELF TO CRAWL AROUND ON THE GROUND LIKE EVERYONE ELSE.
TMP
WHMP
OW.
TMP
WHOAAA, I SEE PANTIES!!

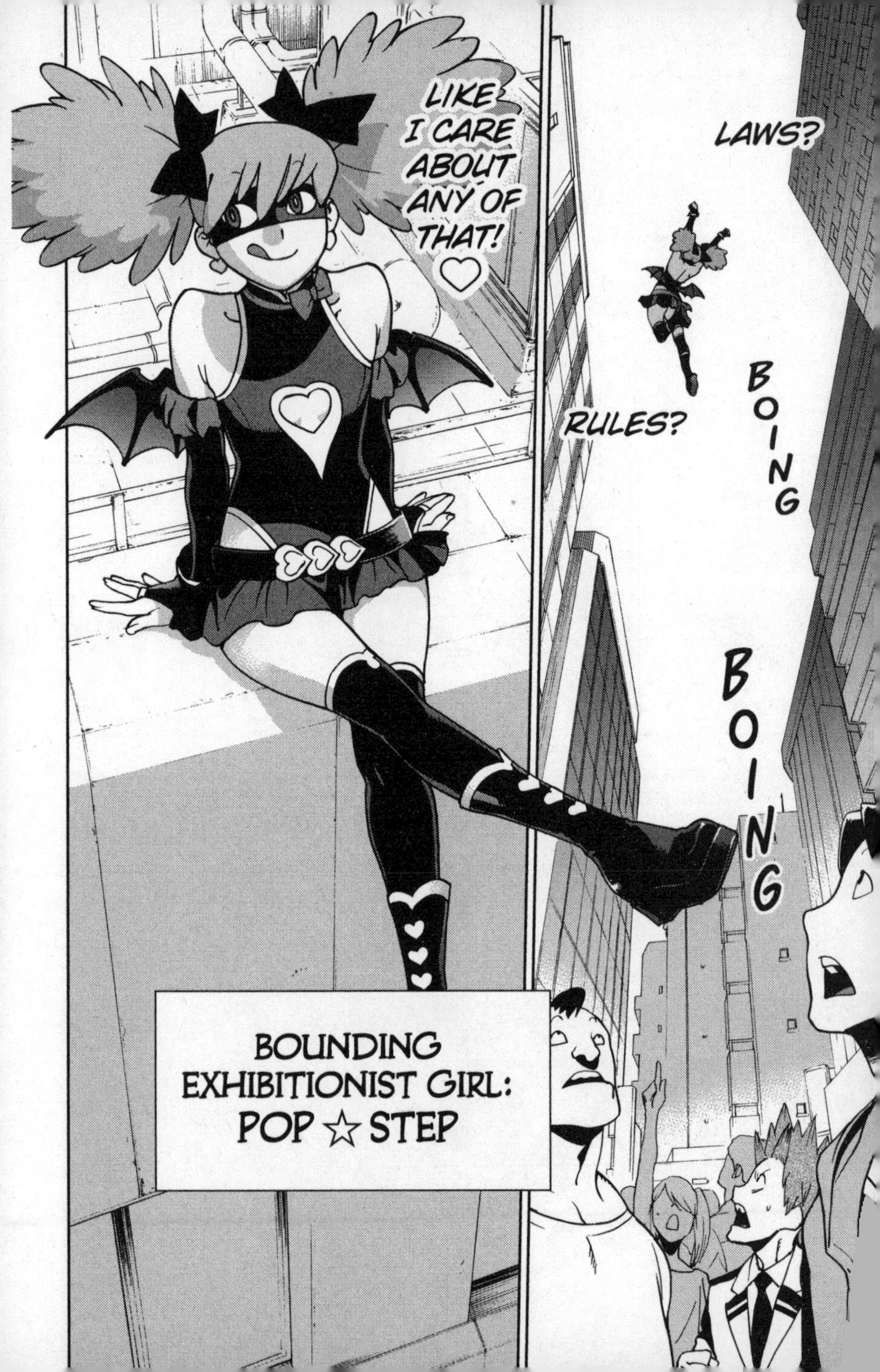
LAWS?
RULES?
BOING
BOING
LIKE I CARE ABOUT ANY OF THAT! ♡
BOUNDING EXHIBITIONIST GIRL: POP ☆ STEP

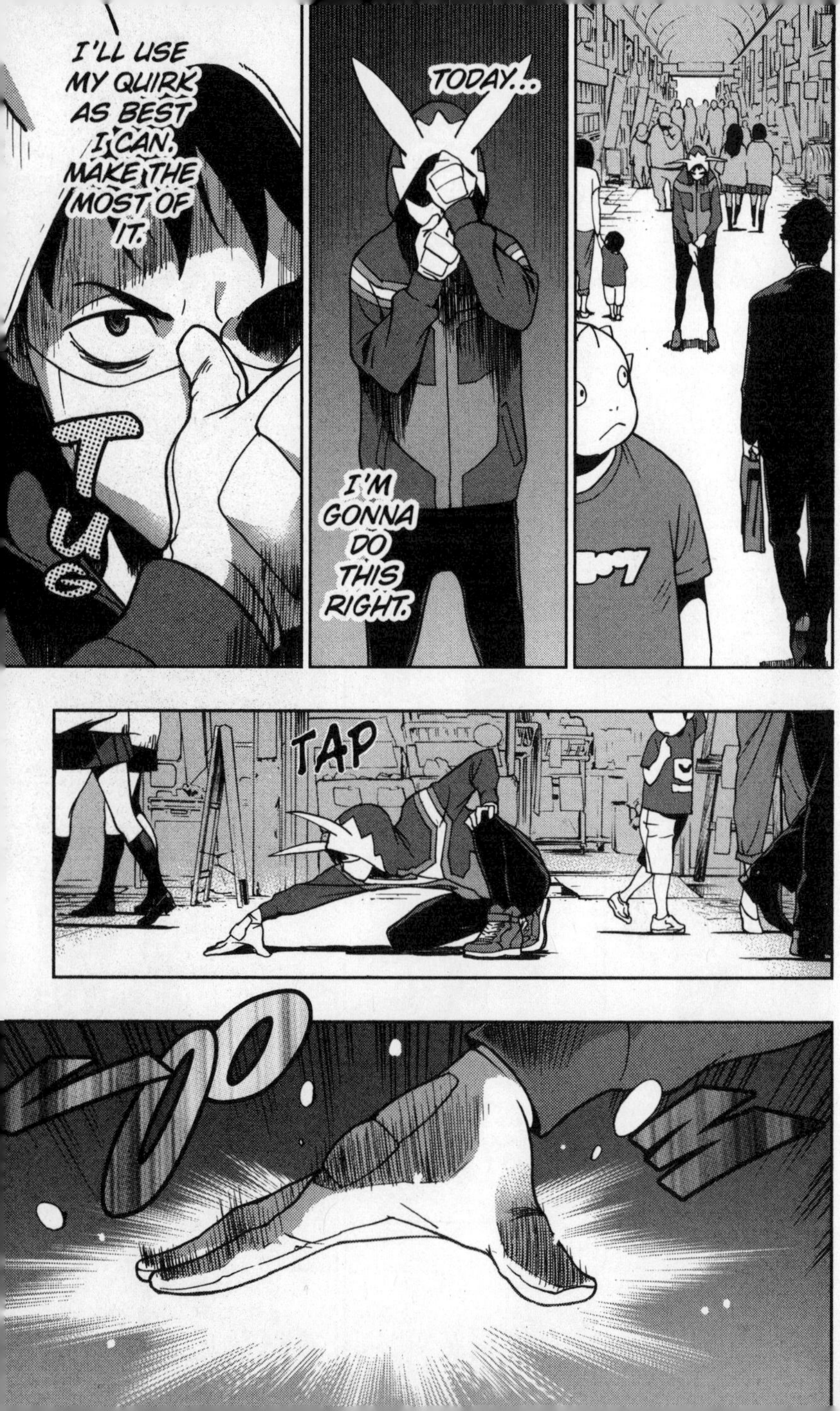
TODAY...
I'M GONNA DO THIS RIGHT.
I'LL USE MY QUIRK AS BEST I CAN. MAKE THE MOST OF IT.
TUG
TAP

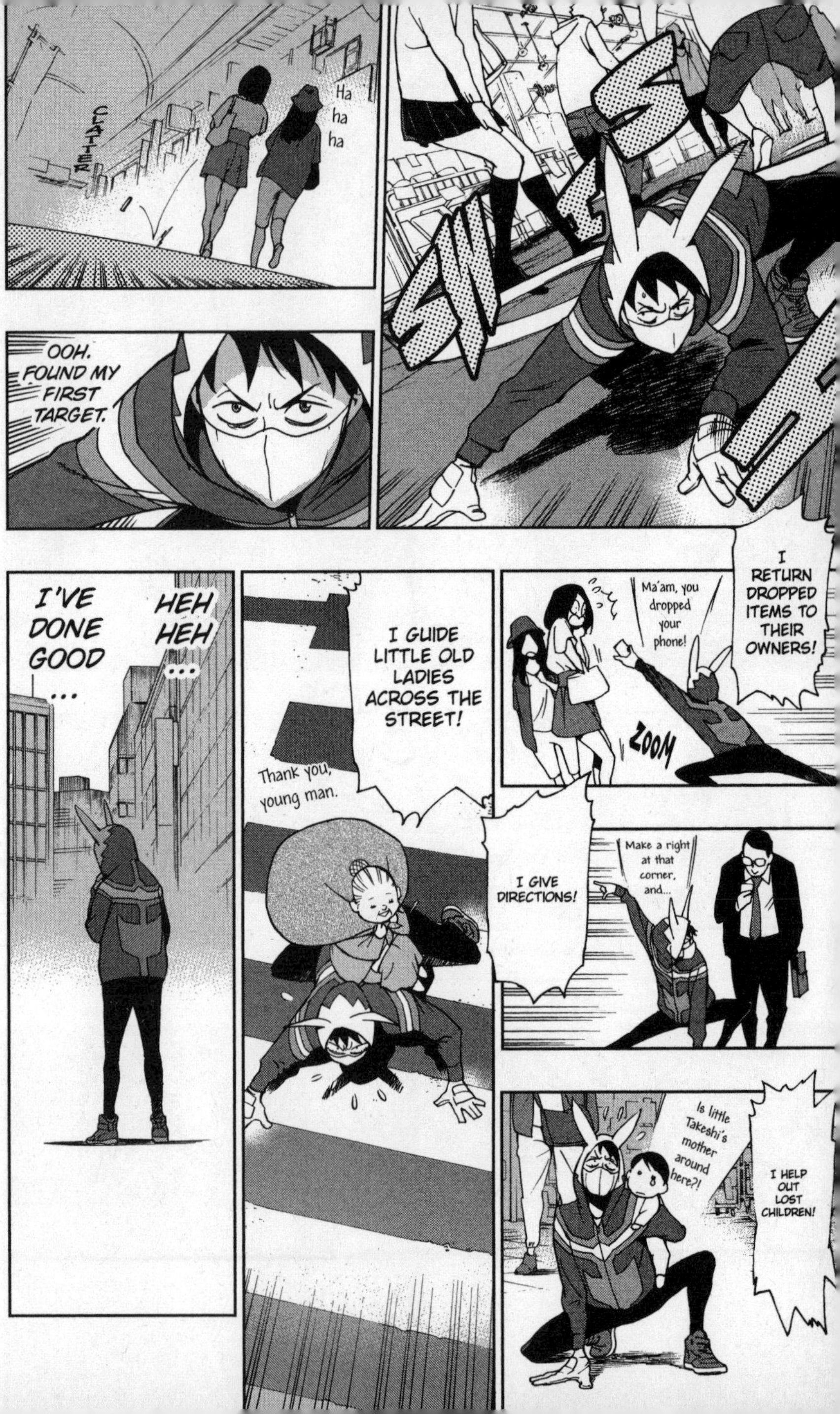
Ha
ha
ha
CLATTER
OOH. FOUND MY FIRST TARGET.
I RETURN DROPPED ITEMS TO THEIR OWNERS!
Ma'am, you dropped your phone!
ZOOM
I GUIDE LITTLE OLD LADIES ACROSS THE STREET!
Thank you, young man.
I GIVE DIRECTIONS!
Make a right at that corner, and...
I HELP OUT LOST CHILDREN!
Is little Takeshi's mother around here?!
HEH HEH...
I'VE DONE GOOD...

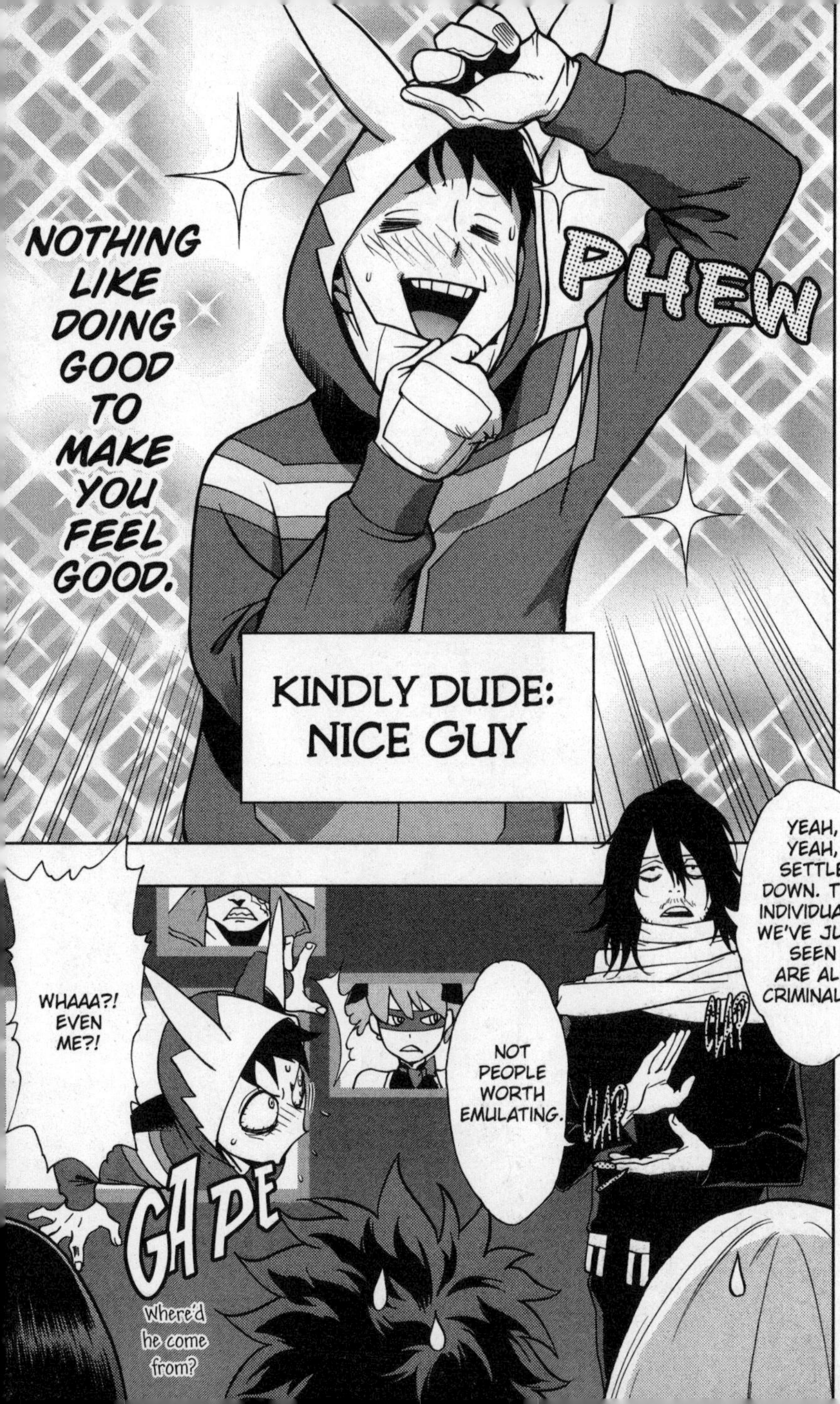
PHEW
NOTHING LIKE DOING GOOD TO MAKE YOU FEEL GOOD.
KINDLY DUDE: NICE GUY
YEAH, YEAH, SETTLE DOWN. THE INDIVIDUALS WE'VE JUST SEEN ARE ALL CRIMINALS.
CLAP CLAP
NOT PEOPLE WORTH EMULATING.
CLAP
WHAAA?! EVEN ME?!
GAPE
Where'd he come from?

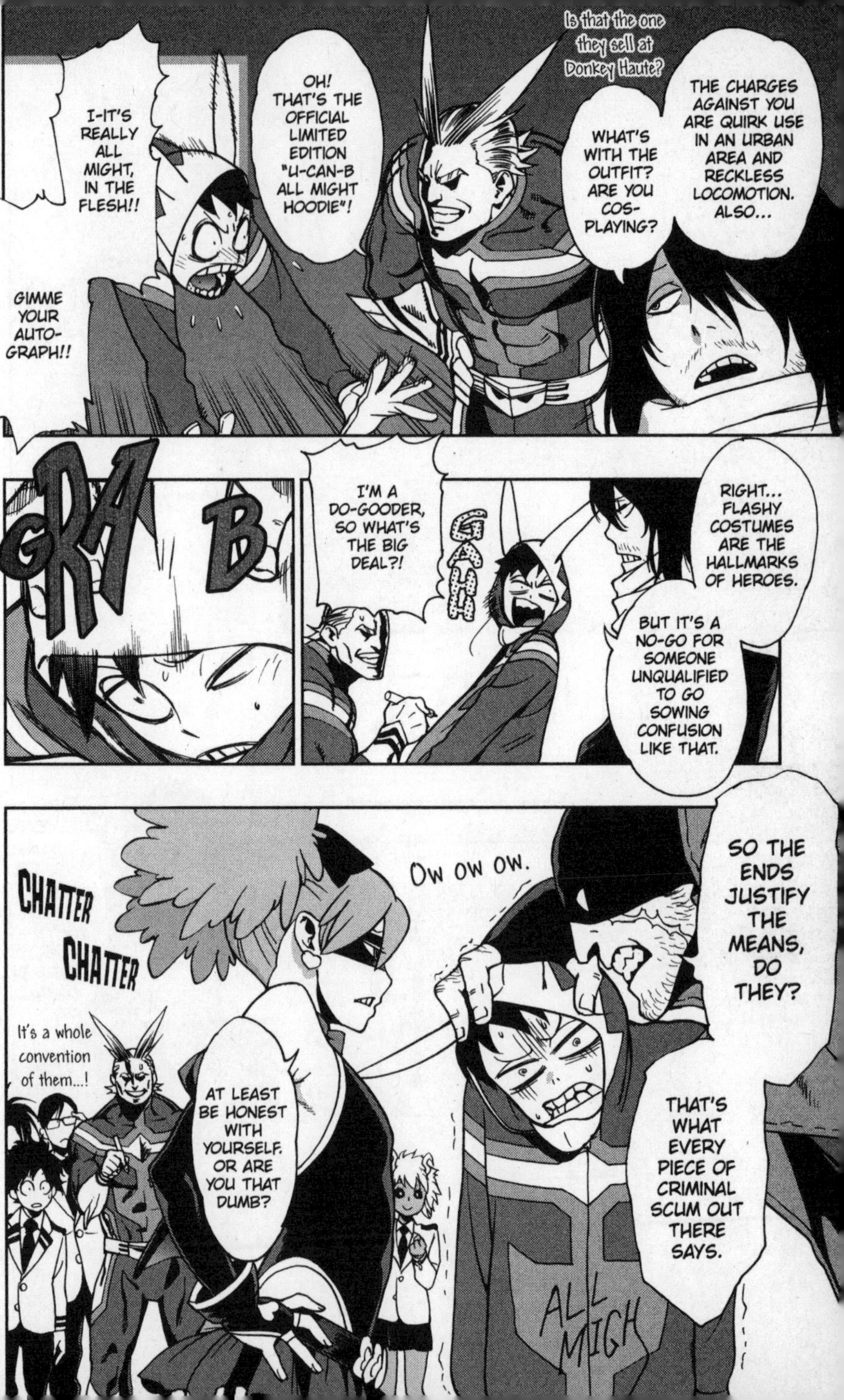
THE CHARGES AGAINST YOU ARE QUIRK USE IN AN URBAN AREA AND RECKLESS LOCOMOTION. ALSO...
WHAT'S WITH THE OUTFIT? ARE YOU COS-PLAYING?
Is that the one they sell at Donkey Haute?
OH! THAT'S THE OFFICIAL LIMITED EDITION "U-CAN-B ALL MIGHT HOODIE"!
I-IT'S REALLY ALL MIGHT, IN THE FLESH!!
GIMME YOUR AUTO-GRAPH!!
RIGHT... FLASHY COSTUMES ARE THE HALLMARKS OF HEROES.
BUT IT'S A NO-GO FOR SOMEONE UNQUALIFIED TO GO SOWING CONFUSION LIKE THAT.
GAH
I'M A DO-GOODER, SO WHAT'S THE BIG DEAL?!
GRAB
SO THE ENDS JUSTIFY THE MEANS, DO THEY?
THAT'S WHAT EVERY PIECE OF CRIMINAL SCUM OUT THERE SAYS.
Ow ow ow.
AT LEAST BE HONEST WITH YOURSELF. OR ARE YOU THAT DUMB?
ALL MIGH
CHATTER
CHATTER
It's a whole convention of them...!

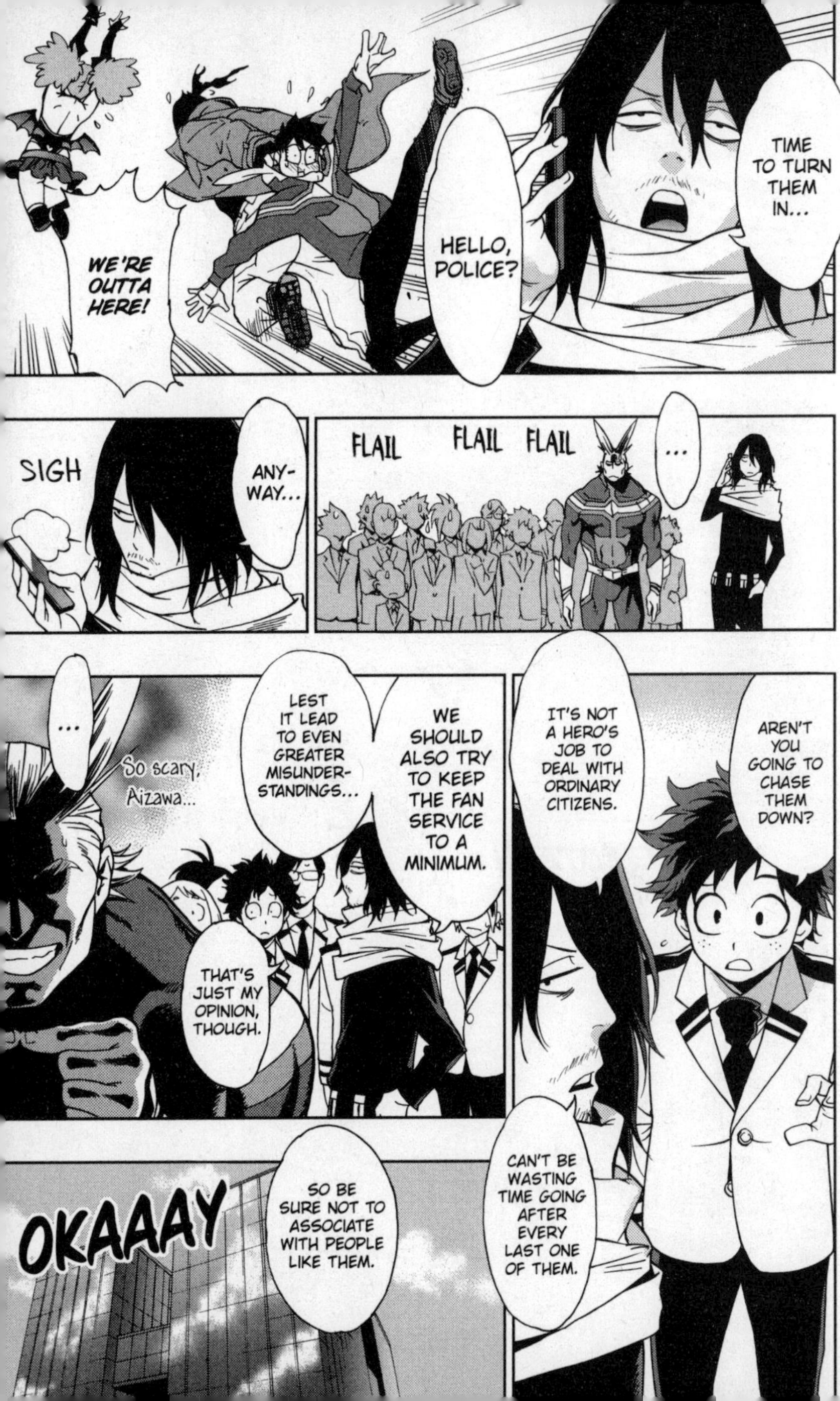
TIME TO TURN THEM IN...
HELLO, POLICE?
WE'RE OUTTA HERE!
...
FLAIL FLAIL FLAIL
ANY-WAY...
SIGH
AREN'T YOU GOING TO CHASE THEM DOWN?
IT'S NOT A HERO'S JOB TO DEAL WITH ORDINARY CITIZENS.
CAN'T BE WASTING TIME GOING AFTER EVERY LAST ONE OF THEM.
WE SHOULD ALSO TRY TO KEEP THE FAN SERVICE TO A MINIMUM.
LEST IT LEAD TO EVEN GREATER MISUNDER-STANDINGS...
...
So scary, Aizawa...
THAT'S JUST MY OPINION, THOUGH.
SO BE SURE NOT TO ASSOCIATE WITH PEOPLE LIKE THEM.
OKAAAY

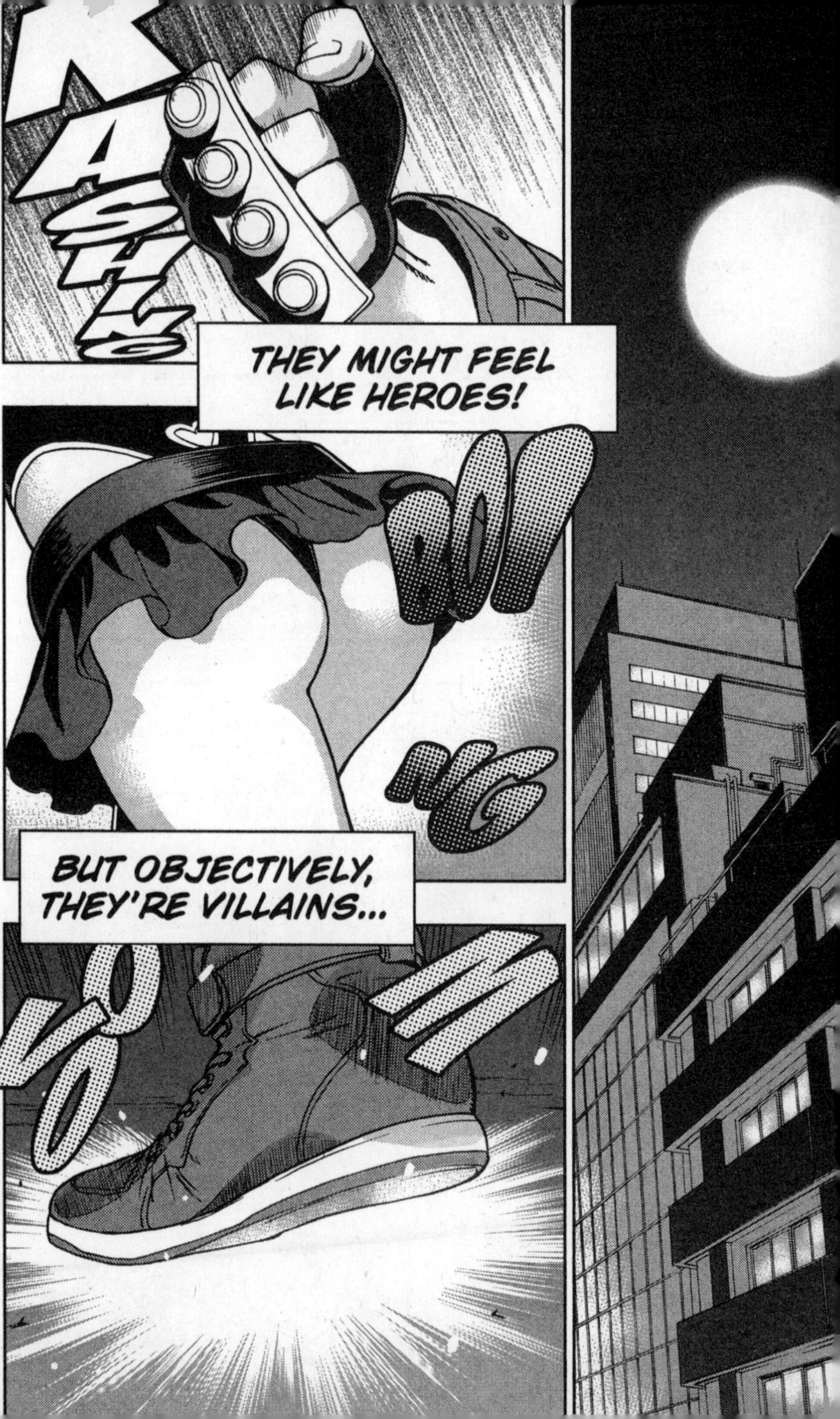
THEY MIGHT FEEL LIKE HEROES!
BUT OBJECTIVELY, THEY'RE VILLAINS...

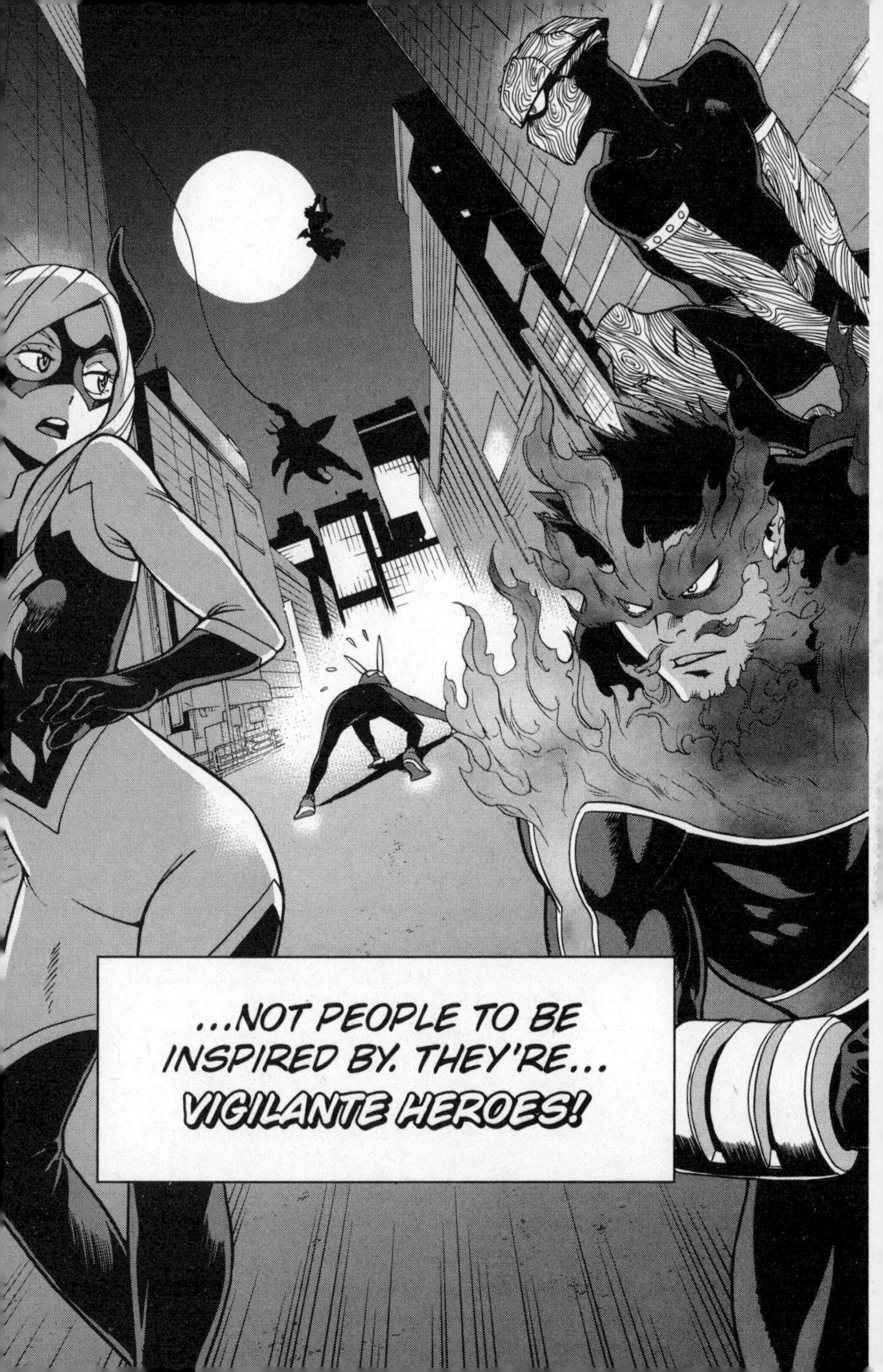
...NOT PEOPLE TO BE INSPIRED BY. THEY'RE...
VIGILANTE HEROES!

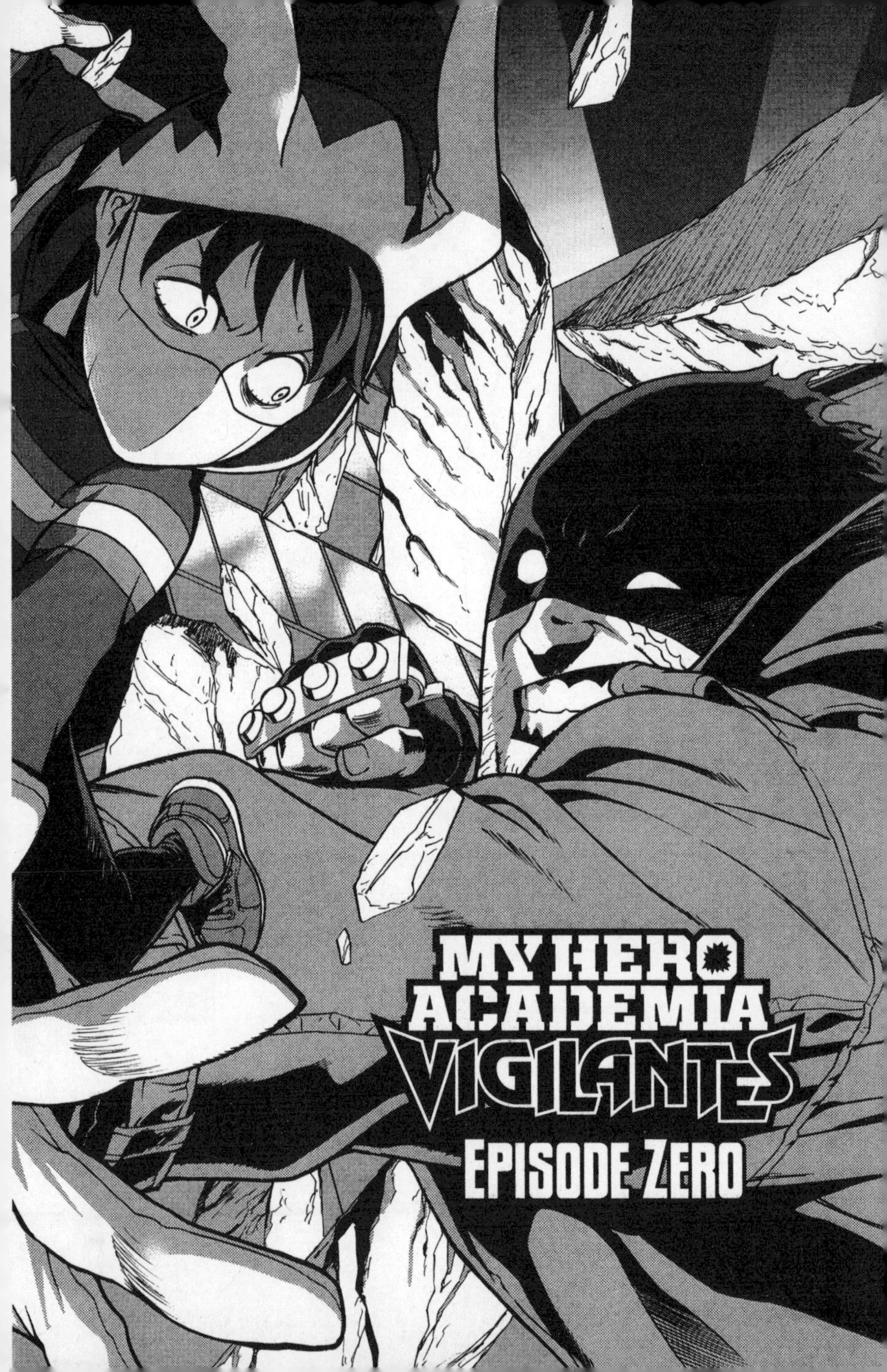
MY HERO ACADEMIA
VIGILANTES
EPISODE ZERO

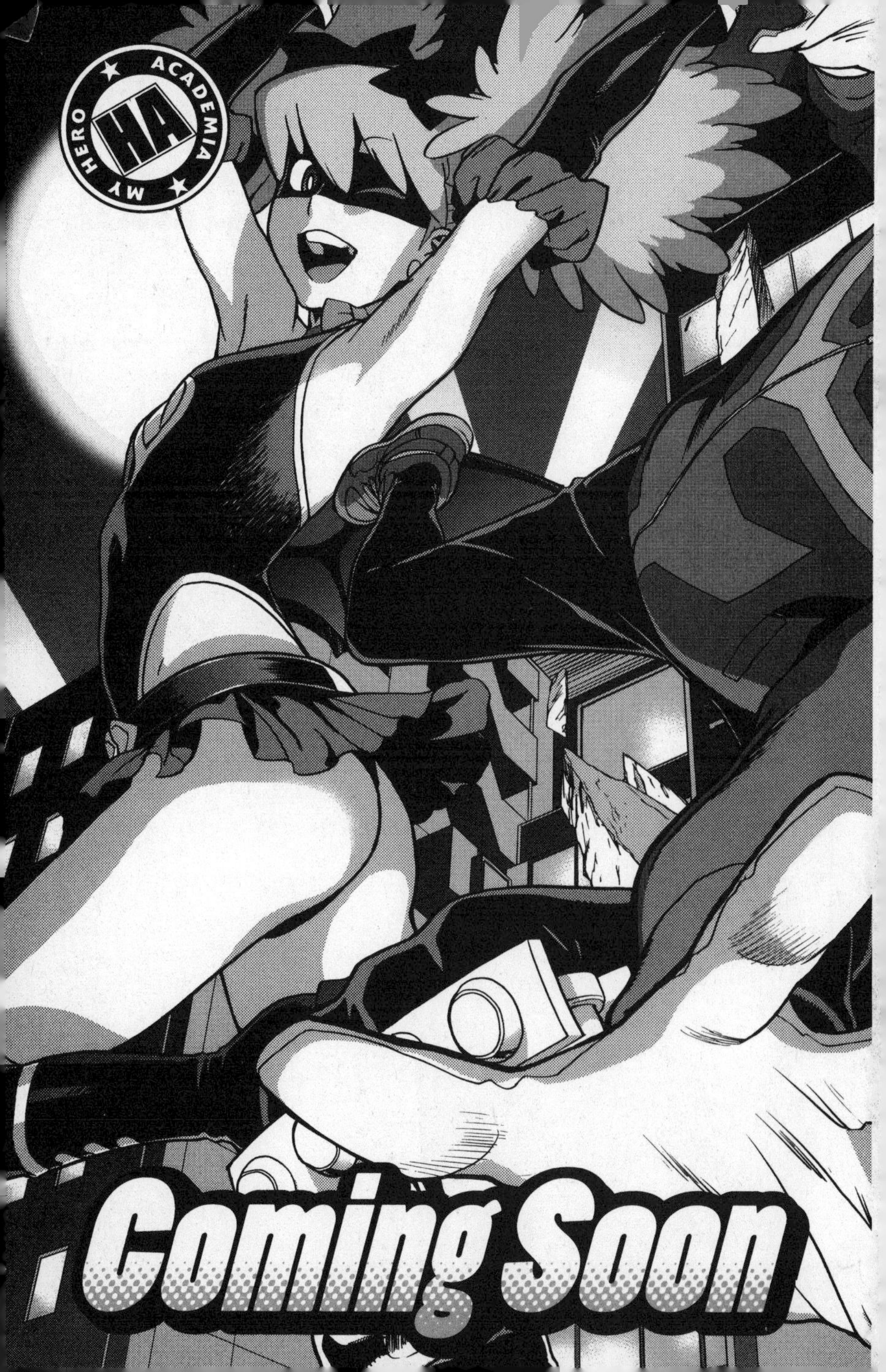
MY HERO ACADEMIA
MHA
Coming Soon

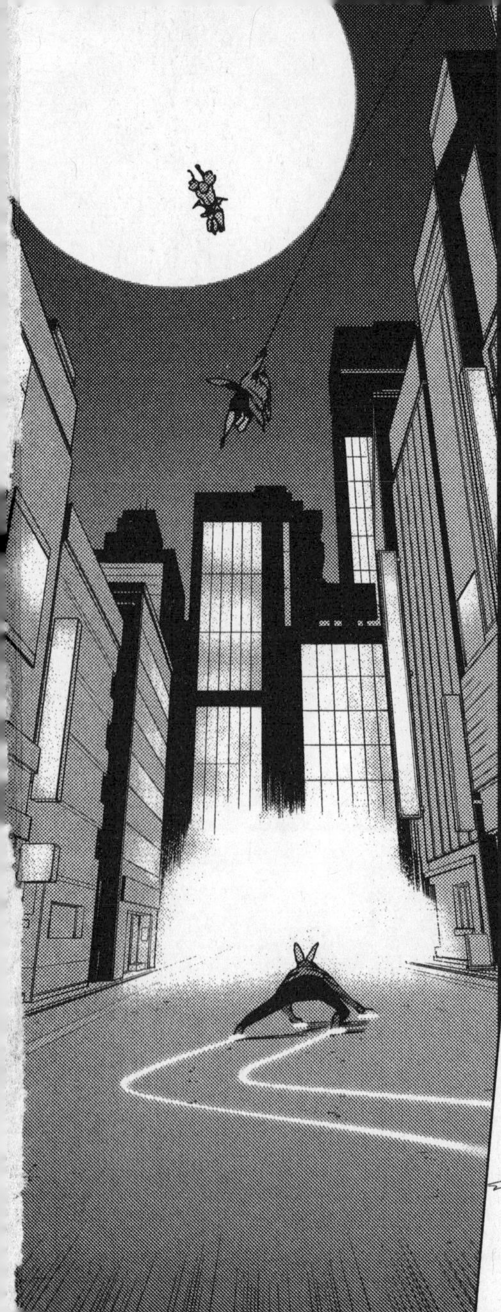

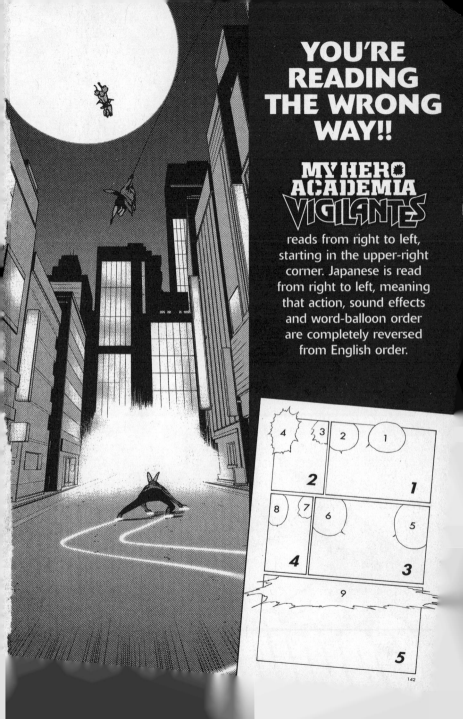

YOU'RE READING THE WRONG WAY!!

MY HERO ACADEMIA VIGILANTES

reads from right to left, starting in the upper-right corner. Japanese is read from right to left, meaning that action, sound effects and word-balloon order are completely reversed from English order.

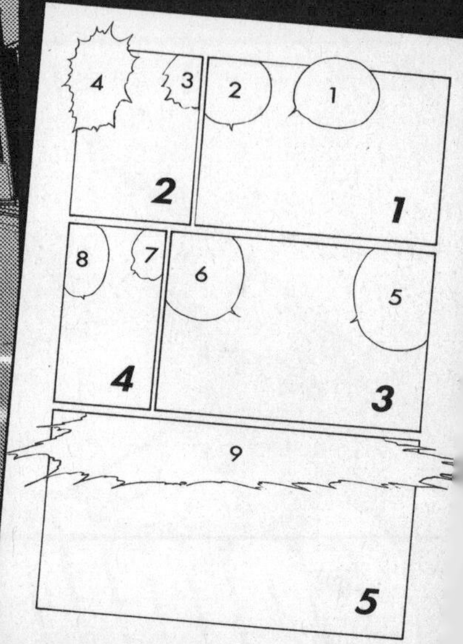

1
2
3
4
1
2
5
6
7
8
3
4
9
5